T0212987

Lecture Notes in Computer Science　9865

Commenced Publication in 1973
Founding and Former Series Editors:
Gerhard Goos, Juris Hartmanis, and Jan van Leeuwen

Editorial Board

More information about this series at http://www.springer.com/series/7409

Atsuyuki Morishima · Lijun Chang
Tom Z.J. Fu · Kuien Liu
Xiaoyan Yang · Jia Zhu
Rong Zhang · Wenjie Zhang
Zhiwei Zhang (Eds.)

Web Technologies and Applications

APWeb 2016 Workshops, WDMA, GAP, and SDMA
Suzhou, China, September 23–25, 2016
Proceedings

 Springer

Editors
Atsuyuki Morishima
University of Tsukuba
Tsukuba
Japan

Lijun Chang
The University of New South Wales
Sydney, NSW
Australia

Tom Z.J. Fu
Advanced Digital Sciences Center
Singapore
Singapore

Kuien Liu
Pivotal Inc.
Beijing
China

Xiaoyan Yang
Advanced Digital Sciences Center
Singapore
Singapore

Jia Zhu
South China Normal University
Guangzhou
China

Rong Zhang
East China Normal University
Shanghai
China

Wenjie Zhang
The University of New South Wales
Sydney, NSW
Australia

Zhiwei Zhang
Hong Kong Baptist University
Kowloon Tong
Hong Kong, SAR China

ISSN 0302-9743 ISSN 1611-3349 (electronic)
Lecture Notes in Computer Science
ISBN 978-3-319-45834-2 ISBN 978-3-319-45835-9 (eBook)
DOI 10.1007/978-3-319-45835-9

Library of Congress Control Number: 2016949587

LNCS Sublibrary: SL3 – Information Systems and Applications, incl. Internet/Web, and HCI

Printed on acid-free paper

This Springer imprint is published by Springer Nature
The registered company is Springer International Publishing AG Switzerland

Message from the APWeb 2016 Workshop Chairs

It is our great pleasure to welcome you to the proceedings of the 18th APWeb workshops. APWeb is a leading international conference on research, development, and applications of Web technologies, database systems, information management, and software engineering. This year, three workshops were held in conjunction with the main conference:

- Second International Workshop on Web Data Mining and Applications (WDMA 2016)
- First International Workshop on Graph Analytics and Query Processing (GAP 2016)
- First International Workshop on Spatial-temporal Data Management and Analytics (SDMA 2016)

The goal of these workshops is to promote new research directions and applications, especially on web data, graph data, and spatial-temporal data management and analytics. Following the evaluation process conducted by the Workshop Program Committee members, the workshop program featured 27 papers selected from 37 submissions. All papers were presented during the workshop session of the main conference, held in Suzhou, China in September 2016.

We would like to thank the authors for choosing APWeb workshops as a venue for presenting their high-quality papers and the Program Committee members for their timely reviews of the papers. We are also very grateful to the workshop organizers from the Advanced Digital Sciences Centre Singapore, the University of New South Wales Australia, and Pivotal Inc. for their essential efforts in selecting the papers and organizing the program. Furthermore, we also gratefully acknowledge the support of the main conference organizers for their great effort in supporting the workshop program.

Finally, we hope that you enjoy reading the proceedings of the APWeb 2016 workshops.

July 2016

Rong Zhang
Wenjie Zhang

Organization

Workshop Co-chairs

Atsuyuki Morishima	University of Tsukuba, Japan
Rong Zhang	ECNU, China
Wenjie Zhang	University of New South Wales, Australia

Workshops

2nd International Workshop on Web Data Mining and Applications (WDMA 2016)

Organizing Committee

Tom Z.J. Fu	Advanced Digital Sciences Center, Singapore
Xiaoyan Yang	Advanced Digital Sciences Center, Singapore

Program Committee

Fan Cheng	National University of Singapore, Singapore
Tian Gan	Institute for Infocomm Research, Singapore
Ming Gao	East China Normal University, China
Qun Huang	Huawei Future Network Theory Lab, Hong Kong, China
Qiao Miao	Advanced Digital Sciences Center, Singapore
Hong Xie	National University of Singapore, Singapore
Baolei Xu	Huawei Nanjing R&D Center, China
Rong Zhang	East China Normal University, China
Yipeng Zhou	Shen Zhen University, China

1st International Workshop on Graph Analytics and Query Processing (GAP 2016)

Program Committee

Rong-Hua Li	Shenzhen University, China
Zheng Liu	Nanjing University of Posts and Telecommunications, China
Miao Qiao	Massey University, New Zealand
Lu Qin	University of Technology Sydney, Australia
Zechao Shang	The Chinese University of Hong Kong, China
Shaoxu Song	Tsinghua University, China

Da Yan   The Chinese University of Hong Kong, China
Junjie Yao   East China Normal University, China
Weiren Yu   Imperial College, UK
Ying Zhang   University of Technology Sydney, Australia
Xiang Zhao   National University of Defense Technology, China
Yuanyuan Zhu   Wuhan University, China

1st International Workshop on Spatio-temporal Data Management and Analytics (SDMA 2016)

General Co-chairs

Jignesh M. Patel   University of Wisconsin, WI, USA
Xiaofang Zhou   University of Queensland, Australia

PC Co-chairs

Hui Zhang   Tsinghua University, China
Kuien Liu   Pivotal Inc., China
Jia Zhu   South China Normal University, China

PC Members

Lei Chen   HKUST, Hong Kong, China
Zhiming Ding   Beijing University of Technology, China
Xiaoyong Du   Renmin University of China, China
Xiaohui Hu   Institute of Software, Chinese Academy of Sciences, China
Peiquan Jin   University of Science and Technology of China, China
Zhixu Li   Soochow University, China
Chengfei Liu   Swinburne University of Technology, Australia
Jie Liu   Institute of Software, Chinese Academy of Sciences, China
Feng Lu   IGSNRR, Chinese Academy of Sciences, China
Hua Lu   Aalborg University, Denmark
Wei Lu   Renmin University of China, China
Yuwei Peng   Wuhan University, China
Weiwei Sun   Fudan University, China
Guangzhong Sun   University of Science and Technology of China, China
Gang Pan   Zhejiang University, China
Shuo Shang   China University of Petroleum-Beijing, China
Haozhou Wang   Pivotal Inc., China
Xing Xie   Microsoft Research Asia, China
Jiajie Xu   Soochow University, China
Jianqiu Xu   Nanjing University of Aeronautics and Astronautics, China
Rui Yang   Tsinghua University, China
Yandong Yao   Pivotal Inc., China

Yang Yue   Shenzhen University, China
Pengpeng Zhao   Soochow University, China
Wen Zhang   Beijing University of Chemical Technology, China
Zheng Xu   The Third Research Institute of the Ministry
                            of Public Security, China

Contents

1st International Workshop on Graph Analytics and Query Processing (GAP 2016)

1st International Workshop on Spatio-temporal Data Management and Analytics (SDMA 2016)

2nd International Workshop on Web Data Mining and Applications (WDMA 2016)

Maximizing the Cooperative Influence Spread in a Social Network Oriented to Viral Marketing

Hong Wu[1,2], Zhijian Zhang[1,3], Kun Yue[1(✉)],
Binbin Zhang[1], and Weiyi Liu[1]

[1] School of Information Science and Engineering,
Yunnan University, Kunming, China
kyue@ynu.edu.cn
[2] School of Information Engineering, Qujing Normal University, Qujing, China
[3] College of Science, Kunming University of Science and Technology,
Kunming, China

Abstract. In many real-world situations, there exist two or more associated products, such as beer and nappy, mobile phone and mobile power pack, bed and mattress etc., in which consumers are likely to purchase these two or more associated products simultaneously. Thus, the associated products can be promoted at the same time, which implies cooperative influence spread of products in viral marketing. In this paper, we focus on maximizing the cooperative influence spread of associated products in a social network. First, we make use of a similarity model, abbreviated as SM, to generate the probabilities of edges. Then, we obtain the cooperative influence spread graph based on single influence spread graphs of these two products and the associated rule. Further, we propose independent cascade model with accepted probability (ICMAP) to describe the cooperative influence spread in a social network, and give an improved greedy algorithm to maximize the cooperative influence spread approximately. Experimental results show the effectiveness and feasibility of the proposed algorithm.

Keywords: Social networks · Cooperative influence spread · Submodularity · Greedy algorithm

1 Introduction

With the emergence of online social networks, such as Facebook, Twitter, Linkedin, Wechat, etc., users can establish the connections (i.e., friendship) and share thoughts, comments, pictures, etc., among these online social networks. The connections of users can form as a social network, upon which the diseases, innovations and information can be spread. According to the recent study [1], people tend to trust the information from their friends, relatives or families more probably than the general advertising media like TVs. Hence, many companies choose online social networks as the media to promote products. For example, *Nike Inc.* used the social networking websites such as *orkut.-com* and *facebook.com* to market product successfully [2]. How do these companies

A. Morishima et al. (Eds.): APWeb 2016 Workshops, LNCS 9865, pp. 3–15, 2016.
DOI: 10.1007/978-3-319-45835-9_1

select initial users to spread the information of products effectively? This problem is called as influence maximization, which is the problem of selecting k seeds in a social network that maximizes the spread of influence under certain influence spread model. In this paper, we focus on maximizing the cooperative influence spread of associated products in a social network.

Kempe et al. [3] first formulated the influence maximization problem as the discrete optimization problem, and proposed the independent cascade (IC) model and linear threshold (LT) model. Based on these two classic diffusion models, some researches proposed novel spread models to reflect different aspects of propagation, such as competitive influence spread [4–6] and negative aspects [7].

However, in the real world, except the competitive and negative influence spread, there also exists cooperative influence spread. For example, a consumer is likely to purchase these two associated products simultaneously, such as beer and nappy, mobile phone and mobile power pack, bed and mattress etc. Thus, we consider modeling the associations among products by a graph model, and maximizing the cooperative influence spread of associated products in this paper.

In order to solve the above problems, we need to consider the following questions.

(1) How to obtain the cooperative influence spread graph of associative products?
(2) How to model the influence spread process of cooperative influence?
(3) How to maximize the cooperative influence spread?

For the question (1), we propose the similarity model (SM) to define the weight of each edge, which reflects the influence strength from one consumer to another. In order to describe the cooperative influence spread, we employ the concept of conditional probability (i.e., confidence), support and associative rule. In this paper, we first obtain the cooperative influence spread graph of associative products by the influence spread graphs of single products, conditional probability, support and associative rule. We further employ the cooperative influence spread graph to effectively promote associative products.

For the question (2), in order to reflect the product promotion in marketing practically as much as possible we extend the IC model to model the cooperative influence spread. We first define an accepted probability λ of consumer with products to describe the preferences of consumers. Then, we extend the IC model to include the accepted probability of consumer, which is called as independent cascade model with accepted probability, abbreviated as ICMAP, (e.g. If Bob receives the iphone 6s and its shell promotion information, then he may neglect this information or read this information and finally purchase this iphone 6s and its shell).

For the question (3), we aim to maximize the cooperative influence spread under the ICMAP, which is NP-hard. Based on the work of Kempe et al. [3], we obtain that the objective function under the ICMAP satisfies monotonicity and submodularity, and thus the greedy algorithm can be used to approximate the optimal result with $1 - 1/e$ based on the theory of Nemhauser et al. [8]. To improve the performance of greedy algorithm, in this paper, we propose an improved greedy algorithm. In the improved greedy algorithm, we directly estimate the influence spread in t days (e.g., 3 days) without the expensive Monte-Carlo simulation process, thus significantly speed up the computation of influence spread.

Extensive experiments on real-world social networks show the effectiveness and feasibility of the method proposed in this paper.

2 Related Work

Kempe et al. [3] proposed LT model and IC model to model the influence spread process in a social network. Along with their work, various extensions [4–6] about these two models were proposed to reflect the characteristics of competitive influence spread. He et al. [4] studied the competitive influence spread under the competitive linear threshold model. Wu et al. [5] proposed the extended LT model to reflect the competitive influence spread process. Liu et al. [6] employed the competitive independence model for the competitive influence spread and considered the problem of selecting a seed set with minimum cost to influence more people than the competitor. In real influence propagation, in addition to the competitive influence spread, there also exists non-competitive influence spread. Datta et al. [9] aimed at maximizing the influence spread for multiple non-competing products $T_{1...t}$. The key difference between their work and ours is that their t non-competing products are not associative. However, in our work, we mainly focus on maximizing the influence spread of associative products. Chen [7] proposed the IC-N model to include the propagation of negative opinion, where there is a quality factor q caused by the product defects. In our work, each consumer has an accepted probability λ, which reflects the probability that consumer is activated and finally purchases the product. Our accepted probability λ can well reflect the real spread situation. In this paper, we extend the IC model proposed by Kempe et al. [3] to incorporate the accepted probability λ of consumer.

In addition to design diffusion model to describe the influence spread process, it is also important to select k seeds effectively to maximize the influence spread under certain diffusion model, which is NP-hard. Kempe et al. [3] proposed the greedy algorithm to approximate the optimal result based on theory of Nemhauser and Wolsey [8], where the objective function should satisfy the monotonicity and submodularity. However, the classic greedy algorithm is time consuming, and several studies have looked into the scalable influence maximization in social networks [10–13]. They either improved the greedy algorithm or proposed new heuristic algorithm. For example, Song et al. [10] adopted a divided-and-conquer strategy with parallel computing mechanism. Gomez- Rodriguez et al. [11] proposed a highly efficient randomized algorithm to estimate the influence of every node in a network with general transmission functions. Tang et al. [12] presented *Two-phase Influence maximization* algorithm, which incorporated novel heuristics that result is up to 100-fold improvements of its computation efficiency. Liang et al. [13] proposed the UserGreedy algorithm to directly estimate the influence spread without expensive simulation process. From the perspective of efficiency, our proposed improved greedy algorithm is similar to that presented in [13]. However, there exists difference in estimation the influence spread aspect. In their work, they proposed an influence-path based method to estimate the influence spread and chose a threshold to prune the paths whose influence probabilities are smaller than threshold. In our paper, we directly estimate the influence in promotion days, which can well reflect the real product promotion.

3 Similarity Model

Given a social network $G = (V, E)$, we make use of the similarity model (SM) of nodes to compute the probabilities of edges by borrowing the idea from the cosine similarity proposed in [14]. Let $Nei(u)$ denote the neighbor nodes of u, which also includes u. The similarity model is defined as follows:

$$SM(u, v) = \frac{|Nei(u) \cap Nei(v)|}{\sqrt{|Nei(u)||Nei(v)|}} \tag{1}$$

Where $|Nei(u) \cap Nei(v)|$ denotes the number of mutual friends of u and v.

Example 1. We give an example to illustrate the process of computing the probabilities of edges by SM. Figure 1(a) shows the original graph. In Fig. 1(b), we use the Eq. (1) to generate the probability of edge $SM(v_1, v_2) = 0.866$. Similarly, we can obtain the probabilities of other edges by SM.

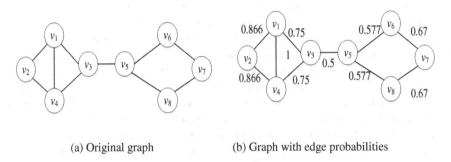

(a) Original graph   (b) Graph with edge probabilities

Fig. 1. An example of generating the probabilities of edges by the SM.

4 Cooperative Influence Spread

In this Section, we introduce how to generate the cooperative influence spread graph G_{AB} and further propose the ICMAP to model the cooperative influence spread.

4.1 Generating Cooperative Influence Spread Graph

Based on the history date, we have known the support St_{AB} and the conditional probability $P(B|A)$ (i.e. the confidence of associative rules [15]) of associative products. How does the edge $e(v_1, v_2)$ simultaneously spread these two associative products A and B?

We can use Rule 1 to generate the cooperative influence spread graph G_{AB} of these two products, which is described as follows.

Rule 1: For all $v \in N(u)$, $P_{AB}(u, v) = P(B|A) \times P_A(u, v)$, here $P_{AB}(u, v)$ denotes the spread probability between consumer u and v with associative products and

$P_A(u, v)$ equal to $SM(u, v)$ of Eq. (1). If $P_{AB}(u, v) \geq St_{AB}$, then the edge can simultaneously spread the influence of A and B. If $P_{AB}(u, v) < St_{AB}$, then the edge only can spread the influence of A or B.

Example 2. We give an example to generate the cooperative influence spared graph G_{AB} based on Fig. 1(b) and Rule 1. In Fig. 1(b), we give $P_{B|A}(u, v) = 0.8$ and $S_{AB} = 0.1$, and then we can obtain $P_{AB}(v_1, v_2) = 0.7$. Similarly, we can obtain the probabilities of other edges. The cooperative influence spread graph G_{AB} is shown in Fig. 2.

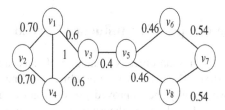

Fig. 2. An example of generating the cooperative influence spread graph G_{AB}

4.2 Independent Cascade Model with Accepted Probabilities

In the IC model, a social network is denoted as a directed graph $G = (V, E)$, where V denotes the individuals of social networks, and E denotes the relationships of individuals. The IC model takes the spread probability $p(v_i, v_j)$ of each edge $e(v_i, v_j)$ and the initial seed sets S_0 as input, and generates the activate set S_t. At step t ($t \geq 1$), for every node $u \in N_{in}(v) \cap (S_{t-1 \setminus t-2})$, u tries to independently activate its out-neighbor v with success probability $P(u, v)$. If successful, then the node v is added into S_t. If multiple nodes activate v successfully, then v is also added into S_t. The process ends at the step t with $S_t = \phi$.

In this paper, we consider the undirected graph in Fig. 2 as a directed graph, where an undirected edge $e(v_i, v_j)$ be viewed as directed edges $e<v_i, v_j>$ and $e<v_j, v_i>$, and propose the ICMAP to model the cooperative influence spread process based on the IC model.

In our ICMAP, each consumer has an accepted probability. We can describe the accepted probability as follows. In reality, Tom is selected as a seed to spread an iphone promotion information, then he will buy the iphone with a probability λ uniformly at random from the interval $[0, 1]$. In a social network $G = (V, E)$, there are two associative products A and B promoting in this social network, and each consumer has an accepted probability λ with these two associative products, i.e. λ_v^{AB}, where λ_v^{AB} denotes the probability of consumer purchasing the products A and B simultaneously. We use an example to illustrate the accepted probability of consumer as follows.

Example 3. In Fig. 3, $S_{AB} = \{v_3\}$ denotes that the consumer v_3 is selected as seed to promote the product A and B. At step $t = 1$, v_3 purchases the product A and B with probability 0.7. At step $t = 2$, v_3 tries to activate its inactive out-neighbors v_1, v_4 and v_5 with probabilities 0.42, 0.42 and 0.28 respectively.

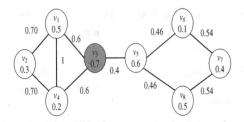

Fig. 3. Cooperative influence spread graph G_{AB} with the accepted probability

5   Maximizing the Cooperative Influence Spread

In this Section, we first define the objective function of maximizing the cooperative influence under the ICMAP. Then, we prove this objective function is monotone and submodular. Further, we employ the improved greedy algorithm to approximate the optimal result with $1 - 1/e$ based on the theory of Nemhauser et al. [8].

5.1   Objective Function for Cooperative Influence Spread

The influence maximization problem is an optimization problem, in which given a graph $G_{AB} = (V_{AB}, E_{AB})$, the probability of edge, the accepted probability of node and the number of the seeds. We want to find a seed set S_{AB} of the size k such that the expected number of nodes is maximized. Now, we first give the objective function (i.e., final profit) of cooperative influence spread under the ICMAP. We give the Rule 2 to reflect the final profit of the cooperative influence under the ICMAP.

Rule 2: In $G = (V, E)$, for $\forall v_j \in V$, the cost and profit of v_j for associative products A and B are C_{AB} and U_{AB} respectively, and the final profit of v_j as the seed of A and B is $\Delta_{AB}(v_j) = U_{AB} \times \sigma_{AB}(v_j) - C_{AB}$, which should satisfy $U_{AB} \times \sigma_{AB}(v_j) \geq C_{AB}$. Here, $\sigma_{AB}(v_j)$ denotes the expectation influence value of v_j as the seed of associative product A and B.

The objective function of maximizing the cooperative influence spread is the problem of finding a seed set S_{AB} at most k that maximizes $\Delta (S_{AB})$, i.e., computing

$$S_{AB}^* = argmax\ \Delta(S_{AB}) \tag{2}$$

Based on Rule 2, we have

$$S_{AB}^* = argmax \sum_{v_j \in S_{AB}} (U_{AB} \times \sigma_{AB}(v_j) - C_{AB} \times |S_{AB}|) \tag{3}$$

The objective function of selecting the optimal seed set to maximize the cooperative influence spread under the ICMAP is NP-hard, and we can prove the monotonicity and submodularity of the objective function as follows.

Obviously, we have

$$\Delta(S_{AB}) \leq \Delta(S_{AB} \cup u) \tag{4}$$

Thus, the objective function $\Delta(S_{AB})$ is monotone.

Now, we prove the submodularity of objective function $\Delta(S_{AB})$.

In Eq. (3), U_{AB} and C_{AB} are constant. Based on the Closeness properties of submodularity in [16], we only need to prove the submodularity of $\sigma(S_{AB})$.

Theorem 1: For any subsets $S_{AB} \subseteq T_{AB} \subseteq V_{AB}$ and any element $u \in V_{AB} \backslash T_{AB}$, we have the following inequality (5).

$$\sigma(S_{AB} \cup \{u\}) - \sigma(S_{AB}) \geq \sigma(T_{AB} \cup \{u\}) - \sigma(T_{AB}) \tag{5}$$

Here, since $\sigma(S_{AB}) = \sum_{i=1}^{t} \sigma(S_{AB}^{t})$, we only need to prove the submodularity of $\sigma(S_{AB}^{t})$.

For any step t, the activated nodes $u \in S_{AB}^{t-1}$ tries to activate its probability $p_{AB}(u, v) \times \lambda_{AB}^{u}$, and v purchase these product A and B with probability $p_{AB}(u, v) \times \lambda_{AB}^{u} \times \lambda_{AB}^{v}$.

And thus, we have

$$\sigma(S_{AB}^{t}) = \sum_{v \in S_{AB}^{t} \backslash S_{AB}^{t-1}} \left(1 - \left(\prod_{u \in S_{AB}^{t-1} \backslash S_{AB}^{t-2}} \left(1 - \left(p_{AB}(u, v) \times \lambda_{AB}^{u} \times \lambda_{AB}^{v}\right)\right)\right)\right) \tag{6}$$

Here, we define $p_{AB}(u, v) \times \lambda_{AB}^{u} \times \lambda_{AB}^{v} = w_{AB}(u, v)$.

Proof: We use the Mathematical Induction to prove the Theorem 1.

At step $t = 1$, the objective is obviously submodular.

At step t, if the objective function is submodular, then we have

$$\sigma(S_{AB} \cup \{u\})^{t} - \sigma(S_{AB})^{t} \geq \sigma(T_{AB} \cup \{u\})^{t} - \sigma(T_{AB})^{t} \tag{7}$$

At step $t + 1$, based on the Eq. (6), we have

$$\sigma((S_{AB} \cup \{u\})^{t+1} - \sigma(S_{AB})^{t+1} =$$
$$\sigma((S_{AB} \cup \{u\})^{t} + \sum_{v \in ((S_{AB} \cup \{u\})^{t+1} \backslash (S_{AB} \cup \{u\})^{t}} \left(1 - \left(\prod_{u \in (S_{AB} \cup \{u\})^{t} \backslash (S_{AB} \cup \{u\})^{t-1}} (1 - w_{AB}(u, v))\right)\right)$$
$$- \sigma(S_{AB})^{t} - \sum_{v \in S_{AB}^{t+1} \backslash S_{AB}^{t}} \left(1 - \left(\prod_{u \in S_{AB}^{t} \backslash S_{AB}^{t-1}} (1 - w_{AB}(u, v)\right)\right)$$

$$\tag{8}$$

Here, we define

$$Inf(S_{AB}^{t+1'}) = \sum_{v \in S_{AB}^{t+1'} \setminus S_{AB}^{t}} (1 - (\prod_{u \in S_{AB}^{t} \setminus S_{AB}^{t-1'}} (1 - w_{AB}(u, v)))) \tag{9}$$

$Inf(S_{AB}^{t+1})$ denotes the influence spread value of S_{AB} at step $t + 1$.

We have the similar expression of $\sigma((T_{AB} \cup \{u\})^{t+1} - \sigma(T_{AB})^{t+1}$. Based on Inequality (7), we only need to prove the submodularity of $Inf(S_{AB})^{t+1}$. At step $t + 1$, the node $u \in S_{AB}^{t} \setminus S_{AB}^{t-1}$ tries to activate its out-neighbor v with probability $p_{AB}(u, v) \times \lambda_{AB}^{u} \times \lambda_{AB}^{v}$. We can see it as the process that flips a biased coin with probability $p_{AB}(u, v) \times \lambda_{AB}^{u} \times \lambda_{AB}^{v}$. Based on the theorem of Kempe et al. [3], we have

$$Inf((S_{AB} \cup \{u\})^{t+1} - Inf(S_{AB}^{t+1'}) \geq Inf((T_{AB} \cup \{u\})^{t+1} \cup \{u\}) - Inf(T_{AB}^{t+1}) \tag{10}$$

Thus, the objective function $\sigma(.)$ is submodular.

6 Approximation Algorithm of Cooperative Influence Spread

Selecting k optimal nodes to maximize the cooperative influence spread under the ICMAP is NP-hard. Based on the theorem proposed by Nemhauser et al. [8], we can use the improved greedy algorithm to approximate the optimal result with $1-/e$ (where e is the base of natural logarithm).

Agorithm 1: Selecting k seeds by improved greedy algorithm, $S=\{S_{AB}\}$ and $k=|S_{AB}|$

Input: $G_{AB} = (V_{AB}, E_{AB}, P_{AB}(u, v), \lambda_{AB}^{v})$ and the number of seeds k.

Output: Seed set S_{AB}.

1: Initialize: $S_{AB} \leftarrow \phi$

2: **for1** i=1 to k do

3:   **for2** each $v_j \in V \setminus S_{AB}$ do

3:   **for3** t=1 to T do

4:     $Inf(S_{AB}^{t+1'}) \leftarrow \sum_{v \in S_{AB}^{t+1'} \setminus S_{AB}^{t}} (1 - (\prod_{u \in S_{AB}^{t} \setminus S_{AB}^{t-1'}} (1 - w_{AB}(u, v)))$

5:     $\sigma_{AB}(S_{AB} \cup \{v_j\}) \leftarrow \sum_{t=1}^{T} inf(S_{AB} \cup v_j)^t$

6:   **end for3**

7:   **end for2**

8:   $\Delta_{AB}(S_{AB} \cup \{v_j\}) \leftarrow (U_{AB} \times \sigma_{AB}(S_{AB} \cup \{v_j\}) - C_{AB} \times |S_{AB} \cup \{v_j\}|$

9:   $u \leftarrow argmax_{v_j \in V \setminus S_{AB}}(\Delta_{AB}(S_{AB} \cup \{v_j\}) - \Delta_{AB}(S_{AB}))$

10: $S \leftarrow S \cup \{u\}$

11: **end for1**

12: return S_{AB}

Example 4. We use an example to illustrate that how to employ the improved greedy algorithm to select seeds to maximize the cooperative influence spread under the ICMAP. In Fig. 4, Given $t = 1$, $C_{AB} = 4$ and $U_{AB} = 10$, we compute σ (.) under the ICMAP as follows.

$\sigma(v_1) = 0.5 + \sigma(v_1 \rightarrow v_2) + \sigma(v_1 \rightarrow v_3) + \sigma(v_1 \rightarrow v_4) = 0.915$
$\sigma(v_2) = 0.3 + \sigma(v_2 \rightarrow v_1) + \sigma(v_2 \rightarrow v_3) + \sigma(v_2 \rightarrow v_4) = 0.342$
$\sigma(v_3) = 0.7 + \sigma(v_3 \rightarrow v_1) + \sigma(v_3 \rightarrow v_2) + \sigma(v_3 \rightarrow v_4) = 0.784$
$\sigma(v_4) = 0.2$

In the first iteration, we select v_1 as the first seed node. We further compute σ $(v_1 \cup \{.\})$ as follows:

$\sigma(v_1 \cup \{v_2\}) = 0.9399$, $\sigma(v_1 \cup \{v_3\}) = 1.3492$ and $\sigma(v_1 \cup \{v_4\}) = 1.015$.

Finally, we select $S_{AB} = \{v_1, v_3\}$ as the seed set. At $C_{AB} = 5$, $U_{AB} = 10$, the final profit is $\Delta_{AB}\{v_1, v_3\} = 10 \times 1.3492 - 5 \times 2 = 3.492$.

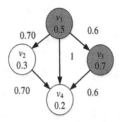

Fig. 4. An example of selecting seeds by using improved greedy algorithm

7   Experiment Results

7.1   Experiment Setup

The ca_Hepth and ca-GrQc are collaboration networks extracted from the e-print arXiv (http://www.arXiv.org), which is the same source used in the experimental study in [3]. The former is extracted from the "High Energy Physics-Theory" and the latter is extracted from the General Relativity. The nodes in these two networks are authors and an edge between two nodes means the two coauthored at least one paper. The p2p-Gnutella08 records the Gnutella peer to peer network from August 8 2002 where nodes represent hosts in the Gnutella network topology and edges represent connections between the Gnutella hosts. We use the SM to generate the influence weight of edges (Table 1).

Table 1. Statistics of three real-world networks in resulting graph

Dataset	ca-HepTh	ca-GrQc	p2p-Gnutella08
Number of nodes	9878	5242	6301
Number of edges	51996	28992	20777

7.2   Performance Studies

First, we tested the effectiveness of improved greedy algorithm. In this experiment, we select 10 seeds with improved greedy algorithm, max-degree algorithm and random algorithm to maximize the cooperative influence. We compared the effectiveness of improved greedy algorithm, max-degree and random algorithm with conditional probabilities $P(B|A) = 0.4$ and $P(B|A) = 0.6$ respectively where spread time step $t = 2$. Figure 5 shows that improved greedy outperforms other two heuristic algorithms. This is because that some of max-degree seed nodes may be clustered, and selecting all of them as the seeds cannot effectively spread the cooperative influence. By the random heuristic, as a baseline heuristic algorithm, some of selected seeds cannot spread the influence effectively.

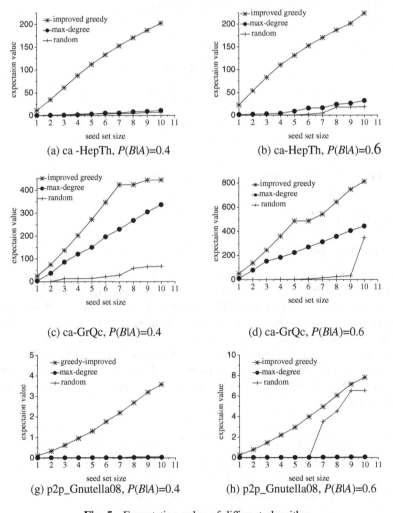

Fig. 5. Expectation value of different algorithm

Further, we tested the conditional probabilities with the expectation value of Algorithm 1 on the ca_Hepth and ca_GrQc. In this experiment, we compare the expectation value of Algorithm 1 with conditional probabilities $P(B|A) = 0.2$, $P(B|A) = 0.4$, $P(B|A) = 0.6$, $P(B|A) = 0.8$ respectively. Figure 6 shows that the expectation value is increased with the increase of the conditional probability, since the value of $P(AB)$ is increased when the conditional probability is increased, and the expectation value of cooperative influence spread is increased.

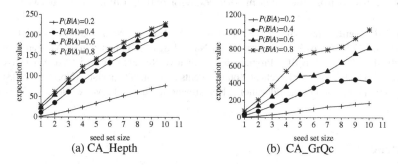

(a) CA_Hepth   (b) CA_GrQc

Fig. 6. Expectation value with different conditional probabilities

Finally, we tested the relationship of final profit with profit U_{AB} on the ca_Hepth and ca_GrQc. In this experiment, if C_{AB} is fixed, then we compare the relationship of final profit with $U_{AB} = 3$, 4, 5 and 6. Figure 7 shows that the final profit is increased with the increase of profit. This is because that the final profit is increased when the profit is increased.

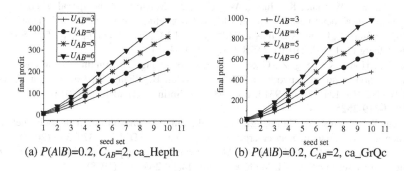

(a) $P(A|B)=0.2$, $C_{AB}=2$, ca_Hepth   (b) $P(A|B)=0.2$, $C_{AB}=2$, ca_GrQc

Fig. 7. Final profit with different U_{AB}

8 Conclusions and Future Work

Aiming at maximizing the cooperative influence spread of associative products, we generate the cooperative influence spread based on the separate influence spread graphs of products and associative rule. Then, we adopt the ICMAP to model the cooperative influence spread, which can well reflect the real information diffusion. Further, we prove the submodularity of objective function that maximizing the cooperative influence spread under the ICMAP, and the improved greedy algorithm is used to solve this objective function.

The improved greedy algorithm proposed in this paper can approximate the optimal result with $1 - 1/e$. However, the improved greedy algorithm is also time consume for selecting seeds to maximize the cooperative influence spread without parallel computing. For our future work, we plan to utilize Spark platform to realize our algorithm. Other than the efficiency, one interesting direction is that obtain the confidence and support threshold from the users history behavior data in online social network.

Acknowledgement. This paper was supported by the National Natural Science Foundation of China (Nos. 61472345, 61402398, 61232002), Natural Science Foundation of Yunnan Province (Nos. 2014FA023, 2013FB010), Program for Innovative Research Team in Yunnan University (No. XT412011), Program for Excellent Young Talents of Yunnan University (No. XT412003), and the Research Foundation of the Educational Department of Yunnan Province (No. 2014C134Y).

References

1. Nail, J., Charron, C., Baxter, S.: The consumer advertising backlash. Forrester research and intelliseek market research report (2004)
2. Johnson, A.: Nike-tops-list-of-most-viral-brands-on-facebook-twitter (2010). http://www.kikabim.com/news/
3. Kempe, D., Kleinberg, J., Tardos, É.: Maximizing the spread of influence through a social network. In: SIGKDD, pp. 137–146 (2003)
4. He, X., Song, G., Chen, W., Jiang, Q.: Influence blocking maximization in social networks under the competitive linear threshold model. In: SDM, pp. 463–474 (2012)
5. Wu, H., Liu, W., Yue, K., Huang, W., Yang, K.: Maximizing the spread of competitive influence in a social network oriented to viral marketing. In: Li, J., Sun, Y., Dong, X.L., Yu, X., Sun, Y., Dong, X.L. (eds.) WAIM 2015. LNCS, vol. 9098, pp. 516–519. Springer, Heidelberg (2015). doi:10.1007/978-3-319-21042-1_53
6. Liu, Z., Hong, X., Peng, Z., Chen, Z., Wang, W., Song, T.: Minimizing the cost to win competition in social network. In: Cheng, R., Cui, B., Zhang, Z., Cai, R., Xu, J. (eds.) APWeb 2015. LNCS, vol. 9313, pp. 598–609. Springer, Heidelberg (2015). doi:10.1007/978-3-319-25255-1_49
7. Chen, W., Collins, A., Cummings, R., et al.: Influence maximization in social networks when negative opinions may emerge and propagate. In: SDM, pp. 379–390 (2011)
8. Nemhauser, G., Wolsey, L., Fisher, M.: An analysis of approximations for maximizing submodular set functions—I. Math. Program. **14**(1), 265–294 (1978)
9. Datta, S., Majumder, A., Shrivastava, N.: Viral marketing for multiple products. In: ICDM, pp. 118–127 (2010)
10. Song, G., Zhou, X., Wang, Y., Xie, K.: Influence maximization on large-scale mobile social network: a divide-and-conquer method. IEEE Trans. Parallel Distrib. Syst. **26**(5), 1379–1392 (2015)
11. Gomez-Rodriguez, M., Song, L., Du, N., Zha, H., Schölkopf, B.: Influence estimation and maximization in continuous-time diffusion networks. ACM Trans. Inf. Syst. **34**(2), 9 (2016)
12. Tang, Y., Xiao, X., Shi, Y.: Influence maximization: near-optimal time complexity meets practical efficiency. In: SIGMOD, pp. 75–86 (2014)

13. Liang, W., Shen, C., Zhang, X.: UserGreedy: exploiting the activation set to solve influence maximization problem. In: Cheng, R., Cui, B., Zhang, Z., Cai, R., Xu, J. (eds.) APWeb 2015. LNCS, vol. 9313, pp. 561–572. Springer, Heidelberg (2015)
14. Leicht, E.A., Holme, P., Newman, M.E.J.: Vertex similarity in networks. Phys. Rev. E **73** (2), 026120 (2006)
15. Han, J., Kamber, M., Pei, J.: Data Mining: Concepts and Techniques. Elsevier, Amsterdam (2011)
16. Krause, A., Guestrin, C.: Beyond convexity: submodularity in machine learning. ICML Tutorials (2008)

A Multi-Model Based Approach for Big Data Analytics: The Case on Education Grant Distribution

Weiqiang Li, Jintao Yang, Wenhan Wu, Wusi Ci, Jie He$^{(\boxtimes)}$, and Lina Fu

Zhejiang University City College, Hangzhou 310015, Zhejiang, China
hej@zucc.edu.cn

Abstract. With the increasing development of big data analytic research, abundant big data analytic models have been the most important tools in many fields of social. Federal Education Grant program is especially important for development of universities all over the world. A reasonable investment for a university could provide students more intensive supports, which eventually resulted in increasing the ratio of talented persons and greater contributions to society. However, the study on the optimization of the investment proportion of education grant is rarely few, and there is even no further study on the integration of it in the field of big data analytics. According to it this article aims to use four different models to invest university selectively and determine an optimal investment ratio.

Keywords: VARMA Model · Internal rate of return model · Mean variance model · GA

1 Introduction

More and more people and organizations pay more attention to education, which becomes a very popular topic in current society. Especially college students, as the most important part of education system, whose great performance in the university campus can promote the development and progress of the society in a certain extent. Based on these reasons, lots of charitable organizations start focusing on funding universities. If existing $1000,000,00 and each university getting $3000,000 on average at least, how much and which one should be paid to? Following this problem, this study mainly focused on presenting a multi-model based approach by using big data analysis method.

Big data analysis has become a trend and has been studied by many studyes. Mazchua [1] analyzed 457 papers about big data Allenby [2] used Bayesian method to analyze large data Pokomy [3] gave the specific data processing process and methods. Besides that, big data analysis has also been applied to many fields. For example, Kanda [4] used the big data analytic method to solve the medical problem, and proposed his own suggestions. In the field of Economics, Hazen [5] used large data applications in operations and supply chain

© Springer International Publishing Switzerland 2016
A. Morishima et al. (Eds.): APWeb 2016 Workshops, LNCS 9865, pp. 16–28, 2016.
DOI: 10.1007/978-3-319-45835-9_2

management; Li [6–8], also analyzed in the manufacturing industry as well as the customer's big data service. However, in the field of resource distribution, there still existing few studyes combine big data in their own study field. Without adopting any big data analysis, Radaev [9] put forward the method of allocating resources to the nuclear radiation of the dangerous source, and Song [10, 11] put forward the strategy of the goal of profit maximization to the rational allocation of resources.

In this article, for the university fund investment, the study mainly uses the spending of the students during the four year of their university and the average wage after they graduated (usually 10 years to obtain the internal rate of return), and the study uses the internal rate of return and mean variance model to get the optimal ratio of the investment. There are lots of universities, it would become difficult to use mean variance model to get the answer, so the study choose to use genetic algorithm to improve the speed of computer processing, and finally an optimal solution could be computed more quickly.

2　Overview

As the Fig. 1 there are a lot of schools in the USA, the data of each school in Internet is also very big. So in this article, we first preprocess online data, then the work uses four models to solve the problem as the Fig. 1 appears. Firstly the work uses the analytic hierarchy process to reduce the number of data. And VARMA Model could get the degree of investment funds for the school and ranked them again. Then we get the internal rate of return and use genetic algorithm to get the best proportion of investment schools in these models, and the algorithm greatly improves the speed of solving the mean variance model.

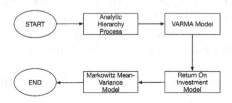

Fig. 1. The process of research

3　Data Collection

In this paper, data mainly comes from the United Stated National Center for education statistics and University information extracted from the web dataset. The database is used by 7804 branch schools in the United States and it includes detailed data of every school, such as location, academic year system and so on. In order not to repeat investing the schools with gained large investment from large investment institution, the study filters data according to Pell grants donating the proportion of undergraduate, and selects schools whose Pell grant disproportionately are less than 60 %. As for the selective level of 60 %, it is in line with the selecting principles that it should exist a large sample of data after filtering and the final selective result is 4341 schools although a lack of large amount of data and some unreliable statistics exist. (The study tries to avoid investing in universities which has been invested by Gates and other foundation.)

By comparing observations roughly, it is found that an index, taking 25th the percentile of the SAT scores at the institution for instance, is vacant in some school while it is recorded completely in another schools. If excluding those school which is lack of relevant data out imply, it is not reasonable and may cause some good school will not be considered. In this way, our paper argued to select and analyze the most worth investment schools respectively from data missing schools and full data schools.

4   Analytic Hierarchy Process Model

As for the analysis of investment in a university, many good methods are not suitable applying in a huge amount of data and the investment amount is limited. Therefore, taking the existing sample size of 4341 schools into account, we think it is of great necessity to reduce the sample size first and seek and confirm the schools to invest in. However, reducing the sample size according to an index of the school purely will ignore many other indicators and may affect our judgment choice so that this study adopts the analytic hierarchy process synthetically on choosing to the schools will invest in.

Analytic hierarchy process is a simple and flexible multi-criteria decision method. The study use AHP Analytic Hierarchy Process method to construct a hierarchical structure model. Elements form several levels based on their attribute relationship. Higher level elements control lower level elements [12].

The study chooses some variables, and the study defines some abbreviation for them (Table 1).

The process of our model construction is shown in the following graph (Fig. 2):

- Target layer: Analyze problem to achieve target results.
- Criterion layer 1: This layer contains a number of factors involved in the implementation of the objective.
- Criterion layer 2: This level contains a number of influence elements involved in the implementation of the rule layer 1.
- Scheme layer: this layer contains a variety of measures and programs which could achieve the aim of optional choices.

In order to establish judgment matrix, we assume that there are n factors, $X = \{x_1, x_2, ..., x_n\}$. To comparing with a factor of the upper layer's influence,

Table 1. Variables Table

Symbols	Meanings
C150_4_POOLED_SUPP	150 % completion rate for four-year institutions
SCORES	ACT or SAT scores
C200_L4_POOLED_SUPP	200 % completion rate for less-than-four-year institutions
GRAD_DEBT_MDN10YR_SUPP	Median debt of completers expressed in 10-year monthly payments
NPT4	Average Net
RET	Retention rate
PREDDEG	Degree awarding
PCTPELL	Percentage of undergraduates receiving Pell grants
UGSD	Number of registered undergraduate students
RPY_3YR_RT_SUPP	3 years repayment rate
PCTFLOAN	Percentage of federal loans to undergraduates
GRAD_DEBT_MDN_SUPP	Average debt

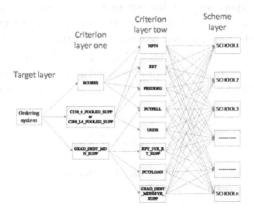

Fig. 2. The process of AHP model

it should determine the weight of this factor in this layer. a_{ij} means comparison results of the factor i to the factor j:

$$a_{ij} = \frac{1}{a_{ij}}$$

$$A = \begin{pmatrix} a_{11} & a_{12} & \cdots & a_{1n} \\ a_{21} & a_{22} & \cdots & a_{2n} \\ \vdots & \vdots & \ddots & \vdots \\ a_{n1} & a_{n2} & \cdots & a_{nn} \end{pmatrix}$$

Among them, different figures represent the important influence degree of different factors, the following table gives specific instructions (Table 2):

Table 2. Definition of the scale of the judgment matrix

Importance scale	Meaning
1	Equal importance
3	Weak importance of one over another
5	Essential or strong importance
7	Very strong importance
9	Absolute importance
2, 4, 6, 8	Intermediate values between adjacent scale values

It is the same that we could list the judgment matrix between the school through the relation between the rule layer and the measure layer. We could get it through the comparison between any two Specific indicators. According to the number of indexes, there are 8 judgment matrixes in measure layer.

We could use the ratio (b_{ij}) of the specific data of each candidate school in this index, during the multiple comparisons, the ratio is $b_{ij} = \frac{B_{ni}}{B_{nj}}$. B_{ni} and B_{nj} are the school data of candidate school i and j in index B_n. It is worth noting that the process needs to be standardized for the school's data, and then map the school's data to the range of 1 to 9. Next, we test the consistency of the judgment matrixes:

Consistency index (CI):

$$CI = \frac{\lambda_{max} - n}{n - 1} \tag{1}$$

The maximum value of the characteristic root is λ_{MAX}

Calculate the consistency ratio CR

$$CR = \frac{CI}{RI} \tag{2}$$

When $CR < 0.1$, we consider that the consistency of the judgment matrix can be accepted, otherwise the judgment matrix should be properly modified.

Wherein CI, CR, λ_{max} is represented consistency test indicators, consistency ratio, judgment matrix biggest feature root and normalized feature vector which is corresponding to the maximum eigenvalue of AHP. They are shown in formula above. n represents judgment matrix size [13].

Through this model, all the composite scores of 4341 schools were obtained. In the case of investment, whose composite scores more than 60 was selected for targeted school in order to make each investment by each school can get a certain number of amount and actual effect, and then the total selective school was about 89 schools.

5   VARMA Model

Because of the indicators in the database are numerous and the analytic hierarchy process (ahp) can not include all indicators, this paper argues that it should further to determine the number of schools through some specific indicators. There is no denying that VARMA model adopted in this paper could achieve purpose.

AR/SVAR model is one of the basic models of macro econometric analysis, It is widely used in economic policy and other macroeconomic issues. However, In recent years, some researchers have found that the VAR/SVAR model has two problems. One problem is that setting up VAR/SVAR model is lack of economic theory basis, another problem is that SVAR model analysis results lack robustness. So, this article we use the VARMA model to obtain the investment funds for the school's effective year, and then rank it.

An N element stationary time series (X_t) could respects:

$$X_t = \mu + \Delta p_t + \psi_1 * \Delta p_{t-1} + ... + = \mu + \sum_{i=0}^{\infty} \psi_i * \Delta p_{t-i} = \mu + \sum_{i=0}^{\infty}(B) * \Delta p_{t-i} \quad (3)$$

The change of graduation rate is Xt and the variable quantity of Pell fund is Δp_t, X_t has zero mean and covariance matrix Σ. Operator is [14]:

$$\psi(B) = \sum_{i=0}^{\infty}(\psi_i) * B^i \quad (4)$$

First order matrix of X^t is:

$$E(X_t) = \mu \quad (5)$$

Second order matrix of X^t is:

$$Var(X_t) = \sum_{i=0}^{\infty}(\psi_i) * \Sigma * \psi_i^T \quad (6)$$

For multivariate time [15] series, $X_t = (x_{1t}, ..., x_{nt})^T, t = 0, \pm 1, \pm 2, ...$ Vector autoregressive model (VAR (1)) is:

$$X_t = \alpha + \phi_1 * X_{t-1} + \Delta p_t \quad (7)$$

In above equation: $n * k$, $E(\Delta p_t * \Delta p_t') = \sum \omega, \alpha = (\alpha_1, ..., \alpha_n)^T$ are constant vector. Because the stationary sequence can be transformed into a zero mean sequence by subtracting the mean. So usually assume $\alpha = 0$ Vector autoregressive model (VAR (p)) is:

$$X_t = \alpha + \phi_1 * X_{t-1} + \Delta p_t, t = p + 1, ..., n \quad (8)$$

Vector autoregressive moving average process (VARMA(p,q)):

$$X_t = \alpha + \phi_1 * X_{t-1} + \Delta p_t + \sum_{k=1}^{q} (\theta_k) * \Delta p_{t-k} \tag{9}$$

$$\phi_p \neq 0, \theta_q \neq 0, \sum \Delta p > 0$$

Vector autoregressive moving average process with input term:

$$X_t = \alpha + \Gamma * \mu_t + \sum_{j=1}^{p} \phi_1 * X_{t-j} + \Delta p_t + \sum_{l=1}^{q} (\theta_k) * \Delta p_{t-k} \tag{10}$$

In this equation, μ_t vector output $s * 1$. X in the name of VARMAX means that it is a Exogenous vector process. So we could get the VARX Model with input term:

$$X_t = \alpha + GD_t + \gamma * \mu_t + \sum_{j=1}^{p} \phi_1 * X_{t-j} + \Delta p_t \tag{11}$$

$$t = p + 1, p + 2, ..., T, \gamma : n * s, G : n * 1, D_t : 1 * 1$$

$G * D_t$ represents the linear time trend deterministic composition item.

Then finding the year when the graduation rate variation lag item coefficient is 0. The year could represent the time duration that the Investment has a significant positive impact on students achievement. We select the longest duration (Not less than 4 years) of 30 schools from 89 schools in the last model.

6   Return on Investment Model

After VARMA model, 30 aimed schools are determined and the allocated amount of each school which is depending on value of investment is distributed. In order to determine the investment value of a school, we use the model to calculate the internal return rate of 30 schools, respectively. In order to determine the value of an school, we could discount the spending of students in the school and the income of students after them graduate from school, and let the net present value (NPV) is equal to 0, and then obtain the corresponding internal rate of return. Internal rate of return usually uses to study project feasibility and investment economics, so in this article, we think that it is feasible to judge the investment of school.

When foundation invests college, the comparison and assurance of cost expenditure and expected return is the original theoretical point of studying individual internal rate of return [16]. So, we regard cost (C_t) as the Average net price for Title IV institutions. n respects years of education, r respects discount ratio. The total present cost of undergraduate education in university is:

$$C = \sum_{t=1}^{n} \frac{C_t}{(1+r)^t} \tag{12}$$

Of course, excluding costs, the discount of benefit is indispensable. In this article, we set Median earnings of students working and not enrolled 10 years after entry is the factor of benefit, this factor could determine as B_T, discount ratio is R, and the years of accepting university education is n, N respects income years.so the total present benefit of undergraduate education in university is:

$$B = \sum_{T=n+1}^{N} \frac{B_T}{(1+R)^T} \tag{13}$$

After analyzing the data of students spending in school and Median earnings of students working and not enrolled 10 years after entry, we find the balance point of invention between loss and benefit. This point is individual Internal Rate of Return (discount ratio) in university. Calculating formula:

$$\sum_{t=1}^{n} \frac{C_t}{(1+r)^t} = \sum_{T=n+1}^{N} \frac{B_T}{(1+R)^T} \tag{14}$$

It is easy to calculate the individual internal ratio of return (R) by using the mathematical iteration in computer.

Finally, After VARMA model, 30 aimed schools are determined and the allocated amount of each school which is depending on value of investment is distributed.

In order to determine the investment value of a school, we use the model to calculate the internal return rate of 30 schools, respectively. Due to the changeability and instability of annual internal return rate, using a year of internal return rate only can not reflect the investment value of the school comprehensively.

7   Markowitz Mean-Variance Model

We choose Markowitz Mean-Variance model, which is good at dealing with the volatility of the return rate, to determined the optimal investment proportion in this paper. Through the further analysis of the school list obtained from the above two models, we find that we can transform the amount of investment allocated to the school into the problem of determining the optimal weight of portfolio in economics. So we seek the optimal portfolio weights from the Markowitz Portfolio (MP) Model. This model uses the method of quantitative analysis in the Markowitz portfolio, and chooses the minimum variance from the investment portfolio based on weighing the risk and expecting return on investment.

7.1   The Development of Model

Assuming that there are N universities in an investment portfolio, $w \in R^N$ represents the investment column vector and its representation method [17] as:

$$w = (w_1, w_2, ..., w_N)^T \tag{15}$$

In this equation, w_i respects that investment of i university, we determine that: $r = (r_1, r_2, ..., r_N)^T$, $r \in R^N$ respects the yield of cost, r_i respects the ratio of the investment of i cost, r respects a N dimensional random column vector, Minimum income is μ_0, the Maximum initial investment level is x_0. $e = (1, 1, ..., 1)^T$, and e is a N-dimensional column vector. [18, 19]

We assume that $\mu \in R^N$ respects the expected yield of cost, so yield is:

$$E(r) = \mu \qquad (16)$$

And $\mu = (\mu_1, \mu_2, ..., \mu_N)^T$, μ_i respects that the expected yield of cost i. μ is an N-dimensional column vector. Assume that $\mu \neq ke$, so μ and e are linearly independent.

We determine covariance matrix between costs is:

$$G := (\sigma_{ij})_{N*N} = E(r - \mu)(r - \mu)^T = E(rr^T) - \mu\mu^T \qquad (17)$$

$$\sigma_{ij} = E(r_i - E(r_i))(r_j - E(r_j)) \qquad (18)$$

Considering of the above equations, we could get the Mean-Variance model:

$$max = \mu/(W^T G W) \qquad (19)$$

$$s.t. \mu^T W = \mu_0$$

$$e^T W = 1$$

7.2   Genetic Algorithm

Because the number of schools is so large after filtering, it needs too much time to run the normal study method, so we choose genetic algorithm to solve the problems of nonlinear programming. Simple Genetic Algorithm can be expressed as:

$$SGA = (C, E, P, M, \Phi, \Gamma, \Psi, T) \qquad (20)$$

In the expression:

C-Individual coding method;
E-Individual fitness evaluation function;
P-Initial population;
M-Population size;
Φ-Selection operator;
Γ-Crossover operator;
Ψ-Mutation operator:
T-the termination condition of genetic operations;

In the Genetic Algorithm, the choice of controls parameter is very critical. The different choice will make difference to Genetic Algorithm's property, and even influence the whole Algorithm's convergence.

In the paper, we choose the group size M = 30, that is each group including 30 schools and each representing a portfolio. The conditions of the Algorithm end; we choose the maximum genetic algebra that is 200 generation. When the algebra achieves the stipulated algebra, the Algorithm ends.

In genetic algorithm, fitness is proposed to measure the how close or how helpful each individual in the group could approach to the most optimal solution. Individuals with higher fitness have higher probability to be inherited, otherwise lower. Fitness function is applied to measure fitness of each individual. Thus, to solve the target function f could be transferred to solve its fitness function Fit (f). For example, in case of maximizing problems, let Fit(f) = f, while in case of minimizing problems, let Fit(f) = −f. The mean variance model is modified to bi-objective model. Meanwhile, considering the diversity of how investors value both risk and profit, as well as two aspects mentioned above, we choose weight coefficient transformation method to solve the problem. Suppose a and 1 C a relatively be the level how investors value risk and profit. Thus transferring the bi-objective nonlinear programming problem to the single-objective nonlinear programming problem, as follows:

$$min f = min|aW^T GW + (1 - a)\mu| \qquad (21)$$

It could be used to combine optimization of asset. And the flow chart is (Fig. 3):

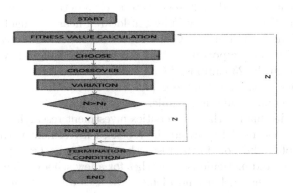

Fig. 3. Genetic algorithm

8   Solution and Result of Model

We program in MATLAB software to achieve the basic genetic algorithm and use it to determine the optimal investment strategy. At last, the work can get the result of the model, and the result can be seen in below Table 3.

The above table shows that the optimal investment amount should be allocated to each school under a certain amount of investment. As can be seen from

Table 3. Final Result

The name of school	Investment volume (million)	The name of school	Investment volume (million)
California State University-Fullerton	5.2356	University of South Florida-Main Campus	3.31056
Texas A & M University-College Station	5.4115	San Jose State University	1.38
California State University-Long Beach	3.7233	Florida International University	4.94
...	...	...	...

the table, schools for investments, which is in a different state and their distribution is relatively discrete. The fund investment is not affected by geographical. This shows that the fund investment is not affected by geographical. At the same time, in the selection of the results, many of them are public universities rather than private universities where people are keen to invest in the United States. This is because this work at first duplication with other large funds. Of course, although most schools are public universities, the work also invest private universities. Then we choose a public university and a private university to verify the rationality of the model in this article. We decided to choose two schools which we randomly selected in 30 schools to make a detailed understanding. We found California State University-Fullerton located near Losangeles, California, in the south of the United States, California. It is the second largest in the state of California. The most important is that all of people thought it was the fastest growing campus in the 23 campus of California State University. And New York University is one of the most famous and best schools in the word. It ranked 20th. So we think our model is credible.

Compared with many other universities investment researches, the model of this paper is a good model to avoid the repeated investment with other funds. Also many scholars did not do the research under the background of big data, most of them only did meticulous researches for a few schools with single model. This article under the background of big data uses different models to choose the school which is worth investment, and determine the optimal investment amount. There are some rationality in logical thinking and some feasibility in practical operation.

9   Conclusion

Our study creatively applied the analysis of big data into the investment of schools selectively due to few researches has linked them together effectively so far. At present, a variety of funds invest schools according to their excellent degree graduates, which could result in a large number of repeated investments.

In order to avoid of the resource waste, that selecting the unrepeated high invest-ment schools and determining the amount of allocation based on different com-prehensive degree of schools are of great feasibility and rationality. Although some problems that we may not find all the schools data or some schools data may not be open to the public exist, our ideas and techniques worth for reference.

Acknowledgement. This work is supported by Zhejiang Provincial Natural Sci-ences Foundation of China (Grant No. LQ14F020002) and project also supported by the National Training Foundation of Innovation and Entrepreneurship for Under-graduates(Grant No.201613021005).

References

1. Rodrguez-Mazahua, L., Rodrguez-Enrquez, C.-A., Snchez-Cervantes, J.L., Cer-vantes, J., Garca-Alcaraz, J.L., Alor-Hernndez, G.: A general perspective of big data: applications, tools, challenges and trends. J. Supercomputing **71**(8), 1–41 (2015)
2. Allenby, G.M., Bradlow, E.T., George, E.I., Liechty, J., McCulloch, R.E.: Perspec-tives on Bayesian methods and big data. Customer Needs Solutions **1**(3), 169–175 (2014)
3. Pokorný, J., Škoda, P., Zelinka, I., Bednárek, D., Zavoral, F., Kruliš, M., Šaloun, P.: Big data movement: a challenge in data processing. In: Hassanien, A.E., Azar, A.T., Snasael, V., Kacprzyk, J., Abawajy, J.H. (eds.) Big Data in Complex Systems. SBD, vol. 9, pp. 29–70. Springer, Heidelberg (2015)
4. Kanda, E.: Use of big data in medicine. Ren. Replace. Ther. **1**(3), 1–4 (2015)
5. Hazen, B.T., Skipper, J.B., Boone, C.A., Hill, R.R.: Back in business: operations study in support of big data analytics for operations and supply chain management. Ann. Oper. Study **243**(1), 1–11 (2016)
6. Li, J., Tao, F., Cheng, Y., Zhao, L.: Big data in product lifecycle management. Int. J. Adv. Manufact. Technol. **81**(1), 667–684 (2015)
7. Sun, Z., Pambel, F., Wang, F.: Incorporating big data analytics into enterprise information systems. In: Khalil, I., Neuhold, E., Tjoa, A.M., Xu, L.D., You, I. (eds.) ICT-EurAsia 2015 and CONFENIS 2015. LNCS, vol. 9357, pp. 300–309. Springer, Heidelberg (2015). doi:10.1007/978-3-319-24315-3_31
8. Liang, Y.H.: Customer relationship management and big data mining. In: Pedrycz, W., Chen, S.-M. (eds.) Information Granularity, Big Data, and Computational Intelligence, vol. 8, pp. 349–360. Springer, Heidelberg (2014)
9. Radaev, N.N., Mel'nikov, M.V.: Efficient distribution of resources for increasing the shielding of nuclear- and radiation-dangerous objects. Atomic Energy **92**(4), 310–316 (2002)
10. Gozalvez, J., Lucas-Estañ, M.C., Sanchez-Soriano, J.: Joint radio resource man-agement for heterogeneous wireless systems. Wirel. Netw. **18**(4), 443–455 (2011)
11. Xu-song, X., Jian-mou, W.: A dynamic programming algorithm on Project-Gang investment decision-making. Wuhan Univ. J. Nat. Sci. **7**(4), 403–407 (2002)
12. Guo, J., Zhang, Z., Sun, Q.: Study and applications of analytic hierarchy proces. Chin. J. Saf. Sci. **18**(5), 148–153 (2008). (in Chinese)
13. Xiong, L., Li, K., Tang, J., Ma, J.: Research on matching area selection criteria for gravity gradient navigation based on principal component analysis and analytic hierarchy process. In: Cases in International Relations, vol. 9815. Longman (2015)

14. Bai, Z., Tong, L., Zhang, J.: The assumptions variance decomposition analysis and application in SVARMA model. Stat. Study **31**(5), 85–94 (2014). (in Chinese)
15. James, C., Koreisha, S., Partch, M.: A VARMA analysis of the causal relations among stock returns, real output, and nominal interest rates. J. Finance **40**, 1375–1384 (1985)
16. Chen, J.: Analysis and measurement of the internal rate of return of higher education. High. Educ. Jiangsu (1), 43–45 (2006). (in Chinese)
17. Soleimani, H., Golmakani, H.R., Salimi, M.H.: Markowitz-based portfolio selection with minimum transaction lots, cardinality constraints and regarding sector capitalization using genetic algorithm. Expert Syst. Appl. **36**(3), 5058–5063 (2009)
18. Luo, K.: The study based MATLAB optimal portfolio problem. Sci. Technol. Inf. **6** (2014). (Chinese)
19. Zhao, Y.: The Application Study on Revised Markowitz Models in Modern Financial Portfolio Selection. Dalian University of Technology, p. 53 (2013). (in Chinese)

Sentiment Target Extraction Based on CRFs with Multi-features for Chinese Microblog

Bingfeng Chen[1(✉)], Zhifeng Hao[1,2], Ruichu Cai[1], Wen Wen[1],
and Shenzhi Du[1]

[1] Faculty of Computer Science, Guangdong University of Technology,
Guangzhou, China
735180@qq.com
[2] School of Mathematics and Big Data, Foshan University, Foshan, China

Abstract. Sentiment target extraction on Chinese microblog has attracted increasing research attention. Most previous work relies on syntax, such as automatic parse trees, which are subject to noise for informal text such as microblog. In this paper, we propose a modified CRFs model for Chinese microblog sentiment target extraction. This model see the sentiment target extraction as a sequence-labeling problem, incorporating the contextual information, syntactic rules and opinion lexicon into the model with multi-features. The major contribution of this method is that it can be applied to the texts in which the targets are not mentioned in the sequence. Experimental results on benchmark datasets show that our method can consistently outperform the state-of-the-art methods.

Keywords: CRFs · Multi-features · Sentiment target extraction · Sentiment analysis

1 Introduction

With the rapid development of social networks, more and more people use microblog for information exchange and sharing. Users are willing to share their views or experience on microblog, which makes a large number of sentiment reviews. With the expansion of such information, it is difficult to use artificial methods to collect and process these massive reviews. Therefore, how to use computer technology to process and mine microblog reviews effectively has become a research hotspot.

The past decade has witnessed a huge exploding interest in sentiment analysis from the natural language processing and data mining communities due to its inherent challenges and wide applications. Sentiment target extraction is a fundamental problem in the field of sentiment analysis and opinion mining [1–4]. Sentiment extraction on Twitter has attracted more and more research in recent years [5]. Microblog sentiment extraction is a very challenging task [6–10], because microblog messages are short, noisy and contains masses of acronyms and informal words.

For some unstructured microblog, sentiment target extraction is a difficult problem, and existing studies seem to have some inadequacies. In this paper, an approach based on standardized microblog text is proposed to improve the segmentation and syntactic

© Springer International Publishing Switzerland 2016
A. Morishima et al. (Eds.): APWeb 2016 Workshops, LNCS 9865, pp. 29–41, 2016.
DOI: 10.1007/978-3-319-45835-9_3

parsing, incorporating the contextual information, syntactic rules and opinion lexicon into the model with multi-features. When the sentiment target appears directly in the text, a conditional random model combined with a classification model is used to solve this problem. For the case that the sentiment target does not appear in the text, we presents an improved model based on Conditional Random Fields (CRFs). It makes the implied target into abstract target, and adding global hidden nodes to CRFs approach to identify targets.

The core idea of this research is to study the sentiment target extraction on Chinese microblog text, which treats it as a sequence labeling problem. We use CRFs to label the text in sentence level, and comprehensive utilization of multi-features to improve the accuracy of model. In the experimental part, we conducted experiments to verify and evaluate the model in two datasets which contain NLP&CC2012 dataset and self-built dataset. Experimental results on two datasets demonstrate that this method outperforms the state-of-art methods, which not only better identify the dominant microblog sentiment targets, but also the hidden sentiment targets.

2   Related Work

Sentiment target extraction in social network and social media starts to attract increasing attentions [11–14]. It is a difficult task in sentiment classification. Several methods have been proposed [15–17]. In the extraction task, sentiment targets usually refer to sentiment features, which are defined as sentiment components or attributes. [16] built two Twitter-specific sentiment lexicons based on the words' associations with emoticons and hashtags containing sentiment words. Then they extracted sentiment features, such as the number of positive and negative words, for each tweet, and combined these features with other textual features for training and classification. [17] proposed to extract contextual knowledge from massive unlabeled messages and incorporate it to enhance the training of microblog sentiment classifiers. [14] proposed a sentiment classification method based on Latent Factor Model. In their method, users and words are represented as distributions over "latent aspects" through matrix factorization. Syntactic parsing tools are utilized to obtain POS tags and dependency relations between words, in order to strengthen the learning of words' representations. Besides, their method relies on microblog syntactic parsing results, which are usually inaccurate and unreliable since microblog messages are noisy and full of informal words.

In our work, we also extract noun targets. Different pruning methods are proposed to remove the noise. To cover infrequent features that are missed, they regard the nearest nouns/noun phrases of the sentiment words identified by frequent features as infrequent features. Other related work on sentiment extraction mainly uses the idea of topic modeling to capture targets in hidden variables. [18] proposed a dependency tree based method for sentiment classification of Japanese and English subjective sentence using conditional random fields with hidden variables. In their method, the sentiment polarity of each dependency sub-tree in a sentence, which is not observable in training data, is denoted by a hidden variable. The polarity of the whole sentence is calculated in consideration of interactions between the hidden variables.

3 The CRFs Model with Multi-features

In this section, we introduce the process and principle of sentiment target extraction. We firstly introduce CRFs model, and then introduce the model of sentiment target extraction and its inference and parameter estimation, At last, we introduce the features that would be used in sentiment target extraction.

3.1 Conditional Random Fields Model

[19] proposed conditional random fields which is a probabilistic models for segmenting and labeling sequence data. CRFs have seen wide application in natural language processing, computer vision, and bioinformatics [20], especially have achieved good effect in Chinese words segmentation, part-of-speech Tag (POS Tag), named entity recognition and information extraction. There are some research have use CRFs to sentiment analysis and sentiment target recognition.

Linear-chain CRFs is a simple and typical model of CRFs, we consider the conditional distribution $p(y|x)$ that follows from the joint distribution $p(y, x)$ of an HMM. The key point is that this conditional distribution is in fact a conditional random field with a particular choice of feature functions. The model structure of linear-chain CRFs is shown in Fig. 1.

$X = \{x_1, x_2, \cdots x_n\}$ is a input sequence, x_i denotes the element of sequence i, there is a total of n elements of the observation sequence. $Y = \{y_1, y_2, \cdots y_n\}$ is a output sequence, it also has a total of n elements of the sequence, y_i denotes the element of sequence i, y_i is the output label result of x_i, in conclusion, the number of input element is equal of output element.

In the probability model of the sentiment target extraction, the conditional probability of a target sequence X and the random variables Y are as follow

$$p(y|x) = \frac{1}{Z(x)} \exp\left(\sum_{k=1}^{K} \lambda_k F_k(x, y)\right) \tag{1}$$

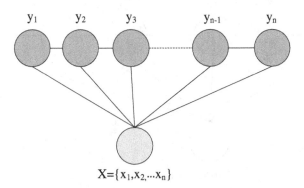

$$X = \{x_1, x_2, \cdots x_n\}$$

Fig. 1. Model structure of linear-chain CRFs

$$Z(x) = \sum_y \exp(\sum_{k=1}^{K} \lambda_k F_k(x, y) \tag{2}$$

$$F_k(x, y) \sum_{i=1}^{n} f_k(y_i, y_j, x, j) \tag{3}$$

where K is the total number of parameter, Z(x) is the normalize factor, $\lambda = \{\lambda_1, \lambda_2, \cdots \lambda_k\}$ is the parameter set of the model. $f_k(y_i, y_j, x, j)$ is a feature function of sequence i, include the node feature and the edge feature, the node feature is relevant with the point of corresponding place, the edge feature is not only relevant with the point of corresponding place, but also relevant with the conjoint point of another place. It's concrete form like

$$f_k(y_i, y_j, x, j) = \begin{cases} f_k(y_i, y_i) & (k \in K^n) \\ f_k(x_i, y_i, x_j, y_j) & (i \neq j, k \in K^e) \end{cases} \tag{4}$$

where K^n denotes the set of node feature, K^e denotes the set of edge feature.

3.2   The Modified Model of CRFs

If the sentiment targets are all in the input observation sequence X, then we can use the CRFs model to label the sequence, extract the sentiment target. However, the sentiment target is sometimes not in the input observation sequence. For example, "So happy!" is a kind of situation just mention above. In order to solve this problem, we observe mass Chinese microblogs and find that there are several kinds of situations which can't find the sentiment target. In most of the cases, there are two typical probabilities, the "blogger" and "topic". We denote blogger is the one who write the microblog, and topic is the main idea of the microblog. So we introduce DCRF (Latent-Dynamic Conditional Random Fields) [21, 22]. In order to label the target "blogger" and "topic", we add two global node g_1 and g_2 into linear-chain conditional random fields. We called the model LLCRF (Linear-chain Latent Dynamic Conditional Random Fields), and the model is shown in Fig. 2.

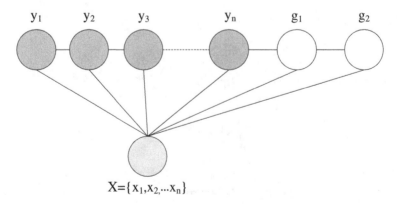

Fig. 2. LLCRF add two global node

Every status node connects with the adjoining node, when y_n and g_2 connect with g_1, the conditional probability is:

$$F_k(\mathbf{x}, \mathbf{y}) = \sum_{i=1}^{n} f_k(y_i, y_{i-1}, x, i) + f_k(y_i, g_1, x, n+1) + f_k(g_1, g_2, x, n+2) \quad (5)$$

In the above probability model, every word in a sentence as a random variable, the two global random variables "blogger" and "topic" are added to the model. The random variable denotes the property of the corresponding sentiment target. In this paper, the attribute value of the sentiment target may be L = {'N-B','N-I','P-B','P-I','O'}, it is the value space of input sequence. "N-B" denotes the begin place of negative sentiment target, "N-I" denotes the following place of negative sentiment target, "P-B" denotes the begin place of positive sentiment target, "P-I" denotes the following place of positive sentiment target, "O" denotes not sentiment target.

Because of the words "topic" and "blogger" are the global targets of the sentence, so it is not the best choice to linear connect with the tail of the sentence. We proposed a modified model to enhance the recognition result of the whole sentiment target, the two global nodes connect with all the other nodes, thus it raises the recognition result of hidden sentiment target. We called this model GLCRF (Global Latent-dynamic Conditional Random Fields), the model is shown in Fig. 3.

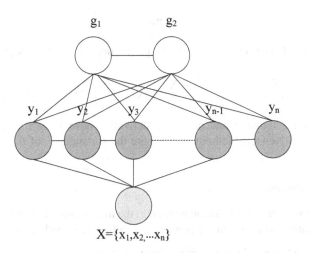

Fig. 3. GLCRF model

Because of the change of graph structure, the conditional probability of GLCRF can be defined by

$$F_k(\mathbf{x}, \mathbf{y}) =$$
$$\sum_{i=1}^{n} f_k(y_i, y_{i-1}, x, i) + \sum_{i=1}^{n} f_k(y_i, g_1, x, i) + \sum_{i=1}^{n} f_k(y_i, g_2, x, i) + f_k(g_1, g_2, x, n+2) \quad (6)$$

3.3   Model Reference and Parameter Estimate

Next we will discuss when given a sentence x, how to get the label s of sentiment target. After word segmentation of the sentence, the output is sequence s, which constitute of the sentiment target label y_i, g_1 and g_2, that is, $s = \{y_1, y_2, \ldots y_n, g_1, g_2\}$, Hence, s is given by

$$s = arg_{i'} max P_\lambda(s'|x) \tag{7}$$

It is hard to use enumeration method to compute the boundary probability of the sentiment target label s_i. In this paper, we use Loopy BP (Loopy Belief Propagation) to compute the boundary probability of the sentiment target label s_i. Loopy BP algorithm can effectively compute the boundary probability of probability graph model. It transmits the beliefs to get the boundary probability by the random variable and factors.

$D = \{ <x^{(m)}, s^{(m)} > \}_{m=1}^M$ is a training set, which has M training samples. We use the logarithm maximum likelihood estimation to estimate the parameter λ of the model, in order to prevent over learning, we use the Gaussian penalty term to do parameter estimation. Define the objective function L_λ, to get the maximum λ of objective function value

$$L_\lambda = \sum_{m=1}^M log P_\lambda(s^{(m)}|x^{(m)}) - \frac{1}{2\sigma^2} \sum_{k=1}^K \lambda_k^2 \tag{8}$$

$$\hat{\lambda} = arg_\lambda max L_\lambda \tag{9}$$

with σ is a given Gaussian prior value, the partial derivative of L_λ is given by

$$\frac{\partial L_\lambda}{\partial \lambda_K} = \sum_{m=1}^M \left[\sum_s F_k\left(x^{(m)}, s^{(m)}\right) - \sum_s P_\lambda\left(s^{(m)}, x^{(m)}\right) F_k\left(x^{(m)}, s^{(m)}\right) \right] - \frac{1}{\sigma^2} \lambda_k \tag{10}$$

Since objective function and its partial derivative have known, it could through L-BFGS of Quasi-Newton Methods to compute the parameter λ of the model.

3.4   Feature Selection

There are five kinds of features would be used in the model, including part-of-speech tag (POS tag), emotion word, syntax dependency, emotion icon, and semantic role label.

Feature 1 (POS tag): POS tag is the basis of lexical analysis, we use a immobilization window as feature, in this paper, we set the number of window is three, on the other hand, we label three word, the current one, the previous one, the behind one.

Feature 2 (Emotion): We structure a dictionary of emotion to tag emotion tendency of every word. Because of the specificity of Chinese microblog, we didn't use the open emotion dictionary like "HowNet Chinese emotion dictionary" and "NTU emotion word set". We structure a mixed dictionary constitute of open emotion dictionary and manual dictionary. The manual dictionary constitute of commonly used word of Chinese microblog.

Feature 3 (Syntax dependency): According to the given grammar structure, analysis the sentence contains what grammar units and the relationship between the units, and then structure a grammar tree. Syntax dependency on sentences in all relations can be expressed as a unified form, represent in the form of binary group, and tag all the type of the relationships, these relationships are not limited to directly adjacent words, the distance words can also be parsed well.

Feature 4 (Emotion Icon): There are a lot of emotion icon in the sentence of Chinese microblog. The icon directly shows the emotion of blogger, and it can also show the emotional polarity and strength.

Feature 5 (SRL): Semantic role label is a concise form of superficial semantic analysis, its mission is to recognize the sender and receiver of the even.

4 Experiments and Discussions

4.1 Data Preprocessing

In this section, we introduce how to process the blog data that we have collected.

Firstly, microblog processing and sentence segmentation. Because of the optional express in Chinese microblog, we have to do some process for the next work. There are a lot of cyber word and abbreviation on microblog, someone get used to use the other punctuation instead of formal punctuation to make pause, some useless link, special character string and so on, all of these, have to process to formal express. In microblog, some topic begins with "#", some contact people begin with "@", these punctuation is all useless, and so we delete all. Every microblog is a textual data; it contains one or more sentence or some emotion icons. Because the input of the model of extract sentiment target is sentence, so we have to separate the microblog to sentences, it will enhance the efficiency of separate words and grammar analysis. Emotion icon is a strong feeling expression, so we extract them for the later work.

Secondly, word segmentation. The input label sequence consists of several words and punctuations, so the first thing is to segment the sentence to words. In the experiment, we use analysis tool of Stanford Word Segmenter to word segmentation.

Thirdly, part-of-speech tagging and syntactic parsing. The model of sentiment target extraction used a variety of features, including part-of-speech tagging and word dependency, therefore we need to part-of-speech tagging and syntactic parsing to each word in the sentence. In the experiment, we used the syntactic parsing Tool of Stanford Parser to deal with. The tool can to part-of-speech tagging sentences after word segmentation, and get the dependencies between words after syntactic parsing. Aiming at the particularity of microblog, we add a user dictionary to improve the effect when in the process of word segmentation, the dictionary is a collection of some commonly used cyber words.

Fourthly, labeling. Because the experiment is supervised learning, so we need to label the experimental data manually.

Fifthly, data standardization. The data from the fourth step have to normalize for each model or application or software package.

4.2 Comparison Between Different Models and Result Analysis

In order to avoid over fitting phenomenon, the experimental results are made five folds cross validation. Experimental data includes two parts: dataset of manual collection and dataset of NLP&CC 2012, data is given in Table 1 for details. All the manual data collect from Sina microblog, crawl the data from Sina open API, then screening and annotations the data manually. There are 1264 sentiment target of manual dataset, and about 395 hidden ones. There are 193 "blogger" and 147 "topic" in the hidden sentiment target. In NLP&CC 2012 dataset, there are 454 hidden sentiment targets, including 37 "blogger" and 417 "topic".

Table 1. The dataset of experiment

Label	Manual dataset	NLP&CC2012	Total
Microblog	897	2228	3125
Sentence	1590	3880	5470
N-B	897	2269	3116
N-I	513	1429	1942
P-B	367	572	941
P-I	163	309	472
O	20676	48985	69661
Hidden sentiment target on total sentiment target (%)	31	16	21

In order to verify the validity of the model, we compare the our model with four models, and adopt all features mentioned above, four models are Naive Bayes (NB), Support Vector Machine (SVM) and Linear-chain Latent-Dynamic Conditional Random Fields (LLCRF) and Global latent-Dynamic Conditional Random Fields (GLCRF). GRMM is a software of probability graph model that widely used in scientific research fields. The experiment of support vector machine is to use libsvm which is a software kit.

Because of the complexity of the model itself and the introduction of many features, LLCRF and GLCRF model training process is time-consuming, the consumption time changes according to the size of the training dataset, but model labeling process is more quickly. At the same time, the experiment found that fusing all kinds of characteristics, all kinds of dictionary and the process of word segmentation and syntax parsing needs to consume more memory.

We use the value of F1 to evaluate the result of the experiment which comprehensive the value of precision and recall. Experimental results are shown in Fig. 4; Fig. 4(a) shows the experimental results of manually collected dataset, Fig. 4(b) shows the experimental results of NLP&CC2012 test dataset, Fig. 4(c) shows the experimental results of manually collected dataset combine with NLP&CC2012 test dataset. From Fig. 4(a), we can see that the experiment result of LLCRF and GLCRF model is better than NB and SVM in label N-B and P-B, but SVM is shown obvious advantage in other labels. F1 value of label O is good at several models, the evaluation results are

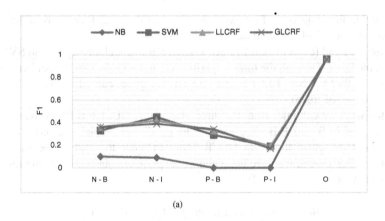

(a)

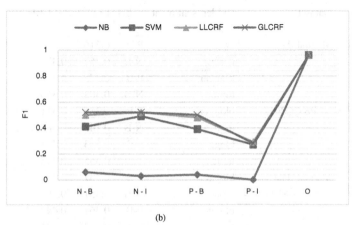

(b)

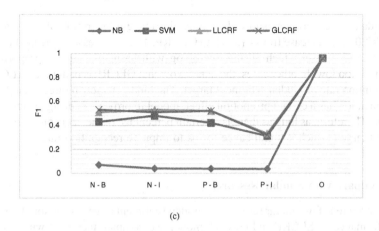

(c)

Fig. 4. (a) Manually collected dataset. (b) NLP&CC2012 dataset. (c) Manual dataset combines with NLP&CC2012 dataset

above 0.9, but the main goal of our work is to extract the other four kinds of the object label, so the label O of not sentiment target is useless.

Figure 4(b) and (c) show that LLCRF and GLCRF model are better than SVM and NB in all the label. Through the three experiments, we can infer that the performance of NB is worst, SVM is bad, LLCRF and GLCRF are good, can effectively marked the sentiment target of microblog.

By the way, we can infer from the three graphs that GLCRF is better than LLCRF in the label of N-B and P-B. Because of "blogger" and "topic" are hidden targets, LLCRF can't recognize them but GLCRF can. In order to validate the recognition effect of GLCRF model, we have done another experiment, and compare the results of hidden sentiment target (Table 2).

Table 2. Recognition result of hidden sentiment target

Dataset	Hidden sentiment target	Label	LLCRF	GLCRF
Manual data	blogger	P-B	0.316	0.371
	topic	N-B	0.357	0.378
	blogger	P-B	0.375	0.397
	topic	N-B	0.308	0.346
NLP&CC2012	blogger	P-B	0.356	0.311
	topic	N-B	0.143	0.086
	blogger	P-B	0.383	0.448
	topic	N-B	0.355	0.415
Manual data + NLP&CC2012	blogger	P-B	0.337	0.405
	topic	N-B	0.351	0.369
	blogger	P-B	0.361	0.442
	topic	N-B	0.373	0.436

The data of experiment show that, only the recognition result of "Blogger" in NLP&CC2012 is decrease from LLCRF to GLCRF. The main reason may be due to the NLP&CC2012 dataset which all the microblog with hashtags, and the proportion of "blogger" is too low. In other cases, the datas show that GLCRF is better than LLCRF in the recognition rate of hidden sentiment target. The hidden target "blogger" and "topic" of identification has a certain promotion effect, model improvement design is just for the sake of it. Therefore, as long as there is a certain percentage of the data contained hidden sentiment target, which is significance for us to improve recognition rate.

4.3   Compare with Similar Research

Until now, there is few similar research of hidden sentiment target extraction. In order to test performance of LLCRF and GLCRF model, we compare the result with open test result of NLP&CC2012 (best1\best2\avg). In order to make the model with NLP&CC2012 test results comparable, we used the same training dataset and testing dataset as competition teams of NLP&CC2012. The value of the table is the higher the better.

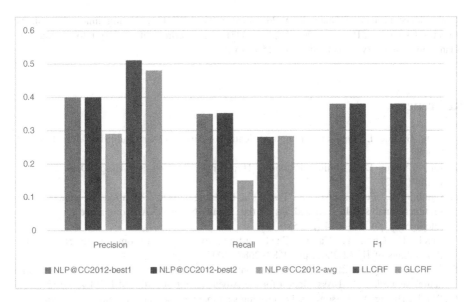

Fig. 5. Compare with NLP&CC2012

The Fig. 5 show that all the result of LLCRF and GLCRF is significantly better than the average result of NLP&CC2012. The precision of LLCRF and GLCRF is better than the two best result of NLP&CC2012.

Above all, the paper proposes the model base CRF can achieve a good result on extract sentiment target. When there are a lot of hidden sentiment target in the text, it is very meaningful of the improvement of LLCRF and GLCRF. The experimental results show that the performance of sentiment target extraction is hardly used in actual, but it is better than similar research.

5   Conclusion

In this paper, we put forward a model with multi-features of sentiment target extraction based on conditional random fields. The model can extract sentiment target not only dominant but also implied. We apply the model to two datasets derived from NLP&CC2012 and manually collected dataset, and compare with different models such as NB, SVM and LLCRF. The experiment results show that GLCRF outperforms state-of-the-art methods for sentiment target extraction.

Acknowledgments. This work is financially supported by NSFC-Guangdong Joint Found (U1501254), Natural Science Foundation of China (61202269, 61472089, 61572143, 61502108, 61502109), Natural Science Foundation of Guangdong province (2014A030306004, 2014A030308008), Key Technology Research and Development Programs of Guangdong Province (2012B01010029, 2013B051000076, 2015B010108006, 2015B010131015), Science and Technology Plan Project of Guangzhou City (2014Y2-00027), Opening Project of the State Key Laboratory for Novel Software Technology (KFKT2014B03, KFKT2014B23), Philosophy and social science project of Guangdong Provenience (GD14XYJ24), Young innovative talents project of Guangdong Province (2015KQNCX027), The experimental teaching reform project of Guangdong university of technology (2015SY45).

References

1. Pang, B., Lee, L.: Opinion Mining and Sentiment Analysis. Now Publishers Inc., Hanover (2008)
2. Liu, B.: Web Data Mining: Exploring Hyperlinks, Contents and Usage Data. Springer, Berlin (2012)
3. Cambria, E., Fu, J., Bisio, F., Poria, S.: Enabling affective intuition for concept-level sentiment analysis. In: Proceedings of the Twenty-Ninth AAAI Conference on Artificial Intelligence, pp. 508–514 (2015)
4. Breck, E., Choi, Y., Cardie, C.: Identifying expressions of opinion in context. In: Proceedings of IJCAI 2007, pp. 2683–2688 (2007)
5. Ren, Y., Zhang, Y., Zhang, M., Ji, D.: Context-sensitive Twitter sentiment extraction using neural network. AAAI-Association for the Advancement of Artificial Intelligence (2016)
6. Wu, F., Huang, Y.: Personalized microblog sentiment extraction via multi-task learning. In: AAAI (2016)
7. Xia, R., Wang, C., Dai, X., Li, T.: Co-training for semi-supervised sentiment extraction based on dual-view bags-of-words representation. In: Proceedings of the 53rd Annual Meeting of the Association for Computational Linguistics and the 7th International Joint Conference on Natural Language Processing, pp. 1054–1063 (2015)
8. Zhou, G., He, T., Zhao, J., Wu, W.: A subspace learning framework for cross-lingual sentiment extraction with partial parallel data. In: Proceedings of the Twenty-Fourth International Joint Conference on Artificial Intelligence (IJCAI), pp. 1426–1432 (2015)
9. Nakagawa, T., Inui, K., Karohashi, S.: Dependency tree based sentiment extraction using CRFs with hidden variables. In: Proceedings of the 2010 Annual Conference of the North American Chapter of the Association for Computational Linguistics, pp. 786–794. Association for Computational Linguistics (2010)
10. Wu, F., Song, Y., Huang, Y.: Microblog sentiment extraction with contextual knowledge regularization. AAAI-Association for the Advancement of Artificial Intelligence (2015)
11. Li, G., Hoi, S.C., Chang, K., Jain, R.: Microblogging sentiment detection by collaborative online learning. In: IEEE ICDM, pp. 893–898 (2010)
12. Song, Y., Lu, Z., Leung, C.W., Yang, Q.: Collaborative boosting for activity classification in microblogs. In: ACM KDD, pp. 482–490 (2013)
13. Li, G., Hoi, S.C., Chang, K., Liu, W., Jain, R.: Collaborative online multitask learning. IEEE Trans. Knowl. Data Eng. 26(8), 1866–1876 (2014)
14. Song, K., Feng, S., Gao, W., Wang, D., Yu, G., Wong, K.F.: Personalized sentiment classification based on latent individuality of microblog users. In: IJCAI, pp. 2277–2283 (2015)
15. Hu, X., Tang, L., Tang, J., Liu, H.: Exploiting social relations for sentiment analysis in microblogging. In: WSDM, pp. 537–546 (2013)
16. Kiritchenko, S., Zhu, X., Mohammad, S.M.: Sentiment analysis of short informal texts. J. Artif. Intell. Res. (JAIR) 50, 723–762 (2014)
17. Wu, F., Song, Y., Huang, Y.: Microblog sentiment classification with contextual knowledge regularization. In: AAAI, pp. 2332–2338 (2015)

18. Nakagawa, T., Inui, K., Kurohashi, S.: Dependency tree-based sentiment classification using CRFs with hidden variables. In: The 2010 Annual Conference of the North American Chapter of the ACL, pp. 786–794 (2010)
19. Lafferty, J., McCallum, A., Pereira, F.: Conditional random fields: probabilistic models for segmenting and labeling sequence data. In: Proceedings of ICML 2001, pp. 282–289 (2001)
20. Sutton, C., McCallum, A.: An introduction to conditional random fields. Mach. Learn. **4**(4), 267–373 (2011)
21. Nakagawa, T., Inui, K., Kurohashi, S.: Dependency tree-based sentiment classification using CRFs with hidden variables. In: Human Language Technologies: The 2010 Annual Conference of the North American Chapter of the Association for Computational Linguistics, pp. 786–794. Association for Computational Linguistics (2010)
22. Morency, L.P., Quattoni, A., Darrell, T.: Latent-dynamic discriminative models for continuous gesture recognition. In: Proceedings of the IEEE Conference on Computer Vision and Pattern Recognition, pp. 1–8 (2007)

EMD-DSJoin: Efficient Similarity Join Over Probabilistic Data Streams Based on Earth Mover's Distance

Jia Xu[1,2], Jiazhen Zhang[1], Chao Song[1], Qianzhen Zhang[1],
Pin Lv[1,2(✉)], Taoshen Li[1,2], and Ningjiang Chen[1,2,3]

[1] School of Computer, Electronics and Information in Guangxi University,
Guangxi, China
{xujia,lvpin,tshli,chnj}@gxu.edu.cn,
{zhangjiazhen,csong,qianzheng}@mail.gxu.cn
[2] Guangxi Colleges and Universities Key Laboratory of Parallel
and Distributed Computing, Guangxi, China
[3] Guangxi Key Laboratory of Multimedia Communication
and Network Technology, Guangxi, China

Abstract. Similarity joins on probabilistic data play a vital role in many practical applications, such as sensor reading monitoring and object tracking based on multiple video sources. Earth Mover's Distance (EMD) proposed in Computer Vision is more effective in returning similar probabilistic data being more consistent to human's perception to similarity. However, the cubic time complexity of EMD hampers its wide application, especially in the analysis of fast incoming data streams. In this paper we, to the best of our knowledge, make the first attempt to address the EMD similarity join over data streams under sliding window semantics. We first design an efficient and effective index framework, named *B+ Forests Index*, which facilitates data pruning and offers proper strategy to deal with out-of-order data. We then propose the EMD similarity algorithm, named *EMD-DSJoin*, based on the proposed index framework. We perform extensive experiments on real-world datasets and verify the effectiveness and efficiency of our proposal.

Keywords: EMD · Data stream · Sliding window similarity join · EMD-DSJoin

1 Introduction

Recent years witness an explosion of data produced by many practical applications. The data applications, such as videos uploaded by users to online video sharing websites and sensor readings gathered by large cyber-physical systems. Different from static data stored in traditional databases, streaming data pose huge demands for faster data analysis, since returning analyzing results in a timely manner is of importance to most of these applications. Hence, designing and implementing efficient data analysis operators for data streams is very important. The similarity join is one of the most significant and time-consuming stream operators. It compares tuples coming from two

© Springer International Publishing Switzerland 2016
A. Morishima et al. (Eds.): APWeb 2016 Workshops, LNCS 9865, pp. 42–54, 2016.
DOI: 10.1007/978-3-319-45835-9_4

data streams and retrieves all qualified tuple pairs of these two streams, such that the similarity between the two tuples in every pair is high. On account of the unbounded property of data streams, such similarity comparisons are only performed on the most recently arriving tuples dropping into a time *sliding window*. This paper focuses on proposing efficient and effective approaches for the sliding window similarity join over probabilistic data streams based on Earth Mover's Distance (*EMD*) [3]. Compared with traditional similarity functions, e.g. L_1 and L_2 *norms*, EMD is more robust in quantifying the similarity of two histogram-representative probabilistic data (in the form of $p = \{p_1, ..., p_n\}$) which have a small distribution shift in their attribute domain [1–3, 5]. Therefore, EMD becomes an attractive similarity measure for applications such as content-based image retrieval, video-based gesture recognition, near duplicate detection, and etc. Hereinafter, histogram-representative probabilistic data is named as *histogram tuple* for short. The EMD similarity join of two data streams owns many applications, such as forest fire monitoring [4] and object tracking based on multiple video sources [13].

Although EMD is very effective in improving the result quality of similarity joins, its high time complexity, i.e. $O(n^3 \log n)$, hampers its wide application in many practical scenarios. Therefore, many research works have been proposed to speed up the procedure of similarity search based on EMD. For example, some researchers propose faster but approximate EMD computation method [12]. A couple of index structures or lower/upper bound filters are also proposed to eliminate unpromising EMD computations of two less similar histogram tuples [4, 11, 12]. However, when the EMD is used to analyze streaming data arriving at high speed, the processing of EMD similarity joins faces the following challenges.

Challenge 1: Due to the cubic complexity of EMD, the similarity join operation on two fast arriving data streams is very expensive. Deriving join results in a timely manner faces great challenges.

Challenge 2: Out-of-order phenomenon is common under the context of data stream environments. How to safely discard expired tuples in the memory so that the integrity of join results is also satisfied is another challenge.

To overcome Challenge 1, we propose a novel framework named *EMD-DSJoin*. EMD-DSJoin transforms the incoming histogram tuples into the space of EMD lower bounds by using the primal-dual theory of linear programming. And then, a group of B^+ tree forests, which we call as B^+ *Forests index*, are constructed based on the space of EMD lower bounds. The B^+-Forests index is of great help in pruning unnecessary comparisons of histograms tuples in terms of EMD. The LB_{IM} [1] lower bound and the UB_p [4] upper bound of EMD are then employed to further eliminate EMD computations. These lower/upper bounds can be computed at a lower cost than EMD, which accelerates the whole similarity join processing based on EMD.

To overcome Challenge 2, we carefully design the data discarding strategy in our B^+-Forests index with the presence of out-of-order tuples in data streams, which ensures the completeness of join results and will not cache too much tuples in the memory. The delay tuple insertion strategy in B^+-Forests index is also well discussed to guarantee the efficiency of query processing.

To summarize, our contributions in this paper are as follows.

- To the best of our knowledge, this is the first attempt to address the EMD similarity join over data streams under sliding window semantics and we propose an effective framework, i.e. *EMD-DSJoin*, which uses the B^+ *Forests* indexing techniques and a couple of lower/upper bounds of EMD to prune EMD calculations and speed up the join processing.
- We propose a couple of strategies to enhance the ability of EMD-DSJoin in coping with out-of-order delay histogram tuples in data streams.
- We design optimization strategy to calculate a proper time span value for every B^+ tree forest, so that the join processing performance of EMD-DSJoin can be further improved.
- We present extensive experiments on real-world datasets to confirm the efficiency and effectiveness of our EMD-DSJoin.

2   Related Work

At present, various works focus on supporting efficient similarity join on data streams [9, 10, 15]. But less them focus on addressing the problem of similarity joins over probabilistic data streams. To the best of our knowledge, this is the first work that specifically solves the EMD similarity join over probabilistic data streams under the sliding window semantic.

Generally, the EMD defines the dissimilarity of two histogram tuples as the minimal cost of transforming one histogram tuple into the other. However, solving this transportation problem renders a high time complexity of $O(n^3 \log n)$. At present, many works have been proposed to accelerate the similarity joins based on EMD. While some efforts are paid to develop approximate EMD calculation method with linear or sub-linear time complexity [12], more efforts have been made to design easy-to-compute lower or upper bounds for EMD [1, 2, 4–6, 12, 14] to prune unnecessary EMD calculations that compare two very similar tuples or two very dissimilar tuples. There are also some works proposing novel index techniques [1, 4, 7, 14] to index histogram tuples w.r.t. EMD, so as to achieve the index-based pruning during the query processing. Among these index techniques, our proposed Tree-based Indexing (TBI) approach [4] is more simple but efficient to index histogram tuples using B^+ tree structure and to perform the index-based pruning of EMD calculations, by employing the dual program of EMD transportation problem. In this paper, we will show how to extend the TBI approach to design efficient and effective index technique, i.e. B^+ Forests Index, to benefit the EMD similarity joins over fast arriving data streams.

There are also several works proposed to speed up the EMD similarity search on large dataset by using distributed computing and popular MapReduce paradigm [4, 6–8]. However, we focus on the optimization of EMD similarity joins over data streams in a centralized computing environment. And our proposal can also be used in a distributed computing environment to benefit the query processing.

3   Preliminaries

In this part, we first formulate the related notions of our problem in Sect. 3.1, and then we elaborate the main idea of our Tree-based Indexing Technique (TBI) [4] in Sect. 3.2.

3.1   Definitions and Notations

In this paper, the probabilistic data is represented by a histogram tuple, in the form of $p = \{p_1, ..., p_n\}$, where p_i records the probability of statistical objects dropping in the ith bin (i.e., attribute domain). The Earth Mover's Distance quantifies the dissimilarity of two histogram tuples by the minimal amount of efforts necessary to transfer one tuple into the other. The formal definition of EMD is given below.

Definition 1 (Earth Mover's Distance). *Given two n-bin histogram tuples $r = \{r_1, ..., r_n\}$ and $s = \{s_1, ..., s_n\}$, and a ground distance matrix $[d_{ij}] \in R^{n \times n}$, the EMD between r and s is the optimum achieved by the following linear program:*

$$min : \sum_{i=1}^{n} \sum_{j=1}^{n} f_{ij} \times d_{ij}, \text{ subject to :}$$
$$f_{ij} \geq 0 \text{ and } \sum_{j=1}^{n} f_{ij} = r_i \text{ and } \sum_{i=1}^{n} f_{ij} = s_i.$$

EMD defines a Work Flow $[f_{ij}]$, such that each f_{ij} is the flow from bin i in r to bin j in s. A *Ground Distance* $[d_{ij}]$ is also provided by users, where every d_{ij} represents the distance between bin i and bin j in the attribute domain. The pairwise computation of EMD takes $O(n^3 \log n)$ time [3].

Definition 2 (EMD Similarity Join with Sliding Window Semantic). *Given two data streams of histogram tuples, i.e. R and S, a similarity threshold θ, and a time sliding window with size $|W|$, for any histogram tuple $r \in R$ (or $s \in S$), EMD similarity join over R and S, denoted by $R \overset{EMD}{\bowtie} S$, returns a set of tuple pairs $\{<r, s>\}$, satisfying $0 \leq |r.timestamp - s.timestamp| \leq |W|$ and $EMD(r,s) \leq \theta$.*

3.2   Tree-Based Indexing Technique for EMD Similarity Search

To boost the EMD similarity data search, we have proposed an efficient and effective technique, which we call Tree-Based Indexing (*TBI*) [4, 5]. On the basis of Primary-Dual theory of linear programming, a histogram tuple is mapped to L different 1-dimensional (1D) keys by using L feasible solutions, i.e. $\{\Phi_1, ... \Phi_L\}$ to the dual program of *EMD*. Then, each histogram tuple s_i is inserted into L B^+ trees independently based on every mapping key under Φ_i, denoted by $key(s_i, \Phi_l)$ with $1 \leq l \leq L$. The constructed L B^+ trees form a B^+ tree forest. Taking Fig. 1 as an example, based on two feasible solutions (e.g. Φ_1 and Φ_2) to the dual program of EMD, a set of histogram tuples, i.e. $s_1, ..., s_{18}$, are projected to two different 1D key spaces, where two B^+ trees, i.e. T_1 and T_2, are built in each mapping space to index all these histogram tuples. The constructed two B^+ trees form a B^+ tree forest that offers effectively support for collaboratively pruning unnecessary EMD computations for EMD similarity search. In particular, given tuple r as the query, θ as the similarity threshold, a range search following the key range shown in Eq. 1 on each B^+ tree derives a candidate result set for the similarity search [4]. In other word, the mapping key value of every tuple s_i that satisfies $EMD(r, s_i) \leq \theta$ must be inside the key range shown in Eq. 1.

$$Key(s_i, \Phi_l) \in [min(\Phi_l) + key(r, \Phi_l) - \theta, \theta - ckey(r, \Phi_l)] \quad (1)$$

Here in Eq. 1, $min(\Phi_l)$ and $ckey$ are two easy-to-compute reals derived only based on r and Φ_l. Then, an intersection of all candidate result sets derived by running the range search on every B^+ tree in the B^+ tree forest renders a much smaller candidate result set for the query r. For example in Fig. 1, the candidate result set (indicated by a dashed frame) derived by T_1 and T_2 are $\{s_6, s_7, s_{11}, s_{12}\}$ and $\{s_5, s_6, s_7, s_8, s_{12}\}$, respectively. The intersection of these two result sets gets $\{s_6, s_7, s_{12}\}$ which is a reduced candidate result set for the query. In Sect. 4, we will show that how to build efficient index structure for streaming probabilistic data by extending the idea of the TBI technique.

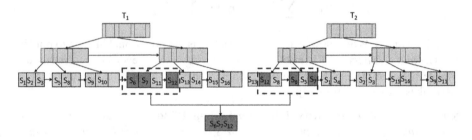

Fig. 1. A B^+ tree forest

4   Index Design

Building effective index is very important to support efficient stream similarity join processing, especially when the similarity function, i.e. EMD, has high computational complexity. However, existing EMD-based index techniques organize the entire stream of histogram tuples using only one single index [1, 4, 7, 14], which definitely renders high overhead for re-adjusting the index whenever expired tuples are discarded. To benefit lower-overhead tuple dropping and index exploration, we introduce an in-memory B^+ *forests index* framework in Sect. 4.1 to overcome the high overheads brought by using a single index. And in Sect. 4.2 we propose a theoretical analysis to determine a proper *archive period* for every B^+ forest, which is a vital parameter in index construction.

4.1   The Framework of B⁺ Forests Index

Given two data streams of histogram tuples, denoted by R and S, the *B⁺ Forests Index* which is composed of a group of B⁺ tree forests, can be built on any of the two streams. The basic idea is to partition the incoming stream tuples in terms of the discrete time intervals and build a B⁺ tree forest per interval. The method of building a B⁺ tree forest to index histogram tuples following the TBI solution proposed in [4], which has been briefly elaborated in Sect. 3.2. This is because the TBI is much more applicable than other indexing methods [1, 7, 14] to index streaming data whose data distribution may change over time [5]. The span of time interval, denoted by P, is also known as the *archive period* of a B⁺ tree forest. Figure 2 illustrates the structure of the B⁺ forests index built on R, where six B⁺ tree forests, namely F1,...,F6, are constructed independently based on six non-overlapping time intervals. Every B⁺ tree forest maintains the minimum and maximum timestamps of the tuples it contains. All B⁺ tree forests are linked in terms of their building time. Based on the sliding window constraint in query processing, expired histogram tuples are dropped from memory in the granularity of B⁺ tree forest-level, rather than tuple-level. As shown in Fig. 2, the sliding window is represented by a black rectangle, with the arrow above it indicating its sliding direction. Any expired B⁺ tree forest (e.g. F_1 in Fig. 2) which is outside the window, is entirely removed from the memory. Under such circumstance, the index re-adjusting overhead for discarding tuples is alleviated, because the deletion of any expired B⁺ tree forest will not affect any other B⁺ tree forests in the window. The B⁺ tree forest F_6 in Fig. 2, which organizes the most recently incoming tuples is referred to as the *active B⁺ tree forest*, denoted by F_{active}. Note that only the active B⁺ tree forest is used to insert the newly incoming tuples.

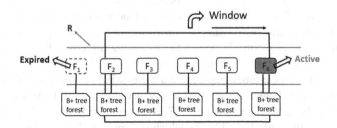

Fig. 2. Window-based B⁺ tree forest

The pseudocode of maintaining a B⁺ forests index for a given time interval is listed in Algorithm 1.

Algorithm 1:   BplusForestsMaintainace
INPUT: data streams R and S, a set of B$^+$ tree forest F, data cache ca, network delay D,   capacity factor c, the archive period P of every B$^+$ tree forest   **OUTPUT:** updated B$^+$ tree forest F
1:    for each incoming tuple p do
2:        if p.source==R then
3:            if $(F = \emptyset \; \| \; (F_{active}.\text{span}() >= P \; \&\& \; F_{active}.\text{size}() >= c*P))$ then
4:                create a new B$^+$ tree forest F_{new};
5:                $F_{active} = F_{new}$;
6:            $F_{active}.\text{insert}(p)$;
7:            update $F_{active}.maxTime$ and $F_{active}.minTime$ based on $p.timestamp$;
8:        else if p.source == S then
9:            ca.add(p);
10:           for each $F_i \in F$ do
11:               if $(p.timestamp - F_i.minTime > |W| + D)$ then
12:                   delete F_i;

Let P and $c*P$ be the archive time period and the maximum capacity of a B$^+$ tree forest respectively, where c is the capacity factor of a B$^+$ tree forest. When a tuple $p \in R$ arrives, it is inserted into either the *active* B$^+$ tree forest F_{active}, or a newly generated B$^+$ tree forest, denoted by F_{new}, if the number of tuples in F_{active} exceeds the B$^+$ tree forest capacity $c*P$ and the time span of F_{active} is large than the B$^+$ tree forest archive period P (lines 2–6). The capacity constraint of a B$^+$ tree forest is used to avoid the generation of a few small B$^+$ tree forests, because some archive periods only contain few tuples. The generated F_{new} will then be used to update F_{active} (line 5). Meanwhile, the minimum and maximum timestamps of F_{active} are updated according to the timestamp value of p (line 7). When the incoming tuple p is from stream S, p is stored into a data cache ca (line 9), waiting for further join with tuples from R. Finally, the difference between the timestamp of p and the maximum timestamp of every forest is checked (line 11). Given the network delay parameter D and the size of sliding window $|W|$, if the difference of a forest F_i is larger than $|W| + D$, F_i can be safely removed from the memory (lines 11–12), which still ensures the integrity of join results in future (for the proof please refer to [15]). This forest-level data discarding strategy improves the discarding efficiency by avoiding timestamp checking for each tuple in a forest.

4.2   Determining an Optimal Archive Period P for B$^+$ Tree Forest

The parameter P, i.e. archive period, determines the time span of a B$^+$ tree forest, which is very vital to the efficiency of the B$^+$ forests index. If P is too small, B$^+$ forests index may contain a lot of B$^+$ tree forests, each of which has very few tuples in it. Querying processing on these small-scale forests may equal to execute a linear scan on the whole data, which is not cost-effective. On the other hand, if P is too large, B^+ forests index may contains only one single large-scale B^+ tree forest, which introduces great overhead in maintaining the index under data deletion and insertions and cannot benefit from our data discarding strategy proposed in Sect. 4.1. This section discusses how to determine a proper value for P.

Recall that every B^+ tree forest maintains the minimum and the maximum timestamps of the histogram tuples in it. During the query processing of sliding window-based joins, we need to check the minimum (and maximum) timestamp of every B^+ tree forest and return those forests for further join processing which are completely contained or partially contained by the sliding window. For the forests being completely contained by the window, every tuple in them definitely arrives in the time period of the sliding window. And for those forests that partially contained by the window, we need to traverse every tuple in the forest and return those tuples dropping into the sliding widow. Under such procedure, the optimal value of P is supposed to minimize the sum of the number of visited B^+ tree forests and the number of traversed tuples in a forest for timestamp checking. The number of visited B^+ tree forests can be calculated by $|W|/P$, where $|W|$ is the size of sliding window. To compute the number of tuples in those partially-contained B^+ tree forest, note that there are at most two B^+ tree forests that may be partially overlapped with the sliding window, with one of them being the active B^+ tree forest. The number of tuples stored in a full B^+ tree forest can be computed by cP, where c is the coefficient between the capacity of a B^+ tree forest and the parameter P. Since the active B^+ tree forest is not yet full, the number of tuples in it can be estimated by $cP/2$. Therefore, the optimal value for P can be derived by solving the objective function shown in Eq. (2).

$$\min_{P}\{\frac{|W|}{P} + cP + \frac{cP}{2}\} \tag{2}$$

Equation 2 can be simplified as $\min_P\{|W|/P + 3cP/2\}$, which achieves its minimum if $|W|/P = 3cP/2$ holds. Thus, the optimal P is derived by Eq. 3.

$$P = \sqrt{2|W|/3c} \tag{3}$$

The optimal value of P can be updated based on the value of c which is updated based on the historical data of the number of histogram tuples in every full B^+ tree forest during query processing.

5 EMD-DSJoin Algorithm

Considering tuple delay is a common phenomenon in data stream processing, we propose a strategy for processing those out-of-order histogram tuples in Sect. 5.1. After that, the pseudocode of our EMD similarity join based on our B^+ forests index, named EMD-DSJoin, is proposed in Sect. 5.2.

5.1 Coping with Out-of-Order Histogram Tuples

To ensure the efficiency of join processing with the presence of out-of-order tuples in data streams, the data insertion strategy of our B^+ forests index (see Sect. 4.1) for those delay tuples should be carefully designed. Let D denote the maximal network delay in the system, R and S denote two data streams and assume that B^+ forests index is built on R. Given a delay tuple $r \in R$ with timestamp $r.ts$, we have $t_{now}-r.ts \le D$, where t_{now} is the timestamp of the newest incoming tuple of R. Note that a B^+ tree forest is removed from memory only when the difference between t_{now} and the maximum timestamp of the forest is larger than $|W| + D$. Thus, it can be proven that the delay tuple r can be always inserted into a B^+ tree forest whose minimum timestamp is smaller and maximum timestamp is larger than $r.ts$. We avoid inserting the delay tuple r into the active B^+ forest like we always do, since it will downgrade the performance of query processing by introducing a serious overlapping of time intervals of different B^+ tree forests, which means that more B^+ tree forests will be included to perform the timestamp checking in query processing. On the other hand, when a delay tuple $s \in S$ arrives, it is simply put into the cache of S in the memory.

5.2 EMD-DSJoin Algorithm Description

The pseudocode of our proposed EMD-DSJoin algorithm for efficient EMD similarity joins over probabilistic data streams is given in Algorithm 2.

The join implementation of EMD-DSJoin follows the idea of classical index join framework of traditional relational database system, which builds efficient indexing structure to avoid the traversing costs of each individual tuple in data streams. To be specific, for each incoming histogram tuple from a data stream, it is inserted into our B^+ forests index following Algorithm 1 (line 2). And then, if the tuple is from the stream R, we traverse each tuples $s_i \in S$ in the data cache ca, and check whether all its join candidates in R corresponding to the sliding window constraint have already arrived (lines 3–5). If all its candidates in R have arrived, we first derive a group of B^+ tree forests who are completely or partially contained by the sliding window of s_i (lines 7–8). For each of such B^+ tree forests, the EMD similarity joins between s_i and tuples in those B^+ tree forests are executed by the function *FilterChain* (line 9). And we return the final join results for the tuple s_i which is the union of every join result returned by each of such B^+ tree forest (lines 10). If the *Timer* object expires, the archive period of every B^+ tree forest P is updated based on the updated value c which is computed based on the latest statistics of the number of tuples in every B^+ tree forest (lines 11–12). The updated P is used to build B^+ tree forests in the following procedure.

In the *FilterChain* function, given any input tuple $s_i \in S$ and a B^+ tree forest F_j, we first execute a range search on F_j based on the proposed key range in Eq. 1, and then derive a potential join candidate set for $r \in R$ in F_j, named *candidate*, with each tuple in it having a timestamp dropping within the sliding window of s_i. And then, we further prune the set *candidate* based on a feasible solution Φ_{new} to the dual program of EMD. A new feasible solution can be derived in an unavoidable EMD computation due to recent query processing and it can be used to update Φ_{new}. We have proven in [5] that the newly-derived feasible solution can help further eliminate lots of unpromising tuples in the candidate set of R in the subsequent query processing, due to the time correlation property of tuples in a data stream. The reduced candidate set *candidate* is further pruned using the proposed lower bound function LB_{IM} of EMD [1] and our proposed upper bound function UB_p for EMD [4]. The upper bound based pruning derives a partial join result set $RS_{upperbound}$ for s_i. Finally, the EMD between s_i and every $r \in candidate$ is computed, and all qualified join results of s_i are put into the set RS_i. After the join processing, the tuple s_i is removed from the cache ca. The final join result set for $s_i \bowtie R$ is thus the union of $RS_{upperbound}$ and RS_i.

Algorithm 2:   EMD-DSJoin

INPUT: data streams R and S, similarity threshold θ, a set of B$^+$ tree forests F, a data cache ca

OUTPUT: $RS=\{(r, s)|$ EMD$(r, s)<=\theta, r\in R, s\in S\}$

1:    for each incoming tuple p do
2:        **BplusForestsMaintainace**(p, ca, F, P);
3:        if p.source $== R$ then
4:            for each $s_i \in ca$ do
5:                if $(p.timestamp - s_i.timestamp> |W| + D)$
6:                    $RS = \emptyset$;
7:                for each $F_i \in F$ do
8:                    if $(F_i.minTime$-$s_i.timestamp \leq |W|) \| (s_i.timestamp$-$ F_i.maxTime \leq |W|)$
9:                        RS.add(**FilterChain** (s_i, θ, F_i));
10:                return RS;
11:    If *Timer*.expire() $==$ TRUE then
12:        P.update(c.update());

---

6 Experimental Results

Environment. We conduct all experiments on a PC with PentiumI Dual-Core @3.2 GHz CPU, 2 GB RAM, 500 GB hard disk and runs 32-bit Windows 7. All methods are implemented by C++.

Datasets. We download three videos, namely the TV play *Sherlock* without subtitle (denoted as video S), the TV play *Sherlock* with subtitle (denoted as video SS), and the movie *Master* (denoted as video M). By reducing the brightness of each frame in the video S by 58f, we derive another video denoted as SLB. We sampled 10,000 frames from each of these videos and extracted a 256-dimensional grey-scale histogram from it. The location of each histogram bin is simply set as the index number of the bin. The *ground distance* between two histogram bins used in EMD is set as the L_2 *norm* between the location values of the two bins. Therefore, every video is now transformed into a data stream containing 10,000 histogram tuples. We test the performance of different methods on EMD similarity join based on three join operations, i.e. $S \bowtie SS$, $S \bowtie SLB$ and $S \bowtie M$.

Relative Settings. We compare our proposal EMD-DSJoin with two baseline solutions, namely RTJ-O and RTJ-S. RTJ-O implements a single large-scale B$^+$ tree forest on the video stream S, while EMD-DSJoin and RTJ-O employ a group of small-scale

B^+ tree forests on S to perform pruning. The pruning technique based on the newly-generated feasible solution to the dual program of EMD, is deployed only in EMD-DSJoin and RTJ-O. The optimization of the archive period of every B^+ tree forest P is only embedded in EMD-DSJoin. The initial value of P used by EMD-DSJoin and RTJ-O is set as $\sqrt{2|W|/3}$ with $c = 1$. P is updated in EMD-DSJoin based on the latest statistics every 2000 s. Table 1 lists the parameter setting with their default values highlighted in bold.

Table 1. Varying parameters (Default values are highlighted in bold.)

Parameters	Varying range
Similarity search threshold for $S \bowtie S$	0.3,0.4,**0.5**,0.6,0.7
Similarity search threshold for $S \bowtie SLB$	0.3,0.4,**0.5**,0.6,0.7
Similarity search threshold for $S \bowtie M$	0.3,0.4,**0.5**,0.6,0.7
The number of B^+ trees in a B^+ tree forest	1,**2**,3,4,5
Sliding window size	600 800 **1000** 1200 1400
Capacity factor c of every B^+ tree forest	**1.4**
Network delay D (in seconds)	**80**
The number of B^+ trees in a B^+ tree forest	4 (is set based on the best experiment results)

6.1 Experimental Evaluation

Figure 3 shows the impacts of different thresholds on CPU time of different methods. The figure displays that with the increase of similarity threshold, the CPU time of each method increases, since a larger threshold introduces more EMD calculations. The figure also shows that EMD-DSJoin gains the best performance, on average 35 % faster than RTJ-O. This is because EMD-DSJoin builds a group of small B^+ tree forests rather than a single big B^+ tree forest on the stream R, which greatly reduces the index maintenance costs corresponding to data insertion (or deletion) triggered by the incoming tuples. Moreover, EMD-DSJoin uses the pruning technique based on the newly generated feasible solution of EMD, which is effective in eliminating more EMD computations than that in RTJ-O. EMD-DSJoin outperforms RTJ-S by on average 5 %, simply since EMD-DSJoin derives an optimal value for P (i.e. the archive period of

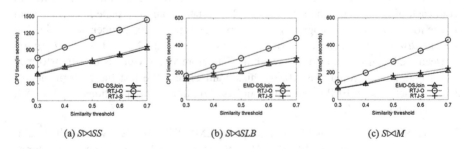

(a) $S \bowtie SS$ (b) $S \bowtie SLB$ (c) $S \bowtie M$

Fig. 3. Effect of different thresholds on CPU time

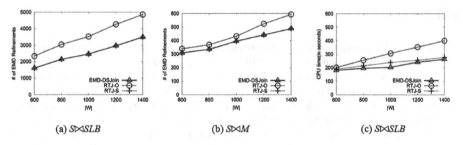

Fig. 4. Effect of sliding window size on the number of EMD refinements and CPU time

every B^+ tree forest), which cuts down the number of tuples and forests visited during time checking phase. The performance gap between EMD-DSJoin and RTJ-O is bigger in Fig. 3(c) than that in Fig. 3(a) or (b). This is because the contents in stream S is quite different from that in M, that enhances the pruning effects of our index structure and the lower/upper bound filters of EMD.

Figure 4(a) and (b) shows the number of EMD refinements of every method by varying the sizes of sliding window for the join operations $S \bowtie SLB$ and $S \bowtie M$ respectively. Apparently, more EMD computations are introduced with the growth of window size. This is because larger size of window indicates more candidates need to be checked in the refinement phase. Due to the utilization of the pruning technique based on the newly generated feasible solution of EMD, EMD-RSJoin and RTJ-S have on average 20 % less EMD computations than that in RTJ-O. Meanwhile EMD-RSJoin and RTJ-S gain the same number of EMD refinements, for they all adopt the same pruning strategy. Since EMD computations are the major cost in EMD similarity join, Fig. 4(c) shows that the reduction of the number of EMD computations in Fig. 4(a) has make EMD-DSJoin run 30 % faster than RTJ-O.

7 Conclusion

To better support similarity join operator on probabilistic data stream, this paper presents EMD-DSJoin, a novel framework for processing the window-based EMD similarity joins. Inspired by the primal-dual projection technique [4], an efficient index framework, named B^+ *Forests Index*, is proposed in EMD-DSJoin, which ensures high-quality similarity search with the presence of out-of-order data in data streams. We conduct extensive experiments based on real-world datasets and show that EMD-DSJoin greatly outperforms two baseline solutions in terms of CPU time and the number of EMD refinements.

Acknowledgments. Jia Xu and Pin Lv are supported by the National Natural Science Foundation of China (No. 61402494, No.61402513 and No. 61402498), Guangxi Natural Science Foundation (No. 2015GXNSFBA139243) and the Scientific Research Foundation of Guangxi University (No. XGZ141182 and No. XGZ150322). Jia Xu and Ningjiang Chen are also supported by the National Key Technology R&D Program (No. 2015BAH55F02).

References

1. Assent, I., Wenning, A., Seidl, T.: Approximation techniques for indexing the earth mover's distance in multimedia databases. In: IEEE ICDE, p. 11 (2006)
2. Assent, I., Wichterich, M., Meisen, T., Seidl, T.: Efficient similarity search using the earth mover's distance for large multimedia databases. In: IEEE ICDE, pp. 307–316 (2008)
3. Rubner, Y., Tomasi, C., Guibas, L.J.: The earth mover's distance as a metric for image retrieval. Int. J. Comput. Vision **40**(2), 99–121 (2010)
4. Xu, J., Zhang, Z., Tung, A.K.H., Yu, G.: Efficient and effective similarity search over probabilistic data based on earth mover's distance. VLDB Endow. **3**(1), 758–769 (2010)
5. Xu, J., Zhang, Z., Tung, A.K.H., Yu, G.: Efficient and effective similarity search over probabilistic data based on earth mover's distance. VLDB J. **21**(4), 535–559 (2012)
6. Xu, J., Lei, B., Gu, Y., Winslett, M., Yu, G., Zhang, Z.: Efficient similarity join based on earth mover's distance using MapReduce. IEEE Trans. Knowl. Data Eng. **27**(8), 1 (2015)
7. Jin, H., Rui, Z., Buyya, R., et al.: Melody-join: efficient earth mover's distance similarity joins using MapReduce. In: IEEE ICDE, pp. 808–819 (2013)
8. Huang, J., Zhang, R., Buyya, R., et al.: Heads-join: efficient earth mover's distance similarity joins on Hadoop. IEEE Trans. Parallel Distrib. Syst. **27**(6), 1660–1673 (2015)
9. Liu, X.L., Wang, H.Z., Li, J.Z., Gao, H., et al.: Similarity join algorithm based on entity. J. Softw. **26**(6), 1421–1437 (2015)
10. Wang, S., Wen, Y., Zhao, H.: Similarity query processing algorithm over data stream based on LCSS. J. Comput. Res. Dev. **52**(9), 1976–1991 (2015)
11. Wichterich, M., Assent, I., Kranen, P., Seidl, T.: Efficient EMD based similarity search in multimedia databases via flexible dimensionality reduction. In: ACM SIGMOD, pp. 199–212 (2008)
12. Shirdhonkar, S., Jacobs, W.: Approximate earth mover's distance in linear time. In: IEEE CVPR, pp. 1–8 (2008)
13. Xu, D., Chang, S.-F.: Video event recognition using kernel methods with multilevel temporal alignment. IEEE Trans. Pattern Anal. Mach. Intell. **30**(11), 1985–1997 (2008)
14. Ruttenberg, B.E., Singh, A.K.: Indexing the earth mover's distance using normal distributions. Proc. VLDB Endow. **5**(3), 205–216 (2011)
15. Lin, Q., Ooi, B.C., Wang, Z., et al.: Scalable distributed stream join processing. In: ACM SIGMOD, pp. 811–825 (2015)

Sentiment Analysis on User Reviews Through Lexicon and Rule-Based Approach

Sobh Zeb[✉], Usman Qamar, and Faiza Hussain

Department of Computer Engineering, College of Electrical and Mechanical
Engineering, National University of Sciences and Technology (NUST),
Islamabad, Pakistan
{sobh.zeb14,faiza.hussain14}@ce.ceme.edu.pk,
usmanq@ceme.nust.edu.pk

Abstract. Computers need data and humans need information. The process of converting data into useful information needs analysis to be done onto it. Reviews of customers are valuable as they are an important source of data for multiple purposes. However, these feedbacks are subjective, so extraction of information is not an easy task. This paper presents a different method of sentiment analysis research on reviews. The main focus is the data mining from multiple trustworthy sites and categorization of this data. The results are efficient and better than available multiple approaches. The paper concludes with recommendations and future work for giving a new direction to ontology-based opinion mining.

Keywords: Sentiment analysis · Opinion mining · Reviews · Feedback · Comments · Marketing · Social media · Subjective data · Ontology · Natural language processing

1 Introduction

Consumers use different types of online forums for social interaction. And via social media, much significant and beneficial information can be extracted. So, Sentiment Analysis is a technique that computationally assesses this data using machine learning algorithms. This information offers many opportunities for marketing people [3]. It plays an important role in evaluation of consumer opinions and to check trust and reputation [4]. It helps us to extract what people think and what are their reactions [2].

The real need behind the extraction is to convert the data into something useful so that reviews become an essential source, base on which, decision could be taken. But for this the first and utmost important task is to convert the data into information or we can also say that to give a proper and more refined shape to the data. Because data leads to information which leads to knowledge and it leads to wisdom which is our goal. The relationship can be shown by the Fig. 1 depicting Data, Information, Knowledge and Wisdom (DIKW) [5].

But with the immense increase in online review sites, social media and personal blogs, many advantages and challenges also arise and now, people use them actively to express their opinions about different things. People contribute on almost everything

© Springer International Publishing Switzerland 2016
A. Morishima et al. (Eds.): APWeb 2016 Workshops, LNCS 9865, pp. 55–63, 2016.
DOI: 10.1007/978-3-319-45835-9_5

Fig. 1. DIKW pyramid

from books, laptops, mobile signals, movies, brands, education etc. [3] Therefore, Opinion Mining is an emerging as well as difficult area that deals with the automated processing of opinions and reviews which are subjective in nature [1].

There can be many possibilities for data classification: users, texts, phrases, words, social media status updates [2]. But sentences or chunks of text which formulates reviews is the center point of this study. As it is very important for sellers to check and survey whether customer is going to buy their products or not? So, the main concerns are:

- What is the general response of people?
- How many reviews are positive and how many negative?
- Are customers satisfied or not?

The answers of these questions not only help the vendors to improve their product or service but also give them new ideas [2]. The analyses and concerns in Opinion Mining are:

- Which part of the sentence is depicting opinion?
- The opinion is written by whom?
- What product/thing is being commented by the user? [14]

It can also be used as a very useful tool to help people make decisions considering reviews of its previous users. People are always interested in getting to know the feedback of other users before purchasing and using a particular product. Because this way they are able to find the reliability of specific product. And at that time sentiment analysis can provide useful information from those comments and reviews of users.

The challenges of sentiment analysis include dual meaning of the same term because it can be perceived differently by different people. Similarly, the same term can be considered positive by some and negative333 by others. So, the correct interpretation is the main motivation of this paper.

Another challenge is the use of heavy technical terms, which are jargon term for some specific domain, which can't be easily identified as positive or negative sentence. E.g., the sentence "An IBM iSeries System Storage DS5020 Express is the equivalent to the x450 IBM server." [10]. Moreover, interpretation of mood of the users in the reviews is also a challenging task.

The paper will emphasize on the literature review in Sect. 2. Methodology will be described in Sect. 3. Later in Sect. 4, results will be presented and discussion will be made in Sect. 5. The conclusion is provided in Sect. 6.

2 Literature Review

As sentiment analysis is a very useful and important research area, many papers have been written for it. As sentiment analysis works as an indicator for many different purposes these sentiments can be categorized into two basic categories i.e. Positive and Negative. It can also be written as n-point scale. E.g., very bad, bad, satisfactory, good, very good. [6] The results from the above mentioned paper shows that hybrid classification can be very helpful to improve the effectiveness of classification. A semi-automatic balancing with aim of one classifier contributing to other classifier is also proposed.

In [7], the idea of sentiment lexicon is given as that negative or positive words can have different directions in different domains. For example, "suck" usually indicates negative sentiment, e.g., "This camera sucks," but it can also imply positive sentiment, e.g., "This vacuum cleaner really sucks."

Semantic word spaces are not of much use as they are unable to express the meaning of longer terms in refined manner. In semantic detection, supervised training and evaluation resources and very powerful mechanism of models is required and semantic tree banks can be used as its remedy. And for this 'Recursive Neural Tensor Network' are used [8].

In [9], a technique for integration of collaborative filtering and sentiment analysis has been proposed. This is a rating inference approach to incorporate reviews of user into the algorithm of collaborative filtering.

In [16], the average accuracy was estimated as 74 % which used simple unsupervised learning algorithm for classifying reviews as recommended or not recommended.

For sentiment analysis the approach of machine learning which can be applied to it, in general, belongs to 'supervised classification' and in particular text classification can be applied. That is why it is known as "supervised learning". In a classification which is based on machine learning two sets of data are required; training and testing set of data.

For text categorization algorithms like Naïve Bayes, Support vector machine and Maximum Entropy have proved themselves as very useful machine learning techniques [13]. For document classification, Naïve Bayes is a popular choice [11, 12].

Text categorization classifies documents based on topic classification. Whereas in sentiment classification we have relatively few classes e.g., 3 stars or positive generalizes across many domains and users [1].

3   Methodology

In this technique, the major steps are:

- Data preparation
- Information Extraction
- Classification of Reviews

3.1   Data Preparation

For the preparation of data, first of all reviews about different products were extracted from Goodreads, BookBrowse and Techradar and many other useful sites and then they were analyzed. For this, XPath was used for the identification of particular required 'reviews nodes'. Also, dataset from UCI machine learning repository was considered which was about hotels and cars' models reviews. The flow of work has been shown in the following Fig. 2:

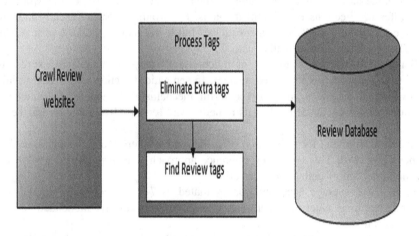

Fig. 2. Work flow

First of all these website were crawled by a web spider and links were saved in a database. And then the nodes having reviews in these websites were studied individually.

3.2   Information Extraction

For reviews extraction, reviews from tags were extracted from the website. And for this structure for each website was taken into account as different websites have different structure. After reviews were extracted, analysis was done on each in order to find its positives or negativeness. Moreover, the neutrality of reviews is also checked in it as there are few reviews which are partial positive and partial negative. So for those review "neutral tag" was assigned. For finding polarity of reviews both lexicon based and rule approaches were used. Using rule-based approach the polarity of positive, negative and neutral opinion words is found and using lexicon method the sentiment polarity of all review words using semantic orientation is calculated. The lexicon used was taken from SentiWordNet. The reason behind choosing both approaches is to increase efficiency of sentiment analysis and to fill the gap if left by any approach. By using both lexicon and rule based approach the polarity is found and calculated by both ways. So for these approaches the work flow followed for the pre-processing is shown in Fig. 3:

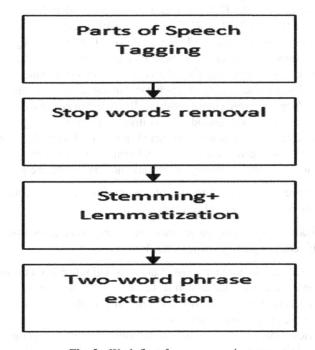

Fig. 3. Work flow for pre-processing

3.3 Classification of Reviews

English words play a vital role in Natural Language Processing (NLP). So, they are used as basis for checking intention. In this section, we first examine the most commonly used words in English. It is not necessary that these are single word i.e. good, bad but can be combination of multiple words i.e. well done, not liking it, not great etc. This work is done by identifying all the terms in the sentence and they are used in the filtration process. After pre-processing is done on data, the polarity of the data can be checked through lexicon and by calculation of semantic orientation of the words.

For finding polarity the adjectives and adverbs are considered very important as they are used to indicate the polarity of the text but only these are not enough as some words may not give the actual polarity e.g., not great etc. So, for accuracy in finding polarity,

First of all, all important patterns of two-word phrases are searched, as they act as rules which check the polarity based on the particular sequence of the data, along with adjectives and adverbs for finding the actual polarity in the sentence [16].

Two categories (positive/negative) are considered for analysis of reviews, as it gives us the clear picture of the polarity of the reviews. The polarity of each review was checked and marked as positive/negative or neutral review by checking the tags of two-word phrases patterns and counting the total number of terms and patterns which are positive, negative. E.g., the patterns like JJ and JJ, JJ and (NN or NNS), (RB, RBR or RBS) and JJ, (NN or NNS) and JJ, (RB, RBR or RBS) and (VB, VBD, VBN or VBG) [16].

These patterns of tags for two-word phrases are very useful in finding the polarity as the sequence or tags act as a useful indicator of the sentiment in the review. After extraction of these two-word phrases the polarity in these phrases and the polarity through adjectives and adverbs were calculated. Each word in the review was matched with the frequent positive/negative words in the database. If number of positive terms was greater than negative, the review was considered positive. If number of negative terms was greater than positive, the review was considered negative. And in third scenario if the number of positive and negative words was equal then it was treated as neutral. Each and every possible word is checked through iterations and then results are generated.

Dataset: For the result, reviews from websites were extracted and a dataset from UCI machine learning repository was also taken.

Training Method: After working on reviews, there were some cases which helped me to consider different perspectives of reviews. For example:

1. "When we're afraid, we lose all sense of analysis and reflection. Our fear paralyses us". This sentence was quoted as part of the review. So here, user's thoughts were expressed in terms of this quote so just the meaning of this quote was needed to be analyzed in order to categorize the review.
2. Another review stated "Is this book a stand alone or part of a series? I liked this book but I didn't love it. It was very predictable for me but it also left me going..." Here the reviewer doesn't specifically 'love' the book but just 'likes' it and at the same time she doesn't dislike it. Moreover the reviewer had issue with its writing style and storyline so she wasn't completely satisfied. But as she chose the neutral tone for writing the review, that is why this review was put in the 'neutral reviews' category.
3. Reviews like: "If this book has the ability to make me cry, then I really do not care about anything else." were a real challenge and despite being positive in nature it wasn't purely considered positive by the program.
4. For review like: I read this interesting book long time ago we need to find important phrase out of two adjective-noun combination. As in this case both interesting and long are adjectives and book and time are nouns. And we need to choose 'interesting book' phrase because this is telling us about opinion of the book.

5. For review like "This book is not bad" simple counting of opinion word cannot be used. This explains the reason of using both lexicons based and rule based approach.

4 Results

For a fair testing and evaluation, a UCI dataset named OpinRankDataset [15] is considered. Then frequent words from dataset are sorted in ascending order and each word is matched within every comment. We summarize our results in Table 1 (Precision Calculation). The trends observed from the table that overall it indicated good performance. A majority of the words were recognized as they are intended. We note that the performance is dropped due to the bulky and heavy reasons provided by the customers.

Table 1. Precision calculation

Polarity	Positive	Negative	Neutral/mixed	Precision
Positive	410	13	20	92.55 %
Negative	7	18	4	62.06 %
Neutral/mixed	11	5	16	50 %

Figure 4 presents the average recall for the True Positive and False Positive. Results of True Positive were the best: it shows that three categories i.e. positive, negative and neutral are recognized the same way as they are in real. While very less amount of results showed False Positive means they are predicted in a wrong category. According to the graph of Fig. 3, blue portion shows True Positive and orange shows False Positive.

True Positive vs False Positive

■ 1 True Positive
■ 2 False Positive

Fig. 4. Pie chart of results (Color figure online)

5 Discussion

Congressional debates on sentiment analysis contain very rich language and cover a wide variety of topics. The sentiment analysis is a very vast domain of research and very useful also as we can guide people about the good/bad productivity or performance of any product by just doing analysis on the reviews by other people.

To handle subjective data is not an easy task as computer understands only binary data i.e. "1" for yes and "0" for no. But there is no straightforward information available for opinion mining for instance, "This food is tacky," "I don't like current version" [2]. And there can be many interpretations of individual feedback, so analyzing and interpreting dispersed and jumbled data is a tricky task. And as all things are difficult before they become easy some issues occurred in this process of sentiment analysis.

The reason is that it's not always possible to generate 100 % correct result in sentiment analysis because factors like sarcasm, irony or vagueness in meaning of sentence are the factors which are difficult to handle. Plus, the jargons and shortcut terminologies and words cause hindrance in this process. As with these factors the chances of pitfall were increased but still the results were not much affected by these factors.

6 Conclusion and Future Work

Sentiment analysis can be considered very useful in many ways e.g., it can be easily used by marketing team as a depiction of success or failure of a product. From this, user satisfaction rate can be drawn. But it is not an easy task and getting 100 % accurate result is almost impossible in natural language. But the approach in this paper aims to provide maximum accurate results for the reviews. This way many practitioners can benefit. As time is money so why one should waste his/her time in figuring out positivity or negativity of the text. This approach will help as a 'guiding tool' to all those who are interested in getting to know views of other people in terms of good/bad before taking any decision about anything. That decision can be about purchasing a new mobile, laptop, choosing a hotel for vacation tour, reading a good book, and buying a new car and much more.

As there are limitations of NLP which need to be handled very carefully, In the future our goal will be work on those factors which affect sentiment analysis significantly. The terms having sarcasm and irony in it are a challenge for the sentiment analysis as by sarcastic statements we are unable to decide whether it's a positive or a negative sentence. And because the presence of the terms having dual meaning is very difficult to analyze that is why these affect efficiency of algorithms also. Moreover, smileys can be given a special attention where a smiley is a good way to reveal the true meaning. That's why special algorithms with capability to specifically handle such terms need to be made and in future it'll be one of our goal to make such algorithm so that identification of such terms become easy.

References

1. Pang, B., Lee, L.: Opinion mining and sentiment analysis. FNT Inf. Retrieval **2**(1–2), 1–135 (2008)
2. www.lct-master.org/files/MullenSentimentCourseSlides.pdf. Accessed 04 July 2016
3. Rambocas, M., Gama, J.: Marketing Research: The Role of Sentiment Analysis
4. Lackermair, G., Kailer, D., Kanmaz, K.: Importance of online product reviews from a consumers perspective. Adv. Econo. Bus. **1**(1), 1–5 (2013)
5. http://www.dqglobal.com/what-is-the-difference-between-data-and-information/. Accessed 04 July 2016
6. Prabowo, R., Thelwall, M.: Sentiment analysis: a combined approach. J. Informetr. **3**(2), 143–157 (2009)
7. Liu, B.: Sentiment analysis and opinion mining. Synth. Lect. Hum. Lang. Technol. **5**(1), 1–167 (2012)
8. Socher, R., Perelygin, A., Wu, J., Chuang, J., Manning, C.D., Ng, A.Y., Potts, C.: Recursive deep models for semantic compositionality over a sentiment treebank. In: Proceedings of the 2013 Conference on Empirical Methods in Natural Language Processing, Stroudsburg, PA, October, pp. 1631–1642. Association for Computational Linguistics (2013b)
9. Leung, C.W.K., Chan, S.C.F., Chung, F.L.: Integrating collaborative filtering and sentiment analysis: a rating inference approach. In: ECAI 2006 Workshop on Recommender Systems, pp. 62–66 (2006)
10. https://web.njit.edu/~da225/NetHelp/Documents/problemswithsentimentanalysis.htm. Accessed 04 July 2016
11. Melville, P., Gryc, W., Lawrence, R.D.: Sentiment analysis of blogs by combining lexical knowledge with text classification. In: Proceedings of the 15th ACM SIGKDD International Conference on Knowledge Discovery and Data Mining, Paris, France, June 28–July 01 (2009)
12. Xia, R., Zong, C., Li, S.: Ensemble of feature sets and classification algorithms for sentiment classification. Inf. Sci. **181**(6), 1138–1152 (2011)
13. Vinodhini, G., Chandrasekaran, R.M.: Sentiment analysis and opinion mining: a survey. Int. J. **2**(6) 2012
14. https://www.w3.org/2012/06/pmod/opinionmining.pdf. Accessed 04 July 2016
15. http://archive.ics.uci.edu/ml/machine-learning-databases/00205/
16. Turney, P.D.: Thumbs up or thumbs down?: semantic orientation applied to unsupervised classification of reviews. In: Proceedings of the 40th Annual Meeting on Association for Computational Linguistics, Philadelphia, Pennsylvania, July 07–12 (2002)

Social Link Prediction Based on the Users' Information Transfer

Chen Yunfang, Wang Tongli, and Zhang Wei[✉]

Nanjing University of Posts and Telecommunications, Nanjing, China
zhangw@njupt.edu.cn

Abstract. Link prediction is one of the hotspots in social network analysis. However, traditional prediction method based on node similarity of network topology does not take the characteristics of user-generated content into account. In this article, the user-generated content based on traditional link prediction method is introduced to predict new user relationships through common neighbors in the social networks. This method is an information-theoretic measure with a predictive interpretation that directly quantifies the strength of the effect of one user's content on another's. Experimental results show that content transfer combined with topology is more consistent with the real social network, which has better performance in link prediction.

Keywords: Link prediction · Transfer entropy · Social network

1 Introduction

Various emerging online social networks narrow the distance between people, and greatly reduce the cost of human communication. People left a lot of data when they are in the exchange of idea on social networks, which provides a wealth of data sources for the social network analysis. In social network analysis, link prediction is one of the most important research directions in which the traditional social network prediction method focuses on static network topology, and focusing on the topology or edges' similarity [1]. One key assumption in sociology is the theory of homophily [2], which postulates that people who have similar characteristics tend to form ties. Moreover, it is likely that the stronger the tie, the higher the similarity [3]. Traditional link prediction method based on topologies similarity only takes the nodes' or the topologies' similarity in social network at one moment into account. Although on some occasions with good results, there are still a number of problems. Firstly, real social relations exist widely dynamic and uncertainty. So real-world networks may also exist relations change, loss, and individuals missing. These factors may be due to the objective reasons or the users and data provides deliberately doing that. However, the changes and loss of the nodes or edges often have a great impact on prediction results. Secondly, the method based on topologies similarity ignores the impact of user-generated content.

User-generated content with initiative, reflects more personal interests and hobbies of the users [4]. So users' relationship inferred from content is real, and can avoid false and invalid links created by zombie users in a social network. We view users as

A. Morishima et al. (Eds.): APWeb 2016 Workshops, LNCS 9865, pp. 64–76, 2016.
DOI: 10.1007/978-3-319-45835-9_6

producers of some arbitrarily encoded information stream. For the two users X and Y, if Y's stream affects X's, then access to Y's signal can, in principle, improve our prediction of X's future activity. So user X can be used to predict the future of user Y. In recent years, some researchers have turned to the content of the users. Armentano, for instance, proposed a followee recommender system based on both the analysis for the content to detect users' interests and the topology of the network in the exploration to find candidate users for recommendation [5]. Despite recent progress, however, content-based analysis of social interactions is still a challenging problem due to the lack of adequate quantitative methods for extracting useful signals from unstructured text and similarity measure. Based on the study of social networks, we introduce the information theory method to quantify content similarity between users. Then the complex networks, information theory and natural language processing can be combined to analyze the evolution of social network from a new perspective.

2 Related Work

In the analysis of social network, the problem of link prediction has been studied extensively, and most of them are only focused on the network topology, for example, PA algorithm [6], JC algorithm [7] and RA algorithm [8]. They are similarity metric based on neighbor nodes to predict user link relations in the future and have a good result. Nevertheless, they are based on a simple network topology, ignoring the semantic social network information and in most cases does not reflect the realities of the social activities.

In the traditional link prediction algorithm, the PA metrical indicates that new links will be more likely to connect higher-degree nodes than lower ones, then it only according to the size as the product of two nodes to determine the similarity. And the JC metrical assumes higher values for pairs of nodes, which share a higher proportion of shared neighbors relative to the total number of neighbors they have. The RA metric considers that the node x can send some resource to y, with their common neighbors playing the role of transmitters for a pair of nodes x and y. It also assumes that each transmitter has a unit of resource, and will averagely distribute it to all its neighbors. So the similarity between x and y can be defined as the amount of resources y received from x. In social networks, transmit resources between users can be regarded as information. However, it may be different for different users to transfer the information from the common neighbors. That is, the two pairs users with the equivalent number of shared neighbors may be different from the resources that are delivered to them. However, RA algorithm will think that the two users have the identical similarity, which is obviously not accurate.

With the rapid development of online social network, communication and cooperation between people have become more convenient. And they have become an important part of our daily life and provide us platforms to exchange information with each other. Since the huge amounts of data on social networks have some obvious characteristics such as high quality, big data, semi-structure and direct reflection of real human society, many researchers from different areas or disciplines pay more and more attention to social networks. Charalampos proposed a tripartite graph to model latent user tastes and applied Katz scores to rank and recommend users [9]. The tripartite graph can be reduced into three bipartite graphs, which model associations between actors and concepts, concepts and resources, and actors and resources. However, the model has some limitations, because it needs additional user concepts or user-generated content's concepts. So it does not fit every social networking platform. Armentano found that many users probably used twitter as a source of information rather than as a social network site through the study of Twitter platform users [5]. Then he proposes a followee recommender system for non-active users based in the analysis for the content to detect users' interests. Even so, he only predicted non-active users to an active one-way relationship between users, and couldn't predict active users to non-active users, active users to active users and non-active users to non-active users, nor solve the language ambiguity problem. In addition, owing to the original topic model assumes that the documents are independent, however, there is a relationship between some documents. Researchers have proposed a relational topic model to predict the relationships of text for document networks [10]. However, the relational topic model limited to the relationship between pair's topics, and the square with the number of parameters on the number of topics. To some extent, these problems limited the scope of its use.

In this article, we will use a theory based on information theory to quantify the relationship between the user-generated content of time series, to infer possible relations between users. Firstly, the transfer entropy [11] combines LDA topic model [12] quantitation the transfer of information between users based on users' text information. The information transferred can be seen as a weight of the strength to the relationship between the linked users. Moreover, because the amount of transferred information between two users in different directions is different, the existing topological structure of users formed a directed weighted network. Meanwhile, Niladri shows that with the right choice for a weighting model, weighted versions may perform better than their unweight counterparts [13]. Then we conducted relations prediction between users on the directed network with the weight. In this article, we need not to assume any network models, just only rely on user-generated content and the current social relations. And it does not depend on any particular social platform, with strong flexibility.

3 Theoretical Foundation

3.1 Transfer Entropy Definition

The entropy of a random variable X with a probability mass function p(x) is defined by

$$H(X) = -\sum_X p(x) \log_2 p(x) \tag{1}$$

We use logarithms to base 2. The entropy will then be measured in bits. The entropy is a measure of the average uncertainty in the random variable. It is the number of bits on average required to describe the random variable.

Entropy is the uncertainty of a single random variable. We can define conditional entropy $H(X|Y)$, which is the entropy of a random variable conditional on the knowledge of another random variable. The reduction in uncertainty due to another random variable is called the mutual information. For two random variables X and Y, this reduction is the mutual information

$$I(X; Y) = H(X) - H(X|Y) = \sum_{x,y} p(x, y) \log \frac{p(x, y)}{p(x)p(y)} \tag{2}$$

We can use mutual information to quantify the overlap of the information content of two systems. Unfortunately, mutual information contains neither dynamical nor direction information. Therefore on the basis of mutual information, Thomas defines the transfer entropy [11]:

$$T_{J \rightarrow I} = \sum P(i_{n+1}, i_n^{(k)}, j_n^{(l)}) \log \frac{p\left(i_{n+1} | i_n^{(k)}, j_n^{(l)}\right)}{p\left(i_{n+1} | i_n^{(k)}\right)} \tag{3}$$

where $i_n^{(k)} = (i_n, \ldots i_{n-k+1})$ is a shorthand notation for words of length k. The most natural choices for l are l = k or l = 1. Usually, the latter is preferable for computational reasons. So the formula (3) can be expressed as a form of entropy:

$$T_{J \rightarrow I} = H\left(I_n | I_{n-1}^{n-k}\right) - H\left(I_n | I_{n-1}^{n-k}, J_{n-1}^{n-l}\right) \tag{4}$$

We can know that transfer entropy between processes X and Y quantify how much better we are able to predict the target process X if we use the history of the process Y and X rather than the history of X alone. Mutual information is symmetric, while $T_{J \rightarrow I}$ is now explicitly non symmetric since it measures the degree of dependence of I to J and not vice versa.

3.2 Transfer Entropy Estimate

Typically, in order to calculate the transfer entropy in the formula (3), we need probability distribution's estimating and data binning, which is a data pre-processing technique used to reduce the effects of minor observation errors. However, it is problematic due to data sparsity. Kozachenko and Leonenko introduced an entropy estimator that was asymptotically unbiased and did not require binning of data [14]. Binless estimators were extended to higher-order quantities like mutual information [15], and divergence between two distributions [16]. The basic idea behind non-parametric binless entropy estimators is to average local contributions to the entropy in the neighborhood of each point, where the neighborhood size is chosen adaptively according to the point's k nearest neighbors [17].

Suppose we have samples i = 1,..., N of points $\left(\vec{x}^{(i)}, \vec{y}^{(i)}\right)$ drawn from some unknown joint distribution. For each point, i, we construct the random variable $\lambda_k(i)$ to represent the distance to the k-th nearest neighbor in the joint x-y space to some metric.

We will use the maximum norm in all dimensions [15]. For example, the distance between points i and j in the joint space would be

$$\left\| \vec{w}^{(i)} - \vec{w}^{(j)} \right\|_{\infty} = \max_l \left| w_l^{(i)} - w_l^{(j)} \right| \tag{5}$$

where $\vec{w}^{(i)} = (x_1^{(i)}, \ldots x_{d_x}^{(i)}, y_1^{(i)}, \ldots, y_{d_x}^{(i)})$ and d_x, d_y are the dimensions of the x and y spaces, respectively. If we project only onto the x (or y) subspace, the number of points strictly within a distance $\lambda_k(i)$ is defined as $n_x(i)$ or $n_y(i)$. We can now proceed to write down the mutual information estimator [15]:

$$\hat{H}(X:Y) = \psi(k) + \frac{1}{N}\sum_{i=1}^{N} \left(\psi(n_x(i)+1) + \psi(n_y(i)+1) - \psi(N) \right) \tag{6}$$

where $\psi(x) = \frac{\mathrm{d}}{\mathrm{dx}} lnr(x) = \frac{\Gamma'(x)}{\Gamma(x)}$. From the above mutual information estimation formula, it is found that the estimated value is only dependent on the distance between the sampling and the number of samples, and does not depend on the dimension of the space.

The estimator has been extended to conditional mutual information. Now we add a third covarying vector, Z, and define $\lambda_k(i)$ as the distance to the k-th nearest neighbor in the full joint x-y-z space, while $n_{yz}(i)$, for instance, represents the number of points strictly within a distance $\lambda_k(i)$ projecting onto the y-z subspace. The conditional mutual information estimation formula [16] is

$$\hat{H}(X:Y/Z) = \psi(k) + \frac{1}{N}\sum_{i=1}^{N} \left(\psi(n_{xz}(i)+1) + \psi(n_{yz}(i)+1) - \psi(n_z(i)+1) \right) \tag{7}$$

According to the formula (3) definition, selecting appropriate sequence of variables X, Y and Z, and conditional mutual information formula can be used to estimate the transfer entropy.

4   Online Social Network Users Link Prediction

Online social-network users produce vast amounts of content every day, which not only reflect the users' interests, but also reflect the changes of users' sentiment. So users who have a similar content will also have great similarities, and this will generate link relationships. Even so, the traditional link prediction method is mainly focused on the node, topology and path, rarely consider the content interaction between users. This is principally because the contents to the user-generated every day presents some unique challenges. (1) User-generated content is usually more casual, which will be mixed with some special network language, expression symbols and language abbreviations. (2) User published content varies, and there are many spelling errors in the content, Web sites and multiple languages. (3) Because of the different interests, the user-generated content information is different. Faced with these problems, correct and effective content quantified is the key to improve link prediction performance. And between users' content overlapped quantitation based on the content quantitation also has an important impact on link prediction. Existing methods simply quantify the similarity of content, and rarely involve the flow of information content.

4.1 Quantization User-Generated Content

In this paper, we use the content generated by each user in a social network as a stochastic process $\{I_i\}$ as shown in the following figure.

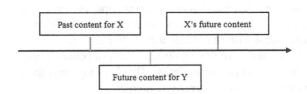

Fig. 1. The content representation of X and Y on the time axis

For a user, the content generated at any time is considered as a random variable, and the set of these variables constitutes a stochastic process. Variety of online interaction between users in a social network, the user typically through their following to get the latest information, sometimes through texts exchange ideas with other users. So we choose the most popular and user-generated text as an information transfer medium. For these contents, the LDA topic model brought a lot of convenience to represent content in recent years. In this paper, our ultimate goal is not to find distinct topics with clear interpretations, but to find the minimal representation that preserves relevant detail. In addition, higher-dimensional representations make entropy estimation more difficult. However, fortunately, the effective dimension of topic vectors for most users is low [17]. So this will not affect our transfer entropy estimate. And from the formula (7) we can see that the entropy estimation method can also be seen that the dimension of variable does not affect the result of final entropy estimation. The transformation of user text information into a vector mainly has the following process. First, we followed the following steps for pre-process the text. (1) We replace all

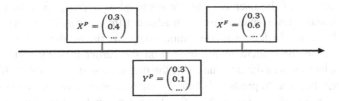

Fig. 2. The vector representation of X and Y on the time axis

"@" with the word "[mention]" (2) We remove all non-Latin alphabet characters and convert to be lower-case. (3) We removed a standard list of English stop-words. (4) We replace all URLs with the word "[url]". Then we trained an LDA topic model implemented in genism [18]. Finally, we constructed the TF-IDF vectors and used them to learn an LDA topic model. The content conversion into a vector is shown in Fig. 2.

4.2 Quantization Information Exchange Between Users

User behavior is rarely considered in traditional link prediction method, so the social network is seen as an unweighted network. For a user in social networks, he has a lot of social relationships, but the users' social relationships are not equally important. As shown in Fig. 3, for the user 1, most of the traditional algorithms will think it will follow user 3 and user 4 with the identical probability. In fact, the user 4 with user 1 and user 3 with user 1 just have the duplicate number of common neighbors, but user 4 and user 3 to user 1's influence are different. That is to say, than the probability of the user 1 followers the user 3 and 4 are also different.

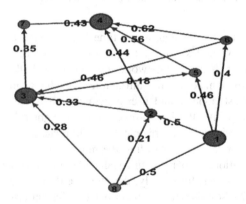

Fig. 3. With the weight social network

In this paper, the transfer entropy is used to quantify the information exchange between users, and the social network with the weight is constructed as shown in Fig. 3. In order to estimate transfer entropy, the near three moments of two users which is similar to Fig. 1 of the user content are regarded as a group. The two users are represented x and y respectively. User x in adjacent time released the contents of the information has a certain degree of correlation, so we can predict the content of the next moment based on the content to the user x on the earlier moment. That is, by its preceding content reduces the uncertainty of the future content information. If knowing y's past content helps us to predict x's future content more accurately, then we can say that y exerts certain influence on x. Namely, it exists a transfer of information between user y and the user x. How much information is transferred between the users can be seen as a link weight of users, reflecting the frequency of communication between users. Note that we demand that y's content should occur after x's previous content otherwise the causal effect of y's content is already being taken into account as affecting x's prior content. Moreover, y could publish many times in between x'scontent but we only consider the most-recent content for simplicity. According to the formula (3) of the transfer entropy definition, we can now write down the information transfer of user X to the user Y as shown in the formula (8).

$$T_{Y \to X} = H(X^F : Y^P | X^P) = H(X^F | X^P) - H(X^F | Y^P, X^P) \tag{8}$$

In the end, we use the formula (7) to estimate the transfer entropy in a pair of user-generated content, and construct the social network with the weight as shown in Fig. 3. In the process of determining the weight of the social network, namely the transfer entropy estimation, smaller k reduces the bias, but larger k reduces the variance [19]. In order to balance these two kinds of errors, we choose k = 3 [15]. Another, sampling number will have certain effects on entropy estimation. Larger number of samples will enhance the prediction results, but also increases the time cost of transfer entropy estimate. In the later experiments, we will give a suitable sample value balanced them.

4.3 User Relationship Prediction Based on Nodes' Information Transfer

In a direction social network with the weight, we still need to determine the similarity of nodes to predict the relationship between users. In this paper, we introduce the information transfer of nodes, and the transfer of information among users in the social network is regarded as the resources allocated to the network, which is specific and has its exact physical meaning. In the social network for a pair of indirectly connected users x and y, user y can influence the user x by the common neighbors of x and y, which will be the transfer of information. For each shared neighbor user w, y to x information transfer through the intermediate node w is part of the w to x information transfer. In the simplest case, we assume that user x will receive the following users' information transfer of w by an equally probable through a common neighbor w. The similarity between x and y can be defined as the amount of information transfer x received from y, which is:

$$S_{xy} = \sum_{w \in \mu(x) \ \cap \mu(y)} \frac{T_{w \to x}}{K(w)} \tag{9}$$

Where function $\mu(x)$ represent the set of following users of the node x, $T_{w \to x}$ represents the transfer entropy, and the function $K(x)$ is the out degree of x in the social network with weight. Formula (9) defines the amount of information transferred between two non-connected users through common neighbors. The more the transfer of information, the greater impact of user y to user x, then user x follows the user y more likely. Clearly, this measure is asymmetric, namely, $S_{xy} \neq S_{yx}$. Similarly, we can calculate the likelihood of y following user x.

Algorithm1: Based on the similarity measure of the users' information transfer

---

Input: a user content dataset D;
Output: node similarity S_{xy} ;
1. For any two users x,y in D
2.   If x in followers of y
3.   Estimate the transfer entropy $T_{(y \to x)}$ if it never be estimated
4.   End if
5. End for
6. For any two users x, y in D
7.   If x not in followers of y
8.   Compute the similarity S_{xy}
9.   End if
10. End for

---

5 Experiment

We make use of data originally collected on a set of 2400 users over a one-month period from 9/20/2010-10-20/2010 by Macskassy [20]. We used all the tweets to help train the topic model, but we did not consider all users when calculating content transfer for pairs of users. After eliminating users with less than 200 tweets, we considered all directed edges between the remaining users. We first select a total of 98 users as the target user in front of five days of the data set, and divide them into training set and test set. After describing the data set, we translate the text into a vector by LDA topic model, and estimate transfer entropy, and then discusses some parameters influencing the link results. Finally, the algorithm with some traditional link prediction algorithms is compared.

We use a standard metric, area under the receiver operating characteristic (ROC) curve [21], to quantify the accuracy of prediction algorithms. In the present case, this metric can be interpreted as the probability that a randomly chosen missing link is given a higher score than a randomly chosen nonexistent link. In the implementation, among n times of independent comparisons, if there are n' times the missing link having higher score and n" times the missing link and nonexistent link having the same score, we define the accuracy as:

$$AUC = \frac{n' + 0.5n''}{n} \tag{10}$$

If all the scores are generated from an independent and identical distribution, the accuracy should be about 0.5 [8]. Therefore, the degree to which the accuracy exceeds 0.5 indicates how much better the algorithm performs than pure chance.

5.1 Prediction Results Under Different Entropy Estimation Parameters

We first set the number of samples to 10, 25, 50, 100 and 200, respectively, to calculate the similarity of any non-connected users of the link prediction. Then we set the N in the formula (10) to 10000, and calculate the AUC value according to the similarity in the training set and unrelated user set. Namely random sample 10000 times from the two sets to compare their similarity and calculate the AUC value, as shown in Fig. 4. The experimental results can be seen that the increase in the number of samples will indeed make the results better, but there is no significant improvement. And the increase in the number of samples will significantly increase the calculation time, so in order to achieve better experimental results and balance the time overhead, we set the number of samples in the following experiments 100.

Although the small number of topics is conducive to the transfer entropy estimation, it is not a very good expression to the difference between the content of different users. So here the number of topic is 10, 50, 100, 125, 150 and 175, respectively, to study the impact of the number of topics on prediction result. The experiment results are shown in Fig. 5. So we think that the number of topics is about 125, which is more consistent with the actual situation of the set. In the following experiment, set the number of topic to 125.

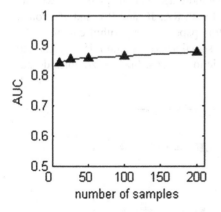 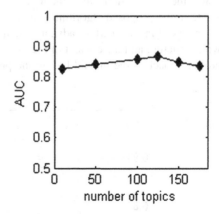

Fig. 4. AUC value curve with the number of samples

Fig. 5. AUC value curve with the number of topics

In Sect. 4.2, we took k = 3. In order to validate its correctness, we conduct an experiment when the sampling value is 100 and the number of topic is 150. The results are shown in Fig. 6. Through the experiment of Fig. 6, we see that results for the value of k are not particularly sensitive, but the AUC asset value is still the best when k = 3, so we took k = 3 in the experiment.

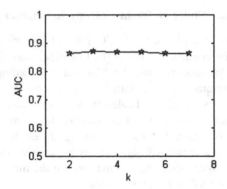

Fig. 6. AUC values curve with k value

5.2   Comparison Between the Algorithm and the Traditional Algorithms

We conduct link prediction based on the paper algorithm and the traditional RA, JC and PA algorithm with different training set size of the entire data set, and the results are shown in Fig. 7. From the experimental results, we can see that with the increase of the nodes, the effect of all algorithms is increased in part, which indicates that the more complete the link relationship to the network, the more accurate the prediction will be. In addition, the proposed algorithm is compared with RA, JC and PA, and it is found that our algorithm has certain advantages. In this paper, our algorithm combines the network structure and the content of the users in social networks, and it is very good to avoid the impact of the invalid link in the prediction results. Such as zombies do not

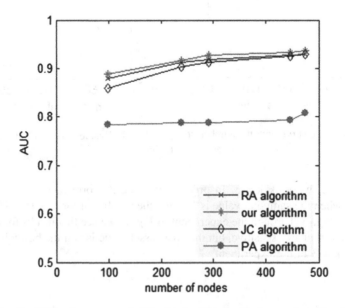

Fig. 7. AUC values curve of different algorithms with the number of nodes

have any valid information in a social network. Although they are in the network structure, they did not transmit any effective resources for the intermediary, which interfere with the accuracy of the RA algorithm, and our algorithm is a good solution in this problem. In addition, the proposed algorithm predicts the directional relationship based on the existent user activity in the actual social network, which is more realistic. Because 77.9 % of Twitter connections are unidirectional, in addition to the fact that 67.6 % of users are not followed by any of their followees are clear indicators that these users probably use twitter as a source of information rather than as a social networking site [5].

6 Conclusion

From the above experimental results, we can see that the social network link prediction based on node information transfer has certain advantages. Compared to traditional social network link prediction, the link prediction based on node information transfer pleasurably quantifies the influence of people's behavior in social networks, which would be predicted more specific and more exact. The information transfer between nodes is a pleasurable measure to quantify the behavior of people in online social networks and the impact of these behaviors of the people around them, to make the prediction more precise. And you can find the zombie users that do not produce any content information and ignore the impact of these zombie users on the prediction.

In this paper, we find the feasibility and advantage of using the nodes' information transfer in social network link prediction. However, some problems are also found during the experiment, such as the accuracy of the transfer entropy estimation, the richness of the content of the user and the complete representation of the content of the user. How to represent the content and improve the accuracy of transfer entropy between users is the key point of the next research work.

References

1. Wang, P., Xu, B., Wu, Y., Zhou, X.: Link prediction in social networks: the state-of-the-art. Sci. China Inf. Sci. **58**, 1–38 (2014)
2. McPherson, M., Smith-Lovin, L., Cook, J.M.: Birds of a feather: homophily. Ann. Rev. Sociol. **27**, 415–444 (2001)
3. Granovetter, M.: The strength of weak ties: a network theory revisited. Sociol. Theory **1**, 201–233 (1983)
4. Han, X., Wang, L., Crespi, N., Park, S., Cuevas, Á.: Alike people, alike interests? Inferring interest similarity in online social networks. Decis. Support Syst. **69**, 92–106 (2015)
5. Armentano, M.G., Godoy, D., Amandi, A.A.: Followee recommendation based on text analysis of micro-blogging activity. Inf. Syst. **38**, 1116–1127 (2013)
6. Barabásia, A.L., Jeonga, H., NÃedaa, Z., Ravasza, E., Schubertd, A., Vicsekb, T.: Evolution of the social network of scientific collaborations. Phys. A. **311**, 590–614 (2002)
7. Liben-Nowell, D., Kleinberg, J.: The link-prediction problem for social networks. J. Am. Soc. Inf. Sci. Technol. **58**, 1019–1031 (2007)

8. Zhou, T., Lü, L., Zhang, Y.-C.: Predicting missing links via local information. ArXiv Prepr. arXiv:0901.0553 (2009)
9. Chelmis, C., Prasanna, V.K.: Social link prediction in online social tagging systems. ACM Trans. Inf. Syst. **31**, 20:1–20:27 (2013)
10. Chang, J., Blei, D.M.: Relational topic models for document networks. In: AIStats, vol. 9 (2009)
11. Schreiber, T.: Measuring information transfer. Phys. Rev. Lett. **85**(2), 461–464 (2000)
12. Blei, D.M., Ng, A.Y., Jordan, M.I.: Latent Dirichlet allocation. J. Mach. Learn. Res. **3**, 993–1022 (2003)
13. Sett, N., Singh, S.R., Nandi, S.: Influence of edge weight on node proximity based link prediction methods: an empirical analysis. Neurocomputing **172** (2015)
14. Kozachenko, L.F., Leonenko, N.N.: Sample estimate of the entropy of a random vector. Probl. Peredachi Informatsii **23**, 9–16 (1987)
15. Kraskov, A., Stögbauer, H., Grassberger, P.: Estimating mutual information. Phys. Rev. E **69**, 066138 (2004)
16. Vejmelka, M.: Inferring the directionality of coupling with conditional mutual information. Phys. Rev. E **77**, 026214 (2008)
17. Ver Steeg, G., Galstyan, A.: Information-theoretic measures of influence based on content dynamics (2013)
18. Řehůřek, R., Sojka, P., et al.: Software framework for topic modelling with large corpora (2010)
19. Wang, Q., Kulkarni, S.R., Verdú, S.: Divergence estimation for multidimensional densities via k-nearest-neighbor distances. IEEE Trans. Inf. Theory **55**, 2392–2405 (2009)
20. Macskassy, S.A.: On the study of social interactions in twitter (2012)
21. Hanley, J.A., McNeil, B.J.: The meaning and use of the area under a receiver operating characteristic (ROC) curve. Radiology **143**, 29–36 (1982)

An Improved ML-*k*NN Approach Based on Coupled Similarity

Xiaodan Yang, Lihua Zhou[✉], and Lizhen Wang

Department of Computer Science and Engineering,
Yunnan University, Kunming 650091, China
838505331@qq.com, {lhzhou,lzhwang}@ynu.edu.cn

Abstract. ML-*k*NN is a well-known algorithm for multi-label classification, but it just assumes the independence of labels and instances. In fact, in the real world, labels or instances are more or less related via explicit or implicit relationships. In this paper, we propose an improved ML-*k*NN approach that takes the coupled similarity of attributes and labels into account, where coupling between attributes is used to find *k* nearest neighbors for instances and coupling between labels is used to predict the labels of unseen instances. Experimental results show that our proposed method outperforms the traditional ML-*k*NN.

Keywords: Multi-label classification · *k*-NN · Coupled similarity

1 Introduction

Data classification has been a problem of great practical importance in several domains, including pattern recognition, machine learning, and data mining. The task of data classification is to predict the label sets of unseen instances through analyzing training instances with known label sets. In traditional single-label classification problem (i.e. two-class and multi-class problems), each instance in the training set is only associated with a label and the task of classification is to output a label for each unseen instance. There are extensive literatures related to traditional single-label classification problem. However, in some real world problems, each instance is associated with a set of labels and the task of classification is to output a label set whose size is unknown before for each unseen instance. This kind of problem is called the multi-label classification problem. It exists in many domains, for example, scene classification [1], automatic text categorization [2], gene functional analysis of bio-informatics [3] and multimedia analysis [4]. The generality of multi-label problems makes it more important to research.

Unfortunately, multi-label classification is more difficult to solve than single-label classification due to the existence of relevance and co-occurrence amongst labels. The method decomposing a multi-label classification problem into multiple independent binary classification problems (one per category) does not consider the relevance between the different labels of each instance and the expressive power of such a system can be weak [5, 6]. [7] proposed an approach to solve multi-label classification problems, which named Multi-Label *k*-Nearest Neighbor (i.e. ML-*k*NN). ML-*k*NN first identified *k* nearest neighbors in the training set for each test instance, and then

© Springer International Publishing Switzerland 2016
A. Morishima et al. (Eds.): APWeb 2016 Workshops, LNCS 9865, pp. 77–89, 2016.
DOI: 10.1007/978-3-319-45835-9_7

determined the label set for the test instance based on the principle of maximum a posteriori possibility, according to statistical information gained from the label sets of neighboring instances of the test instance. ML-kNN is a well-known algorithm for multi-label classification, but it ignores the inter relationship between labels because it only considers one label every time, such that its usage is limited. To overcome the shortcoming of ML-kNN, [8] proposed a coupled k-nearest neighbor algorithm (CML-kNN) that exploited the correlations between class labels by introducing the coupled similarity between class labels. However, both ML-kNN and CML-kNN assume the independence of attributes of instances, such that they do not consider the relationship between values of attributes in the process of identifying k nearest neighbors for an instance, so they fail to capture the global picture of all instances, which is inadequate in multi-label classification.

In fact, in real-world data, attributes are more or less interacted and coupled via explicit or implicit relationships [10]. In this paper, we propose an improved ML-kNN approach (CSML-kNN) based on coupled similarity. CSML-kNN assumes the non-independence of attributes of instances such that takes coupling between labels, intra coupling between values of an attribute and inter coupling between attributes simultaneously into consideration to capture global picture of instance, where coupling between attributes is used to find k nearest neighbors for instances and coupling between labels is used to predict the labels of unseen instances.

The major contribution of this paper is summarized as follows:

First, a new coupled label similarity is introduced to reflect the relationship amongst labels.

Second, an improve ML-kNN algorithm is proposed by integrating the coupled label similarity and coupled attribute similarity to predict the labels of unseen instances.

Third, experimental results on two real-world multi-label classification problems, i.e. *emotions* and *yeast* gene functional analysis, show that CSML-kNN outperforms ML-kNN in some evaluation metrics.

The paper is organized as follows. Section 2 briefly reviews the related work. Section 3 introduces preliminaries and the detailed description of CSML-kNN approach. The experimental results are discussed in Sect. 4. Finally, we conclude this paper in Sect. 5.

2 Related Work

In resent years, multi-label classification has been paid much attention and there have been a variety of methods developed for multi-label classifications. Schapire and Singer proposed BoosTexter that maintains a set of weights over both training instances and their labels, where training instances and their corresponding labels are hard (easy) to predict correctly get incrementally higher (lower) weights [5]. McCallum proposed a Bayesian approach that assumes a mixture probabilistic model to generate each document and learns the mixture weights and the word distributions in each mixture component [6]. Clare and King modified the definition of entropy such that decision tree for multi-label data can be built [11]. Elisseeff and Weston proposed a kernel method for multi-label classification [3]. Zhang and Zhou proposed a neural network algorithm (BP-MLL) that employed a novel error function to capture the characteristics of multi-label learning, i.e., the labels belonging to an instance should be ranked higher than those not belonging to that instance [12]. ML-kNN approach proposed by Zhang and Zhou utilizes maximum a posteriori principle to determine the label set for the unseen instance, based on the statistical information which derives from the label sets of an unseen instance's neighboring instances [7]. Zheng et al. proposed MLRW algorithm based on the random walk model to determine the label set for the unseen instance by carrying out the random walk processing on a multi-label random walk graph system [13].

Cao defined coupling as any relationship or interaction that connects two or more aspects and thought that modeling and learning such couplings is fundamental for complex applications such as big data analytics [14]. Wang et al. proposed coupled similarity metrics for nominal objects and numerical data which consider not only intra-coupled interaction within an attribute but also inter-coupled interaction between attributes [10]–[15]. Liu and Cao presented CML-kNN approach based on ML-kNN exploiting the correlations between class labels, and CML-kNN overcomes the shortcoming of ML-kNN by introducing the coupled similarity between labels [8].

3 CSML-kNN

Let $X = \{x_1, x_2, \ldots, x_m\}$ denote the domain of instances; $A = \{a_1, a_2, \ldots, a_n\}$ be a finite set of attributes; $L = \{l_1, l_1, \ldots, l_q\}$ denote the finite set of labels. A data of multi-labels contains two parts: attribute set and label set. For training instance x_i its attribute set can be described as $x_i(A) = \{x_i(a_1), x_i(a_2), \ldots, x_i(a_n)\}$, where $x_i(a_j)$ represents the j-th attribute value of instance $x_i(x_i(a_j) \in \Re)$; its label set can be presented as $x_i(L) = \{x_i(l_1), x_i(l_2), \ldots, x_i(l_q)\}$, where $x_i(l_j)$ represents the j-th label value of instance $x_i(x_i(l_j) \in \{0, 1\})$. If instance x_i has label l_j, then $x_i(l_j) = 1$, and otherwise $x_i(l_j) = 0$. Thus x_i can be represented as $x_i = \{x_i(a_1), x_i(a_2), \ldots, x_i(a_n), x_i(l_1), x_i(l_2), \ldots, x_i(l_q)\}$. The training instances can be regarded as an information table $S\_training = <X, A, L>$ [9], where its rows denote "instances", columns of A designate "attributes" and columns of L denote "labels", each entry of A represents the value of a specific attribute for a specific instance, and each entry of L stands for the value of a specific label for a specific instance. The form of $S\_training$ is shown in Table 1.

Table 1. The formalization of $S\_training$

X	A				L			
	a_1	a_2	...	a_n	l_1	l_2	...	l_q
x_1	$x_1(a_1)$	$x_1(a_2)$	...	$x_1(a_n)$	$x_1(l_1)$	$x_1(l_2)$	...	$x_1(l_q)$
x_2	$x_2(a_1)$	$x_2(a_2)$	...	$x_2(a_n)$	$x_2(l_1)$	$x_2(l_2)$	...	$x_2(l_q)$
...	...	...	...	...	...	...	...	...
x_i	$x_i(a_1)$	$x_i(a_2)$	...	$x_i(a_n)$	$x_i(l_1)$	$x_i(l_2)$	...	$x_i(l_q)$
...	...	...	...	...	...	...	...	...
x_m	$x_m(a_1)$	$x_m(a_2)$	...	$x_m(a_n)$	$x_m(l_1)$	$x_m(l_2)$	...	$x_m(l_q)$

Accordingly, a test instance x_t whose labels are unknown can be described as $x_t = \{x_t(a_1), x_t(a_2), \ldots, x_t(a_n), ?, ?, \ldots, ?\}$ ("?" means the label is unseen). The task of data classification is to predict the label sets of the test instance x_t through analyzing training instances with known label sets.

Let $H_1^{l_j}$ represent the event that instance x_i has label l_j, $H_0^{l_j}$ represent the event that instance x_i does not have label l_j, and $E_u^{l_j} (u \in \{0, 1, \ldots, k\})$ represent the event that, among the k nearest neighbors of instance x_i, there are u instances having label l_j. Let $P(\cdot)$ denote probability, and $P(\cdot|\cdot)$ denote conditional probability.

The learning phase of ML-kNN includes the computation of $P(H_b^{l_j})$ and $P(E_u^{l_j}|H_b^{l_j})$ ($b = \{0,1\}$) based on the $S\_training$. $P(H_b^{l_j})$ and $P(E_u^{l_j}|H_b^{l_j})$ are defined in Eqs. (1), (2) and (3) respectively [7].

$$P(H_1^{l_j}) = \frac{s + \sum_{i=1}^{m}(x_i(l_j))}{s \times 2 + m}, \quad P(H_0^{l_j}) = 1 - P(H_1^{l_j}) \tag{1}$$

$$P(E_u^{l_j}|H_1^{l_j}) = \frac{s + c[u]}{s \times (k+1) + \sum_{z=0}^{k} c[z]} \tag{2}$$

$$P(E_u^{l_j}|H_0^{l_j}) = \frac{s + c'[u]}{s \times (k+1) + \sum_{z=0}^{k} c'[z]} \tag{3}$$

where s is the smoothing parameter, which generally takes the value of 1. m is the total number of instances. $P(E_u^{l_j}|H_1^{l_j})$ denotes the likelihood that among the k nearest neighbors of instance x_i, there are u instances having label l_j when instance x_i has label l_j. $P(E_u^{l_j}|H_0^{l_j})$ denotes the likelihood that among the k nearest neighbors of instance x_i, there are u instances having label l_j when instance x_i does not have label l_j. $c[u]$ represents instance x_i's k nearest neighbors contain exactly u instances which have label l_j. $c'[u]$ represents instance x_i's k nearest neighbors contain exactly u instances which don't have label l_j.

The testing phase of ML-kNN finds k nearest neighbors for test instance x_t and then computes the posteriori probability $\vec{y}_{x_t}(l_j)$ and real-valued vector $\vec{r}_{x_t}(l_j)$. $\vec{y}_{x_t}(l_j)$ and $\vec{r}_{x_t}(l_j)$ are defined in Eq. (4) and (5) [7].

$$\vec{y}_{x_t}(l_j) = \arg\max_{b \in \{0,1\}} (p(H_b^{l_j}) \times p(E_{\vec{C}_{x_t}(l_j)}^{l_j}|H_b^{l_j})) \tag{4}$$

$$\vec{r}_{x_t}(l_j) = \frac{p(H_1^{l_j}) \times p(E_{\vec{C}_{x_t}(l_j)}^{l_j}|H_1^{l_j})}{\sum_{b \in \{0,1\}} (p(H_b^{l_j}) \times p(E_{\vec{C}_{x_t}(l_j)}^{l_j}|H_b^{l_j}))} \tag{5}$$

where $\vec{r}_{x_t}(l_j)$ is a real-valued vector calculated to rank labels in L. $\vec{C}_{x_t}(l_j) = \sum_{a \in N(t)} x_t(l_j)$ counts the number of neighbors of x_t belonging to the l_j-th class and $N(x_t)$ represents the set of k nearest neighbors of x_t.

ML-*k*NN ignores the fact that labels or instances are more or less related via explicit or implicit relationships. For improving ML-*k*NN, CSML-*k*NN assumes the non-independence of attributes of instances such that takes coupling between labels, and between attributes simultaneously into consideration to capture global picture of instances, where coupling between attributes is used to find k nearest neighbors for instances and coupling between labels is used to predict the labels of unseen instances.

CSML-*k*NN also consists of two phases: one is training phase, and another one is testing phase. In training phase, we firstly compute the prior probabilities. Secondly, we find the k nearest neighbors of each training instance to compute conditional probabilities by using the coupled attribute similarity (CAS) [10], which includes the intra-coupled and inter-coupled interaction. Thirdly, we will compute the coupled label similarity (CLS). In testing phase, we find the k nearest neighbors of each test instance using the coupled attribute similarity (CAS) [10]. Then for each testing instance x_t, $\vec{r}_{x_t}(l_j)$ is determined by integrating the coupled label similarity (CLS). In order to illustrate our CSML-*k*NN approach clearly, we propose a frame, which considers the coupling of attributes and labels simultaneously. The framework of CSML-*k*NN is shown in Fig. 1.

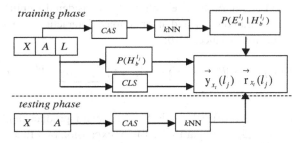

Fig. 1. The framework of CSML-*k*NN

3.1 Coupled Attribute Similarity (CAS)

The couplings of continuous attributes are proposed in terms of both intra-coupled and inter-coupled interactions [16]. Let $<a_j>^p$ $(1 \leq j \leq n)$ be the p-th power of the corresponding values of attribute a_j, the extension of $S\_training = <X, A, L>$ be $S'\_training = <X, A', L>$, where $A' = \{<a_j>^t | 1 \leq j \leq n, 1 \leq t \leq p\}$. The intra-coupled interactions within an attribute is measured by the correlations between attributes and their own powers, while inter-coupled interaction among different attributes is measured by the correlations between attributes and the powers of others. Then a coupled representation for numerical objects is formed by Taylor-like expansion, and the computation of distance between instances can be identified based on it k nearest neighbors of an instance.

The **intra-coupled interaction** within an attribute and the **inter-coupled interaction** among different attributes of A' are defined in Eqs. (6) and (7) respectively [10].

$$R^{Ia}(a_j) = \begin{pmatrix} \theta_{11}(j) & \theta_{12}(j) & \cdots & \theta_{1p}(j) \\ \theta_{21}(j) & \theta_{22}(j) & \cdots & \theta_{2p}(j) \\ \vdots & \vdots & \ddots & \vdots \\ \theta_{p1}(j) & \theta_{p2}(j) & \cdots & \theta_{pp}(j) \end{pmatrix} \tag{6}$$

$$R^{Ie}(a_j|\{a_k\}_{k\neq j}) = \begin{pmatrix} \eta_{11}(j|k_1) & \cdots & \eta_{1p}(j|k_1) & \cdots & \eta_{11}(j|k_{n-1}) & \cdots & \eta_{1p}(j|k_{n-1}) \\ \eta_{21}(j|k_1) & \cdots & \eta_{2p}(j|k_1) & \cdots & \eta_{21}(j|k_{n-1}) & \cdots & \eta_{2p}(j|k_{n-1}) \\ \vdots & & \vdots & & \vdots & \ddots & \vdots \\ \eta_{p1}(j|k_1) & \cdots & \eta_{pp}(j|k_1) & \cdots & \eta_{p1}(j|k_{n-1}) & \cdots & \eta_{pp}(j|k_{n-1}) \end{pmatrix} \tag{7}$$

Where $<a_j>^b$ and $<a_j>^d (1 \leq j \leq n, 1 \leq b, d \leq p, b \neq d)$ is the b-th power and d-th power of the corresponding values of attribute a_j respectively, $\theta_{bd}(j) = R\_Cor(<a_j>^b, <a_j>^d)$, $\{a_k\}_{k\neq j} = \{a_{k_1}, \ldots, a_{k_{n-1}}\}$, $\eta_{bd}(j|k_i) = R\_Cor(<a_j>^b, <a_{k_i}>^d)$, $R\_Cor(\cdot)$ represents the revised Pearson's correlation coefficient.

$$R\_Cor(<a_j>^b, <a_k>^d) = \begin{cases} Cor(<a_j>^b, <a_k>^d) & \text{if } p-value < 0.05, \\ 0 & \text{otherwise.} \end{cases} \tag{8}$$

p-value is used to test the correlation between attributes. If p-value less than 0.05, then we consider the correlation between attribute is considered significant.

According to the intra-coupled and inter-coupled interaction, we then have the coupled representation for instances [10]:

$$CAS(a_j|A', p) = x_i(a_j) \bullet e \times [R^{Ia}(a_j)]^T + x_i(\{a_k\}_{k\neq j}) \bullet \underbrace{[e, e, \ldots, e]}_{n-1} \times [R^{Ie}(a_j|\{a_k\}_{k\neq j})]^T \tag{9}$$

Where $e = [1, 1/(2!), \ldots 1/(p!)]$. $\bullet$ is the Hadamard product, and $\times$ is matrix multiplication. Equation (9) is similar to the Taylor expansion of a function, exhibiting the intrinsic coupled representation for instance x_i on the updated attribute $<a_j>^b$ when the maximal power p tends to infinity.

Based on CAS, the coupled representation of attribute set can be obtained. Then the Euclidean distance between instances can be computed.

Example 1. Table 2 shows an information table $S\_training = <X, A, L>$ with five instances, three attributes and four labels. Table 3 is the extended of Table 2, where $p = 2$, $<a_j>^1$ $(1 \leq j \leq 3)$ represents the original attributes a_j, while $<a_j>^2$ $(1 \leq j \leq 3)$ represents the square of attribute value a_j. According to Table 3, we have $x_1(a_2) = [0.12 \ 0.0144]$, $x_1(a_1, a_3) = [-0.04 \ 0.0016 \ 0.13 \ 0.0169]$. Table 4 shows the coupled representation of attribute set, and the Euclidean distance between x_1 and x_2 is 0.4134.

Table 2. An example of $S\_training$

	a_1	a_2	a_3	l_1	l_2	l_3	l_4
x_1	−0.04	0.12	0.13	0	0	1	0
x_2	−0.06	−0.08	−0.03	1	0	1	0
x_3	0.01	0.19	0.13	0	1	0	1
x_4	−0.02	−0.07	−0.09	1	1	0	0
x_5	−0.07	−0.03	0.07	0	1	0	1

Table 3. The extended table $S\_training$

	$<a_1>^1$	$<a_1>^2$	$<a_2>^1$	$<a_2>^2$	$<a_3>^1$	$<a_3>^2$
x_1	−0.04	0.0016	0.12	0.0144	0.13	0.0169
x_2	−0.06	0.0036	−0.08	0.0064	−0.03	0.0009
x_3	0.01	0.0001	0.19	0.0361	0.13	0.0169
x_4	−0.02	0.0004	−0.07	0.0049	−0.09	0.0081
x_5	−0.07	0.0049	−0.03	0.0009	0.07	0.0049

Table 4. The coupled representation of data set

	$<a_1>^1$	$<a_1>^2$	$<a_2>^1$	$<a_2>^2$	$<a_3>^1$	$<a_3>^2$
x_1	−0.0407	0.0381	0.1341	0.1137	0.13	0.186
x_2	−0.0617	0.0577	−0.0767	−0.0678	−0.03	0.073
x_3	0.01	−0.0093	0.2138	0.0361	0.13	0.1928
x_4	−0.0202	0.0188	−0.0641	0.0049	−0.09	−0.0602
x_5	−0.0723	0.0677	−0.0274	0.0009	0.07	−0.0251

3.2 Coupled Label Similarity(CLS)

The coupling of labels also consists of intra-coupling and inter-coupling. The intra-coupling considers the interaction of two different labels, while the inter-coupling considers the interaction of two different labels with respect to other labels. Due to the co-occurrence frequency reflects the interaction between features and can be used to define what makes two values more or less similar, so, it is incorporated into the existing similarity metrics.

For each pairs l_j and l_k of training multi-label label set, the *intra-coupling label similarity* (*IaCLS*) is defined in Eq. (10) [8] and the *inter-coupling label similarity* (*IeCLS*) is defined in Eq. (11). *IaCLS* reflects the similarity between label pairs. The higher the values are, the more similar label pairs are.

$$Intra(l_j, l_k) = \frac{RF(l_j) \cdot RF(l_k)}{RF(l_j) + RF(l_k) + RF(l_j) \cdot RF(l_k)} \tag{10}$$

$$Inter(l_j, l_k | l_s) = \frac{F(l_j, l_k)}{RF(l_s)} \tag{11}$$

where $RF(l_j)$ and $RF(l_k)$ are the number of instances which have labels l_j and l_k respectively. $F(l_j, l_k)$ is the number of instances which have labels l_j and l_k simultaneously when instances have label l_s, and $RF(l_s)$ is the number of instances which have labels l_s.

By integrating intra-coupling and inter-coupling label similarity, a **Coupled Label Similarity** (CLS) is presented in Eq. (12). The higher the value of $CLS(l_j, l_k)$ is, the more similar label l_j and l_k is

$$CLS(l_j, l_k) = Intra(l_j, l_k) \cdot \sum_{s=1}^{q} Inter(l_j, l_k | l_s) \tag{12}$$

where q is the total number of labels.

Example 2. For the labels in Table 2, we have

$$Intra(l_1, l_2) = 2 \times 3/(2+3+2 \times 3) = 0.55, \ Inter(l_1, l_2 | l_4) = 0/2 = 0,$$

$$CLS(l_1, l_2) = Intra(l_1, l_2) \cdot \sum_{s=1}^{4} Inter(l_1, l_2 | l_s) = 0.55 \times (0.5 + 0.33 + 0 + 0) = 0.46.$$

The coupled label similarity is shown in Table 5.

Tabel 5. Coupled label similarity

	l_1	l_2	l_3	l_4
l_1	1	0.46	0.5	0
l_2	0.46	1	0	0.91
l_3	0.5	0	1	0
l_4	0	0.91	0	1

3.3 Determining Labels of Test Instance x_t

For determining labels of test instance x_t, we first find k nearest neighbors of testing instance x_t based on the coupled attribute similarity, which presented in 3.1, and then we integrate the coupled label similarity into the computation of $\vec{r}_{x_t}(l_j)$. The computation of $\vec{r}_{x_t}(l_j)$ is defined as follows:

If $(CLS(l_j, l_k)) > \lambda$, then

$$\vec{y}_{x_t}(l_j) = \arg\max_{b \in \{0,1\}} (p(H_b^{l_j}) \times \sum_{k=1}^{q} (CLS(l_j, l_k) \times p(E_{C_{x_t}(l_j)}^{l_k} | H_b^{l_k}))) \tag{13}$$

$$\vec{r}_{x_t}(l_j) = \frac{(p(H_1^{l_j}) \times \sum_{k=1}^{q} (CLS(l_j, l_k) \times p(E_{C_{x_t}(l_j)}^{l_k} | H_1^{l_k})))}{\sum_{b \in \{0,1\}} (p(H_b^{l_j}) \times \sum_{k=1}^{q} (CLS(l_j, l_k) \times p(E_{C_{x_t}(l_j)}^{l_k} | H_b^{l_k})))} \tag{14}$$

where $CLS(l_j, l_k)$ donates the coupled label similarity between label l_j and label l_k. $\vec{C}_{x_t}(l_j) = \sum_{a \in N(x_t)} x_a(l_j)(l_j \in L)$ counts the number of neighbors of x_t belonging to the l_j-th class and $N(x_t)$ represents the set of k nearest neighbors of the unseen instance x_t. If $\vec{r}_{x_t}(l_j) > 0.5$, then we can predict the unseen instance x_t has label l_j; otherwise, the unseen instance x_t does not have label l_j. λ is a threshold used to prune weak coupling between labels, because in general strong or positive couplings can play an important role in data analysis, while some objects with weak or negative coupling can bring negative effects. To overcome the negative effects, the weak coupling should not be taken into account. If coupled label similarity (CLS) is greater than λ, the coupling is strong, otherwise it is weak and we will cut it down.

3.4   CSML-*K*NN Algorithm

The complete description of CSML-*k*NN is as follows.

```
Input: A training data set S_training=<X, A, L>,testing
       data xₜ and the number of nearest neighbors k
Output: The label set of testing instance xₜ
 1: Procedure TRAIN
 2:    for j=1 to q do
 3:      └ Calculate P(H₁^lⱼ) and P(H₀^lⱼ)
 4:    for i=1 to m
 5:        │  Identify the k nearest neighbors N(xᵢ) for xᵢ
           │  using coupled attribute similarity
 6:        │  for j=1 to q do
 7:        │  │  for u=0 to k do
 8:        └  └  └ Calculate p(Eᵤ^lⱼ|H₁^lⱼ) and p(Eᵤ^lⱼ|H₀^lⱼ)
 9:    for lⱼ ∈ L do
10:      └ Compute coupled label similarity
11: end Procedure
12: Procedure TEST
13:    Identify the k nearest neighbors N(xₜ) for xₜ
       using coupled attribute similarity
14:    for lⱼ ∈ L do
15:      └ Compute rₓₜ(lⱼ)
16: end Procedure
```

Steps from 1 to 11 are training phase. Steps from 2 to 3 calculate the prior probabilities $P(H_1^{l_j})$ and $P(H_0^{l_j})$ according to Eq. (1). Steps from 4 to 8 identify the k nearest neighbors of instances using the coupled attribute similarity (CAS), then calculate the conditional probabilities $p(E_u^{l_j}|H_1^{l_j})$ and $p(E_u^{l_j}|H_0^{l_j})$ according to Eqs. (2) and (3). Steps 9 to 10 calculate the coupled label similarity (CLS) according to Eq. (12). Steps from 12 to 16 are testing phase. Step 13 identifies the k nearest neighbors of unseen instances x_t using the coupled attribute similarity (CAS). Steps from 14 to 15 compute the $\vec{r}_{x_t}(l_j)$ according to Eq. (14).

4   Experiments and Evaluation

In this section, the experiment data and performance evaluation metrics used in this paper are introduced, and experimental results are presented.

4.1   Experiment Data

Two data sets, *emotions* and *yeast* data, are used to evaluate the performance of CSML-*k*NN. *emotions* data reflects people's emotion towards music. It includes 72 music features for 593 songs categorized into one or more out of 6 classes of emotions [17]. *yeast* data is gene data. Each gene is described by the micro-array expression data which is used to predict the gene functional classes of the Yeast Saccharomyces cerevisiae. It has 103 attributes for 2417 genes categorized into one or more out of 14 classes [3]. *emotions* and *yeast* data are commonly used to evaluate algorithms for multi-labels classification.

4.2   Performance Evaluation Metrics

In this paper, we use *Hamming Loss, One Error, Ranking Loss, Coverage,* and *Average Precision* [5] as measure metric. The meanings of these measure metrics are as follows.

Hamming Loss(H): evaluates how many times an instance label pair is misclassified. The smaller the value of *Hamming Loss*, the better the performance is.

Ranking Loss(R): evaluates the average fraction of label pairs that are reversely ordered for the instance. The smaller the value of *Ranking Loss*, the better the performance is.

One Error(O): evaluates how many times the top-ranked label is not in the set of possible labels. The smaller the value of *One Error*, the better the performance is.

Coverage(C): evaluates how far we need, on the average, to go down the list of labels in order to cover all the proper labels of the instance. The smaller the value of *Coverage*, the better the performance is.

Average Precision(A): evaluates the average fraction of labels ranked above a particular label $l_j \in L$ which is actually in L. The bigger the value of *Average Precision*, the better the performance is.

4.3   Experimental Results

In this section, three experimental results are presented: (1) the values of H, R, O, C, A under different k, (2) the values of H, R, O, C, A under different k nearest neighbors, (3) the values of H, R, O, C, A obtained by CSML-*k*NN and ML-*k*NN.

4.3.1   The Values of *H, R, O, C, A* Under Different λ

Figure 2 shows the values of *H, R, O, C, A* of CSML-*k*NN under different λ, where *k* = 10. In the experiments, we randomly select the training set and testing set for three times, thus the results in Fig. 2 are the average results in three times.

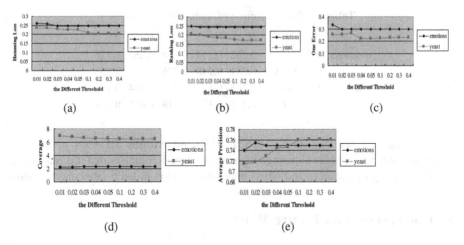

(a)   (b)   (c)

(d)   (e)

Fig. 2. The values of (a) *Hamming Loss*; (b) *Ranking Loss*; (c) *One Error*; (d) *Coverage*; (e) *Average Precision* under different λ

According to Fig. 2, performance is stable and effective when λ ≥ 0.03 for *emotions* data, while λ ≥ 0.1 for *yeast* data. So, in the following experiments, we set λ = 0.03 for*emotions* data and λ = 0.1 for *yeast* data.

4.3.2   The Values of *H, R, O, C, A* Under Different *k*

Table 6 shows the values of *H, R, O, C, A* of CSML-*k*NN under different *k*. Note that *emo* represents *emotions* data.

Table 6. *Emotions* data and *yeast* data with different *k*

	k = 8		*k* = 9		*k* = 10		*k* = 11		*k* = 12	
	emo	yeast	emo	yeast	emo	yeast	emo	yeast	emo	yeast
H	0.256	0.198	0.261	0.197	**0.253**	**0.196**	0.256	0.198	0.265	0.198
R	0.243	0.171	**0.242**	0.171	0.243	**0.170**	0.257	0.171	0.250	**0.170**
O	0.349	0.224	0.343	0.224	**0.335**	0.223	0.349	**0.222**	0.346	0.226
C	2.206	**6.360**	**2.204**	6.370	2.216	6.362	2.278	6.373	2.240	6.365
A	0.732	0.761	**0.735**	0.762	0.734	0.762	0.723	**0.763**	0.726	**0.763**

According to Table 6, we can see that the number of *k* does not significantly affect the performance of our algorithm CSML-*k*NN, which is consistent with ML-*k*NN. So, in the following experiments, we set *k* = 10.

4.3.3   The Values of *H, R, O, C, A* Obtained by CSML-*k*NN and ML-*k*NN [7]

Table 7 shows the values of *H, R, O, C, A* of CSML-*k*NN and ML-*k*NN, where 10-fold cross-validation is used. The results are the average results of 10-fold cross-validation.

Table 7. The comparison of multi-label approaches

		H	R	O	C	A
emotions	ML-*k*NN	0.262	0.254	0.374	**2.253**	0.716
	CSML-*k*NN	**0.251**	**0.248**	**0.326**	2.258	**0.733**
yeast	ML-*k*NN	0.205	0.175	0.227	6.434	0.756
	CSML-*k*NN	**0.203**	**0.173**	**0.218**	**6.428**	**0.761**

From Table 7, we can see that CSML-*k*NN outperforms ML-*k*NN in all measurement metrics except for *Coverage* in *emotions* data. It indicates that it is reasonable to take coupling of instances and labels into consideration in multi-label classification.

5   Conclusions and Future Work

In this paper, we propose an improved ML-*k*NN approach that takes the coupled similarity of attributes and labels into account, where coupling between attributes is used to find *k* nearest neighbors for instances and coupling between labels is used to predict the labels of unseen instances. Experimental results show that CSML-*k*NN method outperforms the traditional ML-*k*NN, thus it is reasonable to take coupling of instances and labels into consideration in multi-label classification.

In this study, we just focus on the numerical multi-label data. One of our future work is to deal with categorical [18] or mixed type multi-label data.

Acknowledgement. This work is supported by the National Natural Science Foundation of China under Grant No. 61262069, No. 61472346, the Natural Science Foundation of Yunnan Province under Grant No. 2015FB114, No. 2015FB149, No. 2016FA026, Program for Young and Middle-aged Skeleton Teachers, Yunnan University, and Program for Innovation Research Team in Yunnan University under Grant No. XT412011.

References

1. Boutell, M.R., Luo, J., Shen, X., Brown, C.M.: Learning multi-label scene classification. Pattern Recogn. **37**(9), 1757–1771 (2004)
2. Lewis, D., Yang, Y., Rose, T., Li, F.: RCV1: a new benchmark collection for text categorization research. Mach. Learn. Res. **5**, 361–397 (2004)
3. Elisseeff, A., Weston, J.: A kernel method for multi-labeled classification. In: Advances in Neural Information Processing Systems, vol. 14, pp. 681–687 (2002)

4. Snoek, C., Worring, M., Gemert, J.V., Geusebroek, J., Smeulders, A.: The challenge problem for automated detection of 101 semantic concepts in multimedia. In: ACM International Conference on Multimedia, pp. 421–430. ACM, New York (2006)
5. Schapire, R.E., Singer, Y.: Boostexter: a boosting-based system for text categorization. Mach. Learn. **39**(2–3), 135–168 (2000)
6. McCallum, A.: Multi-label text classification with a mixture model trained by EM. In: Working Notes of the AAAI 1999 Workshop on Text Learning (1999)
7. Zhang, M., Zhou, Z.: ML-*k*NN: a lazy learning approach to multi-label learning. Pattern Recogn. **40**(7), 2038–2048 (2007)
8. Liu, C., Cao, L.: A coupled *k*-nearest neighbor algorithm for multi-label classification. In: 19th Pacific-Asia Conference on Knowledge Discovery and Data mining, pp. 179–187 (2015)
9. Kaytoue, M., Kuznetsov, S.O., Napoli, A.: Revisiting numerical pattern mining with formal concept analysis. In: 22nd International Joint Conference on Artificial Intelligence, pp. 1342–1347 (2011)
10. Wang, C., She, Z., Cao, L.: Coupled attribute analysis on numerical data. In: 22th International Joint Conference on Artificial Intelligence, pp. 1736–1742 (2013)
11. Clare, A.J., King, R.D.: Knowledge discovery in multi-label phenotype data. In: Siebes, A., De Raedt, L. (eds.) PKDD 2001. LNCS (LNAI), vol. 2168, pp. 42–53. Springer, Heidelberg (2001)
12. Zhang, M., Zhou, Z.: Multi-label neural networks with applications to functional genomics and text categorization. IEEE Trans. Knowl. Data Eng. **18**(10), 1338–1351 (2006)
13. Zheng, W., Wang, C., Liu, Z., Wang, J.: A multi-label classification algorithm based on random walk model. Chin. J. Comput. **33**(8), 1418–1426 (2010)
14. Cao, L.: Coupling learning of complex interactions. Inf. Process. Manag. **51**, 167–186 (2015)
15. Wang, C., Cao, L., Li, J., Wei, W., Ou, Y.: Coupled nominal similarity in unsupervised learning. In: The 20th ACM International Conference on Information and Knowledge Management, pp. 973–978. ACM, New York (2011)
16. Cao, L.: Non-IIDness learning in behavioral and social data. Comput. J. **57**(9), 1358–1370 (2014)
17. Trohidis, K., Tsoumakas, G., Kalliris, G., Vlahavas, I.P.: Multi-label classification of music into emotions. In: 2011 9th International Conference on Music Information Retrieval, vol. 2011, no. 1, pp. 325–330 (2008)
18. Wang, C., Cao, L.: Coupled attribute similarity learning on categorical data. IEEE Trans. Neural Netw. Learn. Syst. **26**(4), 781–797 (2015)

A Novel Recommendation Method Based on User's Interest and Heterogeneous Information

Jiatong Wang$^{(\boxtimes)}$, Zhenqian Fei, Shuyu Qiao, Wei Sun, Xiaoxin Sun, and BangZuo Zhang

School of Computer Science and Information Technology, Northeast Normal University, Changchun 130117, China {wangjt453, feizq092, qiaosy976, sunwl32, sunxx772, zhangbz}@nenu.edu.cn

Abstract. It's a consensus that trust relationship is significant to improve the recommendation efficiently. But in most cases, trust relationship information is so sparse and difficult to use. Actually, the trust relationship is the response of interest among users, that is, it is an effective method to find the appropriate trust relationships by mining users' interests accurately. There are so many factors that can affect users' interest as well, such as age, occupation and so on. Based on these factors we can construct a heterogeneous information network, this paper deeply mine more accurate trust relationship through the interest and similarity from the heterogeneous information network among users, and merges the trust relationship to the matrix decomposition techniques. Moreover, we innovative conduct our experiment to test the recommendation algorithm based on trust, which has not been studied so far in MovieLens100k dataset. Experimental results demonstrate that our method outperforms other counterparts both in terms of accuracy.

Keywords: Trust relationship · Heterogeneous information network · Recommender system

1 Introduction

With the high speed development of Internet technology and World Wide Web, today is an era of information explosion. The explosion of information has led to lower utilization of it, facing the massive information, people cannot quickly and accurately obtain the information what they need, and neither effectively convey information to others. People puts forward higher requirements and new conceptions, such as information storage, collection, propagation, big data and so on, it have been face huge challenges. To solve this problem, people have proposed many methods, one of the most common and most effective way is personalized recommendation [1], which pushes the useful information to the user by analyzing user's past behavior data, thereby increasing the effective utilization of information. In fact, Netflix [2, 3] has expressed in the propaganda: 60 % of users find their own interested movies and videos by recommender system. The great success of recommender system has been

© Springer International Publishing Switzerland 2016
A. Morishima et al. (Eds.): APWeb 2016 Workshops, LNCS 9865, pp. 90–101, 2016.
DOI: 10.1007/978-3-319-45835-9_8

confirmed in the practical application. In the same time, we have to admit that there are more space to improve the personalized recommendation, and it is the goal of this paper as well.

In the past two decades, personalized recommender system has gotten a great development, lots of recommendation algorithm has been put forward to improve the efficiency. The most widely used algorithm is the collaborative filtering. Traditional collaborative filtering algorithms [4] calculate the similarity among users to find the neighbors who have similar tastes or preferences by users' past behavioral characteristics. Usually, the similarity of the active users and other users has been computed, and then select several users who have the highest similarity as the user' near neighbor. The common calculate similarity measure are Pearson correlation coefficient (PCC) [5], cosine similarity and so on. But in the real world, people tend to consider more factors, for example, whether the neighbor users who give the recommendation are his friends, whether the neighbor users have a reliable trust, and so on. The traditional collaborative filtering algorithms are only focused on computing the similarity between users, but they do not take trust relationships into account. In fact, if two users have similar preferences and interests, they should like the same thing, and more easily accept another's recommendations. It means the similarity of user is relevant with the trust relationship [6, 7]. It is a good opportunity to get more precise recommendation results if we can find out more accurate relationship between trust relationship and similarity.

Of course, there are so many factors that can affect the relationship between people, not only trust relationship, but also other factors, such as, geography, occupation, age and so on. When considering such factors, they can form a massive and complex network, that is, a heterogeneous information network, which is a newly emerging research field [8–10] in recent years, and give a new thought to consider the user's relationship. Heterogeneous information network is composed of nodes different nodes and the links, which is more appropriate to the real world relationship network [11]. For example, in the real world, we will judge whether we are interested in a movie by the ratings of other users who has watched it, or by the attributes of movie, such as the actor, the director and the movie style. Of course, if they are our trust friends, it will have a greater influence to us.

The users and items can be connected to form a heterogeneous information network by different attributes. If choose different attribute, there will have a different paths to connect users and items, called meta-path. The meta-path is a relations sequence between two objects, and the links belong to these two objects. Different meta-path indicates different semantics and the different influence for the result.

In order to have better recommendation results by trust relationship, this paper proposes a method merge user' rating similarity and their heterogeneous information network similarity to achieve precise recommendation by using matrix decomposition technology. This paper uses the popular MovieLens100k dataset. At the beginning of experiment, we need preprocess the dataset. Then, we find out trust relationship set among users by calculating the similarity with setting the threshold. Finally, experiment verify the effectiveness of the proposed method by the evaluation metric, mean absolute error (MAE) and root mean square error (RMSE) to illustrate the significantly improvement of the recommendation quality. It is the first time to use the recommendation algorithm with trust relationship in MovieLens100k dataset.

In order to deeply mine trust relationship, this paper combines the similarity of heterogeneous networks and the similarity of rating scores in the matrix decomposition technology to give an efficient prediction. The main contributions of this paper are as follows.

1. It deeply mine the users' behavior similarity and the similarity of heterogeneous information network between users to find out the precise trust relationship.
2. It innovatively runs the recommendation algorithm based on trust relationship in the MovieLens100k dataset, which hasn't such work yet and opens a new direction.
3. The proposed method has been vilified by the experimental results, which shows our proposed algorithm outperform the state-of-art algorithms.

The remaining of this paper is organized as follows. In Sect. 2, we provide the relevant concept of several major approaches for recommender systems based on trust relationship and heterogeneous information network, and some related works. Section 3 presents module and framework of our proposed method. The experimental results and the analysis are demonstrated in Sect. 4. The last part makes the conclusions and give the future works in Sect. 5.

2 Related Works

In the traditional collaborative filtering algorithm, the most classical algorithms can be classified as the memory-based and model-based [5, 12]. Memory-based CF mainly relies on the similarity measure of users or items, and was efficient in early recommender system. It isn't suitable for the real-time operation with the rapid increasing in data volume in recent years, so model-based CF becomes more popular. Since the end of Netflix competition in 2009, the matrix factorization method, such as SVD++ [13] has gotten more attention, which is better for improving the prediction accuracy of the recommender system. Lots of researchers find that the similarity measure and the trust relationship between users can be considered together in the model-based CF, which can greatly improve the accuracy.

In 2008, Ma et al. has proposed a social regularization method (SoRec) [14] by constraint of social relationships. The main idea is to achieve a user-feature matrix factorized by ratings and trust relationship. In 2010, Jamali and Ester put forward a new model (SocialMF) [15] on the base of SoRec by integrating the results of the active user's user-specific vector with trust users. In 2011, Ma et al. have further proposed a method that the active user's user-specific vector should be considered the average of the trusted neighbors with using a regularization to form a new matrix factorization model (SoReg) [16].

In 2015, Guo et al. have proposed a matrix decomposition method that combines the user's trust relationship and the impact of the explicit and implicit rating data, which is based on SVD++, and extended the implicit trust factors (TrustSVD) [17]. All of these methods employ the social relations, but in [18–20] have been proved that, the unilateral relationship of trust is more valuable than the bilateral relationship (such as friends) for the recommendation. And when using the trust relationship for recommender system, the trust relationship matrix is very sparse, in order to get better recommendation, we have to find a more valuable implicit trust relationship.

Of course, we need to use the user interest relation to find the accurate trust relationship. In 2013, Shi et al. [21] have proposed a novel similarity measurement method, called HeteSim, which combines the objects and the surrounding attributes to explore the similarity relationship. The trust relationship also can be measured by the similarity between friends. In 2016, Wang et al. [6] used a new Pearson similarity to propose the trust relationship in the Filmtrust dataset, and integrate matrix decomposition technology with the original trust relationship, and the results show more satisfactory. However, the similarity between users is not only due to the rating scores, but also many other relevant factors, for example, the user's occupation, age and so on. [21] has proposed the similarity of heterogeneous information networks, used some information of movies like actor, director, style and others, and used HeteSim to calculate and produce high quality recommendations.

3 The Proposed Method

In this Section, we give a detailed explanation of the proposed method. Subsection 3.1 explains the implicit trust relationship mines from rating information; Subsect. 3.2 illustrates the framework of heterogeneous information network; Subsect. 3.3 introduce the famous matrix decomposition technique, named TrustSVD; Subsect. 3.4 puts forward the algorithm HPTrustSVD.

3.1 Users' Implicit Trust Relationship

In the same area of interest, if two people have a trust relationship, it confirm they have similar interest. In other words, people's trust relationship is based on their interest. So it is not surprising that two persons don't know each other when they have trust relationship. If we want to acquire the trust relationship between them, we can only rely on the user's interest. The most classical similarity formula is Pearson correlation coefficient [5] as in Eq. (1).

$$PearsonSim_{u,v} = \frac{\sum_{i \in I_{u,v}} (r_{u,i} - \bar{r}_u)(r_{v,i} - \bar{r}_v)}{\sqrt{\sum_{i \in I_{u,v}} (r_{u,i} - \bar{r}_u)^2} \sqrt{\sum_{i \in I_{u,v}} (r_{v,i} - \bar{r}_v)^2}} \quad (1)$$

where $PearsonSim_{u,v} \in [-1,1]$, u and v denotes two users, respectively. $I_{u,v}$ denotes the list of the co-ratings given by user u and user v, $\bar{r}_u$ and $\bar{r}_v$ denotes their average rating scores.

But there will have a problem: if two user' only one co-rated, the Pearson correlation coefficient is 1, that is, they have the highest similarity, no matter what the rating score is. Obviously it violate the common sense, so Wang et al. make some changes as in Eq. (2).

$$NewSim_{u,v} = \begin{cases} 1 & u = v \\ (1 - 1/n)(Sim_{u,v} + 1)/2 & u \neq v \end{cases} \tag{2}$$

where n is the number of co-rating score between two users, we put the number of co-rating scores in Eq. (2), and used to deal with the above problem. What's more, it makes the score range between 0 and 1, and will benefit the next works.

After calculating the similarity among users based on Pearson correlation coefficient, we set a threshold θ. If the similarity reaches a predetermined threshold, it is defined the new trust relationship as in Eq. (3).

$$PTrustSet = \{(u,v) \mid NewSim_{u,v} \geq \theta;\ u,v \in U\} \tag{3}$$

where U denotes all the users, θ is a parameters range from 0 to 1. By this means, we can mine the trust relationships between users deeply.

3.2   Heterogeneous Information Network

Firstly, we introduce information network: given a graph directed G, it form an information network, which include lots of nodes and links. We need to observe these nodes and links, if the type number of nodes or links is greater than one, the network is called heterogeneous information network, otherwise homogeneous information network.

In MovieLens100k dataset, there are many users' attributes, which constitute a heterogeneous information network. In this network, we can calculate the heterogeneous information similarity between users according to their age, occupation, gender or other factors. Shi et al. normalized the HeteSim formula as in Eq. (4).

$$HeteSim(a, b \mid P) = \frac{PM_{P_L}(a)\, PM_{P_R}(b)}{\sqrt{\|PM_{P_L}(a)\|\, \|PM_{P_R}(b)\|}} \tag{4}$$

Where P represents the meta-path of two nodes, PM_L and PM_R represent the meta-path from the beginning of the middle node to the left and right, thus it can be written as matrix multiplication according to the relationship between two nodes.

In this paper, all the HeteSim formulas are obtained through normalization. We can get a set of similarity obtained by the HeteSim, and combine it with the rating score similarity that is calculated by Subsect. 3.1, and then set θ that reaches a certain threshold as the trust relationship as in Eq. (5).

$$HPTrustSet = \{(u,v) \mid NewSim_{u,v} + HeteSim_{u,v} \geq \theta;\ u,v \in U\} \tag{5}$$

So we can combine two kinds of similarities to infer a more accurate trust relationship.

3.3 TrustSVD Algorithm

The most famous method of matrix decomposition algorithm, it is SVD, which decomposes the rating matrix R into two low-rank matrices P and Q to reduce dimensionality of the original matrix, in other words $R \approx P^T Q$. The prediction $\hat{r}_{u,j}$ is done by taking an inner product, as in Eq. (6).

$$\hat{r}_{u,j} = q_j^T p_u \tag{6}$$

The predicted ratings and other vacancies values will be filled by matrix decomposition. But every one has different standard that measure the extent of users' preferences. For example, some people may give a full mark as long as they feel a little interest, while others rarely give high marks. In order to this problem, SVD++ method add the baseline estimates bui and users' ratings implicit feedback information as in Eq. (7).

$$\hat{r}_{u,j} = b_{ui} + q_j^T \left(p_u + |I_u|^{-\frac{1}{2}} \sum_{i \in I_u} y_i \right) \tag{7}$$

where I_u represents the datasets which user u has rated, b_u and b_i represent the observed deviations of user u and item i, μ is the overall average rating.

So we can get: $b_{ui} = \mu + b_u + b_i$, rating r_{ui} is denoted by b_{ui} and accounts for the user and item effects. y_i provides information about users' implicit feedback, and it also provide an additional indication of the user's preference, with increasing prediction accuracy. $q_j^T y_i$ is the influence of having been rated item i.

Guo et al. added explicit trust information users on the basis of SVD++ and presented TrustSVD. To get more accurate predicted ratings, we show the specific rating model as follow Eq. (8).

$$\hat{r}_{u,j} = \mu + b_u + b_i + q_j^T \left(p_u + |I_u|^{-\frac{1}{2}} \sum_{i \in I_u} y_i + |T_u|^{-\frac{1}{2}} \sum_{v \in T_u} w_v \right) \tag{8}$$

where T_u represents the set of users' trust; $q_j^T w_v$ can be know as the influences of active user u from trust user v. This method is added decomposition of trust relationship matrix.

3.4 Our Proposed Method

We get users' the implicit trust relationship by users' the rate information and Heterogeneous similarity, then we combine it with trustSVD, it's named HPTrustSVD as in Eq. (9).

$$L = \frac{1}{2}\sum_u \sum_{j \in I_u} (\hat{r}_{u,j} - r_{u,j})^2 + \frac{\lambda_t^{hp}}{2}\sum_u \sum_{v \in T_u} (hp\hat{t}_{u,v} - hpt_{u,v})^2$$

$$+ \frac{\lambda}{2}\sum_u |I_u|^{-\frac{1}{2}} b_u^2 + \frac{\lambda}{2}|U_j|^{-\frac{1}{2}} b_j^2 + \sum_u (\frac{\lambda}{2}|I_u|^{-\frac{1}{2}} + \frac{\lambda_t^{hp}}{2}|hpT_u|^{-\frac{1}{2}})\|p_u\|_F^2 \quad (9)$$

$$+ \frac{\lambda}{2}\sum_j |U_j|^{-\frac{1}{2}}\|q_j\|_F^2 + \frac{\lambda}{2}\sum_i |U_i|^{-\frac{1}{2}}\|y_i\|_F^2 + \frac{\lambda}{2}|hpT_v^+|^{-\frac{1}{2}}\|w_v\|_F^2$$

$\hat{r}_{u,j}$ is different from Eq. (8), that hpT_u is substitute for T_u, and the hpT_u is our implicit trust. A trust relationship can be predicted by the inner product of a truster-specific vector and a trustee-specific vector $hp\hat{t}_{u,v} = w_v m_u$, exT_u and hpT_u represent the set of explicit and implicit trust of users in HPTrsutSVD, respectively; w_v is the feature vector of trusters and trustees, and $q_j^T w_v$ is the impact of the users who active user trust implicitly, hpT_v^+ is the set of users who trust user v. Some variable parameters are continue to use the same parameters in the original TrustSVD. It is of great significant contribution for other researchers to use implicit trust in MovieLens100k dataset, because the dataset has no real trust.

This paper refer to the TrustSVD algorithm of Guo et al., which give a relatively small penalty factor to more active and frequent user or more popular items. In contrast, users or items which is the cold start will be given larger penalty factor.

To solve the loss of function by gradient descent, we can calculate the partial derivatives of the parameters as follows:

$$\frac{\partial L}{\partial b_u} = \sum_{j \in Iu} e_{u,j} + \lambda |I_u|^{-\frac{1}{2}} b_u, \quad \frac{\partial L}{\partial b_j} = \sum_{u \in Uj} e_{u,j} + \lambda |U_j|^{-\frac{1}{2}} b_j$$

$$\frac{\partial L}{\partial p_u} = \sum_{j \in Iu} e_{u,j} q_j + \lambda_t^{hp} \sum_{v \in T_u^{hp}} e_{u,v}^{hp} w_v + \left(\lambda |I_u|^{-\frac{1}{2}} + \lambda_t^{hp} |hpT_u|^{-\frac{1}{2}}\right) p_u$$

$$\frac{\partial L}{\partial q_j} = \sum_{u \in Uj} e_{u,j} \left(p_u + |I_u|^{-\frac{1}{2}}\sum_{i \in I_u} y_i + |hpT_u|^{-\frac{1}{2}}\sum_{v \in hpT_u} w_v\right) + \lambda |U_j|^{-\frac{1}{2}} q_j \quad (10)$$

$$\forall i \in I_u, \frac{\partial L}{\partial y_i} = \sum_{j \in I_u} e_{u,j}|I_u|^{-\frac{1}{2}} q_j + \lambda |U_j|^{-\frac{1}{2}} y_i$$

$$\forall v \in hpT_u, \frac{\partial L}{\partial w_v} = \sum_{j \in I_u} e_{u,j}|hpT_u|^{-\frac{1}{2}} q_j + \lambda_t^{hp} e_{u,v}^{hp} p_u + \lambda |hpT_v^+|^{-\frac{1}{2}} w_v$$

where $e_{u,j} = \hat{r}_{u,j} - r_{u,j}$ represents the error of predicted ratings, and $e_{u,v}^{hp} = hp\hat{t}_{u,v} - hpt_{u,v}$ represents the error of the explicit trust prediction.

4 Experimental Results and Analysis

4.1 Dataset

We use MovieLens100k dataset that has founded by GroupLens team of Computer Science and Engineering, Minnesota University. This dataset is the most classical one in collaborative filtering, it consists of $100,000$ ratings from 942 users on 1682 movies, and in which each user has 20 film ratings at least. In the movie data, there are so many attributes, like actor, type, director and so on. As for user, there are attributes like age, sex, occupation, zip code and so on. These attributes can be formed a heterogeneous information network. But we focus on mining the user's trust relationship, so we don't consider about those attributes of movies. In the experiments, 80 % of the dataset is used as the training set for the algorithm, and the remaining is used as test set to measure the performance.

4.2 Evaluation Metrics

This paper use two evaluation metrics to compare the performance. One is the mean absolute error (MAE), and the other is the root mean square error (RMSE), the formula is as in Eqs. (11) and (12), respectively.

$$MAE = \frac{\sum_{u,i \in S} |r_{ui} - \hat{r}_{ui}|}{|I|} \tag{11}$$

$$RMSE = \sqrt{\frac{\sum_{u,i \in S} (r_{ui} - \hat{r}_{ui})^2}{|I|}} \tag{12}$$

where r_{ui} is the user u's rating score for item i, $\hat{r}_{ui}$ is the predicted rating score by user u for item i, I denotes the number of items. These two formulas are used to measure deviation, and the smaller deviation value means the better prediction.

4.3 Attributes Selection

In this paper, we focus on considering the relationship among users, so the attributes of movies would not be considered. In MovieLens100k dataset, attributes of users include age, sex, occupation, zip code. Among these attributes, zip code refers to geographical location of users, which has no direct relations with interest of users, so we don't take it into consideration.

In the HeteSim formula, when we consider gender and occupation, as long as two persons have the same gender or occupation, the similarity result is 1 according to formula (4), which is not unexpected, because everyone only has one age and one occupation, there is only one value in the matrix's row, and that can not be changed.

But for age, there will be some impact for users within a certain age range, so we divided users into groups by age, every four years as a group, by which one user can stay in several groups simultaneously. For example: a user is 24 years old, so he belongs to the group of 20–25, and also belongs to the group of 22–27. In the experiments, we set the age of four as a group, each year increments up.

Therefore the formula contains heterogeneous similarity with age, gender, occupation is as in Eq. (13).

$$HeteSim_{u,v} = \alpha AgeSim_{u,v} + \beta GengderSim_{u,v} + \gamma OccSim_{u,v} \tag{13}$$

4.4 Analysis and Comparison

Our main idea is mining trust relationship by attributes and behavior information of users. In HeteSim algorithm, each attribute plays a different role, therefore we set the values of α, β, γ as 0.05, 0.01, 0.09 respective in the Eq. (13). And the $\lambda = 0.9$, $\lambda_t^{ht} = 0.4$, these values are certified by experiment. We set the impact of gender on interest of users is the smallest, and occupation play a greater role on interest of users. According to Eq. (3), Wang et al. have acquired trust relationship set by behavior information (PtrustSVD). According to Eq. (5), we merge Heterogeneous Information similarity based on method of Wang et al. (HPTtrustSVD). Figure 1 shows the performance comparisons on MAE and RMSE respectively, in which the horizontal axis is the range of θ values. We can learn from the following figures that our algorithm outperforms than the other one which only use the rating scores similarity without heterogeneous information network. And the best values of MAE can reach 0.699516, and the best values of RMSE also can reach 0.899334.

We know different value of θ can lead to different number of trust relationship. In Fig. 1, we can find that it's the best performance when the value of θ is 0.45. When the value of θ less than 0.45, the number of trust relationships will increase lead to performance degradation, even worse. Of course, the more trust relationship in the model, the role's importance is decrease. Therefore, the key point of improving the performance is how to select an adequate and accurate threshold to control the number of the trust relationship.

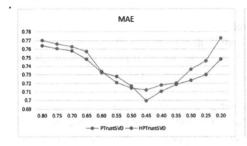
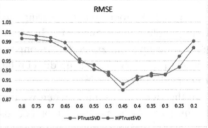

Fig. 1. The MAE and RMSE results of PTrustSVD and HPTrustSVD by θ

So far, there is no one recommender system algorithm that based on trust relationship in MovieLens100k dataset, so we compare it with several classical approaches to prove the effectiveness of our proposed method. We use a 5-fold cross-validation for learning and testing. In each time we randomly select 80 % of data as training set and the rest 20 % for test. Table 1 shows the results of our model compare with several other state-of-arts algorithms.

Table 1. HPTrustSVD's comparison with others methods

Method	MAE	RMSE
UserAvg	0.834814	1.041613
UserAvg	0.816861	1.024324
NMF	0.791817	1.022864
SVD++	0.765267	0.996121
RegSVD	0.763899	0.994060
PTrustSVD	0.71202	0.901826
HPTrustSVD	0.699516	0.899334

It is obviously that the result of our method is extremely efficient. When the value of θ is 0.45, the trust relationship is so accurate enough that it has a good effect on recommendation. HPTrustSVD method has a highly accurate prediction to trust relationship before matrix decomposition, and it can get a more efficient result than PTrustSVD method.

The experimental results verify that our proposed algorithm can effectively improve recommendation performance base on the basis of user interest and the heterogeneous information network similarity.

5   Conclusion and Future Work

In this paper, we propose HPTrustSVD method which integrate the heterogeneous information network similarity based on the similarity among users to infer the trust relationships. Then, apply to the recommendation algorithm based on trust. Finally the experimental results demonstrate the method's efficient performance. There is an innovation is that our recommender algorithm is based on trust at classical Movie-Lens100k dataset.

We integrate the heterogeneous information network similarity, which is increasing based on the original user similarity. In this case, trust relationship will constantly increase. So we have to consider how to control the amount of trust relationship and try to find more accurate trust relationship with removing some useless or inaccurate trust relationship in future work. Additionally, we only consider the trust relationship, which is positive influence, but there is a very important influence on distrust relationship, which is so difficult that can not solve in the recommendation algorithm based on trust relationship. We are supposed to research these problems to achieve better results on recommendation approaches.

Acknowledgments. This work is supported by the National Natural Science Foundation of China (No. 71473035), MOE (Ministry of Education in China) Project of Humanities and Social Sciences (No. 14YJA870010), Jilin Provincial Science and Technology Key Project (No. 20150204040GX), Project of Jilin Provincial Industrial Technology Research and Development (No. 2015Y055), National Training Programs of Innovation and Entrepreneurship for Undergraduates (201410200042), Natural Science Fund of Northeast Normal University (2014015KJ004).

References

1. Adomavicius, G., Tuzhilin, A.: Towards the next generation of recommender systems: a survey of the state-of-the-art and possible extensions. IEEE Trans. Knowl. Data Eng. **17**, 634–749 (2005)
2. Bennet, J., Lanning, S.: The Netflix Prize. In: KDD Cup and Workshop (2007). www.netflixprize.com
3. Bell, R., Koren, Y.: Lessons from the Netflix Prize challenge. SIGKDD Explor. **9**, 75–79 (2007)
4. Herlocker, J.L., Konstan, J.A., Borchers, A., Riedl, J.: An algorithmic framework for performing collaborative filtering. In: Proceedings of the 22nd ACM SIGIR Conference on Information Retrieval, pp. 230–237 (1999)
5. Masthoff, J.: Recommender Systems Handbook. Springer US, New York (2010)
6. Wang, J., Hu, J., Qiao, S., Sun, W., Zang, X., Zhang, B.: Recommendation with Implicit Trust Relationship Based on Users' Similarity. ICMSIE, DEStech Publications Inc., Lancaster (2016)
7. Ma, H.: On measuring social friend interest similarities in recommender systems. In: Proceedings of the SIGIR 2014, Gold Coast, Queensland, Australia, 6–11 July 2014
8. Yu, X., Ren, X., Sun, Y., Gu, Q., Sturt, B., Khandelwal, U., Norick, B., Han, J.: Personalized entity recommendation: a heterogeneous information network approach. In: Proceedings of the 2014 ACM International Conference on Web Search and Data Mining (WSDM 2014) (2014)
9. Yu, X., Ren, X., Gu, Q., Sun, Y., Han, J.: Collaborative filtering with entity similarity regularization in heterogeneous information networks. In: Proceedings of the IJCAI 2013 HINA Workshop (2013)
10. Sun, Y., Han, J., Yan, X., Yu, P.S., Wu, T.: PathSim: meta path-based top-K similarity search in heterogeneous information networks. PVLDB **4**(11), 992–1003 (2011)
11. Yu, X., Ren, X., Sun, Y., Sturt, B., Khandelwal, U., Gu, Q., Norick, B., Han, J.: HeteRec: entity recommendation in heterogeneous information networks with implicit user feedback. In: Proceedings of 2013 ACM International Conference Series on Recommendation Systems (RecSys 2013), Hong Kong, October 2013
12. Wang, Q., Sun, M., Xu, C.: An improved user-model-based collaborative filtering algorithm. J. Inf. Comput. Sci. **8**(10), 1837–1846 (2011)
13. Koren, Y.: Factorization meets the neighborhood: a multifaceted collaborative filtering model. In: Proceedings of the 14th ACM SIGKDD International Conference on Knowledge Discovery and Data Mining (KDD), pp. 426–434 (2008)
14. Ma, H., Yang, H., Lyu, M.R., King, I.: SoRec: social recommendation using probabilistic matrix factorization. In: Proceedings of CIKM 2008, pp. 931–940. ACM, New York (2008)

15. Jamali, M., Ester, M.: A matrix factorization technique with trust propagation for recommendation in social networks. In: Proceedings of the 4th ACM Conference on Recommender Systems (RecSys), pp. 135–142 (2010)
16. Ma, H., Zhou, D., Liu, C., Lyu, M.R., King, I.: Recommender systems with social regularization. In: Proceedings of the 4th ACM International Conference on Web Search and Data Mining (WSDM), pp. 287–296 (2011)
17. Guo, G., Zhang, J., Yorke-Smith, N.: TrustSVD: collaborative filtering with both the explicit and implicit influence of user trust and of item ratings. In: Proceedings of the 29th AAAI Conference on Artificial Intelligence, Austin, USA, 25–30 January 2015
18. Ma, H.: On measuring social friend interest similarities in recommender systems. In: Proceedings of SIGIR 2014, Gold Coast, Queensland, Australia, 6–11 July 2014
19. Guo, G., Zhang, J., Thalmann, D.: Merging trust in collaborative filtering to alleviate data sparsity and cold start. Knowl. Based Syst. **57**, 57–68 (2014)
20. Massa, P., Avesani, P.: Trust-aware recommender systems. In: Proceedings of RecSys 2007, Minneapolis, MN, USA, pp. 17–24 (2007)
21. Shi, C., Kong, X., Yu, P.S., Xie, S., Wu, B.: Relevance search in heterogeneous networks. In: Proceedings of the 15th International Conference on Extending Database Technology (EDBT 2012), Berlin, Germany (2012)

Knee Point-Driven Bottleneck Detection Algorithm for Cloud Service System

Xiao-Long Liu, Xue-Bai Zhang, Hsiang Chao,
and Shyan-Ming Yuan$^{(\boxtimes)}$

Department of Computer Science, National Chiao Tung University,
Hsinchu, Taiwan, ROC
shallen548@gmail.com, asuracocoa@gmail.com,
shine30001@hotmail.com, smyuan@cs.nctu.edu.tw

Abstract. Currently, providers of Software as a service (SaaS) can use Infrastructure as a Service (IaaS) to obtain the resources required for serving customers. Performance problems in a SaaS system are difficult to diagnose, because they may be caused by various system components. This study proposes a knee point-driven bottleneck detection algorithm, the specific resource bottleneck in the target system can be detected by analyzing the collected metrics. The detection result provides a scale up recommendation for the service provider to facilitate reconfiguring the service system. The experimental results revealed that the proposed system can detect a potential bottleneck in a service system accurately. After solving the detected bottleneck the performance of the target cloud service can be improved efficiently.

Keywords: Bottleneck detection · Knee point · Cloud testing · Resource allocation

1 Introduction

In the age of cloud computing [1], a growing number of system maintainers and service providers of software as a service (SaaS) are willing to move their backend infrastructure from their local servers onto cloud-based servers. Accordingly, SaaS providers can alleviate a tremendous amount of server maintenance effort for tasks such as maintaining availability and backups as well as load balancing [2]. Because infrastructure technologies have evolved and cloud services have become popular with businesses, the quality of service (QoS) of cloud services has become extremely high. Commercial offerings must deliver the QoS expected by consumers, and consumers prefer to select a cloud service that can offer services with a high QoS [3].

However, for certain cloud applications such as launching a popular game online or reserving tickets for movies, concerts, or transportation, the QoS can hinder service providers. This dissatisfactory QoS is primarily caused by insufficiently deployed computing instances or resources. In other words, in such cases, service providers have inaccurately predicted customer demand, which causes a high volume of requests concurrently sent to a few computing instances. Auto-scaling mechanism [4] is one technique used in infrastructure provider that enables service providers to maintain

© Springer International Publishing Switzerland 2016
A. Morishima et al. (Eds.): APWeb 2016 Workshops, LNCS 9865, pp. 102–111, 2016.
DOI: 10.1007/978-3-319-45835-9_9

their resources and reduce wasted resources by automatically increasing or reducing them whenever required. Certain cloud services support autoscaling functionality, such as AWS CloudWatch [5] and RightScale [6]. They monitor information on CPU utilization, disc I/O, and network I/O on the server side for triggering system configurations. However, no predictive functions are available that might predict performance degradation that are instantly caused by a lack of computing instances.

For the staging of the service lifecycle, every system should be verified whether the performance of the system is sufficiently good to satisfy users in terms of capability and availability. The performance of a service relies on having a powerful and complex system of distributed servers. For example, a Web service may require an Apache Web server at the front end to display the Web page and accept user requests; an application server in the middle to manage dynamic requests (e.g., those regarding PHP coding and Common Gateway Interface), which may require querying the database; and a database server in the tail end to be queried. Even in this simple three-tiered structure, the number of instances in each tier is not necessarily limited to one. Service providers strive to determine the most influential weak point in the system flow, and then improve overall system performance by enhancing the weak point. This weak point is called "the bottleneck." Nevertheless, after service bottleneck detection, information on how to allocate adaptive instances to a different tier of services can be provided efficiently. In a distributed server system, the bottleneck detection problem becomes more difficult as the system becomes increasingly complex.

This paper proposes a bottleneck detection algorithm that can eliminate weak points and ensure a high QoS in a cloud service system. By increasing the workload in the target system, the change in metric information on utilization is collected from monitors, and the algorithm is used to analyze whether the current system has a bottleneck. For each metric, its knee point is located first, with the maximum workload of each metric estimated afterward to detect the bottleneck in the system. The bottleneck detection procedure can be conducted repeatedly until the overall system performance satisfies the service provider's expectations. The experimental results revealed that the proposed system can accurately detect a potential bottleneck, and that the overall performance can be improved after resolving the bottleneck in the target service. Therefore, the proposed algorithm was demonstrated as a suitable one for service providers to evaluate their system performance on both system testing stage and cloud service operational stage.

The rest of the context is organized as following: We discuss the related works in Sect. 2; Sect. 3 introduces the proposed bottleneck detection algorithm; The experimental results are presented in Sect. 4; Finally, we conclude this paper in Sect. 5.

2   Related Works

A system bottleneck occurs when requests start to queue and have a limited throughput [7]. Regarding system resource utilization, a bottleneck can be classified into three types: a single bottleneck, saturation without a single bottleneck, and a rapidly alternating bottleneck. A single bottleneck occurs when service systems reach the maximum throughput because a single resource is fully utilized. By contrast, saturation without a single bottleneck occurs when no hardware resources are fully utilized. An alternating bottleneck occurs in turn among different system resources when one system resource becomes the main bottleneck at any moment.

To detect transient alternating bottlenecks in an n-tier system, Wang et al. [8] proposed a fine-grained load/throughput analytical method. The first step in this method involves measuring a server load and throughput in continuous fine-grained time intervals. This provides a saturation point N^* for the minimum load that is beyond a server's limit. This saturation point facilitates determining the time intervals in which the server is saturated based on the measured load, and analyzing if short-term saturation occurs in alternating patterns. However, regarding the analytical results, this method can only detect bottlenecks that are caused by Java Virtual Machine Garbage Collection and VM allocation. Cohen et al. [9] presented an n-tier server bottleneck detection model to detect bottlenecks caused by different system components. First, requests are created to test servers by using load generators, and metrics related to different components are collected. Afterward, the Tree-Augmented Bayesian Networks (TANs) model is correlated with the collected metrics and service level objective (SLO) defined by the service provider. The TANs model identifies the component with metrics that are highly correlated with the SLO violation as a potential bottleneck in this system. Jung et al. [10] presented another model to detect n-tier server bottlenecks. In their model, the durations of all requests in each tier are collected, and the fastest-growing duration is identified as the bottleneck tier. The metrics that surpass the threshold value are then selected to train the J48 decision tree. By using the decision tree, the bottleneck between the metrics and the SLO violation can be detected. Instead of using the machine-learning techniques for bottleneck detection that have been used by Cohen et al. and Jung et al., Malkowski et al. [11] proposed a statistic intervention analysis algorithm to identify bottlenecks. In their model, the confidence interval of the SLO is calculated to automatically characterize the potential change in metric graph trends and assess its correlation with SLO violations.

The authors of these studies have claimed that they can determine the bottleneck point by analyzing the change in metric as the load increases. However, all of the bottleneck detection mechanisms necessitate defining the threshold of the SLO. However, the threshold definition would be inconvenient for service providers because SLO satisfaction involves variance in specific measurable characteristics such as availability, throughput, frequency, response time, and quality [12]. Therefore, selecting the metric and the threshold required for promising a service quality that satisfies the service-level agreement can be challenging. To simplify the detection mechanism, Yao et al. [13] proposed a novel knee point detection algorithm. In their approach, throughput is defined as the number of user requests that pass all the server tiers successfully. The change rates of the entire metric utilization and that of the throughputs in all tiers are collected. The bottleneck tier is identified based on the earliest knee point of the throughputs observed among all the tiers. The precise bottleneck resource is then identified by comparing the earliest knee point and the lowest maximum load. However, the method by Yao et al. necessitates defining the throughput of different servers in different services, and is inconvenient for detecting potential bottlenecks that coexist in the system. Therefore, the present study proposes an improved bottleneck detection algorithm that provides a system applicable for various services and enables the convenient identification of all potential resource bottlenecks.

3   The Proposed Bottleneck Detection Algorithm

This section details the proposed bottleneck detection algorithm. During testing, the metrics information on utilization (e.g., the CPU, network, disc, and memory usage) is collected from monitors, and the algorithm is used to analyze whether the current system has a bottleneck. For each metric, its knee point is located first, with the maximum workload of each metric estimated afterward to detect the bottleneck in the system. The knee point [14] is the point where the change rate of the metric is significantly lower while the workload is higher than normal. Before the knee point, the utilization of each metric increases with a linear growth property in accordance with the workload, whereas afterward, the utilization cannot grow further with the property because of a potential bottleneck.

Figure 1 displays an example of normalized metric utilization plotted against the workload throughout one test duration. To locate the knee point of this metric, a linear line connecting the first test point to the last test point was generated (i.e. dash line C in Fig. 1). Subsequently, for each test point x in the figure, two lines can be generated. The first line connects the first test point to the current test point x (i.e., dashed line A_x in Fig. 1). The second line connects the last test point to the current test point x (i.e., dashed line B_x in Fig. 1). In accordance with the generated lines C, A_x, and B_x, the length of the orthogonal line (i.e., H_x in Fig. 1), which connects the test point x to line C, can be calculated in accordance with the following equation:

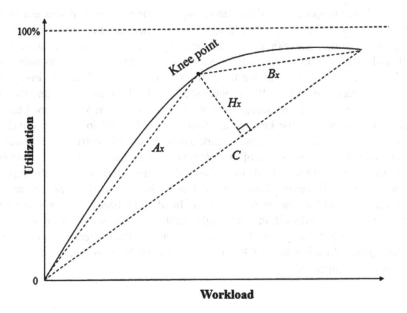

Fig. 1. Location of the knee point

$$H_x = A_x \sin(\cos^{-1}((A_x^2 + C^2 - B_x^2)/2A_xC)). \tag{1}$$

where sin and cos are the sine rule and cosine rule, respectively. For each test point x, a corresponding orthogonal line H_x can be calculated. Finally, the test point with the longest orthogonal line is the knee point of this metric.

In accordance with the located knee point, the maximum workload of each metric is estimated to detect the bottleneck in the system. Assume that point K_m is the knee point of the metric m, and is located in position (U_{Km}, W_{Km}), where U_{Km} is the metric utilization of K_m, and W_{Km} is the corresponding workload. The correlation between the metric utilization U_x and the workload W_x of test point x, located before the knee point K, can be approximately defined as a linear function, as follows:

$$U_x = \frac{U_{Km}}{W_{Km}} W_x. \tag{2}$$

Therefore, assuming that all of the test points in this test duration follow the linear function, if the metric utilization reaches its maximum workload (i.e., 100 %), the maximum workload W_m^{max} of metric m can be calculated using the following equation:

$$W_m^{max} = \frac{W_{Km}}{U_{Km}}. \tag{3}$$

After computing the maximum workloads of all metrics in the system with the same method, a set of maximum workloads can be generated as $\{W_1^{max}, W_2^{max}, W_3^{max} \ldots, W_n^{max}\}$. The metric with the lowest maximum workload in this set is the bottleneck resource.

To clarify the proposed algorithm, an example of the bottleneck resource detection process is shown in Fig. 2. In this example, we assumed that the service system was expected to support at least 800 clients concurrently. The normalized utilizations of the cpu/db and io/db metrics that resulted from the cloud service testing procedure were plotted against the workload as the red and green lines, respectively, in Fig. 2. The cpu/db metric represented the CPU resource status in the database server, and the io/db metric represented the disc resource status in the database server. We assumed that K_{io} and K_{cpu} were located as the knee point of metrics cpu/db and io/db, respectively. In accordance with Eq. (2), the maximum workload of the cpu/db metric was estimated as 337, and the maximum workload of the io/db metric was calculated as 651. However, the estimated maximum workloads of 337 and 651 were both lower than the expected workload of 800. Therefore, both the CPU and disc in the database server were regarded as potential bottlenecks in the system. In addition, because 337 was the lower estimated maximum workload, the CPU in the database server was detected as the main bottleneck resource in the system. Therefore, to overcome the bottleneck and ensure the expected QoS, allocating more CPU resources to database instances of the target system was recommended.

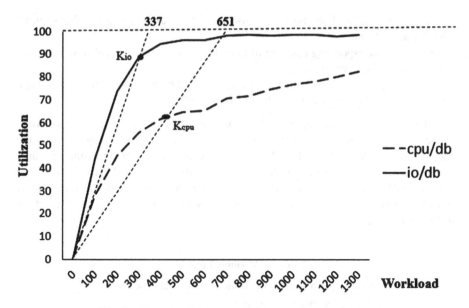

Fig. 2. Example of the proposed auto-scaling mechanism

4 Experimental Results and Evaluation

This section presents the simulation results of the proposed bottleneck detection algorithm. In the experiments, four physical machines and the TPC Benchmark™ W (TPC-W) [15] were used. An online book store was deployed as a three-tiered Web service involving a Web server, application server, and database server. Each physical machine had an Intel(R) i7-4770 chipset with four hyper-threading 3.4 GHz cores, 32 GB RAM, 2 TB 5400 RPM disc, and a 100 Mbps network adapter. One physical machine was installed with a virtual machine to deploy the database server. Another physical machine was installed with two virtual machines to deploy the Web server and application server. The remaining two physical machines were used as hypervisors to perform testing, in which two virtual machines were installed on each hypervisor, with each virtual machine able to generate several test clients as emulated workloads.

To test the experimental web service we performed the experiments by using the shopping mix mode, where browse interactions and order interactions accounted for 80 % and 20 % of all interactions, respectively. For all of the experiments, we assumed that the service system could support at least 1,200 clients concurrently, because the private network environment could only steadily manage 1,200 clients at a time. The experimental service-testing procedure is outlined as follows:

- Step 1. Allocate the resource of virtual machine for each tier server.
- Step 2. The test was started with zero workloads. The system stress was then iteratively increased by 100 workloads until 1,300 workloads were reached while the system metrics were monitored simultaneously.

- Step 3. The proposed bottleneck detection algorithm was used to detect the potential bottleneck resource.
- Step 4. The corresponding resource of the bottleneck server was scaled up using the provided scaling recommendation.
- Step 5. The process was repeated from Step 1 until the service system could manage 1,200 workloads concurrently without a bottleneck.

In the service-testing procedure of the experiments, the metrics that were monitored involved all of the servers' resource statuses (i.e., CPU, disc, and memory usage) in the system, which are listed in Table 1. Each metric represented a corresponding resource status of each server. For example, the cpu/web metric represented the CPU resource status of the Web server, the mem/app metric represented the memory resource status of the application server, and the io/db metric represented the disc resource status of the database server.

Table 1. Monitored metrics

Resource	Web server	Application server	Database server
CPU	cpu/web	cpu/app	cpu/db
Memory	mem/web	mem/app	mem/db
Disk	io/app	io/app	io/db

4.1 Experiment with Initial Resource Allocation

In this experiment, shopping mix mode was used to test the target system. The test clients' Web interactions focused on browsing the target Web site with certain ordering processes. The initial virtual machine resource allocations for the system servers are listed in Table 2. The test results of the initial resource allocation are plotted in Fig. 3. To facilitate reading the figures in this paper, we plotted only the most evidently changing metrics, and did not plot metrics that did not have a knee point or display significant changes. Figure 3 displays only the results of the cpu/app, cpu/db and io/db metrics, because their variations were extremely obvious.

Table 2. Initial resource allocation

Resource	Web server	Application server	Database server
CPU	VCPU*1	VCPU*1	VCPU*1
Memory	4G	4G	4G
Disk	HDD	HDD	HDD

As shown in Fig. 3, the utilization of the cpu/app metric was nearly 100 % with 700 workloads. With the influence of the cpu/app metric, the utilization of the cpu/db and io/db metrics could not increase after 700 workloads. The bottleneck detection results of the initial resource allocation test are listed in Table 3. They revealed that a cpu/app metric had a significant knee point with 700 workloads, and the maximum workload was estimated as 715.18. Because the estimated maximum workload was

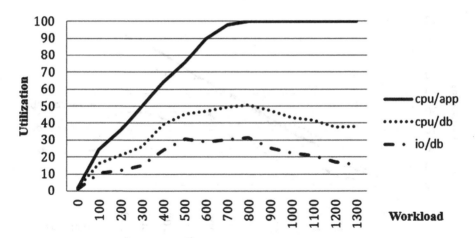

Fig. 3. Testing results of initial resource allocation

lower than the expected workload of 1,200, the CPU of the application server was detected as the main bottleneck resource in this experiment. Therefore, in this case, the system recommended allocating more CPU resources to the application server, and to scale it up for the next test.

Table 3. Bottleneck detection results of initial resource allocation

Factor	cpu/app
Knee point	700
Maximum workload	715.18

4.2 Experimental Results After Scaling

In accordance with the recommended allocating, in this test we reallocated more CPU resources to the application server. The resource allocation after the recommend scaling of the service system is shown in Table 4.

Table 4. Resource allocation after scaling

Resource	Web server	Application server	Database server
CPU	VCPU*1	**VCPU*2**	VCPU*1
Memory	4G	4G	4G
Disk	HDD	HDD	HDD

After scaling of the resource allocation, the service system was tested using the shopping mix mode again. The test results after the scaling are plotted in Fig. 4. Compared with the testing result of the initial resource allocation (i.e. Fig. 3), the utilizations of the cpu/db and io/db metrics could increase significantly after 700 workloads. This was because the bottleneck (i.e. the cpu/app metric) in the server system had been solved. After the bottleneck detection, the estimated maximum workloads of

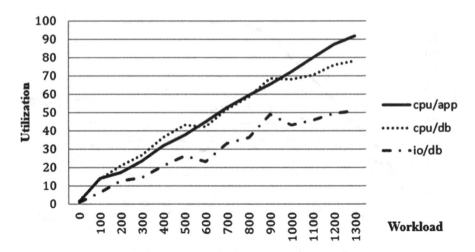

Fig. 4. Testing results after scaling

the cpu/app and cpu/db metrics were 1379.42 and 1320.45, respectively, as shown in Table 5. Therefore, all the estimated maximum workloads of metrics in the service system were more than 1,200, indicating no resource bottlenecks. The experiment results in the shopping mix mode indicated that: the CPU of the application server was the most critical resource while browsing was the main web interaction with the service system.

Table 5. Bottleneck detection results after scaling

Factor	cpu/app	cpu/db
Knee point	1200	900
Maximum workload	1379.42	1320.45

The experimental results presented above demonstrated that the proposed system can accurately detect and resolve a bottleneck in a target service by iteratively increasing the system load and monitoring the system metrics simultaneously. By analyzing the metric change as the load is increased, the bottleneck point can be detected. After scaling the corresponding resource of the bottleneck, an overall improvement in performance is observable. The bottleneck detection and scaling procedures can be repeatedly performed until the overall system performance satisfies user expectations.

5   Conclusions

This paper proposed a bottleneck detection algorithm that ensures the QoS for cloud services. After evaluating the knee point of each metric the weak point of the target service can be eliminated efficiently by using the proposed bottleneck detection algorithm. In the experiments, we used shopping mix mode in TPC-W benchmark to test a target three-tiered Web service. The experimental results revealed that the proposed system can accurately detect potential bottleneck resources, and that overall performance can be improved after scaling up the bottleneck resources in the target service. In the future, more web interaction mix modes and benchmarks would be used to further evaluate the proposed bottleneck detection algorithm.

Acknowledgement. This paper was supported by the National Science Council of Taiwan under Grant NSC103-2221-E-009 -133 -MY2, and W & J soft Inc. under Grant 104C140.

References

1. Armbrust, M., Stoica, I., Zaharia, M., Fox, A., Griffith, R., Joseph, A.D., Katz, R., Konwinski, A., Lee, G., Patterson, D., Rabkin, A.: A view of cloud computing. Commun. ACM **53**(4), 50 (2010)
2. Cusumano, M.: Cloud computing and SaaS as new computing platforms. Commun. ACM **53**(4), 27–29 (2010)
3. Abdelmaboud, A., Jawawi, D.N.A., Ghani, I., Elsafi, A., Kitchenham, B.: Quality of service approaches in cloud computing: a systematic mapping study. J. Syst. Softw. **101**, 159–179 (2015)
4. Lorido-Botrán, T., Miguel-Alonso, J., Lozano, J.A.: Auto-scaling Techniques for Elastic Applications in Cloud Environments. Department of Computer Architecture and Technology, UPV/EHU, EHU-KAT-IK (2012)
5. Amazon Web Services. Amazon Cloud Watch. Amazon. http://aws.amazon.com/cloudwatch
6. RightScale. Cloud Portfolio Management. RightScale. http://www.rightscale.com
7. Wang, Q., Kanemasa, Y., Li, J., Jayasinghe, D., Shimizu, T., Matsubara, M., Kawaba, M., Pu, C.: An experimental study of rapidly alternating bottlenecks in n-tier applications. In: IEEE 6th International Conference on Cloud Computing (CLOUD) (2013)
8. Wang, Q., Kanemasa, Y., Li, J., Jayasinghe, D., Shimizu, T., Matsubara, M., Kawaba, M., Pu, C.: Detecting transient bottlenecks in n-tier applications through fine-grained analysis. In: IEEE 33rd International Conference on Distributed Computing Systems (ICDCS) (2013)
9. Cohen, I., Chase, J.S., Goldszmidt, M., Kelly, T., Symons, J.: Correlating instrumentation data to system states: a building block for automated diagnosis and control. In: The 6th Conference on Symposium on Opearting Systems Design & Implementation (OSDI) (2004)
10. Jung, G., Swint, G., Parekh, J., Pu, C., Sahai, A.: Detecting bottleneck in n-tier it applications through analysis. In: 17th IFIP/IEEE International Workshop on Distributed Systems: Operations and Management (DSOM), Dublin, Ireland (2006)
11. Malkowski, S., Hedwig, M., Parekh, J., Pu, C., Sahai, A.: Bottleneck detection using statistical intervention analysis. In: Clemm, A., Granville, L.Z., Stadler, R. (eds.) DSOM 2007. LNCS, vol. 4785, pp. 122–134. Springer, Heidelberg (2007)
12. Ludwig, H.: Web services QoS: external SLAs and internal policies or: how do we deliver what we promise? In: The Fourth International Conference on Web Information Systems Engineering Workshops, Roma, Italy (2004)
13. Yao, J., Jung, G.: Bottleneck detection and solution recommendation for cloud-based multi-tier application. In: Franch, X., Ghose, A.K., Lewis, G.A., Bhiri, S. (eds.) ICSOC 2014. LNCS, vol. 8831, pp. 470–477. Springer, Heidelberg (2014)
14. Zhang, X., Tian, Y., Jin, Y.: A knee point-driven evolutionary algorithm for many-objective optimization. IEEE Trans. Evol. Comput. **19**(6), 761–776 (2015)
15. TPC. TPC-W – Homepage. http://www.tpc.org/tpcw/

Confirmatory Analysis on Influencing Factors When Mention Users in Twitter

Yueyang Li[1(✉)], Zhaoyun Ding[1], Xin Zhang[1], Bo Liu[2], and Weice Zhang[3]

[1] College of Information Systems and Management,
National University of Defense Technology, Changsha 410073, China
{liyueyang14,zyding,zhangxin78}@nudt.edu.cn
[2] Airforce Electromagnetic Spectrum Management Center, Nanjing, China
[3] Nanchang Institute of Army, Nanchang, China

Abstract. Nowadays, Twitter has become an important platform to expand the diffusion of information or advertisement. Mention is a new feature on Twitter. By mentioning users in a tweet, they will receive notifications and their possible retweets may help to initiate large cascade diffusion of the tweet. To enhance a tweet's diffusion by finding the right persons to mention, in this paper, we propose three factors that probably have impact on tweet's diffusion. Specifically, these factors are user vulnerability, user's online status and spatial location. In this paper, the issue 'whom to mention when tweeting' is transformed to the issue 'choosing users who have higher probability to retweet. By analyzing users retweet behaviors, online status and users' location in Twitter, we confirm these three factors. Experiments were conducted on a real dataset from Twitter containing about 49,253 users and 563,758 tweets in a target community, and results show that these three factors all have significant impacts on retweeting and information diffusion.

Keywords: Twitter · Retweet · Mention · Recommendation

1 Introduction

Micro-blogging systems like Twitter have become the most important ways for people to communicate with others and share information in recent years. In twitter, users tweet (post a message) about any topics within the 140-character limit and follow others to receive their tweets. Furthermore, with retweeting (forward a tweet), information can be effectively relayed beyond adjacent neighbors, virtually giving every user the power to spread information broadly. Therefore, retweeting have become the key mechanism for information diffusion and enhancing users' influence in Twitter.

However, recent studies [1–3] show that the diffusion power of tweets from different users varies significantly: 0.05 percent of Twitter users attract almost 50 percent of all attention within Twitter and the spread of a tweet from an ordinary user is rather limited, with an average retweet rate of 0.11. This suggests a very limited diffusion for most tweets. Fortunately, as a new feature on Twitter, Mention can help ordinary users to improve the visibility of their tweets and go beyond their immediate reach in social

© Springer International Publishing Switzerland 2016
A. Morishima et al. (Eds.): APWeb 2016 Workshops, LNCS 9865, pp. 112–121, 2016.
DOI: 10.1007/978-3-319-45835-9_10

interactions. Mention is tagged as @username. All the users mentioned by a tweet will receive a mention notification. By using Mention, one can draw attention from specific users. Properly using mention can quickly help an ordinary user spreading his tweets.

Due to the significance of the mention, some studies have focused on mention recommendation in their foregoing work. One of the most representative work was proposed by Wang et al. [4]. They propose a recommendation scheme named as 'whom-to-mention', which take user interest, Content-dependent user relationship and user influence into consideration when choosing whom to mention in their tweets. And confirmed these factors are related.

To the best of our knowledge about Mention Recommendation, most of the previous work is based on the content factors. However, the goal of mention recommendation is to find candidates who can help spread a tweet. Instead of topical relevance. Therefore, to better help an ordinary user spreading their thought in Microblogging systems, there are several problems should be considered:

Recommendation Length Restriction: Due to the strict length restriction of a tweet, only a small number of users can be mentioned in a tweet. Moreover, a tweet mentioning a lot of users is likely to be treated as a spam tweet, which will decrease others' interest in retweeting it. Thus, to accomplish the mention recommendation task, the algorithm needs to be optimized for mentioning only a small number of users.

Recommendation Overload Problem: Traditional recommendation systems such as those used in Amazon may recommend one item to large numbers of users, which results in popular products. However, in the mention recommendation system, a user being recommended too many times will suffer from the severe mention overload problems. Tons of mention notifications will not only interrupt user's daily use of microblogs, but also result in frustration and decrease user's interest in retweeting.

Space and Time Problem: with the explosive growth of mobile Internet and mobile intelligent devices, more and more people use Twitter and other social network platform by smartphone or pad whenever and wherever possible. Time and location elements play more and more important effects on recommendation system. In other work about mention recommendation, space and time are seldom considered.

Users' personalities: In traditional recommendation system, collaborative filtering, content-based recommendation are the main two methods. Collaborative filtering is main based on users' social network relationships, recommending items to them through analyzing their friends' interests and attentions. But content-based recommendation is based on the user's past behaviors, such as purchase history data in shopping website, browsing history in news site and search engine, following history in social network. However, we need think of more users' personalities besides user interests and social relations in Mention Recommendation, such as user's online habit, whether liking retweets and so on.

To cope with all the above mentioned challenges, three other factors are proposed in this paper through our long-term analysis for some special users and their tweets and retweets. Specifically, these factors are briefly introduced as follows:

1. User vulnerability

   Different users have different sentiment and different behaviors on one tweet, someone like retweeting but someone not. We define user vulnerability as the probability a user retweet a tweet. The probability higher, the user's vulnerability higher.

2. Online status

   Users usually preferred to retweet the instant information. If users are online in next time and they discover the information is outdated, the probability of retweets would become lower. Moreover, due to the overload problems on Twitter, large number of other mentioned tweets maybe drown earlier mentioned tweets and caused these earlier mentioned tweets to be read with a lower probability.

3. User's spatial location

   Users usually preferred to retweet the information take placed in our surrounding and interact with users near to them. If a news or topic we see in Twitter is far away from us and that will not cause large-scale influence, we rarely to pay close attention to it, the probability of retweets would become lower.

In this work, we mainly focus on user vulnerability, users' online status and users' spatial location and verify the influences of these three factors for retweets.

2 Related Work

2.1 Twitter

Among various microblogging systems, Twitter is the most popular service by far. Twitter is a social networking and microblogging service that allows users to send and read 140-character short messages known as tweets, enabling users to share and discover topics of interest in real-time. Users choose to follow other notable users to gain real-time updates on news and statuses. Once authored by a user, tweets are immediately delivered to the author's subscribers or followers. For a reader, tweets from all users whom she follows are gathered together and displayed in a single chronological list for consumption. Twitter also provides a set of application programming interface (http://dev.twitter.com/), which allows third party applications to send and receive tweets.

Tweets are publicly visible by default, but senders can restrict message delivery to just their followers. Users can tweet via the Twitter website, compatible external applications (such as for smartphones), or by Short Message Service (SMS) available in certain countries.

Users may subscribe to other users' tweets—this is known as "following" and subscribers are known as "followers" or "tweeps", a portmanteau of Twitter and peeps. Individual tweets can be forwarded by other users to their own feed, a process known as a "retweet". Users can also "like" (formerly "favorite") individual tweets.

Twitter allows users to update their profile via their mobile phone either by text messaging or by apps released for certain smartphones and tablets.

2.2 Retweet

In addition to its typical usage, which is to broadcast a short text to the public, tweets are often used to converse with individuals or groups [5, 6]. When a user wants to specify another user in a tweet, she can use the form of mentioning '@username', which is subsequently parsed and translated into a clickable hyperlink to the mentioned user. These user links enable the discovery of other interesting persons to follow and often facilitate a conversation. Furthermore, for a user, tweets containing that user's name will appear in a special "replies tab" (accessible at http://twitter.com/replies for logged-in users) notifying that the tweet was intended for her. If more than one person are included in a tweet using the @username format, each person will see the update in her own replies tab.

Retweet is one particular case of mentioning. When a user finds an interesting tweet written by another Twitter user and wants to share it with her followers, she can retweet the tweet by copying the message, typically adding a text indicator (e.g. RT, Via) followed by the user name of the original author in @username format [7].

As discussed by Boyd et al. [8], retweeting is associated with various social motivations such as entertaining a specific audience, commenting on someone's tweet, publicly agreeing with someone. Moreover, people often add more content or slightly modify the original when retweeting. Twitter users created a number of different ways to retweet such as "RT @" and "via @" [8]. Retweeting has become so widespread that Twitter added a feature in 2009 to allow users to retweet easily with one-click.

Some work also start research 'why we retweet'. Zhiheng Xu et al. do a deep analysis of user retweet behavior [9]. Jan Boehmer et al. studied the factors influencing intentions in specific field (sport news) [10].

2.3 Mention Recommendation

Mention is a new feature in micro-blogging systems, but it play a vital role in diffusing information and enhancing users' influence in Twitter. By mentioning users in a tweet, they will receive notifications and their possible retweets may help to initiate large cascade diffusion of the tweet. So, Mention Recommendation is to enhance a tweet's diffusion by finding the right persons to mention.

By mentioning a non-follower of the tweet author, the non-follower may retweet it to his followers and spread the tweet to a new group of users, which usually leads to further cascade diffusion; By mentioning a follower of the author, the mention serves as a useful notification, especially when the follower follows a large number of other users and a tweet can be easily swamped in the enormous number of tweets. It's also critical for a tweet to be viewed promptly as 25 % replies to a tweet happen within 67 s, 75 % within 17 min and 75 % message flow lasts less than an hour [11]. Therefore, without proper notification, a tweet may easily be neglected as one's followers fail to read it in time.

3   Data

In order to prove that these three factors are influential to retweet, we collected data from Twitter containing the following information. For a user, we get his/her userid, name (screen name), location, number of followers and friends and so on. For a tweet, we get the author of the tweet, time when the user posted the tweet, the content of the tweet, and the created time of the tweet (only retweets have).

3.1   Preprocessing

We randomly choose some seed users as initial target group of our experiments. We only extract some users useful for our experiments. First, we eliminate the garbage users, including the users whose followees is much higher than followers, and high proportion of retweets or even only have retweets in his/her all tweets. Second, we removed the users who don't have location information in their profiles when we verify the factor of spatial location. For each tweet, we can get its creation time, so we cannot remove any tweets of when we verify the factor of online status of users.

We randomly choose 49,253 users as monitoring objects in the experiments. Generally, we pay more attention on users who have a number of followers and a few followees as influential, so we define user influence:

$$UI = \frac{countOfFollowers}{countOfFollowees + 1} \tag{1}$$

We define those users whose UI less than 0.1 as garbage users, and removed them from monitoring objects. There are 44,658 users remaining. Then we collected their all tweets posted from October 1, 2105 to December 31, 2015 and saved to database, including user table and tweet table. And we also collected their data from January 1 2016 to March 31, 2016, use them as comparison when assess user vulnerability.

4   Statistical Experiments

4.1   User Vulnerability

For every user in our experiment, we count his/her amount of tweets and retweets. And using their retweet rates as the users' vulnerability. If a user has higher retweet rate, that indicates he/she is more vulnerable. 'We start from a tweet from the tweets data table, then find the userid who post it, and we can find the user and his/her all tweets (include retweets) easily in tweets data table through the userid. For every tweet text, we can count as retweet if it start with 'RT'. So, we can calculate every user's retweetability in a period of time that our monitoring objects.

$$R_i = \frac{M1_i}{M2_i} \tag{2}$$

Here, the R_i indicated the retweet rate of user i, and $M1_i, M2_i$ indicated the retweet amount and tweet amount.

We count every user's retweets and tweet, then calculate the retweet rate from 2015.10 to 2015.12 (phase 1), some of statistical data are shown in Table 1.

Table 1. A fraction of users' retweet statistical data from October to December, 2015

Num	Userid	countOfRetweet	countOfTweet	retweetRate
1	100122533	13	29	0.448276
2	100147610	1	1	1
3	1001642364	85	85	1
4	100167612	0	2	0
5	100172757	24	183	0.131148
6	100175420	23	162	0.141975
7	1001788356	7	15	0.466667
8	100184413	91	748	0.121658
9	100198190	252	624	0.403846
10	100201420	0	7	0

In order to certify that everyone's retweet behavior is not randomly occurred and everyone's actions have regularity and stability in Twitter, we collected these users' data from 2016.01 to 2016.03 (phase 2) and compared to everyone's retweet rates in the two different time slot. In this experiment, because of being disturbed by other factors, we processed the data and give up the data whose count of tweet less than 50 in either phase 1 or phase 2, and also give up the data whose retweet rate is 0 or 1. Finally we got 5,009 valid data. Some of data are shown in Table 2.

Table 2. A fraction of users' retweet statistical data after processing (comparing phase 1 with 2)

num	userid	2015.10-2015.12			2016.01-2016.03		
		countOfRetweet	countOfTweet	retweetRate	countOfRetweet	countOfTweet	retweetRate
8	100184413	91	748	0.121657754	64	375	0.170666667
9	100198190	252	624	0.403846154	151	357	0.422969188
11	100233785	108	324	0.333333333	35	70	0.5
21	1005931626	92	111	0.828828829	102	114	0.894736842
23	10065202	148	709	0.208744711	44	150	0.293333333
26	100693518	34	105	0.323809524	82	120	0.683333333
27	100693538	26	233	0.111587983	18	76	0.236842105
32	1007793098	55	111	0.495495495	12	57	0.210526316
38	100882076	8	221	0.036199095	62	859	0.07217695
45	1010959956	10	362	0.027624309	1	109	0.009174312
...	...	...	...	...	...	...	...

Then, we apply formula to compute retweet stability index as follow:

$$RS_i = \frac{retweetRate1_i}{retweetRate2_i} \tag{3}$$

$retweetRate1_i$, $retweetRate2_i$ indicated respective retweet rate in phase 1 and phase 2 of user i, RS_i indicated retweet stability index of user i.

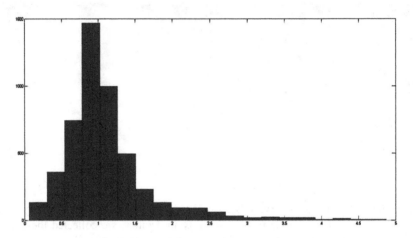

Fig. 1. 5,009 users' retweet stability distribution

In Fig. 1, X-axis indicated the retweet stability index, the length of each interval was divided 0.25. Y-axis indicated the user number of every interval. Obviously, (0.75, 1], (1, 1.25], (0.5, 0.75], and (1.25, 1.5], the four intervals have more numbers, they have 4,311 users data of 5,009, account for 86.1 %. After fitting these data, we found that retweet stability distribution is basically obey the normal distribution and its average index is 1.

So, this experiment shown that users in Twitter have relatively stable vulnerability. They usually won't retweet frequently in a time span but seldom retweet in another time span, and vice versa. As we know, different user has different retweet rate, so we could choose users who have high retweet rate when we in search of better users to mention.

4.2   Online Status

In order to expand the diffusion of tweets by @ recommendation on Twitter, it is important to consider whether mentioned users are online. When planning tweet, we will get twice the results with half the effort if we know the highest time of clicks and participation. Master these information will get unexpected results, and we have been exploring social media twitter best practices, for example, the length, the frequency and timing. Especially the timing, is the factor needed to further exploration.

But users' online status are not presented directly in Twitter. So we need conversion to analyze other information that we can measure directly for verifying the users' online status impact on retweet. Messages Twitter users saw in their homepage is sorted by time, latest tweet always is saw firstly, outdated tweet would be submerged. In our collected data, we can get created time for every tweet, and retweet time for every retweet about time element. So we can calculate Δt for every retweet. For every retweet, the smaller of Δt, the greater of the retweet user online when it was posted.

$$\Delta t = t_1 - t_2 \tag{4}$$

Here, t_1 indicate the retweet time, t_2 indicate the created time.

We collected 563,758 retweets posted by all 49,253 monitoring users in three month (from 2015.10 to 2015.12), then calculated their Δt, and the statistical data shown in Fig. 2. X-axis indicated time(s), every span is 0.5 h. The last span indicated Δt is more than 24 h. Y-axis indicated amounts. If Δt less than 2 h, the retweet fall in the first time span.

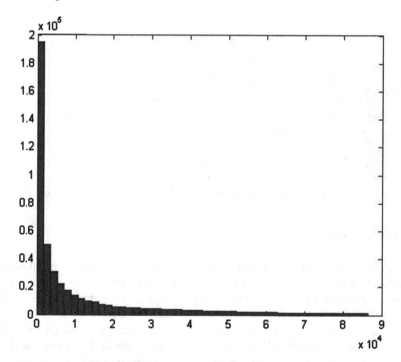

Fig. 2. The distribution of 563,758 retweets

As shown in Figure, the greater Δt, the less retweet number. 194,911 retweets' Δt is less than 0.5 h, account for more than 34.5 %; 297,572 is less than 4 h, account for more than 52 %;328,420 is less than 4 h, account for more than 58 %; 349,703 is less than 6 h, account for more than 62 %; 366,098 is less than 8 h, account for more than 65 %. This suggests that the majority of retweets happened in relatively short time, it happened in the period that the users online probability are higher.

4.3 Location Similarity

In this experiment, we also use the 563,758 retweets collected in last experiment. For each collected retweet, we can easily find its poster. And in retweet text, we can also find out the source of user. Through analyzing location of the poser and source user, we can discover something interesting. After finding out the poser and the source user, we could use their userid as search condition to retrieval their location wrote in each profile in our user data table. If any of locations is null, giving up this retweet. There are 71,872 valid data left. Then we compare the two locations and judge whether same/similar or nor. Finally, we calculated the location similarity for entire retweets.

As shown in Fig. 3, about 1/3 data have same or similar location, This is a relatively high proportion because so many locations exist. This means that you will get definitely higher retweet rate if choose people who have same location with you to mention when you tweet.

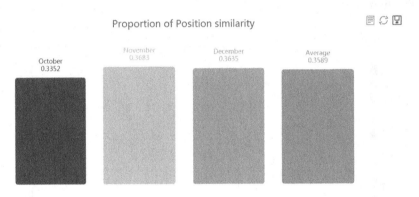

Fig. 3. Proportion of Position similarity of retweet user and tweet user

5 Conclusions

We propose three factors that probable impact Twitter users' retweet behavior (user vulnerability, user online status and location similarity) when we @ some users, and offer some methods to confirm them. We proved that these three factors all have obvious influences for retweets by our collected data and experiments.

After confirming these factors, Mention Recommendation based on these three factors and interests match will be our main research work in the future, which will help finding the better users to mention on Twitter, accelerating and enlarging the tweet diffusion and improving personal influence.

References

1. Zhao, W.X., Jiang, J., Weng, J., He, J., Lim, E.-P., Yan, H., Li, X.: Comparing Twitter and traditional media using topic models. In: Clough, P., Foley, C., Gurrin, C., Jones, G.J., Kraaij, W., Lee, H., Mudoch, V. (eds.) ECIR 2011. LNCS, vol. 6611, pp. 338–349. Springer, Heidelberg (2011)
2. Bakshy, E., Hofman, J., Mason, W., Watts, D.: Everyone's an influencer: quantifying influence on Twitter. In: Proceedings of WSDM 2011, pp. 65–74 (2011)
3. Wu, S., Hofman, J., Mason, W., Watts, D.: Who says what to whom on Twitter. In: Proceedings of WWW 2011, pp. 705–714 (2011)
4. Wang, B., Wang, C., Bu, J., Chen, C., Zhang, W.V., Cai, D., He, X.: Whom to mention: expand the diffusion of tweets by @ recommendation on micro-blogging systems. In: Proceedings of the 22nd International Conference on World Wide Web (WWW 2013), Rio de Janeiro, Brazil, May 2013, pp. 1331–1340 (2013)
5. Honeycutt, C., Herring, S.: Beyond microblogging: conversation and collaboration via Twitter. In: Proceedings of the HICSS 2009, pp. 1–10 (2009)
6. Java, A., Song, X., Finin, T., Tseng, B.: Why we Twitter: understanding microblogging usage and communities. In: Proceedings of the WebKDD/SNA-KDD 2007, pp. 56–65 (2007)
7. Suh, B., Hong, L., Pirolli, P., Chi, E.H.: Want to be retweeted? Large scale analytics on factors impacting retweet in Twitter network. In: 2010 IEEE Second International Conference on Social Computing (SocialCom), pp. 177–184 (2010)
8. Boyd, D., Golder, S., Lotan, G.: Tweet, tweet, retweet: conversational aspects of retweeting on Twitter. In: Proceedings of the HICSS 2010, pp. 1–10 (2010)
9. Xu, Z., Yang, Q.: Analyzing user retweet behavior on Twitter. In: 2012 IEEE/ACM International Conference on Advances in Social Networks Analysis and Mining, pp. 46–50 (2012)
10. Boehmer, J., Tandoc Jr., E.C.: Why we retweet: factors influencing intentions to share sport news on Twitter. Int. J. Sport Commun. **8**, 212–232 (2015)
11. Ye, S., Wu, S.: Measuring message propagation and social influence on twitter.com. In: Bolc, L., Makowski, M., Wierzbicki, A. (eds.) SocInfo 2010. LNCS, vol. 6430, pp. 216–231. Springer, Heidelberg (2010)

A Stock Recommendation Strategy Based on M-LDA Model

Min-fan He[(✉)]

School of Mathematics and Big Data, Foshan University,
Guangdong 528000, China
heminfan1980@126.com

Abstract. Reports from stock analysis are an important source of information in the quantitative investment. How to capture the valuable information from the massive research reports quickly and accurately, and make a good stock recommendation method is one of the important issues in big data quantitative investment. Based on a kind of semi-supervised topic models (M-LDA) and by setting some fundamental emotion labels along with some certain topic labels, we are able to discover the representative words of the research reports for both explicit and latent topics. And then, by calculating the frequency of words in the topics, we designed a stock recommendation strategy. Experiments were carried out the report data from 2011 and 2014 and the results show that this method is effective to find out higher winning-rate stocks.

1 Introduction

Quantitative investment is a process which make use of mathematical models and computer technology to achieve specific investment strategies and ideas. Unlike traditional technical analysis, quantitative investment combine the historical empirical data and models as its investment experience, and thus produce an optimal prediction of investment with the aid of modern computer technology.

Text mining, also known as text data mining [1] or text knowledge discovery [2], aims to extract interesting and important patterns and knowledge from unstructured text documents, which can be considered as an extension of the data mining or knowledge discovery.

Devitt and Ahmad [3] predict the future trend of the finance through the emotional recognition of the text of the financial review. Researchers gradually find out growing effeteness of text mining for quantitative investment. In 2015, the thematic investment was very popular. The quickly locating of the theme of investment and investment targets helps us comprehensively understand the finance data, and serve better information for the quantitative investment. In recent years, Blei et al. [4, 5] proposed a topic model receiving a lot of attention. Many scholars had applied it to the financial research fields. Through analyzing the text of the analyst research report, individual stock can be estimated and evaluated based on the understanding of public opinion. And also according to the, We also attempt to get an effective stock recommendation strategy based on the sentimental polarity and multiple perspectives analyses.

© Springer International Publishing Switzerland 2016
A. Morishima et al. (Eds.): APWeb 2016 Workshops, LNCS 9865, pp. 122–128, 2016.
DOI: 10.1007/978-3-319-45835-9_11

2 Model and Algorithm

In order to obtain the topic distribution and topic-relevant hot-words in the research report, we labeled a part of the data with known topic-labels and the rest with unknown labels. In the case of lacking of marked theme partially, finding semi-supervised model, is not only to dig out the known theme, but also to dig out the underlying theme. However, the traditional LDA, an unsupervised topic model, is not suitable. Therefore, a mixture of tag semi-supervised model called M-LDA (Mixture LDA in 2015) [6, 7] proposed by Li Ximing is referred. This knowledge will help us pointing out the data mining and implement methods from the stock analyst's research report data (Fig. 1).

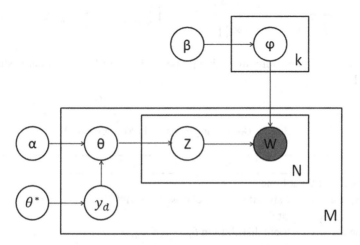

Fig. 1. M-LDA model

2.1 M-LDA Model

The design of M-LDA model was proposed for supervised machine learning algorithm, dealing with data sets with tags. The design of the model is mainly based on the following two points:

1. LDA topics K is divided into two parts, one is the category y_d data set, its number was denoted as K_t. Another part is still implicit topic of the data set, its number was denoted as K_h, where $K = K_t + K_h$;
2. In the probability distributions of document - topic, the labels of emotional categories set y_d were given relatively higher weights than the implicit topics. The weight and threshold were controlled by introducing parameter θ^*.

The M-LDA model mixes the topic layer with known categories and hidden topics. It means that the known category is regarded as a part of the topic, and assigned a higher weight in the process of training model.

The topic distribution of the traditional LDA model is based on the prior parameter α generation. According to the idea of the model design, the improved M-LDA model is a mixture of the subject distribution by the known class, which can be represented with conditional function as

$$f(\alpha, y_d, \theta^*, K_d) = \begin{cases} \theta_{di} = \frac{\theta^*}{K_d}, i \in y_d \\ \sim Dir'(\alpha, y_d), \text{else} \end{cases} \qquad (2.1)$$

Where $K_d = |y_d|$, $Dir'(\alpha, y_d)$ represents the Dirichlet distribution subjected to the priori parameters α and the Dirichlet distribution of category labels set y_d:

$$Dir'(\alpha, y_d) = \frac{\Gamma\left(\sum_{k \notin y_d} \alpha_k\right)}{(1 - \theta^*)^{\sum_{k \notin y_d} \alpha_k} \times \prod_{k \notin y_d} \Gamma(\alpha_k)} \prod_{k \notin y_d} \theta_k^{\alpha_k - 1}, \sum_{k \notin y_d} \theta_k = 1 - \theta^* \quad (2.2)$$

The process of generating the training text set for the M-LDA model is showed as follows (Table 1):

Table 1. Document generation in M-LDA model

steps:
For each of the k topic
Generate words distribution $\emptyset_k$, choose $\emptyset_k \sim Dir(\beta)$
For each document d
Generate Mixed topic distribution $\theta_d \sim f(\alpha, y_d, \theta^*, K_d)$
For each of the n word w_i
Generate topic $z_{dn} \sim Multinomial(\theta_d)$
Generate word $w_{dn} \sim Multinomial(\emptyset_{s_{dn}})$

In the M-LDA model, given the probability distribution of θ and φ, the joint probability of a training set W and a topic z is given by:

$$P(W, z | \Phi, \theta) = \prod_{d=1}^{D} \prod_{k=1}^{K} \prod_{v=1}^{V} \emptyset_{kv}^{N_{kv}} \theta_{dk}^{N_{dk}} \left(\theta_{dk} = \frac{\theta^*}{K_d}, \text{ if } k \in y_d\right) \qquad (2.3)$$

Where, θ obey the conditional probability distribution, and the likelihood function can be calculated by integrating over θ, φ and z, as follow

$$P(W | \alpha, \beta) = \sum_z (C^* \prod_{d=1}^{D} \frac{\Gamma(\sum_{k \notin y_d} \alpha_k)}{\prod_{k \notin y_d} \Gamma(\alpha_k)} \frac{\prod_{k \notin y_d} \Gamma(\alpha_k + N_{dk})}{\Gamma(\sum_{k \notin y_d}(\alpha_k + N_{dk}))} \prod_{k=1}^{K} \frac{\Gamma(\sum_{v=1}^{V} \beta_v)}{\prod_{v=1}^{V} \Gamma(\beta_v)} \frac{\prod_{v=1}^{V} \Gamma(\beta_v + N_{kv})}{\Gamma(\sum_{v=1}^{V}(\beta_v + N_{kv}))}) \quad (2.4)$$

Where

$$C^* = \frac{\left(\theta^* \sum_{d=1}^{D} \sum_{k \in y_d} N_{dk}\right)}{\prod_{d=1}^{D} K_d^{\sum_{k \in y_d} N_{dk}}} (1 - \theta^*)^{\sum_{d=1}^{D} \sum_{k \in y_d} N_{dk}} \qquad (2.5)$$

2.2 Parameter Estimation and Optimization

In the M-LDA model, the Gibbs-EM algorithm was used to estimate the Dirichlet prior parameters. In E step, with given parameters α and β, we count the topic Z by applying Gibbs sampling algorithm. And the following formula is acquired from formula derivation:

$$P\left(z_{dn} = k | z^{-dn}, W, \alpha, \beta\right) \propto \begin{cases} \frac{\theta^*}{K_d} \times \frac{N_{kw_{dn}} + \beta_{w_{dn}} - 1}{\sum_{v=1}^{V}(N_{kv} + \beta_v) - 1} & \text{if } k \in y_d \\ (1 - \theta^*) \times \frac{N_{dk} + \alpha_k - 1}{\sum_{k \neq y_d}(N_{dk} + \alpha_k) - 1} \times \frac{N_{kw_{dn}} + \beta_{w_{dn}} - 1}{\sum_{v=1}^{V}(N_{kv} + \beta_v) - 1} & \text{else} \end{cases}$$
$$(2.6)$$

In the M step, prior parameters α and β were optimized by maximizing the joint the probability $p(W, z | \varphi, \theta)$, through iterative formula derivation showed below (Table 2):

$$\alpha_k \leftarrow \alpha_k \frac{\sum_{d=1}^{D}(\psi(N_{dk} + \alpha_k) - \psi(\alpha_k))}{\sum_{d=1}^{D}\left(\psi\left(\sum_{k \neq y_d}(N_{di} + \alpha_i)\right) - \psi\left(\sum_{k \neq y_d} \alpha_i\right)\right)} \qquad (2.7)$$

$$\beta_v \leftarrow \beta_v \frac{\sum_{k=1}^{K}(\psi(N_{kv} + \beta_v) - \psi(\beta_v))}{\sum_{k=1}^{K}(\psi\left(N_k + \sum_{i=1}^{V} \beta_i\right) - \psi(\sum_{i=1}^{V} \beta_i))} \qquad (2.8)$$

Table 2. Parameter optimization of M-LDA model

Algorithm steps:
Initialized the distribution of subjects and the parametersα and β
Repeat
E Step
Use formula (2.6) to do Gibbs sampling and regenerate the theme distribution
M Step
Use the formula (2.7) to optimize parameterα
Use the formula (2.8) to optimize parameterβ
The end of Gibbs algorithm convergence

By applying training data to the LDA model, the implicit topics of the posterior distribution are acquired. The prior parameters α and β are optimized. The reasoning process based on Gibbs sampling algorithm is used to calculate the document d' topic formula as indicated follows:

$$P(z'_{dn} = k | z'^{-d'n}_{d'}, w_{d'}, U, \alpha^*, \beta^*) \propto \frac{N^{-d'n}_{d'k} + \alpha^*_k}{N^{-d'n}_{d'} + \sum_{i=1}^{K} \alpha^*_i} \times \frac{N'^{-d'n}_{kw_{dn}} + N_{kw_{d'n}} + \beta^*_{w_{dn}}}{N'^{-d'n}_k + N_k + \sum_{i=1}^{V} \beta^*_i} \quad (2.9)$$

Where, N'_{kv}: the word V in the document is assigned to the quantity of the topic K. and $N'_k = \sum_{i=1}^{V} N'_{ki}$. Mean while, when the algorithm is convergent, we can evaluate the category information according to the topic of the distribution $\theta_{d'}$ of the document d', and the formula is as follows:

$$\theta_{d'k} = \frac{N_{d'k} + \alpha^*_k}{N_{d'} + \sum_{i=1}^{K} \alpha^*_i} \quad (2.10)$$

3 Stock Recommendation Strategy Based on M-LDA Model

3.1 Topic and Hot Words

We found that the positive or negative emotions of the analysts is more difficult to label. Since it is possible to obtain the implied emotion category, we select part of the 2011–2014 research reported data that are crawled from the most popular website of stock market in China (http://data.eastmoney.com/report/). This data was marked by five labels such as positive fundamentals, negative fundamentals, Reform of state-owned enterprises, a drop in oil prices, and the remaining data was not marked. Each topic includes 2000 research reports while the rest of the data in the case of lacking of labeling, we found out the first five words of the highest frequency related to each topic (including both explicit and latent topics) (see Table 3).

Table 3. Keywords of known class/implicit theme

Emotional category/latent topic	Hot word thesaurus
Positive fundamentals	Purchase; transition; private placement; inflection point; super expectation
Negative fundamentals	Descending in achievements; loss; go against; panic; decline
Reform of state-owned enterprises	National asset; reformation; enterprise reformation; overall listing; government
Belt and road	East Asia economic circle; European economic circle; port; cement; the fusion
A drop in oil prices	Crude oil investment; futures; gold; the dollar; energy
Implicit topic 1	Grow up; expansion; underestimated; ascension; growth
Implicit topic 2	Industrial 4.0; internet; the internet of things; intelligent production; wisdom
Implicit topic 3	Double; huge; the dragon's head; major; overweight
Implicit topic 4	Go against; panic; watching; reduce; underweight

During the experiment, set the following parameters: weight parameter θ^* is selected in the interval [0.3 0.8]: 0.3, 0.4, 0.5, 0.6, 0.7, 0.8. $\alpha = \frac{50}{K}$, $\beta = 0.1$, where $K = K_t + K_h$, $K_t = 6$, $K_h = 4$.

3.2 Stock Recommendation Strategy

Based on this, the following stock-picking strategy recommendations can be utilized.

Strategy One: It is recommended by seeing the Positive fundamentals of stock as a reference.

Step 1: According to M-LDA, the topic of each research report and hot words of each topic was obtained.

Step 2: The stocks which marked with "positive fundamentals" label was selected. Then 100 stocks with most frequent hot words in the "positive fundamentals" labels were selected as the recommended stocks for each year.

Strategy Two: Combining stock content topics and fundamentals, a more fine-grained recommended stocks program is utilized for recommendation. Specifically, the following strategies were used:

Step 1: Obtain research report's topic content based on M-LDA (for example, "Reform of state-owned enterprises", "Belt and Road").

Step 2: The same content topic research reports are merged into a document clusters.

Step 3: In a document cluster of a given content topic, select 10 stocks which have the highest frequency of hot words in the "positive fundamentals" label as the recommended stocks.

4 Experimental Result

According to the aforementioned stocks recommendation scheme in Sect. 3.2, we analyze the research report from 2011 to 2014, and then obtain the result given in Tables 4 and 5.

Table 4. Experimental results by Strategy One

Year	Absolute return	Cumulative abnormal return (vs CSI 300 index)	Cumulative abnormal return (vs CSI 500 index)
2011	−13.45 %	12.48 %	21.49 %
2012	10.41 %	2.75 %	11.2 %
2013	32.34 %	40.23 %	14.79 %
2014	51.23 %	28.95 %	13.45 %

The results of the experiment shows that the stock picking strategy is stable according to the data from 2011 to 2014. The various indicators can beat CSI 500 index and CSI 300 Index, meanwhile, we found that the more refined Strategy Two is better than Strategy One.

Table 5. Experimental results by Strategy Two

Topic	Absolute return	Win rate	Cumulative abnormal return (vs CSI 300 Index)	Cumulative abnormal return (vs CSI 500 index)
Reform of state-owned enterprises	25.74 %	54 %	30.45 %	36.47 %
Belt and road	30.45 %	57 %	40.15 %	27.59 %
A drop in oil prices	32.34 %	49 %	40.23 %	14.79 %

5 Conclusions

The traditional multi-factor quantitative stock selection model is closed and unable to capture the market hot spots. There are about 50,000 research reports by securities analyst each year. Compared to the financial media, the research report has obvious advantages in terms of professionalism, credibility, norms of real-time degree. Therefore, it is one of the most important sources for text data mining. Refer to the M-LDA model, hot words related to the topic are found and tapped by setting part of the fundamentals' emotional labels and some determined labels. Two kinds of stock recommendation strategies have been proposed. The experimental results show that the two recommended strategies are stable and effective.

References

1. Hearst, M.A.: Text date mining: issues, techniques, and the relationship to information access. In: Presentation Notes of UW/MS Workshop on Data Mining, July 1997
2. Feldmanand, R., Dagan, I.: Knowledge discovery in textual data bases (KDT). In: Proceeding of the First International Conference on Knowledge Discovery and Data Mining (KDD 1995), Montreal, Canada, August 20–21, pp. 112–117. AAAI Press (1995)
3. Devitt, A., Ahmad, K.: Sentiment polarity identification in financial news: a cohesion based approach. In: Carroll, J. (ed.) Proceedings of the Association for Computational Linguistics (ACL), pp. 984 – 991. ACL, Morristown (2007)
4. Blei, D.M., Ng, A.Y., Jordan, M.I.: Latent dirichlet allocation. J. Mach. Learn. Res. **3**, 993–1022 (2003). doi:10.1162/jmlr.2003.3.4-5.993
5. Blei, D.M., Ng, A.Y., Jordan, M.I.: Correlated topic models. In: Schölkopf, B. (ed.) Advances in NIPS, pp. 147–154. MIT Press, Hyatt Regency (2006)
6. Li, X.: Study on topic model based multi-label text classification and stream text data modeling, Jilin University (2015)
7. Li, X., Ouyang, J., Zhou, X.: Supervised topic models for multi-label classification. Neurocomputing **149**, 811–819 (2015)

Short-Term Forecasting and Application About Indoor Cooling Load Based on EDA-PSO-BP Algorithm

ZhiWei Huang[1]([✉]), Li Yan[2], XinYi Peng[3], and Jia Tan[4]

[1] Architectural Design Institute, South China University of Technology,
Guang Zhou 510640, Guang Dong, China
jerray@qq.com
[2] School of Foreign Language, South China University of Technology,
Guang Zhou 510640, Guang Dong, China
[3] School of Software, South China University of Technology,
Guang Zhou 510800, Guang Dong, China
[4] School of Computing, South China University of Technology,
Guang Zhou 510800, Guang Dong, China

Abstract. In order to improve the precision of cooling load prediction, the authors of this essay proposes neural network model based on EDA-PSO-BP algorithm. We used PSO optimization algorithm combined with BP neural network to do cooling load prediction experiments of indoor sample data of a building. The results showed that compared with other three kinds of prediction algorithms, the error of this algorithm is minimum and its running speed is the fastest.

Keywords: PSO · BP neural network · Cooling load prediction · EDA

1 Introduction

In building energy consumption, heating and air conditioning account for a considerable proportion. According to statistics, Indoor air conditioning load accounts for more than 40 % of the electrical load of some cities in summer. China's building energy consumption will reach 108.9 billion tons by 2020. Air conditioning load amounts to the full load capability of ten Three Gorges Power Station in summer peaks, which is an important factor in causing the power shortage in city. To meet the country's requirement of energy-saving control, it's important to have a short-term prediction and precise control for indoor cooling load targeted at energy conservation. Our recent study focuses on making use of existing resources to build scientific prediction model.

Using BP neural network algorithm to forecast load such as electrical load, cooling load [1, 2] has made adequate progress. But this method has the disadvantage of slow convergence and relatively low precision [3, 4]. Some scholars combined GA-BP with PSO-BP to forecast power load, and it has seen research result. But both GA and PSO are likely to converge to pseudo optimums when there are many local optimums [5, 6]. In this paper, based on estimation of distribution algorithms (EDA), through adding

© Springer International Publishing Switzerland 2016
A. Morishima et al. (Eds.): APWeb 2016 Workshops, LNCS 9865, pp. 129–135, 2016.
DOI: 10.1007/978-3-319-45835-9_12

feedback factor, the authors build indoor cooling load prediction model targeted at energy conservation. By making use of global convergence capability and robustness of PSO with PSO algorithm and BP neural network combined, it's possible to shorten neural network training time based on keeping, even improving precision. In this paper, the authors forecast building's cold load by combining PSO algorithm with neural network.

2 BP Neural Network Model Based on Improved PSO

PSO can improve the generalization and mapping ability, the convergence speed and the learning ability of neural network. For BP neural network, weights and thresholds of all neurons can be expressed as the individual particles in the particle swarm. Take the average error of training sample through the neural network as fitness function to calculate the fitness of each particle, weight and threshold is the optimal solution required by particle swarm in the search space. According to the characteristic of cooling load, we first optimize PSP,

Mathematically expressed, suppose there is particle swarm consisting of n number of particles in m dimensional search space, and when the i th particle is at time t,use vector $X_i = [x_{i1}, x_{i1}, \ldots, x_{im}]$ to indicate its position, vector $V_i = [v_{i1}, v_{i1}, \ldots, v_{im}]$ to indicate its speed. The adjustment of the particle's position is determined by speed, so the position of the particle i can be expressed by the following formula:

$$X_i(t+1) = X_i(t) + V_i(t+1) \tag{1}$$

Suppose that the i th particle is at time t, position of its best adaptive value is called the personal best position, expressed by vector $P_i = [p_{i1}, p_{i1}, \ldots, p_{im}]$, while the best position that all particles in particle swarm have passed through is called the global optimal position, expressed by $P_M(t)$.

Suppose that f(x) is fitness function, To particle i, The current best position at time t + 1 is determined by the following formula

$$P_i(t+1) = \begin{cases} P_i(t), f(X_i(t+1)) \geq f(P_i(t)) \\ X_i(t+1), f(X_i(t+1)) < f(P_i(t)) \end{cases} \tag{2}$$

The global optimal position is expressed as:

$$P_i(t+1) = \begin{cases} P_i(t), f(X_i(t+1)) \geq f(P_i(t)) \\ X_i(t+1), f(X_i(t+1)) < f(P_i(t)) \end{cases}$$

$$P_g(t) = \{\{P_0(t), P_1(t), \cdots, P_d(t)\} | f(P_g(t)) = \min\{f(P_0(t)), f(P_1(t)), \cdots, f(P_n(t))\}\} \tag{3}$$

And at time t + 1, the velocity of particle i is determined by the following formula:

$$v_{ij}(t+1) = v_{ij}(t) + c_1 r_{1j}(t)[p_{ij}(t) - x_{ij}(t)] + c_2 r_{2j}(t)[p_{gj}(t) - x_{ij}(t)] \tag{4}$$

In the case of improved distribution estimation:

$$v_{ij}(t+1) = rand * v_{ij}(t) + D * [p_{gj}(t) - x_{ij}(t)]$$

Of which: $D = 0.4 + 0.5 * EC\text{min}/EC$

After improvement, $v_{ij}(t)$ represents the velocity of particle i on the dimension j, $x_{ij}(t)$ indicates the position at time t, rand is a random numbers varying from 0 to 1, D is feedback correction coefficient varying from 0.4 to 0.9. EC is feedback error value, the higher than ECmin (minimum error), the closer the value to globally optimal solution. The nearer to ECmin, the closer the value to local optimal solution.

3   Algorithm Process

Process of improved EDA-PSO to optimize the BP neural network is as follows:

(1) Randomly initialize the position and velocity of particles in the particle swarm, in which the position of particle is actually the weight value of BP neural network.
(2) For each particle in the particle swarm, calculate its fitness, and mark the optimal position of the individual as p. In all the particles'p, select one as the global optimal position marked as P_M.
(3) Respectively update the velocity and position of each particle, equivalent to the updating of linked weights of BP neural network.
(4) Calculate the fitness of all particles in the particle swarm.
(5) For each particle, compare the current fitness of particle with that of the personal best position p. If the current particle is more optical, use the information of current particle to update p's information.
(6) Compare the fitness values of all p with those of all pg, and update pg.
(7) If the termination criterion is satisfied, output pg and fitness value, and stop the algorithm. Otherwise, go to step 3.
(8) Particle position of the final output is the optimal weight, also as BP neural network linked weight.

4   Numerical Simulation

4.1   EDA-PSO-BP Prepare

Factors affecting indoor cooling load are generally divided into stability factor and instability factors.

First, stability factor refers to equipment load in a building. Due to its strong stability, it has a relatively small impact on the forecast.

Second, instability factor is the major consideration of the impact of prediction, which include the factors of weather, time, historical data with inertia characteristics and human, of which weather factors include temperature, humidity, solar radiation and wind speed; time factors include whether it is working day and its time; inertial historical factors include the data of the last hour, the data at the same time of the previous day, the data at the same time of the previous two days, etc.; human factor is the number of people inside the building (Table 1).

Table 1. Parameters

Sequence number	Parameter	Code name
1	Point-in-time	N1
2	Outside temperature	N2
3	Outside humidity	N3
4	Room temperature	N4
5	The number of indoor	N5
6	t-1 moment cooling load	N6
7	t-12 moment cooling load	N7
8	t-24 moment cooling load	N8
9	t-48 moment cooling load	N9
10	t-1w moment cooling load	N10
11	Actual value	N11

Third, the error feedback (EC), the distribution of the target cooling load.

Data show the indoor conditions of a building, the following table is a collection of data in a day of September, 2015. Data patterns are shown in Table 2.

Table 2. The data of cooling load after the normalization

N1	N2	N3	N4	N5	N6	N7	N8	N9	N10	Value
0.00	0.26	0.80	0.62	0.00	0.00	0.00	0.00	0.00	0.00	0.00
0.11	0.33	0.62	0.66	0.46	0.00	0.63	0.80	0.81	0.87	0.72
0.22	0.39	0.48	0.68	0.29	0.72	0.71	0.71	0.73	0.88	0.70
0.33	0.47	0.36	0.70	0.72	0.70	0.69	0.69	0.91	0.95	0.72
0.44	0.48	0.27	0.75	0.90	0.72	0.44	0.47	0.54	0.66	0.58
0.56	0.51	0.25	0.68	0.62	0.58	0.54	0.59	0.67	0.75	0.75
0.67	0.49	0.25	0.65	1.00	0.75	0.60	0.60	0.70	0.81	0.80
0.78	0.47	0.27	0.64	0.72	0.80	0.73	0.74	0.74	0.83	0.74
0.89	0.38	0.58	0.57	0.73	0.74	0.66	0.66	0.69	0.73	0.69
1.00	0.37	0.56	0.61	0.82	0.69	0.21	0.21	0.11	0.18	0.21

4.2   EDA-PSO-BP Results

The samples in 2011 and 2015 were collected for model training to forecast cooling load on 13, September 2015. The results of forecasting are as follows (Table 3):

Table 3. Forecasting results on 13, September 2015

Moment	Actual value	Predicted value	Absolute error value	Relative error values
0	0.00	0.00	0.00	0.00
1	0.00	0.00	0.00	0.00
2	0.00	0.00	0.00	0.00
3	0.00	0.00	0.00	0.00
4	0.00	0.00	0.00	0.00
5	0.00	0.00	0.00	0.00
6	0.00	0.00	0.00	0.00
7	0.00	0.00	0.00	0.00
8	8.51	8.4	0.11	1.31 %
9	223.39	220.88	2.51	1.14 %
10	256.08	249.09	6.99	2.81 %
11	228.4	222.45	5.95	2.67 %
12	227.63	224.68	2.95	1.31 %
13	194.49	191.91	2.58	1.34 %
14	233.3	221.125	12.175	5.51 %
15	238.785	237.05	1.735	0.71 %
16	247.64	239.885	7.755	3.23 %
17	258	249.105	8.895	3.57 %
18	0.00	0.00	0.00	0.00
19	0.00	0.00	0.00	0.00
20	0.00	0.00	0.00	0.00
21	0.00	0.00	0.00	0.00
22	0.00	0.00	0.00	0.00
23	0.00	0.00	0.00	0.00

Imitative effect is shown in Fig. 1:

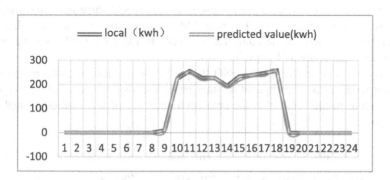

Fig. 1. Forecast graph

The relative error is shown in Fig. 2:

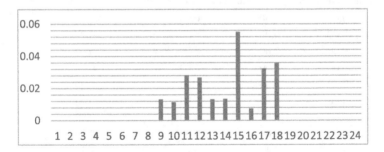

Fig. 2. The relative error of the predicted and the actual value

Figure 2 shows: use this algorithm to predict, its maximum relative error is 5.51 %, the minimum relative error is 0.71 %, the average relative error is 2.36 %. The results show that it fully meets the application requirements of the cooling load forecasting.

5   Conclusion

To compare the performance of the algorithm, use three algorithms respectively to forecast cooling load of former building sample in September 2015. Comparative results are shown in Table 4:

Table 4. Training performance comparison of different prediction methods

Forecasting methods	Required precision	Training times	Training time/s
BP	0.01	1473	162
PSO-BP	0.01	626	106
EDA-PSO-BP	0.01	446	97

From Table 4 we can know that if use standard BPNN, there is so many training times, and training time is long. By using PSO optimization, training effect has been significantly improved. While compared to PSO-BP, EDA-PSO-BP has better effect. The detailed results are as follows in Table 5:

From the above analysis, EDA-PSO-BP prediction method proposed in this paper has faster training speed compared to other prediction methods, i.e. fast convergence. Its forecasting results show that the prediction accuracy of this prediction method is also improved.

Table 5. Average relative error and root mean square error

Forecasting methods	Average relative error (%)	Root-mean-square error
BP	8.1	24.34
PSO-BP	3.6 %	13.21
EDA-PSO-BP	2.4 %	11.59

References

1. Gibson, G.L., Kcraft, T.T.: Electric demand prediction using artificial neural network technology. ASHREA J. **3**, 60–68 (1993)
2. Yalcintas, M., Akkurt, S.: Artificial neural networks applications in building energy predictions and a case study for tropical climates. Int. J. Energy Res. **29**(10), 891–901 (2005)
3. Kandel, E.R., Schwarts, J.: Principles of Neural Science, pp. 1–49. Elsevier, Amsterdam (1985)
4. Lippmann, R.P.: An introduction to computing with neural nets. IEEE ASSP Mag., 12–35 (1987)
5. Kennedy, J., Eberhart, R.: Particle swarm optimization. In: Proceedings of the IEEE International Conference on Neural Networks, vol. 34, issue 3, pp. 103–107 (1995)
6. Xiao, N., Lei, Z., Bo, Z., et al.: PSO grey model to power load forecasting. China Manag. Sci. **15**(1), 69–73 (2008)

1st International Workshop on Graph Analytics and Query Processing (GAP 2016)

Identifying Relevant Subgraphs in Large Networks

Zheng Liu[✉], Shuting Guo, Tao Li, and Wenyan Chen

School of Computer Science and Technology,
Nanjing University of Posts and Telecommunications, Nanjing, China
{zliu,q12010109,towerlee,b12040209}@njupt.edu.cn

Abstract. Structural relationships between objects are used to model as graphs in many applications. In this paper, we study the problem of identifying relevant subgraphs in large networks. Relevant subgraphs in large networks contain network elements which are maintained by network administrators. We formalize the problem and propose a framework consisting of two major phases. The relevance scores of all vertex pairs are computed in the offline phase, while relevant subgraphs are identified in the online phase. We analyze the relevance score measure carefully and design an efficient algorithm for relevant subgraph identification by repeatedly expanding candidate subgraphs and merging overlapping ones. Our experiments based on real data sets show that our relevant subgraphs are of high quality and can be found efficiently, which are useful for network administrators during network operation and maintenance.

1 Introduction

Graph patterns are able to represent complex structural relationships between objects in various domains. Finding subgraphs that retain the best connection between vertices on graphs has many applications in social networks [3,7], Web analysis [5], recommendation systems [10], knowledge graphs [15] and etc. In this paper, we study the problem of identifying the relevant subgraphs in large networks, which are utilized by network administrators in daily network operation and maintenance.

The rapid development of information technology (IT) and communication technology (CT) results in large-scale, high-performance networks, which are supported by network infrastructures. Network infrastructures refer to the combination of all computing and network hardware components, as well as software resources, e.g., computing servers, routers, switches, virtual machine platforms, operating systems. The reliability of upper-level business and service of networks highly depends on the quality of operating and maintaining network infrastructures, which is obvious not an easy task for administrators of large networks. Network administrators confront various issues such as equipment failures, communication errors, system mis-configurations and many other situations. Modern networks with cloud computing technology are hierarchical and heterogeneous,

© Springer International Publishing Switzerland 2016
A. Morishima et al. (Eds.): APWeb 2016 Workshops, LNCS 9865, pp. 139–151, 2016.
DOI: 10.1007/978-3-319-45835-9_13

which makes this task more difficult. Some best practices from industry organizations such as ITIL[1], ITU-T[2] and TM Forum[3] indicate that an integrated monitoring platform with human intervention is a solution to this problem [16].

In large networks, the smallest units for monitoring are called network elements. Usually there are monitoring tools running on network elements, which continuously monitor their status and detect potential problems by computing metrics for hardware and software performance at regular intervals. The monitoring tools would issue an alert if the metrics are not acceptable according to pre-defined thresholds, and emit an event log if the alert does not disappear after a certain time. All event logs are consolidated in the integrated monitoring platform for analysis. The integrated monitoring platform filters part of these event logs based on pre-defined rules from domain experts and notices network administrators to handle the left ones. Network administrators are responsible for the problem determination and resolution according to the contents in these event logs, to ensure that network services are running smoothly.

Event logs do not happen isolatedly in networks, which means when a network element reports an alert, it is quite possible that other nearby or service-depended network elements will also issue alerts. When network administrators are determining and solving problems, they often have to go through these network elements with alerts, as well as other connected network elements for root cause analysis. With limited manpower, it is not practical for network administrators to inspect a large area of network elements. A better way is to only inspect a small connected network elements containing the ones with alerts, which will lower the human cost and improve the efficiency of problem determination and resolution in daily operation and maintenance.

Let G denote the graph corresponding to a certain network, where each network element is considered as a vertex in G and connections between elements are edges in G. Let U denote a vertex set representing network elements with event logs. In this paper, *we study the problem of identifying one or a certain number of relevant subgraphs $g_1, \ldots, g_k$ from G, given a vertex set U, where vertices in U are contained in the union set of vertices of subgraph $g_1, \ldots, g_k$.* The notations used in this paper are summarized in Table 1. The main contributions of this paper are summarized below.

- We formalize the problem of identifying important subgraphs in networks and propose using neighborhood random walk to measure the relationships between vertices based on a careful analysis of relevance score measure.
- We develop an efficient algorithm to discover relevant subgraphs based on an expanding and merging strategy.
- We present an evaluation of our proposed approach by using large real data sets form a telecommunication network demonstrating that our method is able to find relevant subgraphs effectively and efficiently.

---

[1] Information Technology Infrastructure Library, http://www.axelos.com/itil.

[2] ITU Telecommunication Standardization Sector, http://www.itu.int/en/ITU-T.

[3] TM Forum, https://www.tmforum.org.

Table 1. Notations

Symbol	Definition
G	A graph
U	A vertex set containing vertices with event logs
g	A relevant subgraph
v_j	A vertex on a graph
$N(v_j)$	The set of neighbors of vertex v_j
$d(j)$	The sum of edge weights between vertex v_j and $N(v_j)$
A	The adjacency matrix of graph G
P	The transition matrix of graph G
D	The diagonal matrix where $d_{jj} = d(j)$
Π	The vertex relevance score matrix of graph G

The rest of this paper is organized as follows. Section 2 discusses the related work and Sect. 3 introduces the overall solution framework. We present our proposed approach in Sect. 4. Experimental results are presented in Sect. 5. And finally, Sect. 6 concludes this paper.

2   Related Work

The problem of finding subgraphs that retain the best connection between vertices on graphs has attracted considerable research efforts in literature, on applications such as social networks [3,7], Web analysis [5], recommendation systems [10], etc. Cheng et al. [3] proposed an approach that can find subgraphs with best connections between objects. They partitioned a large graph into a set of communities as the context of vertices, then calculated the intra-community and inter-community connections for subgraph discovery. Hintsanen et al. [7] solved the most reliable subgraph problem by using stochastic search of candidate paths, as well as Monte-Carlo simulation. Faloutsos et al. [5] presented fast algorithms for discovery of connection subgraph based on electricity analogues and dynamic programming. A heuristic method in near-real time is proposed for huge, disk-resident graphs. Koren et al. [10] introduced a new proximity measure for finding proximity graphs which are useful in recommendation systems. Proximity graphs could be found by solving an optimization problem with efficient approximation.

In terms of distance and similarity measures, the concept of random walk has been widely used to develop various measures that are suitable for different tasks. Jeh and Widom [8] designed a measure called SimRank, which defines the similarity between two vertices in a graph by their neighborhood similarity. SimRank between two vertices v_i and v_j is essentially the expected meeting distance of two random walks that respectively start from v_i and v_j and randomly surfer in the graph. Palmer and Faloutsos [12] defined a similarity function, named

REP, to measure the similarity between categorical attributes. They first converted a categorical dataset to an attribute-attribute graph. Then, REP between two attributes x and y is defined to be the refined escape probability that a random walk that starts from x will return to x before reaching y. Pons and Latapy [14] proposed to use short random walks of length l to measure the similarity between two vertices in a graph for the task of community detection. Pan et al. [13] utilized random walk with restarts for automatic captioning for multimedia data. In this work, we propose a relevance score measure based on neighborhood random walks, which takes the advantage of both short random walks and random walks with restart.

There are also several studies [2,4,6] that identifying dense areas in large and sparse graphs, especially in the domain of social science. Dense areas are usually considered as communities, which are not suitable to be relevant subgraphs for network operation and maintenance.

3   Solution Framework

We present the framework of our solution in this section, which consists of two major phases as shown in Algorithm 1.

The first phase is *relevance score computation*, which is done offline. In this phase, all the relevance score between vertex pairs are calculated and cached. We analyze the relevance score measure in details in Sect. 4.1, as well as the computation method.

The second phase is *relevant subgraph discovery*, which is done online whenever there are event logs needed to be handled by network administrators. We proposed an algorithm that repeatedly expands and merges candidate subgraphs. In each loop, the algorithm first expands candidate subgraphs by selecting and including a vertex from the candidate vertex set for each candidate subgraph. Then two candidate subgraphs are merged into a larger one if they are sharing common vertices. We discuss in details the expanding and merging procedures of relevant subgraph discovery in Sect. 4.2.

Algorithm 1. The Solution Framework

Input: a graph G, a vertex set U
Output: The subgraphs $\{g\}$
  1: Offline Phase: Compute relevance scores for vertex pairs in G ;
  2: Online Phase: Identify relevant subgraphs containing vertices in U.

---

4   Identifying Relevant Subgraphs

In this section, we present our careful analysis of relevance score measure, followed by our approach of relevant subgraph discovery.

4.1   Relevance Score Computation

Consider a graph G, the relationship between vertex pairs could be modeled in several ways, e.g. short path distance, local density, random walks. In this paper, we explore this issue using neighborhood random walks on graphs to help identifying relevant subgraphs. We first review some basic concepts of random walks on graphs. Let A denote the adjacency matrix of a weighted graph G, where $A(i, j)$ maintains the weight for the edge (v_i, v_j). A random walk on G is performed in the following way. A particle starts at a certain vertex v_0. Suppose it walks to a vertex v_s in the s-th step and it is about to move to one of the neighbors of v_s, denoted as $v_t \in N(v_s)$, with probability p_{st}, where p_{st} is $A(s, t)/\sum_{v_k \in N(v_s)} A(s, k)$, and $N(v_s)$ contains all neighbors of vertex v_s.

The vertex sequence of a random walk is a Markov chain. Let D be the diagonal matrix with the diagonal value $d(s) = \sum_{v_k \in N(v_s)} A(s, k)$, then the transition probability matrix P of the Markov chain for graph G is

$$P = D^{-1}A.$$

The probability of going from v_i to v_j through a random walk of length l can be obtained by multiplying the transition probability matrix l times and is given as $P^l(i, j)$.

An Infinite Step Approach: $(l \to \infty)$
One possible relevance score measure from vertex v_i to vertex v_j is defined as the steady-state probability $P^l(i, j), l \to \infty$, which is the probability that the particle starting from v_i will be on vertex v_j after an infinite number of steps. While it might be working in some fields such as biology [1], it has a big drawback. When G is not a bipartite graph, with the memoryless property of Markov chains, the steady-state probability distribution follows the equation below [11]:

$$\forall i, \lim_{l \to +\infty} P^l(i, j) = \frac{d(j)}{\sum_{v_s \in V} d(s)}. \tag{1}$$

Here, V is the set of vertices of graph G. Recall that $d(s) = \sum_{v_t \in N(v_s)} A(s, t)$. Equation (1) states that the probability of random walk to a certain vertex v_j from any initial vertex v_i shares the same limit value. In other words, random talk to a certain vertex is independent from the initial vertex. Therefore, such a measure cannot be effectively used to measure the relevance of two vertices.

An Infinite Step Approach with Restart: $(l \to \infty$ and $0 < c < 1)$
It is important to note that the relevance score measure needs to easily capture the nearby local structural information, which means a vertex should be more relevant to the vertices nearby. Here the issue is the locality of vertex pairs. Note that a random walk with an infinite number of steps $(l \to \infty)$ can possibly visit the entire graph and might go to as far as possible from where it starts. One possible approach is to use a restart probability c $(c < 1)$. Here $c(1 - c)^l$ implies the probability of jumping back to the initial starting vertex in the l-th step. Since $c < 1$, when l is small (close to the initial starting vertex), the

probability of jumping back is high; and when l is large (away from the initial starting vertex), the probability of jumping back becomes small [13]. It requires to compute the transition probability matrix P until it converges, which is a time consuming process. In the literature, a small $c \ll 0.5$ is usually used. However, in our problem setting, with a small $c \ll 0.5$, there are possibilities that random walks will visit vertices that are far away from the initial vertex, and make it uncertain how the local structural information is captured. The problem cannot be solved by simply using a large c value, because the meaning of random walk with a larger c value becomes less obvious.

A Fixed Step Approach with Restart: (fixed l and $0 < c < 1$)
With a fixed l, we focus on the local structural information using neighbors of a vertex, v_i, from which the random walk starts. The vertex, v_i, to start random walks is the vertex that is involved in an edge change. The neighbors of v_i are the vertices that v_i can reach in l steps. Random walks are only conducted in the l-step neighborhood of the vertex v_i with a restart probability c. Our following algorithm is designed in a way that a user can enlarge the l value if needed at run time. We adopt the similar expected f-distance in [8,9]. In the expected f-distance, a parameter c is used. We prove that such a parameter c is the restart probability used in [13] with minor difference which can be ignored. The proof is presented in Appendix A. In short, neighborhood random walk distance, which is also called the *vertex relevance*, is the expected f-distance defined on random walks whose length is smaller or equal to l.

Definition 1. Neighborhood Random Walk Distance (Vertex Relevance): *Let P be the $n \times n$ transition probability matrix of a graph G. Given l as the length that a random walk can go, the neighborhood random walk distance $\Pi^l(i,j)$ from v_i to v_j is defined as follows:*

$$\pi(i,j) = \sum_{\tau: v_i \leadsto v_j; length(\tau) \leq l} p(\tau) c(1-c)^{length(\tau)}, \qquad (2)$$

where $0 < c < 1$, and τ is a path from v_i to v_j whose length is $length(\tau)$ with transition probability $p(\tau)$.

The matrix form of the neighborhood random walk distance is as follows.

$$\Pi^l = \sum_{\gamma=1}^{l} c(1-c)^\gamma P^\gamma. \qquad (3)$$

Here, P is the transition probability matrix for graph G, and Π is the neighborhood random walk distance matrix for graph G. By Eq. (3), the iterative form of the vertex relevance score is

$$\Pi^l = \sum_{\gamma=1}^{l} c(1-c)^\gamma P^\gamma = c(1-c)^l P^l + \Pi^{l-1}. \qquad (4)$$

Algorithm 2. The Expanding Algorithm

Input: The adjacency matrices A of graph G; the relevant score matrix Π; the vertex set U;

Output: The relevant subgraphs $\{g\}$

1: /* Initialization; */
2: **for** each vertex v_i in U **do**
3:     $g_i = \{v_i\}$;
4:     **for** each g_i **do**
5:         Initialize max heap H_i;
6:         **for** each neighbor v_k of v_i on graph G **do**
7:             insert $\Pi(i, k)$ to max heap H_i;
8:         **end for**
9:         $\epsilon_i = \max(\Pi(i, :)) \times bratio$;
10:     **end for**
11: **end for**
12: **while** *true* **do**
13:     /* Expanding step; */
14:     **for** each subgraph g_k **do**
15:         v_m = the first vertex in H_k;
16:         **if** $\max(\Pi(I(V(g_k), m)) > \epsilon_k$ **then**
17:             Add v_m to subgraph g_k;
18:             remove v_m from max heap H_k;
19:             **for** each neighbor v_n of v_m **do**
20:                 **if** v_n not in g_k and v_n not in H_k **then**
21:                     Insert $\langle v_n, \Pi(m, n) \rangle$ into the heap H_k;
22:                 **else**
23:                     **if** v_n in H_k **then**
24:                         update v_n in H_k based on $\Pi(m, n)$;
25:                     **end if**
26:                 **end if**
27:             **end for**
28:         **end if**
29:     **end for**
30:     /* Merging step; */
31:     **while** $\exists g_i \cap g_j \neq \emptyset$ **do**
32:         $g_i = g_i \cap g_j$;
33:         $g_j = \emptyset$;
34:         $H_i = H_i \cap H_j$;
35:         $\epsilon_i = \max(\epsilon_i, \epsilon_j)$
36:     **end while**
37:     **if** If all subgraph $\{g\}$ is not changed **then**
38:         break;
39:     **end if**
40: **end while**

4.2 Relevant Subgraph Discovery

With the vertex relevance matrix Π, we now explain how to identify relevant subgraphs from those vertices in the given vertex set U. Recall that U represents those vertices whose corresponding network elements report event logs. It is obvious that the found relevant subgraphs should cover all vertices in U. Other vertices in subgraphs should be relevant to the vertices in U, and also relevant to each other. We develop a repeated expanding and merging strategy for relevant subgraph discovery. The basic idea is to include vertices whose relevance scores to vertices in candidate subgraphs are large. The whole algorithm is presented in Algorithm 2.

The initialization part is from line 1 to 11. The initial candidate subgraphs are built from vertices in U where each subgraph contains only one vertex from U. Each candidate subgraph has a max heap to maintain the relevance scores of candidate vertices for expanding. The candidate vertices are neighbors of vertices in current candidate subgraphs. The threshold ϵ at line 9 is the stop criteria of candidate subgraphs. In our experiments, we discover that the vertex relevance scores follow the power law distribution. So we set the value of ϵ as the max relevance score of lastly included vertex in a proper proportion $bratio$, which is 0.2 in this paper.

From line 13 to 29, the algorithm expands current subgraph g_k by including the vertex v_m with the max value in max heap H_k, and add the neighbor vertices of v_m into H_k if they are not in H_k. For those neighbor vertices already in H_k, the algorithm updates their relevant scores in H_k if their relevant scores from v_m are larger. At line 16, $I(V(g_k))$ is the indices of vertices in g_k on graph G.

The merging step is from line 30 to 39, where if any two candidate subgraphs are sharing common vertices, they are merged into one larger candidate subgraph, as well as their corresponding max heaps and thresholds. The expanding and merging procedures are repeated until all subgraphs are not changed.

5 Experimental Evaluation

In this section, we present the experimental results on three real datasets to show both the effectiveness and the efficiency of our proposed approach. All experiments are done on a Macbook Air with Intel i5 CPU at 1.6 GHz and 4 GB memory, running OS X 10.10.5. The algorithm is implemented in Python.

5.1 Datasets

We collected real event logs from a telecommunication network of a small city for one month. The topology of the network is not changed during the collection period. By representing network elements as vertices and links between them as edges, we built the corresponding graph with 11367 vertices and 16522 edges. We divided the event logs into three datasets **LOG1**, **LOG2** and **LOG3**. Each dataset covers event logs for ten consecutive days. The number of event logs in each dataset is shown in Table 2.

Table 2. Number of event logs in each dataset

Datasets	LOG1	LOG2	LOG3
# of event logs	2489	10376	16644

For each dataset, we split the time period into time windows, whose length is one minute. Then we identify subgraphs for event logs in each time window. It is worth noting that in practice, the length of the time windows for event logs are determined by temporal mining techniques, which is beyond the scope of this paper. The distribution of the number of event logs in these time windows are present in Fig. 1.

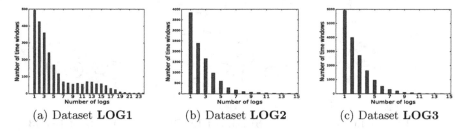

(a) Dataset **LOG1**   (b) Dataset **LOG2**   (c) Dataset **LOG3**

Fig. 1. Dataset characteristics

5.2 Effectiveness

Let us first introduce our criterion of the relevant subgraphs. Let g denote a found subgraph. We evaluate the goodness of relevant subgraphs as

$$Goodness = \frac{\sum_{v_j \in g \cap U, v_k \in g} \Pi(j,k)}{\sum_{v_j \in g \cap U, v_k \in G} \Pi(j,k)}, \tag{5}$$

where Π is the relevant score matrix of vertex pairs. The goodness is essentially the fraction of the relevant score between vertices in U and vertices in G that are captured by relevant subgraphs.

Figure 2 presents the average goodness for different values of restart probability c, when varying the length l of neighborhood random walks from 2 to 5. As we can see that our algorithm captures most of the relevances from the vertex set U. When $l = 3$, the goodness is more than 85 %. For a longer length of l, The goodness value drops, which is because that more and more vertices are relevant to vertices in U.

We use $c = 0.15$ and $l = 5$ in the following experiments. We show three real relevant subgraphs in Fig. 3, one for each dataset. The dark vertices in each figure are the vertices in U, which are the network elements reporting event logs. The

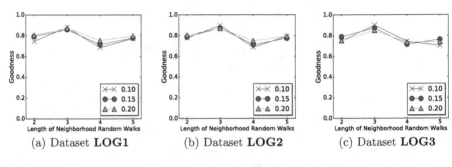

Fig. 2. The goodness

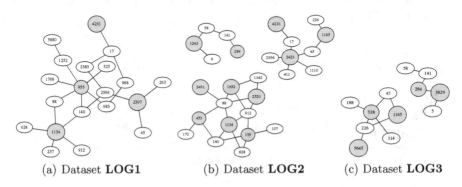

Fig. 3. Relevant subgraphs

relevant subgraphs can help network administrators for problem determination and resolution, because they capture the relationship of relevance between the vertices with event logs, and other vertices. Network administrators could avoid going through a large area of network elements for problem analysis.

5.3   Efficiency

Table 3 reports the computation time of relevance scores for our datasets varying the length of l. As l goes larger, the time becomes longer.

Table 3. Relevant score computation time

Length of neighborhood random walk	2	3	4	5	6
Time (s)	0.0921	0.4708	2.0797	5.9183	16.8016

The running time of relevant subgraph identification is reported in Fig. 4. In Fig. 4(a), We vary the length of time window from one minute to four minutes. For each length of time window, we report the average running time of identifying

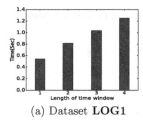

(a) Dataset **LOG1**

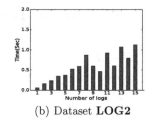

(b) Dataset **LOG2**

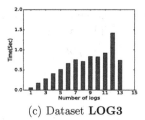

(c) Dataset **LOG3**

Fig. 4. Running time

relevant subgraphs. With longer time windows, the number of event logs in each window is larger (U is larger.), so the running time is longer as a result. In Fig. 4(b) and (c), we report the average running time for different number of logs in time windows, where the length of time window is one minute. As we can see that in general, the average running time increases as the number of event logs in time windows increases. The running time drops sometimes when the number of logs increases in Fig. 4(b) and (c) is because that the number of candidate subgraphs shrinks after merging the overlapping ones.

6 Conclusion

We study the problem of identifying relevant subgraphs in large networks in this paper. We formalize the problem and propose a framework consisting of two major phases. Relevant subgraphs are generated online based on relevance scores computed in the offline phase by repeatedly expanding and merging candidate subgraphs. Experimental results show that our approach can identify relevant subgraphs of high quality efficiently.

Acknowledgments. This work was supported in part by Nanjing University of Posts and Telecommunications under Grants No. NY215045 and NY214135, and Ministry of Education/China Mobile joint research grant under Project No. 5–10.

Appendix

A Relationship Between Expected f-Distance and Random Walk with Restart

The vertex relevance matrix using the expected f-distance is not much different from one using random walk with restart. The proof is presented below. Based on the iterative form of the definition of random walk with restart, the vertex relevance score matrix Π''^l of graph G_i can be expressed as following.

$$\Pi''^l = (1 - c)\Pi''^{l-1}P + cI, \tag{6}$$

where c is the restart probability, P is the transition matrix of G and I is identity matrix. Then we have

$$
\begin{aligned}
\Pi'^l &= (1-c)\Pi'^{l-1}P + cI \\
&= (1-c)((1-c)\Pi'^{l-2}P + cI)P + cI \\
&= (1-c)^l P^l + c\sum_{\gamma=1}^{l-1}(1-c)^\gamma P^\gamma + cI \\
&= c(1-c)^l P^l + c\sum_{\gamma=1}^{l-1}(1-c)^\gamma P^\gamma + (1-c)^{l+1}P^l + cI \\
&= \sum_{\gamma=1}^{l}c(1-c)^\gamma P^\gamma + (1-c)^{l+1}P^l + cI \\
&= \Pi^l + (1-c)^{l+1}P^l + cI.
\end{aligned}
\tag{7}
$$

The last line of Eq. (7) contains three items. The first item is the vertex relevance matrix Π_i^l using the expected f-distance. The third item cI affects only the diagonal entries of the vertex relevance matrix, which is ignored since we do not consider the vertex self-relevance. Then, the difference using random walk with restart and the expected f-distance results in the second item $(1-c)^{l+1}P_i^l$. When l goes to infinity, the vertex relevance matrices using expected f-Distance and random walk with restart are the same except the diagonal entries. Even when l is small, the corresponding entries of two matrices do not differ so much since $(1-c)^{l+1}P^l$ is very small comparing with $\Pi^l = \sum_{\gamma=1}^{l}c(1-c)^\gamma P^\gamma$.

References

1. Çamoğlu, O., Can, T., Singh, A.K.: Integrating multi-attribute similarity networks for robust representation of the protein space. Bioinformatics **22**(13), 1585–1592 (2006)
2. Chakrabarti, D.: AutoPart: parameter-free graph partitioning and outlier detection. In: Boulicaut, J.-F., Esposito, F., Giannotti, F., Pedreschi, D. (eds.) PKDD 2004. LNCS (LNAI), vol. 3202, pp. 112–124. Springer, Heidelberg (2004)
3. Cheng, J., Ke, Y., Ng, W., Yu, J.X.: Context-aware object connection discovery in large graphs. In: ICDE, pp. 856–867. IEEE (2009)
4. Dourisboure, Y., Geraci, F., Pellegrini, M.: Extraction and classification of dense communities in the web. In: Proceedings of the 16th WWW, pp. 461–470. ACM (2007)
5. Faloutsos, C., McCurley, K.S., Tomkins, A.: Fast discovery of connection subgraphs. In: Proceedings of the Tenth ACM SIGKDD, pp. 118–127. ACM (2004)
6. Gibson, D., Kumar, R., Tomkins, A.: Discovering large dense subgraphs in massive graphs. In: Proceedings of the 31st VLDB, pp. 721–732. VLDB Endowment (2005)
7. Hintsanen, P., Toivonen, H., Sevon, P.: Fast discovery of reliable subnetworks. In: ASONAM, pp. 104–111. IEEE (2010)
8. Jeh, G., Widom, J.: Simrank: a measure of structural-context similarity. In: Proceedings of the Eighth ACM SIGKDD, pp. 538–543. ACM (2002)

9. Jeh, G., Widom, J.: Scaling personalized web search. In: Proceedings of the 12th WWW, pp. 271–279. ACM (2003)
10. Koren, Y., North, S.C., Volinsky, C.: Measuring and extracting proximity graphs in networks. ACM TKDD **1**(3), 12 (2007)
11. Lovász, L., et al.: Random walks on graphs: a survey. Comb. Paul Erdos Eighty **2**, 353–398 (1996)
12. Palmer, C.R., Faloutsos, C.: Electricity based external similarity of categorical attributes. In: Whang, K.-Y., Jeon, J., Shim, K., Srivastava, J. (eds.) PAKDD 2003. LNCS, vol. 2637, pp. 486–500. Springer, Heidelberg (2003)
13. Pan, J.-Y., Yang, H.-J., Faloutsos, C., Duygulu, P.: Automatic multimedia cross-modal correlation discovery. In: Proceedings of the Tenth ACM SIGKDD, pp. 653–658. ACM (2004)
14. Pons, P., Latapy, M.: Computing communities in large networks using random walks. In: Yolum, I., Güngör, T., Gürgen, F., Özturan, C. (eds.) ISCIS 2005. LNCS, vol. 3733, pp. 284–293. Springer, Heidelberg (2005)
15. Ramakrishnan, C., Milnor, W.H., Perry, M., Sheth, A.P.: Discovering informative connection subgraphs in multi-relational graphs. ACM SIGKDD Explor. Newslett. **7**(2), 56–63 (2005)
16. Tang, L., Li, T., Shwartz, L., Pinel, F., Grabarnik, G.Y.: An integrated framework for optimizing automatic monitoring systems in large it infrastructures. In: Proceedings of the 19th ACM SIGKDD, pp. 1249–1257. ACM (2013)

User-Dependent Multi-relational Community Detection in Social Networks

Peizhong Yang, Lihua Zhou$^{(\boxtimes)}$, and Hongmei Chen

School of Information, Yunnan University, Kunming 650091, China
285342456@qq.com, {lhzhou,hmchen}@ynu.edu.cn

Abstract. Multi-relational community detection is a very important task in social network analysis because in the real world social networks are mostly multi-relational. In this paper, we propose a user-dependent method to detect communities in multi-relational social networks. We define a multi-relational community as a shared community over multiple single-relational graphs while the quality of a partitioning of nodes is assessed by a multi-relational modularity, and we design a desirable set of communities to represent the requests of users and use Normalized mutual information (NMI) between the desirable set of communities and the sets of communities detected in each single-relational graph as the weights for measuring the importance of all kinds of relationship types. We then use a greedy agglomerative manner to identify communities. Experiments have been conducted on synthetic networks to evaluate the effectiveness of the proposed approach.

Keywords: Multi-relational social network · Community detection · Multi-relational modularity

1 Introduction

Communities, groups of actors that are frequently interacted, are considered to be a significant property of real-world social networks and play important roles. Detecting communities is not only of particular prominence but have immediate applications [1–3]. Thus, community detection and analysis are important tasks for mining the structure and function of social networks. In recent years, community detection has been receiving a great deal of attention from many fields [4–6].

Social networks are usually modeled by graphs, where the nodes represent actors, and edges indicate interactions amongst actors. Depending on the context, we may use interchangeably node and actor, graph and network. At present, most existing community detection algorithms are designed to find densely connected groups of nodes from only one single graph that represents only a relatively homogenous relationship (such as friendship) amongst actors. However, in the real world, social networks are mostly multi-relational, i.e., persons or institutions are related through different relationship types [7], such as trade, communication, colleague, friendship, and interest relationships. Each type of relation spans a social network of its own [8], thus the interactions amongst actors in different relationship types can be represented by multiple single-relational graphs, each reflects one kind of relation. Of course, community

© Springer International Publishing Switzerland 2016
A. Morishima et al. (Eds.): APWeb 2016 Workshops, LNCS 9865, pp. 152–163, 2016.
DOI: 10.1007/978-3-319-45835-9_14

detection in multi-relational social networks involves multiple single-relational graphs. Although the existing community detection algorithms for single-relational networks can be used independently in each single-relational graph, the communities obtained just represent local structures; they may not help to fully understand the whole society, because it overlooks the inter-dependencies and feedbacks amongst multiple relational interactions. In the real world, these different relationship types usually jointly affect people's social activities [9], and whenever inter-dependencies and feedbacks between multiple relational interactions are significant [8]. Hence, it is necessary to develop community detection algorithms that are suitable for multi-relational social networks.

Unfortunately, detecting communities in multi-relational social networks faces more difficulty than in single-relational networks. In a multi-relational social network, there are different interactions amongst the same nodes in different relationship types, and these different relationship types may play distinct roles with respect to different requests of users [9]. For example, in the 3-relational network of Fig. 1, the interactions amongst actors are different in the three relations, and the relation (a) is the most important one, the relation (b) is the second if node 8, 9, 10 and 11 are required to belong to the same community, but the relation (b) is the most important one if node 8 and 10 are required to belong to a community, 9 and 11 are required to belong to a community, but 8, 10 and node 9, 11 are required to belong to different communities, while the relation (c) becomes the most important one if node 8, 9, 10, 11 are required to belong to different communities. If we do not distinguish three relations and treat them equally, then communities detected should not satisfy the specified needs or preferences of users.

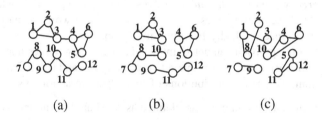

(a)   (b)   (c)

Fig. 1. A 3-relational network

To find communities in multi-relational social networks, the following problems quite deserve our attention:

- How to define and measure the communities in multi-relational networks?
- How to distinguish the importance of relations to match the requests of users such that communities are user-dependent?
- How to detect the user-dependent multi-relational communities?

For the first problem, in this paper we define the multi-relational communities as the components of a partitioning with respect to the set of all nodes in a multi-relational network. The multi-relational communities are relevant to interactions amongst actors in multiple relations and are satisfying in multiple relations, so they represent a more global structure. We also define the *multi-relational modularity* to measure the quality of a partitioning with respect to the set of all nodes in a multi-relational network. Detecting multi-relational communities means finding only one partitioning over multiple single-relational graphs such that this partitioning can maximize the *multi-relational modularity*. This unique partitioning is easier to understand, although considering one unique partitioning that is relevant for several relation types cannot be as good on a given relation type as partitioning found by a single-relational algorithm that specifically optimizes it for this particular relation. As maximizing modularity is a NP-complete problem [10], we will actually try to find a partitioning that having the higher *multi-relational modularity* possibly.

For the second problem, we design a desirable set of communities to represent the requests of users and use the *Normalized mutual information (NMI)* [11] between the desirable set of communities and the sets of communities detected independently in each single-relational graph as the weights to measure the importance of all kinds of relations. The community structures in each single-relational graph can be detected by existing single-relational network algorithms, such as *Louvain Method* [12], *GN algorithm* [13]. *NMI* measures the similarity between two community structures, thus a relation with high-weight indicates that the relation type itself matches the requests of users well. This approach incorporates the diverse requests from different users into the weights of relations, thus communities detected can satisfy the specified needs or preferences of users.

For the last problem, we develop a *greedy agglomerative manner* to identify user-dependent multi-relational communities, which starts from the nodes as separate communities (singletons), communities are iteratively merged to be larger communities for improving the *multi-relational modularity* until no pairs of communities are merged. This *greedy agglomerative manner* does not require a priori knowledge on the number and size of the communities, and it matches the real-world scenario, in which communities are formed gradually from bottom to top.

In summary, our approach can detect multi-relational communities that are relevant to interactions amongst actors in multiple relationship types, and it takes the requests of users into account. The main contributions of this paper are as follows:

- The multi-relational communities are defined as the shared communities underneath different interactions rather than any one of single-relational graphs.
- The *multi-relational modularity* is defined as a quality function to quantitatively assess the quality of a partitioning of nodes.
- A desirable set of communities is designed to represent the requests of users and *NMIs* between the desirable set of communities and the sets of communities detected in each single-relational graph are used as the weights to measure the importance of all kinds of relationship types.
- A greedy agglomerative manner is proposed to identify communities. The proposed manner does not require a priori knowledge on the number and size of communities.

The rest of this paper is organized as follows: Section 2 reviews related work; Sect. 3 introduces the concept of multi-relational communities and the approach to detect user-dependent multi-relational communities; Sect. 4 presents the experimental results on the synthetic data set; and then Sect. 5 concludes this paper.

2 Related Work

So far, community detection in single-relational networks has been extensively studied and many methods have been proposed based only on topological information of networks [4]. Of which, maximization of modularity is a widely accepted method. The *modularity*, proposed by Newman and Girvan [13], is a well-known quality function to measure quantitatively the quality of a partitioning of a network into communities, by comparing the number of edges inside a given group with the expected value for a randomized graph of the same size and degree sequence. The modularity of partitioning $\tau = \{S_1, S_2, \ldots, S_c\}$ in network G, with $|E|$ the total number of edges, e_S the number of edges inside a community S and d_S the total degree of S, is defined as $Q(G, \tau) = \sum_{S \in \tau} \frac{e_S}{|E|} - \left(\frac{d_S}{2|E|}\right)^2$. The best partitioning for the network is the one with the maximum of modularity. To optimize the modularity, Blondel et al. [12] designed a hierarchical greedy algorithm, named the *Louvain Method* that allows detecting communities quickly and efficiently with enlightening results in large networks. Aynaud and Guillaume [14] modified the *Louvain Method* to detect multi-step communities in evolving networks, where the evolving networks are described as a sequence of static graphs at different time steps, each reflects a particular snapshot, and the multi-step communities are relevant for (almost) every time step during a given period. Shang et al. [15] used an improved genetic algorithm (MIGA) to optimize the modularity. Sun and Gao [6] proposed a framework of mapping undirected to directed graphs and redefined modularity on their framework, such that this new definition not only contains the information in Q, but also the number of nodes within communities and the number of nodes in the whole network.

In recent years, multi-relational social networks have attracted the attention of many researchers. They analyzed multi-relational networks form different aspects, such as link prediction [16, 17], social recommendation [18], network analysis [8], positional and role analysis [19], and community detection.

To detect communities in multi-relational social networks, Tang et al. [20] proposed four strategies (*network integration, utility integration, feature integration,* and *partition integration*) to integrate the interaction information presented in different relations, and then utilized the spectral clustering to discover communities. However, all four strategies do not distinguish the importance of various relations and consider users' expectations. Cai et al. [9] proposed a regression-based algorithm to learn the optimal relation weights, and then they combined various relations linearly to produce a single-relational network and utilized threshold cut as the optimization objective for community detection. This approach can best meet the user's expectation and capture effectively subtle semantics. However, it failed to consider the mutual influence between relations and nodes. Ströele et al. [7] used four different relationship types (*project participation, co-authored publications, advisory work, and technical production*) to modeled a multi-relational scientific social network where each edge carries a different weight, representing how close two researchers are to one another, and then they used a Max-flow grouping algorithm to identify the social structure and research communities. This method does not also consider the mutual influence between relations and nodes although the weight of all relationship types between two researchers are considered in the process of determining the weight of each edge. Wu et al. [21] proposed a novel co-ranking framework, *MutuRank*, to determine the weights of various relation types and actors simultaneously, and then they combined the probability distributions of relations linearly to produce a single-relational network and presented a Gaussian mixture model with neighbor knowledge to discover over-lapping communities. *MutuRank* makes full use of the mutual influence between relations and actors, but it is independent of the users' needs or preferences. Rodriguez and Shinavier [22] presented the multi-relational path algebra to map multi-relational networks to single-relational networks, by means of a series of operations on a tensor representation of a multi-relational network. From this single-relational representation, all of the known single-relational network algorithms can be applied to detect communities.

Different from the existing studies above in which community detection is carried out in a single-relational network that is integrated from multiple networks, our study detects only one partitioning over multiple single-relational graphs rather than a single-relational graph.

3 Multi-relational Community Detection

Community detection in multi-relational social networks involves multiple single-relational graphs. In this paper, detecting multi-relational communities means finding only one partitioning of all nodes underneath different interactions rather than any one of single-relational graphs. To this end, we extend the modularity of Newman and Girvan [13] as *multi-relational modularity* to measure the strength of the partitioning.

In the next, we first present the definitions of the *multi-relational communities* and the *multi-relational modularity*, and then we introduce the method to determine weights of relations and give the algorithm for detecting multi-relational communities.

3.1 Definitions

Let the multi-relational network G on a set of relations $R = \{1, 2, \ldots, r\}$ be $G = \{G_1, G_2, \ldots, G_r\}$, where r be the number of relations types, $G_i = (N_i, E_i)$ be an undirected graph with $|N_i|$ nodes (actors) and $|E_i|$ edges (interactions), representing the interactions amongst actors in the relation $i(i \in R)$, i be the relation index. Let A_i be the adjacent matrix associated with G_i, $i = 1, 2, \ldots, r$, $A_i(x, y) \in [0, 1]$ represents the normalized strength of interaction between x and y for any pair of nodes $x, y \in N_i$ in the relation $i(i \in R)$. Especially, if the network is an unweighted graph, then $A_i(x, y) = 1$ if $(x, y) \in E_i$ for any pair of nodes $x, y \in N_i$ and 0 otherwise in the relation $i(i \in R)$. Let $N = \bigcup_{i \in R} N_i$, the set of all nodes in a multi-relational network. In general, not all relations have the same importance, let w_i represents the weight of relation i,

$$w_i \geq 0, \sum_{i=1}^{r} w_i = 1.$$

Definition 1. *Multi-relational communities.* Let $\tau = \{S_1, S_2, \ldots, S_c\}$ be a partitioning of all nodes in N, where $S_i \subseteq N$ ($i = 1, 2, \ldots, c$), $\bigcup_{i=1,2,\ldots,c} S_i = N$, then S_i is called as a *multi-relational community* and τ is called as a *multi-relational community structure* of G.

In general, there are many kinds of partitions for the nodes of N, but not all partitions are equally good. To assess the quality of a partition, we extend the single-relational modularity to multi-relational scenario. Thus, the partitioning with the maximum of modularity is the best.

Definition 2. *Single-relational modularity and multi-relational modularity.* Let $\tau = \{S_1, S_2, \ldots, S_c\}$ be a partitioning of nodes in N, where $S_i \subseteq N$ ($i = 1, 2, \ldots, c$). A *single-relational modularity* is the modularity of the partitioning τ on a single-relational graph only considering the nodes in this *single-relational graph*, while the *multi-relational modularity* is defined on multiple single-relational graphs. Let $Q(G_i, \tau)$ be the *single-relational modularity* with respect to G_i, $Q(G, \tau)$ be the *multi-relational modularity* with respect to G, then $Q(G_i, \tau)$ and $Q(G, \tau)$ are defined by the Eqs. (1) and (2) respectively.

$$Q(G_i, \tau) = \sum_{S \in \tau} \frac{e_{iS}}{|E_i|} - \left(\frac{d_{iS}}{2|E_i|} \right)^2 \tag{1}$$

$$Q(G, \tau) = \frac{1}{\sum_{i \in R} w_i} \sum_{i \in R} w_i Q(G_i, \tau) \tag{2}$$

Where $e_{iS} = \frac{1}{2} \sum_{\substack{x,y \in S \\ x,y \in N_i}} A_i(x, y)$, it is the sum of the weights of the edges amongst nodes that inside the subset S ($S \in \tau$) in the single-relational graph G_i; $d_{iS} = \sum_{\substack{x \in S \\ x,y \in N_i}} A_i(x, y)$, it is the sum of the weights of the edges attached nodes of S in G_i; $|E_i| = \frac{1}{2} \sum_{x,y \in N_i} A_i(x, y)$, it is the sum of the weights of all edges in G_i. After reordering the summation of Eq. (2), we have

$$Q(G, \tau) = \frac{1}{\sum_{i \in R} w_i} \sum_{S \in \tau} \left(\sum_{i \in R} w_i \frac{e_{iS}}{|E_i|} - \sum_{i \in R} w_i \left(\frac{d_{iS}}{2|E_i|} \right)^2 \right) \tag{3}$$

Given a set of single-relational graphs $G = \{G_1, G_2, \ldots, G_r\}$, detecting user-dependent multi-relational communities means finding a partitioning that maximizes $Q(G, \tau)$.

According to the Eq. (2), we have $\Delta Q(G, \tau) = \frac{1}{\sum\limits_{i \in R} w_i} \sum\limits_{i \in R} w_i \Delta Q(G_i, \tau)$, i.e. the
multi-relational modularity gain is the average of the modularity gains for each
single-relational network. So, it can be easily computed locally.

The modularity gain $\Delta Q(G_i, \tau)$ obtained by merging S_k and $S_l (S_k, S_l \in \tau)$ can be
computed by the Eq. (4).

$$\Delta Q(G_i, \tau) = \left(\frac{e_{i\{S_k + S_l\}} - e_{i\{S_k\}} - e_{i\{S_l\}}}{|E_i|} \right) - \left[\left(\frac{d_{i\{S_k + S_l\}}}{2|E_i|} \right)^2 - \left(\frac{d_{i\{S_k\}}}{2|E_i|} \right)^2 - \left(\frac{d_{i\{S_l\}}}{2|E_i|} \right)^2 \right] \quad (4)$$

Where $e_{i\{S_k\}}$ be the sum of the weights of the edges amongst nodes within S_k in G_i;
$d_{i\{S_k\}}$ be the sum of the weights of the edges attached nodes of S_k in G_i; $|E_i|$ be the sum
of the weights of all the edges in G_i; $S_k + S_l$ be the union set of S_k and S_l.

3.2   Determining Weights of Relations

In general, not all relations have equivalent importance with respect to different
requests of users. To evaluate the importance of each relation, we design a desirable set
of communities and use the *Normalized mutual information* (*NMI*) [11] between the
desirable set of communities and the sets of communities detected in each
single-relational network to measure the importance of all kinds of relationship types.

3.2.1   The Desirable Set of Communities

The *desirable set of communities* (*DS*) is a collection of communities in which the
memberships of nodes are specified according to users' requests, i.e. the nodes that are
required by users to belong to a community are assigned same memberships, while the
nodes that are required by users to belong to different communities are assigned different memberships, and there is a community that contains all nodes.

Example 1. In the 3-relational network shown in Fig. 1, if node 8, 9, 10 and 11 are
required to belong to a community, then $DS_1 = \{\{8, 9, 10, 11\}, \{1, 2, 3, 4, 5, 6,$
$7, 8, 9, 10, 11, 12\}\}$; if node 8 and 10 are required to belong to a community, 9 and
11 are required to belong to a community, but 8, 10 and node 9, 11 are required to
belong to different communities, then $DS_2 = \{\{8, 10\}, \{9, 11\}, \{1, 2, 3, 4, 5, 6,$
$7, 8, 9, 10, 11, 12\}\}$; if node 8, 9, 10 and 11 are required to belong to different
communities,   then $DS_3 = \{\{8\}, \{9\}, \{10\}, \{11\}, \{1, 2, 3, 4, 5, 6, 7, 8, 9, 10,$
$11, 12\}\}$.

3.2.2   The Sets of Single-Relational Communities

In this study, we use *Louvain Method* [12] to detect the communities in each
single-relational graph. Let CS_i be the set of communities detected in G_i by the *Louvain
Method*. The *Louvain Method*, as a heuristic method that is based on modularity
optimization, allows detected communities with good accuracy in large networks.

Example 2. In Fig. 1, the *Louvain Method* detects three community structures respectively in the three single-relational graphs: $CS_1 = \{\{1, 2, 3\}, \{4, 5, 6\}, \{7, 8, 9, 10, 11, 12\}\}$, $CS_2 = \{\{1, 2, 3\}, \{4, 5, 6\}, \{7, 8, 10\}, \{9, 11, 12\}\}$, $CS_3 = \{\{1, 2, 3, 8\}, \{4, 6, 10\}, \{7, 9\}, \{5, 11, 12\}\}$.

3.2.3 Normalized Mutual Information (NMI)

The *Normalized mutual information (NMI)* [11] is an evaluation metric used to measure the accuracy of an algorithm for community structure identification. Given two sets of communities $\tau_1 = \{C_1, C_2, \ldots, C_c\}$ and $\tau_2 = \{D_1, D_2, \ldots, D_d\}$, $NMI(\tau_1, \tau_2)$ measures quantitatively how similar or different between τ_1 and τ_2, $NMI(\tau_1, \tau_2) \in [0, 1]$. If $\tau_1 = \tau_2$, $NMI(\tau_1, \tau_2) = 1$; if τ_1 and τ_2 are completely different, $NMI(\tau_1, \tau_2) = 0$.

Example 3. In Fig. 1, the *NMIs* between $DS_i, i = 1, 2, 3$ of Example 1 and $CS_j, j = 1, 2, 3$ of Example 2 are as following:

$$NMI(DS_1, CS_2) = 0.2015, \quad NMI(DS_1, CS_2) = 0.067, \quad NMI(DS_1, CS_3) = 0;$$
$$NMI(DS_2, CS_1) = 0.1297, \quad NMI(DS_2, CS_2) = 0.3452, \quad NMI(DS_2, CS_3) = 0.0415;$$
$$NMI(DS_3, CS_1) = 0.1006, \quad NMI(DS_3, CS_2) = 0.2349, \quad NMI(DS_3, CS_3) = 0.3072;$$

3.2.4 The Weights of Relations

Let $\mathbf{w_R} = (w_1, w_2, \ldots, w_r)$ denotes the weight distributions of relationship types in R, where $w_k \geq 0$, $\sum\limits_{k=1}^{r} w_k = 1$, w_k is defined by the Eq. (5).

$$w_k = \frac{NMI(DS, CS_k)}{\sum\limits_{i=1}^{r} NMI(DS, CS_i)} \tag{5}$$

Example 4. In Fig. 1, $w_1 = 0.75$, $w_2 = 0.25$, $w_3 = 0$ with respect to DS_1; $w_1 = 0.251$, $w_2 = 0.668$, $w_3 = 0.080$ with respect to DS_2; $w_1 = 0.157$, $w_2 = 0.365$, $w_3 = 0.478$ with respect to DS_3.

The case that $w_1 = 0.75$, $w_2 = 0.25$, $w_3 = 0$ with respect to DS_1 indicates that the relation (a) is the most important one and the relation (b) is the second one if node 8, 9, 10 and 11 are required to belong to a community. It is quite clear that all weights measure the importance of all kinds of relationship types correctly under different information needs.

3.3 An Algorithm for Detecting Multi-relational Communities

In this study, we develop a *greedy agglomerative manner* to identify multi-relational communities. The main idea of the *greedy agglomerative manner* is to start from the nodes as separate communities (singletons), communities that can result the highest positive modularity increment are iteratively merged into a larger community until no such merging operation can be performed any further. The pseudo-code for the *greedy agglomerative algorithm* is given in *MuReCD* (Multi-Relational Community Detection) algorithm.

MuReCD algorithm:

Input: a multi-relational network $G = \{G_1, G_2, ..., G_r\}$, the desirable set of communities DS

Output: the community structure of G

Steps:

1.Detecting the sets of single-relational communities CS_i and compute $NMIs$ between the desirable set of communities DS and CS_i

2.Computing the weight distributions of relationship types based on Equation (5)

3. $\tau New = \{\{1\}, \{2\}, ..., \{|N|\}\}$

4.do

5. $(S_i, S_j) = \underset{S_k, S_l \in \tau New}{\arg \max} \Delta Q(G, \tau New - \{S_k\} - \{S_l\} + \{S_k + S_l\})$

6.   if $\Delta Q(G, \tau New - \{S_i\} - \{S_j\} + \{S_i + S_j\}) > 0$ // $S_i + S_j$: The union set of S_i and S_j

        $\tau New = \tau New - \{S_i\} - \{S_j\} + \{S_i + S_j\}$ //merging S_i and S_j

7.   end if

8.while merging operation be executed

9.Output τNew

The Step 3 initializes each node as a singleton community, and all singleton communities form τNew; the loop of Step 4 ~ Step 8 forms the final community structures by merging communities with the highest positive modularity increment gradually from bottom to top.

The time complexity of *MuReCD* algorithm is $O(|N| \log |N|)$ at worst case. Note that, $|N| - 1$ iterations are an upper bound and the algorithm will terminate as soon as no pair of communities would be merged any further. It is possible that the algorithm ends up before all nodes are merged into a community.

4   Experimental Validation

We produce 3 benchmark networks by using Lancichinetti and Fortunato's method [23] to simulate a 3-relational network under following parameters: the number of vertices $N = 1000$, the average degree $k = 15$, the maximum degree $\max k = 20$, the mixing parameter, i.e. the portion of crossing edges $mu = 0.1$, the minimum for the community sizes $\min c = 30$, the maximum for the community sizes $\max c = 60$, the number of overlapping vertices $on = 0$. The benchmark structure is shown in Fig. 2.

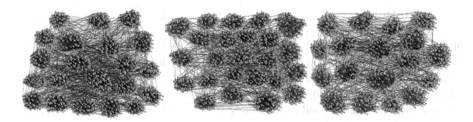

Fig. 2. A 3-relational network with 1000 nodes

To evaluate the performance of our approach, we use the accuracy rate (AR) as measure metric. Let $C \in DS$, then $AR(C)$ and $AR(DS)$ is defined in Eqs. (6) and (7) respectively.

$$AR(C) = \frac{\arg\max_{S_i \in \tau} \delta(C, S_i)}{|C|} \qquad (6)$$

$$AR(DS) = \arg\min_{C_i \in DS} AR(C_i) \qquad (7)$$

Where τ is the community structure detected by *MuReCD* algorithm, $\delta(C, S_i)$ is the number of same elements in C and S_i, i.e. $\delta(C, S_i) = |C \cap S_i|$, $|C|$ is the size of C.

Traditional community mining algorithms are independent of the user-submitted query. Thus, the three relations are treated equally, i.e. $w_i = 0.33$, $i = 1, 2, 3$. We take this as the baseline and denote it as *TCMA* for short. Table 1 shows the comparisons of AR between *TCMA* and *MuReCD* under different nodes specified by users, where $|q_u|$ is the number of nodes specified by users, and $|DS|$ is the number of communities that nodes in q_u belong to.

Table 1. $AR(DS)$ of *TCMA* and *MuReCD* under different nodes specified by users

$|q_u|$	$|DS|$	AR w.r.t *TCMA*	AR w.r.t *MuReCD*
21	1	0.666	0.9523
38	2	0.6111	0.95
39	3	0.5909	1.0
47	4	0.5	1.0
55	5	0.5714	0.975
74	6	0.4	0.9091

From Table 1, we can see that *MuReCD* outperforms *TCMA*. It indicates that the results obtained by *MuReCD* are more agreed with user's demand.

5 Conclusions

In this paper, we propose a user-dependent method to detect communities in multi-relational social networks. To evaluate our methods, experiments on synthetic networks have been conducted. The experimental results validate the effectiveness of our approach since it substantially improves prediction accuracy and it convincingly discovers interesting relations and communities.

Acknowledgement. This work is supported by the National Natural Science Foundation of China under Grant No. 61262069, No. 61472346, the Natural Science Foundation of Yunnan Province under Grant No. 2015FB114, No. 2015FB149, No. 2016FA026, Program for Young and Middle-aged Skeleton Teachers, Yunnan University, and Program for Innovation Research Team in Yunnan University under Grant No. XT412011.

References

1. Chen, W., Liu, Z., Sun, X., Wang, Y.: A Game-theoretic framework to identify overlapping communities in social networks. Data Min. Knowl. Disc. **21**(2), 224–240 (2010)
2. Yang, T.B., Chi, Y., Zhu, S.H., Gong, Y.H., Jin, R.: Detecting communities and their evolutions in dynamic social networks: a Bayesian approach. Mach. Learn. **82**, 157–189 (2011)
3. Navakas, R., Džiugys, A., Peters, B.: A community-detection based approach to identification of inhomogeneities in granular matter. Physica A **407**(1), 312–331 (2014)
4. Fortunato, S.: Community detection in graphs. Phys. Rep. **486**, 75–174 (2010)
5. Mucha, P.J., Richardson, T., Macon, K., Porter, M.A., Onnela, J.P.: Community structure in time-dependent, multiscale, and multiplex networks. Science **328**, 876–878 (2010)
6. Sun, P.G., Gao, L.: A framework of mapping undirected to directed graphs for community detection. Inf. Sci. **298**(20), 330–343 (2015)
7. Ströele, V., Zimbrão, G., Souza, J.M.: Group and link analysis of multi-relational scientific social networks. J. Syst. Softw. **86**(7), 1819–1830 (2013)
8. Szell, M., Lambiotte, R., Thurner, S.: Multirelational organization of large-scale social networks in an online world. Proc. Natl. Acad. Sci. U.S.A. **107**(31), 13636–13641 (2010)
9. Cai, D., Shao, Z., He, X., Yan, X., Han, J.: Community mining from multi-relational networks. In: Jorge, A.M., Torgo, L., Brazdil, P.B., Camacho, R., Gama, J. (eds.) PKDD 2005. LNCS (LNAI), vol. 3721, pp. 445–452. Springer, Heidelberg (2005)
10. Brandes, U., Delling, D., Gaertler, M., Goerke, R., Hoefer, M., Nikoloski, Z., Wagner, D.: Maximizing modularity is hard (2006). arXiv:Physics/0608255
11. Danon, L., Danone, D.-G.A., Duch, J., Arenas, D.: Comparing community structure identification. J. Stat. Mech: Theor. Exp. **2005**, P09008 (2005)
12. Blondel, V.D., Guillaume, J.-L., Lambiotte, R., Lefebvre, E.: Fast unfolding of communities in large networks. J. Stat. Mech: Theor. Exp. **P10008**, 1–12 (2008)
13. Newman, M.E.J., Girvan, M.: Finding and evaluating community structure in networks. Phys. Rev. E **69**, 026113 (2004)
14. Aynaud, T., Guillaume, J.-L.: Multi-step community detection and hierarchical time segmentation in evolving networks. In: Proceedings of the Fifth SNA-KDD Workshop on Social Network Mining and Analysis, in Conjunction with the 17th ACM SIGKDD (KDD 2011), San Diego, CA, 21–24 August (2011)

15. Shang, R., Bai, J., Jiao, L., Jin, C.: Community detection based on modularity and an improved genetic algorithm. Physica A **392**(5), 1215–1231 (2013)
16. Davis, D., Lichtenwalter, R., Chawla, N.V.: Multi-relational link prediction in heterogeneous information networks. In: International Conference on Advances in Social Networks Analysis and Mining (ASONAM 2011), Kaohsiung, Taiwan, 25–27 July, pp. 281–288. IEEE Computer Society (2011)
17. Krohn-Grimberghe, A., Drumond, L., Freudenthaler, C., Schmidt-Thieme, L.: Multi-relational matrix factorization using Bayesian personalized ranking for social network data. In: The fifth International Conference on Web Search and Web Data Mining (WSDM 2012), Seattle, WA, USA, 8–12, February, pp. 173–182 (2012)
18. Jiang, M., Cui, P., Wang, F., Yang Q., Zhu, W.W., Yang, S.Q.: Social recommendation across multiple relational domains. In: The 22th ACM International Conference on Information and Knowledge Management (CIKM), Maui, Hawaii, US, October 29–November 2, pp. 1422–1431 (2012)
19. Dai, B.T., Chua, F.C.T., Lim, E.P. and Faloutsos, C.: Structural analysis in multi relational social networks. In: Proceedings of the Twelfth SIAM International Conference on Data Mining, Anaheim, California, USA, 26–28 April, pp. 451–462 (2012)
20. Tang, L., Wang, X., Liu, H.: Community detection via heterogeneous interaction analysis. Data Min. Knowl. Discovery **25**(1), 1–33 (2012)
21. Wu, Z., Yin, W., Cao, J., Xu, G., Cuzzocrea, A.: Community detection in multi-relational social networks. In: Lin, X., Manolopoulos, Y., Srivastava, D., Huang, G. (eds.) WISE 2013, Part II. LNCS, vol. 8181, pp. 43–56. Springer, Heidelberg (2013)
22. Rodriguez, M., Shinavier, J.: Exposing multi-relational networks to single relational network analysis algorithms. J. Inform. **4**(1), 29–41 (2010)
23. Lancichinetti, A., Fortunato, S., Kertesz, J.: Detecting the overlapping and hierarchical community structure in complex networks. N.J. Phys. **11**, 033015 (2009)

Compressing Streaming Graph Data Based on Triangulation

Liang Zhang$^{(\boxtimes)}$, Ming Gao, Weining Qian, and Aoying Zhou

Institute for Data Science and Engineering, East China Normal University,
Shanghai, China
52101500013@ecnu.cn, {mgao,wnqian,ayzhou}@sei.ecnu.edu.cn

Abstract. There is a wide diversity of applications for graph compression in web data management, scientific data processing, and social data analysis. In real-life applications like social media data processing, elements in a graph, typically vertices and edges, are arriving continuously. Compressing the graph before storing it in a database is important for real-time processing and analysis, while being a challenging yet interesting problem. A streaming lossless compression method, named as *STT (streaming timeliness triangulation)*, is introduced in this paper. It is a time-efficient method for compressing a streaming graph, which differs itself from static graph compression methods in that: (1) it's able to compress streaming graph without occupying extra storage; (2) it can achieve both low compression ratio and high throughput over the streaming graph; (3) it supports efficient graph query processing directly over compressed graphs. Thus, it can support a wide range of streaming graph processing tasks. Empirical study over a paper co-author graph and a real-life large-scale social network graph has shown the superiority of the newly proposed method over existing static graph compression methods.

Keywords: Graph compression · Streaming data · Social graph · Graph query

1 Introduction

Graphs are widely used in Web-related applications to represent different kinds of data, such as linkage structure of web pages, social networks, and semantic networks. The recent explosion in number and scale of real-life structured data sets has created a pressing need for efficiency in processing and analysing massive graphs. For example, in the context of on-line services, the web graph amounts to at least one trillion of links. In particular, Facebook recently reported more than 1 billion of users and 140 billions of friend connections. The unprecedented proliferation of data not only provides us with new opportunities and benefits, but also poses hard computational challenges.

© Springer International Publishing Switzerland 2016
A. Morishima et al. (Eds.): APWeb 2016 Workshops, LNCS 9865, pp. 164–175, 2016.
DOI: 10.1007/978-3-319-45835-9_15

Among the computational models that have been proposed to deal with massive data sets, graph compression processing has received an ever-increasing attention in the last few years. Graph compression is a natural approach to transforming a large-scale graph into some data structures with less storage consumption.

However, for static graph compression algorithms, acquisition of an entire graph topology is usually an essential. Also, the majority of such algorithms require a graph to be fully stored in the main memory, while some others may require graph to be partially stored in sequences. These would all lead to an excessive computation. Furthermore, graph structures never remain unchanged. Updates, deletions, and insertions underwent over a period of time would lead to the reduction in compressing performance. As a result, graphs were once compressed by static algorithms need to be re-compressed every once in a while. However, many static methods failed to support processing incremental data. Achieving the original graph by decompressing the compressed data was, thus, a necessity before re-compression. For graphs that demand frequent updates, constant decompression-and-recompression will generate great computing costs. Last but not least, none update is allowed on graphs during static compression execution. This makes graph handling even harder in the present time. Streaming graph compression is an approach to transforming streaming graph with lower requirements of storage to be consumed before saving the data to a disk. A streaming graph has some features as followings. Data arrives in real-time. Orders of data arrivals are independent to each other and uncontrollable. Data is massive without predictable regularity. Last but not least, once data is processed, unless specifically saved, re-processing is inapplicable, or very costly. We compared static graph compression models and the streaming model as demonstrated in Fig. 1. Since the graph was compressed beforehand, less extra space on the disk would be occupied, which was subsequent to less computing costs. Usually, finding a suitable streaming compression methods for a large-scale graph, such as friendship networks from a popular social networking website, is a difficult task. Thus, we proposed a streaming compression algorithm, *STT*, that complete topology is not needed before the compression. Real-life graph compression becomes applicable without excessive computing costs in one pass.

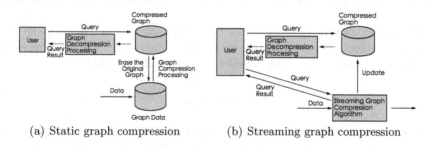

(a) Static graph compression   (b) Streaming graph compression

Fig. 1. Comparison of static and streaming graph compression models.

The aim of this paper is to find a general streaming algorithm, which will carry out well-compressed results relying only on structures of graphs. An algorithm named as *STT* is introduced. Characteristics of *STT* algorithm are as follows.

- It's able to compress graph streams without occupying extra storage.
- It achieves both low compression ratio and high streaming throughput, which is demonstrated by real-life graphs.
- For some common graph queries, it achieves positive query processing performance with an equivalent compression ratio.

The remainder of this paper is organized as following. The streaming graph compression problem is formalized in Sect. 2. In Sect. 3, our *STT* streaming graph compression algorithm is introduced in details. In Sect. 4, experimental results over two large-scale real-life social graphs are reported. After the related work, which is introduced in Sect. 5, Sect. 6 is for concluding remarks.

2   Problem Statement

We assume a graph $G = (V, E)$ with a set of nodes V and a set of edge E. Each edge is a pair of vertices, an entry (u, v) denotes an edge points from node u to node v in a directed graph, or denotes the correlation between node u and node v. We discuss lossless graph compression in this paper.

Definition 1. *Graph compression, given two graphs G and $G'(V', E')$, we say G' is a lossless compression of G if it can get a compact result graph with less storage cost and do not lose any nodes or graph structure, and the graph G can be recovered when it is uncompressed.*

Then we define problems that exist in streaming graph compression. We consider a simple streaming graph model, which data arrives in a stream with sets of edges. We extend the model by allowing a cache replacement strategy based on the edge timeliness. We would like a compressed streaming graph to support the same operations of an original one, while occupying significantly less space and providing high throughput. Our algorithm tries to updates the cache by node timeliness, and list all triangle elements in the cache to achieve high compression ratio.

The compression ratio is one of the most paramount indicators to judge the compression effect. The compression ratio means the ratio of the uncompressed size of a graph against the compressed size, the smaller, the better.

$$compression\ ratio\ cr = \frac{G}{G_C},\ 0 < cr < 1 \tag{1}$$

The streaming throughput is another important indicator when evaluating a streaming algorithm, which is defined as the number of uncompressed edges that can be handled in one second. A good streaming algorithm should handle more data in unit time.

3   Streaming Compression Algorithm - *STT*

We presented an algorithm, *STT (streaming timeliness triangulation)*, that works on the basis of maintaining a cache to hold part of the streaming data, and achieves compression based on merging node pairs, which connected to each other and their common neighbors to triangle elements.

3.1   *STT (Streaming Timeliness Triangulation)* Algorithm

It has been observed that most real-life graphs have an important characteristic in common, i.e. the distribution of node degrees are highly biased. The majority of nodes have very low degrees while the minority have high degrees. We have to take an excessive quantity of resources to list the triangles that formed by a high degree node and its neighboring low degree nodes. A triangle could be defined as a set of three nodes such that each possible edge among any two of them was presented in the graph. In complex network studies, one often deals with huge graphs, typically with several million or even up to a few billions nodes and edges. Both time and space required by triangle listing computations are then key issues. We can find that there might be $\Theta(n^3)$, or $\Theta(m^{\frac{3}{2}})$ triangles in a graph with n nodes and m edges [9]. However, in practice, graphs are often sparse. We applied an improved edge-iterator triangulation algorithm on our compression algorithm to speed up the triangle listing task. It could list all triangles in a graph in $\Theta(m^{\frac{3}{2}})$ time and need only $O(m)$ space, the details is shown in Algorithm 1.

Another characteristic shared by the most of the real-life graphs, which has been observed recently, is that edges in graphs are timeliness. The status of which a node gains focus of attention with suddenness might stay valid only for a certain period of time. These nodes might get degree explosively increased in a short time, and known as hot items during that time, but they would possibly be neglected after a while.

Based on the both two characteristics of real-life graphs discussed above, we proposed a streaming graph compression algorithm, named as *STT* with low compression ratio and high streaming throughput. It tried to keep recent hot items in the cache, which were frequently accessed in the latest period of time to optimize compression performance. We listed the triangle elements in the cache to achieve compression by using partial structure of the graph [2], and stored the triangle elements as $T = \{([x,y],z)|z \in W = \{common\ neigher\ nodes\ of\ connected\ node\ pair\ x\ and\ y\}\}$.

We maintained a cache with fixed size to store a few past data, and applied the triangulation algorithm discussed above to list all increasing triangle elements on the data. Algorithm 1, *STT* algorithm, takes graph streaming as input. Line 1 to 7 updated the cache with the streaming cache algorithm discusses below, that tried to replace an out-of-date entry with new node pair. Line 8 to 13 created an empty adjacency list, A, for the nodes do not appear in the cache. Line 14 to 23 iteratively processed following steps. For each node in the cache, y, and for each neighboring node of y, we set it as x. If we found a non-empty

---

Algorithm 1. STT, streaming timeliness triangulation

Require: linked node pairs $P\{(u,v)|u,v \in V\}$ transferred in streaming mode, cache
  replacement threshold r_t
Ensure: $S'(V, T, E)$
1: **repeat**
2:    select a random entry e in the cache
3:    **if** $t_e < r_t$ **then**
4:        find an out-of-date entry successfully
5:    **end if**
6: **until** find an out-of-date entry
7: replace e with (u,v)
8: **if** u do not appear in cache **then**
9:    $A(u) \leftarrow \emptyset$; {adjacency list of node u}
10: **end if**
11: **if** v do not appear in cache **then**
12:    $A(v) \leftarrow \emptyset$; {adjacency list of node v}
13: **end if**
14: **for each** $A(x) \in cache \cup A(u) \cup A(v)$ **do**
15:    **for each** $y \in A(u)$ **do**
16:        **for each** $w \in A(x) \cap A(y)$ **do**
17:            $W \leftarrow W \cup w$; $E \leftarrow E \setminus (x,w)$; $E \leftarrow E \setminus (y,w)$; {form a triangle element}
18:            $hit(x,y)$++; {hit counter}
19:        **end for**
20:        $A(y) \leftarrow A(y) \cup \{x\}$;
21:    **end for**
22:    $T \leftarrow T \cup \{[x,y], W\}$;
23: **end for**
24: $V \leftarrow V \cup V'$;
25: **return** $S'(V, T, E)$

---

common node set W in $A(x)|\cap A(y)$, we would output the triangle set $\{[x,y], W\}$
and remove the edge set $\{(x,w) \cup (y,w)|w \in W\}$ from E. Then we add node y
to array $A(x)$.

3.2 Steaming Cache Algorithm

The streaming cache keeps the node pairs that are likely to be used in the near
future. With a high efficient streaming cache algorithm, we processed our compression with more triangle elements found during the streaming pass through.

There are some typical cache algorithms, such as First in First out(FIFO),
Least Frequently Used(LFU), Least Recently Used(LRU) and Random Replace-
ment(RR), etc. Each algorithm has its own advantages and disadvantages, and
they may play out differently in different situations. There are two primary figures for evaluating a cache algorithm: the latency, and the hit rate [11]. The
hit rate of a cache describes how often a searched item is actually found in the
cache. More efficient replacement policies keep track of more usage information
in order to improve the hit rate. The *latency* of a cache describes how long after
requesting the desired item the cache can return that item. Faster replacement

strategies typically keep track of less usage information or to reduce the amount of time required to update that information. Each replacement strategy is a compromise between hit rate and latency.

Our cache algorithm takes strengths from RR, LFU, and LRU. It always selects a random item in the cache, which leads to a high streaming throughput performance. Besides, it also considers preservation of items with high access rate without using any extra counter. The items will be removed when they are not accessed over a period of time. Even though, it was hit many times earlier. Furthermore, we can keep recently used items correctly and make sure that it will not be replaced too early.

We defined a replacement frequency value to judge whether the entries in the cache is out-of-date or not. Then, we proposed our cache algorithm as a hot entry that has a timeliness parameter $t = \frac{n \times h}{s}$ exceeding the replacement frequency set to keep it staying in the cache; and that includes n nodes and has been hit by h times over past s million seconds. We randomly chose an entry in the cache to find if it could be replaced. If it was still a hot entry, as the value of t was high, we would randomly choose another entry again. The worst situation was that we might scan the whole cache before we get the result, but it rarely happened because there would be few hot entry in the stream within a short period of time.

3.3   Analysis

Our algorithm utilizes triangulation structures in the cache to compress the streaming graph. Intuitively, in a large-scale graph, there exist many dense subgraphs, of which contains many triangles. Efficient data structures for representing these triangles lead to compact storage of the whole graph. Our algorithm makes the cache keep recent dense subgraphs in the stream to get a compact compression result.

The time complexity of the proposed approach is of particular interest, due to the times of cache miss is indeterminate. For a cache, we use $|C|$ to denote the maximum adjacency lists could be held in it. The number of out-of-time adjacency lists in the cache is $|O|$. The probability of cache hit is $p = \frac{|O|}{|C|}$. As the graph follows a power-law distribution, the probability follows a geometric distribution, the expected attempt times until we can get a cache hit is $n = \frac{|C|}{|O|}$. We ran incremental compression in the cache, the compression time of each input can be ignored. The time complexity of our algorithm can be estimated as

$$T = n \times T_m + T_h + T_s = O(\frac{|C|^2}{|O|}) \tag{2}$$

$n =$ expected attempt times before cache hit, $T_m =$ time to make cache access when there is a miss, $T_h =$ time when there is a cache hit, $T_s =$ time to compression the entries in the cache. Most web graphs are scale-free networks, and their degree distributions follow the power-law, at least asymptotically. In studying the degree distributions, Barabasi found that in a scale-free network, when we pick a random node u, the probability of its degree d is a natural number k as $\mathbb{P}(d = k) \propto \frac{1}{k^\gamma}$, where γ is a parameter whose value is typically in the range between 2 and 3, though occasionally it may lie outside these bounds [5]. It leads to a large value of $|O|$, and we can get a low value of T when $|C|$ is constant.

4   Experiment

We ran all experiments on a single PC with a 3.06 GHz Intel processor, 8 GB of RAM(1066 MHzs DDR3 SDRAM). We ran our STT algorithm, comparing against some typical cache algorithms and static graph compression methods, which described in Sect. 5, on two real-life graphs with power-law node degree distribution, as shown in Fig. 2. The social follow graph is an undirected graph, which represents social followings of users fetched from Sina Weibo as time goes on, and can be treated as a typical streaming graph. When one user followed another, there would be a directed link between these two users, which pointed from the follower to the followed. It contains *2,675,412* nodes and *11,857,851* edges. The co-author graph was a paper-writing collaboration directed graph published by DBLP database, and took the value of 'mdate' to describe the publish time of the paper, as a time line of the streaming graph. If two researchers collaborated on at least one paper, there would exist an undirected edge that inter-connected between them. It contains *659,390* nodes and *5,656,152* edges.

We conducted an innovative research on the streaming graph compression algorithm, so we could not find other reach results on this problem. Thus, we can only compare our compression effect against static compression methods.

4.1   Compression Ratio and Compression Efficiency

In our method, cache size and cache replacement frequency are most important parameters that affected compression performance. They had direct control on the compression ratio and streaming throughput. We observed the impact of replacement frequency and cache size on the performance of our method with two graphs. By observing changes occurred in compression ratios and streaming processing abilities, against variations in replacement frequency, as showed in

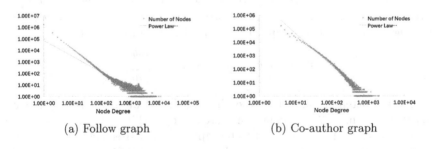

(a) Follow graph   (b) Co-author graph

Fig. 2. Node degree distribution.

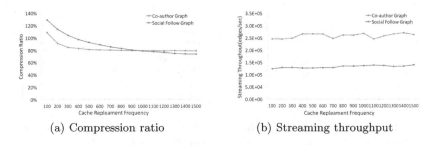

(a) Compression ratio   (b) Streaming throughput

Fig. 3. Impact of the replacement frequency on compression performance.

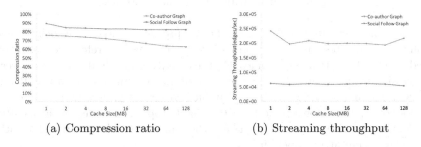

(a) Compression ratio   (b) Streaming throughput

Fig. 4. Impact of the cache size on compression performance.

Figs. 3 and 4, we found that compression ratios get lower with higher replacement frequencies while streaming process efficiencies appear to have less tendency in such correlation.

A high replacement frequency means that data in a cache will be replaced with better consistency, which avoids the entries that contain lots of historical references in the past but is no longer hit from staying in the cache. Hence, we can get a high hit rate by always keeping up-to-date hot entries in the cache. Having that makes it easier to find a triangle from the cache for incoming streaming data, so as to improve the compression result that has a significant effect on a sparse graph like the social follow graph. However, when the replacement frequency gets high, benefits generated from the timeliness of real-life graph decreases. Therefore, the compression ratio tends to be stable. In some situation, a dense graph, like co-author graph, may lead to a negative effect when the cache is replacing too fast that some hot entries may be thrown by mistakes. On the other hand, we updated the entries in the cache more frequently leading to the occupation of more computation cost, so the processing ability may be slightly reduced.

4.2 Effectiveness of Different Caching Strategies

In the comparison experiment, we compared our method against other cache algorithms on the performance of compression ratio and throughput capabilities. The result, in Fig. 5, showed our algorithm performed better on both graphs than

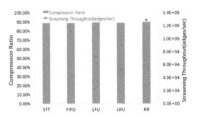 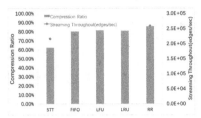

(a) Streaming compression perfor-   (b) Streaming compression performance on follow graph   mance on co-author graph

Fig. 5. Compare with other cache algorithms.

the others that described in Sect. 3.2. The compression ratio on the social follow graph was similar because the graph was too sparse that the reference algorithm ended with under-satisfied outcomes. On the co-author graph, it achieved a great compression result by our algorithm because of its high timeliness feature. It was common that many authors who had published lots of papers and cooperated with lots of scientists for a period of time might stop announcing few ideas after a while. Our algorithm can easily find out these provisional hot entries efficiently and replace them at a proper time.

In the outcomes of stream handling ability, the RR performed the best because it did not need to process any history information that would take additional computation cost during processing. Our algorithm also randomly found an entry in the cache that had been out of time without scanning the whole, nor maintaining a history log. We might need to try several times to find an entry met conditions, but not too many, so the performance of ours was better than that of LRU and LFU that need to handle the extra log, and was similar to FIFO that always replace the oldest one with poor compression ratio. The performance difference of streaming throughput on the two graphs appeared to be obvious. This is caused by the higher quantity of nodes in the follow graph. Hence, a relatively larger amount of streams is needed to processing edges in the follow graph.

4.3 Query Processing Over Compressed Graphs

We compared our streaming compression methods with some static graph compression algorithms that are described in Sect. 5. The performance of compression process, compression ratio and average common neighbor query responding time is shown in Fig. 6.

In the comparison experiment, our algorithm achieved a similar compression ratio to other static algorithms, which took the advantage of handling the whole graph structure during processing. Our streaming algorithm processed compression along with arriving of the graph, which save much more time and storage cost, while the static compression methods started processing until the whole graph was stored locally that wasted time on waiting for the graph transmission.

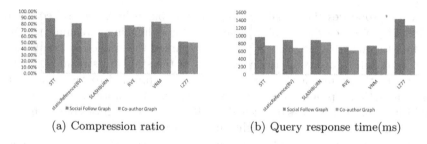

(a) Compression ratio   (b) Query response time(ms)

Fig. 6. Compare with static graph algorithms on query performance.

The response time of the common neighbor query is often used in graph mining. There has been increasing interests in research on links between objects in networks recently, of which, the most fundamental research is link prediction. Cui proposed a common-neighbor-based approach for link prediction [6], and Chaturvedi also studied the common neighbor leading link prediction method in social network [4]. As a general rule, the greater number of common neighbors that two nodes share, the greater possibility that there will be a link between them in the future.

We used the common neighbor query to satisfy the need of discovering common neighbors between two nodes in many graph applications. In the graph compressed by our *STT* algorithm, we do not need decompression to get the common neighbor set in many cases. Therefore, we can significantly reduce query time when we can get the set we query from triangle elements in the compressed graph, while the graph compressed by other static graph compression methods may need to be decompressed before getting the result. We produced 1000 random node pairs and recorded average query time on querying the common neighbors of these node pairs on compressed graphs. The reference based compression method need to scan other rows in the adjacency list for element referenced, it may take slightly longer time than other node merge scheme methods, which only need to scan the comparison table. The reorder scheme need to regain the original IDs before running the query on the graph, it took additional processing time and space to store the ID mapping table. The LZ77 performed worst because it had to decompress the whole graph before doing the query.

Based on the observation, we proved that our algorithm is capable of producing a compressed result that is similar to other static graph compression algorithms in the aspect of compression ratio, while take less time, and similar efficiency in the common neighbor query. Additionally, it also capable of processing streaming data.

5 Related Work

Graph compression has a rich history. In this section, we describe several existing compression algorithms. The majority of graph compression algorithms target to reduce storage cost of graphs, while their compressed results must maintain the certain properties of original graphs. Many problems have been raised due to the difficulty of processing graph compression algorithms in a streaming setting, including the most classic ones [2]. This has sparked the studies on graph algorithms that aim to overcome the constraints of the standard streaming model. However, of the results for graph streams, many appeared to be negative, as many foundational problems required either substantial working memory or a prohibitive number of passes over the data [10]. Several categories of graph compression algorithms had been brought out, and we will discuss below.

When graphs are represented in adjacency list, each element in adjacency list requires log_n bits for storage. Adler proposed the FIND-REFERENCE algorithm, which was specifically designed for graph structures with many shared links [1]. They attempted to find nodes that share several common neighbors corresponding to cases of which one node might have copied the links shared among the others. Once an appropriate neighbor was identified, the difference, or delta, between the adjacency lists of the two nodes could be identified.

U Kang and Christos envisioned a graph as a collection of hubs connecting spokes, with super-hubs connecting the hubs, and so on [8]. They proposed that the real-life graph could be shattered easily by removing hub nodes from them, and proposed the SLASHBURN algorithm, which grouped the non-zero elements in the adjacency matrix of graph G, and gave the hubs that connecting more spokes lower id.

Gilbert proposed a way to combine similar nodes into one to compress the graph. They used node or edge attributes and topological information to measure similarities between nodes. They brought out a Redundant Vertex Elimination (RVE) scheme to merge two nodes, which had some minimum number of common neighbors, into a single node and inherit their edges [7].

Buehrer and Chellapilla proposed the Virtual Node Miner (VNM) compression method [3], which was based on the idea of identifying bi-cliques, and used virtual nodes as indirection connecting level to link two node sets in order to reduce the number of edges. They presented that the overlap in link structure present in the graph could be summarized by adding a relatively small number of virtual nodes, which were one-level indirection of intersecting bipartite graphs.

The dictionary method achieves without the use of a variable-size code. Instead, they rely on the whole phrase recurrence. Using a dictionary, they encode variable-length phrases to fixed-length codes. LZ77 uses a sliding window consisting of a look-ahead buffer. The encoder scans the buffer backward trying to locate a match for the characters and be saved as length-distance pairs.

6   Conclusion

The problem of streaming lossless compression of large-scale graphs is studied in this paper. The algorithm of *STT (streaming timeliness triangulation)* is introduced. The basic idea is to keep hot entries in the cache with high access rate in short time, and make it thrown out when it is out of time to raise the hit ratio of the cache, while finding more triangle elements to raise the compression ratio. We show that our algorithm is effective in graph streaming that both low compression ratio and high streaming throughput can be achieved. Furthermore, this compression method is friendly to common neighbor queries, which is a basic building block for many graph processing tasks. Experimental results over real-life graph show the efficiency of our proposed method.

Our future work includes the revision of this compression method to dynamically adjust the size of the cache, and improve the replacement parameter to reach a better result. We are keen in finding more efficient streaming compression of large-scale graphs approaches.

Acknowledgement. This work is partially supported by National Hightech R&D Program (863 Program) under grant number 2015AA015307, and National Science Foundation of China under grant number 61432006.

References

1. Adler, M., Mitzenmacher, M.: Towards compressing web graphs. In: Data Compression Conference, DCC 2001, Snowbird, Utah, USA, 27–29 March 2001, pp. 203–212 (2001)
2. Boldi, P., Vigna, S.: The webgraph framework I: compression techniques. In: Proceedings of the 13th International Conference on World Wide Web, WWW 2004, New York, NY, USA, 17–20 May 2004, pp. 595–602 (2004)
3. Buehrer, G., Chellapilla, K.: A scalable pattern mining approach to web graph compression with communities. In: Proceedings of the International Conference on Web Search and Web Data Mining, WSDM 2008, Palo Alto, California, USA, 11–12 February 2008, pp. 95–106 (2008)
4. Chaturvedi, A., Acharjee, T.: An efficient modified common neighbor approach for link prediction in social networks. IOSR J. Comput. Eng. (IOSR-JCE) **12**, 25–34 (2013)
5. Choromański, K., Matuszak, M., Mikisz, J.: Scale-free graph with preferential attachment and evolving internal vertex structure. J. Stat. Phys. **151**(6), 1175–1183 (2013)
6. Cui, H.: Link prediction on evolving data using tensor-based common neighbor. In: 2012 Fifth International Symposium on Computational Intelligence and Design (ISCID), vol. 2, pp. 343–346. IEEE (2012)
7. Gilbert, A.C., Levchenko, K.: Compressing network graphs. In: Proceedings of the LinkKDD Workshop at the 10th ACM Conference on KDD (2004)
8. Kang, U., Faloutsos, C.: Beyond 'caveman communities': hubs and spokes for graph compression and mining. In: 11th IEEE International Conference on Data Mining, ICDM 2011, Vancouver, BC, Canada, 11–14 December 2011, pp. 300–309 (2011)
9. Latapy, M.: Main-memory triangle computations for very large (sparse (power-law)) graphs. Theor. Comput. Sci. **407**(1), 458–473 (2008)
10. McGregor, A.: Graph mining on streams. In: Encyclopedia of Database Systems, pp. 1271–1275 (2009)
11. Smith, A.J.: CPU cache memories. In: SIGMETRICS, p. 219 (1989)

1st International Workshop on Spatio-temporal Data Management and Analytics (SDMA 2016)

Scene Classification in High Resolution Remotely Sensed Images Based on PCANet

Dongmei Huang[1], Yanling Du[1], Qi He[1(✉)], Wei Song[1],
and Kefu Liu[2]

[1] College of Information Technology,
Shanghai Ocean University, Shanghai, China
qihe@shou.edu.cn
[2] East Sea Branch of the State Oceanic Administration, Shanghai, China

Abstract. Rich information provided by high resolution remotely sensed images allow us to classify scenes by understanding their spatial and structural patterns. The key of scene classification task with remotely sensed images lies in feature learning efficiency and invariant image representations. While deep neutral network-based approaches achieved good classification accuracy for remotely sensed images, they often have to train millions of parameters and involve heavily iterative computation. In this paper, we propose a new framework for scene classification based on a simple PCANet which is introduced into high remotely sensed image classification for the first time. First, we verify the eligibility of PCANet on classifying large scale scenes from high resolution remotely sensed images. Then we explore the impact of PCANet parameters including filter size, number of filters, and block overlap ratio on classification accuracy. Lastly, we do comprehensive experiments with the public UC-Merced dataset to exemplify the effectiveness of the approach. Experimental results show that the proposed framework achieved on par with the state-of-the-art deep neutral network-based classification accuracy without training a huge amount of parameters. We demonstrate that the proposed classification framework can be highly effective in developing a classification system that can be used to automatically scan large-scale high resolution satellite imagery for classifying scenes.

Keywords: Deep learning · Image classification · High resolution remotely sensed image · PCANet · Feature learning

1 Introduction

Earth observation system through remote sensing techniques is a research field where a huge variety of physical signals are measured from instruments on board space and airborne platforms. Nowadays, the increase of spatial and spectral resolutions of remotely sensed images provides a more widely range of potential applications in earth observation tasks, such as military detection, precision agriculture, fisheries targeting, environment and resource surveillance. The classification of remotely sensed image has

© Springer International Publishing Switzerland 2016
A. Morishima et al. (Eds.): APWeb 2016 Workshops, LNCS 9865, pp. 179–190, 2016.
DOI: 10.1007/978-3-319-45835-9_16

long attracted the attention of the remote sensing community because classification results are fundamental sources for many environmental and socioeconomic applications. Scientists and practitioners have made great efforts in developing advanced classification approaches and techniques for improving classification accuracy.

Remotely sensed image classification based on visual content is a very challenging task, largely because there is usually a large amount of intra-class variability, arising from different weather conditions, complex land covers, image-processing and image classification approaches, multimodal sensors, and the analyst's experiences [1]. Conventional approaches to image classification require the design and selection of appropriate features to improve the classification accuracy. In practice, the features design and selection process are laborious, as they are highly dependent on the application and the types of data being used. And this process requires much of experts experience in specific domain and understanding of the physical process that governs how light is reflected from the materials. Examples of handcrafted features commonly used in remotely sensed applications include spectral indices (for example, NDVI [2], EVI [3] and NDWI [4]), spatial features (for example, texture and shape [5], wavelets [6] and Gabor texture features [7]), local features (for example, SIFT [8] and HOG [9]). Numerous efforts have been made to counter the intra-class variability by manually designing low-level features for classification tasks. Although the low-level features can be handcrafted with success for certain data and tasks, designing effective features for new data and tasks usually requires new domain knowledge because most hand-crafted features cannot simply be adapted to new conditions [10, 11].

Currently, the deep learning methods have garnered significant attention because they achieved great success in object recognition and detection [10]. The methods can learn features layer-wise and extract abstract and invariant high level features automatically for better image classification [12]. However, learning a network that is useful for particular classification is not easy. These methods face very serious challenges, mainly manifest in:

(1) *Millions of parameters to be trained.* The deep neutral networks depend on large-scale datasets to train millions of parameters for improving the classification accuracy [11]. For instance, the large deep convolutional neural network, trained in the ImageNet dataset, contains eight learned layers from which five convolutional and three fully connected layers, 60 million parameters and 650000 neurons [12].

(2) *High-computational problems involved.* The computational expense to train such extremely deep neutral networks is overwhelming. For example, the distributed computing infrastructure (known as DistBelief) manages to train a neural network using 16000 CPU cores in the experiments [13]. The classification of images turns out to be very challenging, particularly for high resolution remotely sensed images because of the high dimensionality of the pixels, the high spatial and spectral redundancy and collinearity, and their potentially nonlinear nature [14].

Very recently, a simple deep learning baseline PCANet for image classification is proposed and achieves great performance in classification of faces, digits, and texture images. It is able to eliminate the image variability and provides reasonably competitive accuracy [12] without training many parameters. PCANet is actually a PCA network. They prove that a two-staged PCANet outperforms the single-staged one, and a deeper architecture does not necessarily lead to further improvement. PCANet has been shown to have the ability to be compared with the off-the-shelf Convolutional Neural Networks (CNN) with respect to performance on various tasks. However, the effectiveness of PCANet for complicated, large scale and high resolution remotely sensed image classification has not been evaluated.

In this paper, a generalized classification framework based on PCANet is proposed for high resolution remotely sensed images by reducing significant intra-class variability without training many parameters. In the rest of the paper, after a thorough analysis of related work (Sect. 2), we provide the basic background on PCANet and the classification framework (Sect. 3). Then we make a series of experiments to examine the classification framework with different parameters settings of PCANet and present the classification results (Sect. 4), and finally draw conclusions (Sect. 5).

2 Related Work

In recent years, there has been intense research on remotely sensed scene classification, focusing on the use of suitable image features for specific classification tasks. From perspective of feature extraction scale, the classification methods can be divided into pixel-based and object-oriented. Bruzzone and Carlin [15] exploit spatial context by segmenting the images firstly, then combine spectral statistics associated with the segment along with the geometrical features computed from the segment for pixel-based classification. Similarly, pixel-based and object-oriented features to image classification were proposed. The feature vector contains spectral and textural pixel-level features, also includes spectral measurements, and geometrical attributes associated with the segments object-level features [16]. Morphological profiles were introduced into classifications to generate pixel features [17]. However, these methods highly depend on the quality of segmentation and the specific applications. In fact, local features like local binary patterns (LBP) [18], scale-invariant feature transform (SIFT) [8], and histograms of oriented gradients (HOG) [9], with their invariance to geometric and photometric transformations, have proven effective in a variety of computer vision applications. They can be extracted both in pixel and object way, and the dimension of the feature space is extremely high. Getting an expressive but compact representation is vital for the image classification.

Lately, the bag of visual words (BOVW) model is a successful approach to reach this goal [19]. BOVW encodes the SIFT feature to its closest visual word, and uses histogram for image representation. In order to take the spatial context into consideration, Lazebnik [20] proposed the spatial pyramid match kernel (SPMK) method. It divided the image into sub-regions and extracted each sub-region features respectively. Jiang [21] performed a randomized spatial partition (RSP), aiming at a better characterization of the spatial layout of the images. The translation and rotation-invariant pyramid-of-spatial-relations (PSR) model [22], spatial co-occurrence kernel (SCK) [19] and its pyramidal version (SPCK) [23] were proposed to capture both absolute and relative spatial arrangements of images. These methods and their variants, which are free of hand-crafted features, have applied in remotely sensed image classification. But the learning features for classification get limited accuracy because of their shallow learning architectures [24–26].

Deep learning makes it possible to extract high-level image features which are more appropriate for complex real-world scene classification. Especially the deep convolution neural networks (CNNs) have achieved dramatic success in image classification, such as handwriting recognition [12], face detection [27], and scene classification [28–30]. However, the deep CNNs, which typically include millions of parameters, should be trained using sufficiently large volume training datasets. As a consequence, the deep learning approaches have significant limitations in practical applications for the large-scale training datasets and extremely high computation cost.

3   High Resolution Remotely Sensed Images Classification Framework Based on PCANet

An initial motivation of our study is the desire to put forward a simple and general framework which is suitable for high resolution remotely sensed images and various applications without training millions of parameters and large computational expense.

In this section, we propose a framework based on PCANet for high resolution remotely sensed image classification that should be very easy to train and to adapt to different data and applications.

3.1   PCANet-Based Classification Framework

This paper advocates a deep framework to generate invariant high level features for improving classification accuracy. For high resolution remotely sensed images with large volume and complex characteristics, one shallow layer always would not be enough in describing the complicated relations between original images and the intra-class variabilities.

Here, we employ a PCANet for high resolution remotely sensed images feature learning and design a deep learning network which is suitable for high complex remotely sensed images. The PCANet-based classification framework is illustrated in Fig. 1. It consists of five primary steps: (1) training dataset generation, (2) filters learning, (3) PCA filters convolution, (4) repeat steps (2)–(3) based on the results of the previous step, (5) feature indexing and feature pooling, and (6) classification. We generate training dataset by resizing, rotation, and translation of the remotely sensed images. We use PCANet to learn features. We apply hash binarization to feature index and use block-wise histogram to feature pool. And the final features are then fed to a linear support vector machine (SVM) classifier.

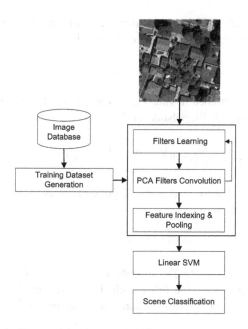

Fig. 1. Framework of scene classification based on PCANet

3.2 Structure of PCA Network

In order to give a detailed description of PCANet for high resolution remotely sensed image classification, we propose the structure of multi-layer PCANet which is illustrated in Fig. 2. Suppose that the training images set $\{I_i\}_{i=1}^{N}$ contains N images and each image with the size of $m \times n$. The patch size is $k_1 \times k_2$ at all stages. The parameters need to learn from the input images $\{I_i\}_{i=1}^{N}$ there are only the PCA filters. The components of PCANet are described in detail as follows.

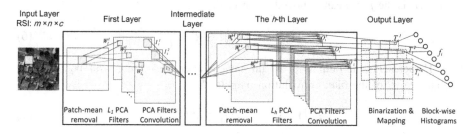

Fig. 2. Structure of the multi-layer PCANet

The First Layer of PCANet. For any one image I_i in training images set, a $k_1 \times k_2$ patch slides from each pixel, we then subtract the patch mean from each patch and obtain $\bar{X}_i = [\bar{x}_{i,1}, \bar{x}_{i,2}, \cdots, \bar{x}_{i,\tilde{m},\tilde{n}}]$, where $\tilde{m} = m - k_1/2$, $\tilde{n} = n - k_2/2$, $\bar{x}_{i,j} = x_{i,j} - \frac{1^T x_{i,j}}{k_1 k_2} 1$

is a mean-removed patch. And $\mathbf{1}$ is an all-one vector with proper dimension. In order to obtain the same matrix for all input images we combine the vectors as (1).

$$X = [\bar{X}_1, \bar{X}_2, \cdots, \bar{X}_N] \in R^{k_1 k_2 \times N\tilde{m}\tilde{n}} \tag{1}$$

Assuming that the number of filters in layer i is L_i. The reconstruction error is minimized by orthonormal filters bank, i.e.,

$$\min_{V \in R^{k_1 k_2 \times L_1}} \|X - VV^T X\|_F^2, \; s.t. \; VV^T = I_{L_1}, \tag{2}$$

where I_{L_1} is a $L_1 \times L_1$ matrix, that is the L_1 principle eigenvectors of XX^T. The PCA filters can be expressed as,

$$W_l^1 = mat_{k_1,k_2}\left(q_l\left(XX^T\right)\right) \in R^{k_1 k_2}, \qquad l = 1, 2, \cdots, L_1, \tag{3}$$

here, the function $mat_{k_1,k_2}(vector)$ is to convert the $vector \in R^{k_1 \times k_2}$ to a matrix $W \in R^{k_1 \times k_2}$ and $q_l(XX^T)$ represents the l-th principal eigenvector of XX^T. The significant principal eigenvectors capture the main variation of all of the mean-removed training patches.

The Higher Layers of PCANet. Majority of operations are consistent with the first layer of PCA. The l-th filter output of the first PCA layer is depicted as,

$$I_i^l = I_i * W_l^1, \quad i = 1, 2, \cdots, N, \tag{4}$$

where * denotes the convolution of two dimensions. We make each image zero-padded in the boundary before it convolves with PCA filters. Similar to the first layer, we subtract the patch mean from each patch, and obtain:

$$\bar{Y}_i^l = [\bar{y}_{i,l,1}, \bar{y}_{i,l,2}, \cdots, \bar{y}_{i,l,\tilde{m}\tilde{n}}] \in R^{k_1 k_2 \times \tilde{m}\tilde{n}}, \tag{5}$$

where $\bar{y}_{i,l,j}$ is the j-th mean-removed patch in I_i^l.

$$Y^l = [\bar{Y}_1^l, \bar{Y}_2^l, \cdots, \bar{Y}_N^l] \in R^{k_1 k_2 \times N\tilde{m}\tilde{n}}, \tag{6}$$

here, Y^l represents the outputs of all the images after convolving with W_l^1. And we concatenate all of the filter convolution outputs Y^l,

$$Y = [Y^1, Y^2, \cdots, Y^{L_1}] \in R^{k_1 k_2 \times L_1 N\tilde{m}\tilde{n}} \tag{7}$$

We can obtain PCA filters of the higher layers as:

$$W_l^h = mat_{k_1,k_2}\left(q_l\left(YY^T\right)\right) \in R^{k_1 \times k_2}, \quad l = 1, 2, \cdots, L_h, \quad h \geq 2, \tag{8}$$

For each input I_i^l of the higher layer, one will output L_h images of size $m \times n$, and each convolves I_i^l with W_l^h for $l = 1, 2, \cdots, L_h$:

$$O_i^l = \{I_i^l * W_l^h\}_{l=1}^{L_h} \tag{9}$$

The number of output images at the higher layer is $L_1 L_2 \cdots L_h$. The PCANet can be easily build more layers if a deeper architecture is found to be beneficial.

The Output Layer of PCANet. The h-th layer has L_{h-1} input images I_i^l whose outputs are $\{I_i^l * W_l^h\}_{l=1}^{L_h}$. The PCA layer outputs are binarized and we obtain $\{H(I_i^l * W_l^h)\}_{l=1}^{L_h}$, here $H(\cdot)$ is a Heaviside step function, whose value is one for positive entries and zero otherwise.

For each pixel of the L_h outputs we convert them to decimal numbers. And the map function is:

$$T_i^l = \sum_{l=1}^{L_h} 2^{l-1} H(I_i^l * W_l^h), \tag{10}$$

Each pixel is an integer in the range $[0, 2^{L_h} - 1]$. Each of the L_1 images T_i^l, $l = 1, 2, \cdots, L_1$ is partitioned into B blocks. We compute the histogram of the decimal values in each block and concatenate all B histograms into one vector and denote this vector as Bhist (T_i^l). After this encoding process, the "feature" of the input image I_i is then defined to be the set of block-wise histograms, i.e.,

$$f_i = [Bhist(T_i^1), \cdots, Bhist(T_i^{L_{h-1}})]^T \in R^{(2^{L_h})L_{h-1}B}. \tag{11}$$

4   Experiments and Results

The main objective of this paper is to explore the generalization and efficiency of proposed framework for high resolution remotely sensed image classification. The experiments are conducted following a classification protocol, in which the dataset is split into training and testing sets and image feature vectors from the training set are used to feed a machine learning classifier. The test set is then used for evaluating the learned classifiers in terms of classification accuracy.

4.1   UC-Merced Data Collection

We validate the scene classification on the UC-Merced dataset [19]. The UC-Merced dataset released in 2010, was cropped from large optical images of the US Geological Survey, taken over various regions of the United States. The UC-Merced dataset consists of 2100 256×256 color images from 21 scene classes, with 1-ft/pixel resolution. The dataset contains highly overlapping classes and has 100 images per class. Figure 3 depicts some images per land use class of interest.

Fig. 3. Examples of the UC-Merced scene classes dataset. (Color figure online)

4.2 Experimental Setup

We select images from per class in varying proportions for training and leave the remaining for testing. The parameters of the method is very simple and easy to set, we do extensive experiments to explore the optimal parameters combination for high resolution remotely sensed image classification.

(1) *Impact of the number of training images.* We report the classification accuracy of the proposed approach for different numbers of high resolution training remotely sensed images. At the same time, we also explore the impact on training time. As the training time highly depends on the computation environment, here we only describe how the training time relative to the change of parameter settings. The total of the images is 2100, the proportion of the training and testing data set vary 6:4 to 9:1, namely the training set is from 1260 to 1890. The filters size is set to 5, 7, 9, 11, 13, respectively. The other parameters are set to $L_1 = 40$, $L_2 = 8$, a block size of 8×8, and the block overlap ratio 0.5. The results are illustrated in Fig. 4. The accuracy of the proposed method is gradually improves as the number of training set increases, and obtains perfect classification accuracy when there are 1890 training images and the filter size is $k_1 = k_2 = 5$. Different training images obtain optimal accuracy at varying filter sizes. The 1890 training images achieve best classification result with filter size 5, while the 1680 training images with filter size 9. Apparently, the training time is increasing with the increase of training images number and filter size.

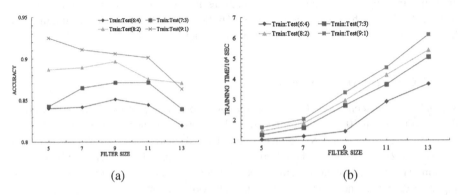

Fig. 4. (a) Classification accuracy and (b) training time of the PCANet-based method on the varying number of training set

(2) *Impact of the number of filters.* Based on the classification accuracy illustrated above, we choose the two best ratio of training to testing 8:2 and 9:1, the corresponding numbers of training images are 1680 and 1890, respectively, to examine the impact of the number of filters on the classification performance. The parameters are set to block size 8×8 and the block overlap ratio 0.5. We vary the number of filters in the first layer L_1 from 30 to 60, and the second layer L_2 is set to a fixed value 8. The results shown in Fig. 5 illustrate that the highest accuracy is achieved at 60 filters with filter sizes $k_1 = k_2 = 9$ for the 1680 of training images, and at 40 filters with filter size $k_1' = k_2' = 5$ for the 1890 of training images.

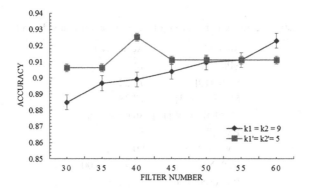

Fig. 5. Classification accuracy for varying number of filters in the first layer $(L_2 = 8)$

(3) *Impact of the block overlap ratio.* We next examine the impact of the block overlap ratio on the classification accuracy. We set the number of filters is $L_1 = 45$, $L_1' = 40$ for 1680 and 1890 training images based on the classification results, respectively. The filter sizes are $k_1 = k_2 = 9$ and $k_1' = k_2' = 5$, and the block size is 8×8. We change the block overlap ratios (BORs) from 0.1 to 0.9. It is clearly shown in Fig. 6 that 1680 and 1890 training images achieve their maximum accuracy for BOR equal to 0.6 and 0.5, respectively. And the more training images the higher accuracy.

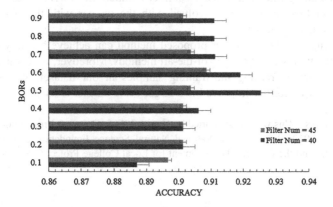

Fig. 6. Classification accuracy for varying block overlap ratios (BORs)

(4) *Comparison with state-of-the-art methods.* We compare our best result achieved with various state-of-the-art methods that have reported classification accuracy on the UCM dataset. As shown in Table 1, the proposed method largely outperforms all the methods except for the deep CNN-based approach CaffeNet [30]. However, The CaffeNet should training millions of parameters which are complicated to train and consumes a very expensive amount of computations. In contrast with most of these methods that use either a huge amount of labor with low-level hand-engineered features [19, 20, 22, 23] or sophisticated learning strategy with millions of parameters training [30], our method is more straight forward and simpler.

Table 1. Classification accuracy comparison of state-of-the-art methods on the UCM dataset

Methods	Accuracy (%)
SPM [20]	74
SCK [19]	72.52
SPCK++ [23]	77.38
CCM-BOVW [19]	86.64 ± 0.81
PSR [22]	89.1
OverFeat [30]	90.91 ± 1.19
CaffeNet [30]	93.42 ± 1.00
Proposed method	92.52 ± 1.12

5 Conclusion

In this paper, we have comprehensively investigated the proposed new framework for high resolution remotely sensed scene classification task. We extract invariant features with PCANet, and trained linear SVM to classify highly overlapping scene classes. The advantages of proposed method are obviously shown in: (1) efficiently extracting high-level features with training the principal filters, and conveniently setting the initial parameters including filter size, block size, filter number, block overlap ratio and layer; (2) simple and low computation involved with the on par with the state-of-the-art methods classification accuracy.

The experiments show that our proposed method can achieve a nearly equal performance compared with other state-of-the-art methods. Moreover, we obtained a better performance when increasing the training samples in our dataset. We believe the performance can be further improved if a larger scale dataset is used.

Acknowledgments. This work is supported by National Basic Research Program of China (973 Program) Grant 2012CB316206, the National Natural Science Foundation of China (NSFC) Grant 61272098, and the Capacity Development for Local College Project Grant 15590501900.

References

1. Romero, A., Gatta, C., Camps-Valls, G.: Unsupervised deep feature extraction for remote sensing image classification. IEEE Trans. Geosci. Remote Sens. **54**(3), 1349–1362 (2016)
2. Tucker, C.: Red and photographic infrared linear combinations for monitoring vegetation. Remote Sens. Environ. **8**, 127–150 (1979)
3. Huete, A., Justice, C., Liu, H.: Development of vegetation and soil indices for MODIS-EOS. Remote Sens. Environ. **49**, 224–234 (1994)
4. Gao, B.: NDWI a normalized difference water index for remote sensing of vegetation liquid water from space. Remote Sens. Environ. **58**, 257–266 (1996)
5. Davis, S., Landgrebe, D., Phillips, T., Swain, P., et al.: Remote Sensing: The Quantitative Approach, p. 405. McGraw-Hill International Book Co., New York (1978). 1
6. Ouma, Y.O., Tetuko, J., Tateishi, R.: Analysis of co-occurrence and discrete wavelet transform textures for differentiation of forest and non-forest vegetation in very-high-resolution optical-sensor imagery. Int. J. Remote Sens. **29**, 3417–3456 (2008)
7. Reis, S., Taşdemir, K.: Identification of hazelnut fields using spectral and Gabor textural features. ISPRS J. Photogram. Remote Sens. **66**, 652–661 (2011)
8. Lowe, D.: Distinctive image features from scale-invariant keypoints. Int. J. Comput. Vis. **60**(2), 91–110 (2004)
9. Dalal, N., Triggs, B.: Histograms of oriented gradients for human detection. In: IEEE International Conference on Computer Vision and Pattern Recognition, pp. 886–893 (2005)
10. Hinton, G.E., Salakhutdinov, R.R.: Reducing the dimensionality of data with neural networks. Science **13**(5786), 504–507 (2006)
11. Chan, T.-H., Jia, K., Gao, S.H., et al.: PCANet: a simple deep learning baseline for image classification? (2014). arXiv preprint arXiv:1404.3606
12. Deng, J., Dong, W., Socher, R., et al.: Imagenet: a large-scale hierarchical image database. In: Proceedings of the IEEE Conference on Computer Vision and Pattern Recognition, Miami, FL, USA, pp. 248–255 (2009)
13. Le, Q., Ranzato, M., Monga, R., et al.: Building high level features using large scale unsupervised learning. In: International Conference on Machine Learning (2012)
14. Castelluccio, M., Poggi, G., Sansone, C., Verdoliva, L.: Land Use Classification in Remote Sensing Images by Convolutional Neural Networks. http://arXiv.org/abs/1508.00092. Accessed 12 Apr 2016
15. Bruzzone, L., Carlin, L.: A multilevel context-based system for classification of very high spatial resolution images. IEEE Trans. Geosci. Remote Sens. **44**(9), 2587–2600 (2006)
16. Shackelford, A.K., Davis, C.H.: A combined fuzzy pixel-based and object-based approach for classification of high-resolution multispectral data over urban areas. IEEE Trans. Geosci. Remote Sens. **41**(10), 2354–2363 (2003)
17. Bellens, R., Gautama, S., Martinez-Fonte, L., et al.: Improved classification of VHR images of urban areas using directional morphological profiles. IEEE Trans. Geosci. Remote Sens. **46**(10), 2803–2813 (2008)
18. Ojala, T., Pietikainen, M., Maenp, T.: Multiresolution gray-scale and rotation invariant texture classification with local binary patterns. IEEE Trans. Pattern Anal. Mach. Intell. **24**(7), 971–987 (2002)
19. Yang, Y., Newsam, S.: Bag-of-visual-words and spatial extensions for land-use classification. In: International Conference on Advances in Geographic Information Systems, pp. 270–279 (2010)
20. Lazebnik, S., Schmid, C., Ponce, J.: Beyond bags of features: spatial pyramid matching for recognizing natural scene categories. In: IEEE International Conference on Computer Vision and Pattern Recognition, pp. 2169–2178 (2006)

21. Jiang, Y., Yuan, J., Yu, G.: Randomized spatial partition for scene recognition. In: Fitzgibbon, A., Lazebnik, S., Perona, P., Sato, Y., Schmid, C. (eds.) ECCV 2012, Part II. LNCS, vol. 7573, pp. 730–743. Springer, Heidelberg (2012)

22. Chen, S., Tian, Y.: Pyramid of spatial relations for scene-level land use classification. IEEE Trans. Geosci. Remote Sens. **53**, 1947–1957 (2015)

23. Yang, Y., Newsam, S.: Spatial pyramid co-occurrence for image classification. In: IEEE International Conference on Computer Vision, pp. 1465–1472 (2011)

24. Coates, A., Ng, A.Y., Lee, H.: An analysis of single-layer networks in unsupervised feature learning. In: Proceedings of the International Conference on Artificial Intelligence and Statistics, Ft. Lauderdale, FL, USA, pp. 215–223 (2011)

25. Zhang, F., Du, B., Zhang, L.: Saliency-guided unsupervised feature learning for scene classification. IEEE Trans. Geosci. Remote Sens. **53**, 2175–2184 (2015)

26. Hu, F., Xia, G., Wang, Z., et al.: Unsupervised feature learning via spectral clustering of multidimensional patches for remotely sensed scene classification. IEEE J. Sel. Top. Appl. Earth Obs. Remote Sens. **8**, 2015–2030 (2015)

27. Li, H., Lin, Z., Shen, X., et al.: A convolutional neural network cascade for face detection. In: CVPR (2015)

28. Razavian, A.S., Azizpour, H., Sullivan, J., Carlsson, S.: CNN features off-the-shelf: an astounding baseline for recognition. In: Proceedings of the IEEE Conference on Computer Vision and Pattern Recognition Workshops, Columbus, OH, USA, pp. 512–519 (2014)

29. Gong, Y., Wang, L., Guo, R., Lazebnik, S.: Multi-scale orderless pooling of deep convolutional activation features. In: Fleet, D., Pajdla, T., Schiele, B., Tuytelaars, T. (eds.) ECCV 2014, Part VII. LNCS, vol. 8695, pp. 392–407. Springer, Heidelberg (2014)

30. Penatti, O.A., Nogueira, K., dos Santos, J.A.: Do deep features generalize from everyday objects to remote sensing and aerial scenes domains? In: Proceedings of the IEEE Conference on Computer Vision and Pattern Recognition Workshops, Boston, MA, USA, pp. 44–51 (2015)

Finding Top-k Places for Group Social Activities

Xiaosheng Feng[1(✉)], Nikos Armenatzoglou[2], Hao Xu[1], Xiang Zhao[1,3],
and Pan Hui[4]

[1] National University of Defense Technology, Changsha, China
[2] Pivotal Inc., San Francisco, USA
xiangzhao@nudt.edu.cn
[3] Collaborative Innovation Center of Geospatial Technology, Wuhan, China
[4] Hong Kong University of Science and Technology, Hong Kong, China

Abstract. Geo-social network applications utilize check-in information to suggest places for social activities. This paper focuses on recommending points of interest (POIs) to groups of users based on the current location of users and the popularity and suitability of the POIs from history. To address the problem, we propose a new type of query, namely, *group-based geo-social top-k places* (GkP) query, which takes spatial proximity and social fitness into consideration. This is among the first attempts, and we present the preliminary results. In particular, we investigate the problem formulation, especially the modeling of spatial proximity and social fitness. Two baseline algorithms, distance-driven and relevance-driven, respectively, are conceived. Initial empirical results confirm that GkP queries meet the needs of potential applications, and the proposed algorithms are sufficient to handle GkP queries.

1 Introduction

With the proliferation of mobile devices, geo-social networks are significantly widespread globally. Geo-social networks support social network functionality along with location-based services. On geo-social networks, users can make new friends, check-in to points of interest (POIs), interact with their friends, arrange social activities, etc. A typical commercial geo-social network, `Foursquare`, currently has more than 55 million of users and 7 billions of check-ins in total.

Motivated by the vast amount of available social and spatial data, recent research has focused on POI-based recommendations. By *offline* mining the historical check-in data, [2,6,13] investigated the recommendation of POIs. These approaches overlook the real-time nature of the problems that users are mobile, and have not taken the current locations of users into consideration. See this disadvantage, [4,5,10] proposed real-time recommendation systems. Nevertheless, they focus on suggesting POIs to single users, but not to groups of specified users. Moreover, all the aforementioned methods and known spatial queries, e.g., aggregate nearest neighbor (ANN) query [8], do not consider popularity and suitability of POIs to hosting an event for a group of users.

In this paper, we focus on recommending POIs to groups of users based on users' current locations, as well as the popularity and suitability of POIs.

© Springer International Publishing Switzerland 2016
A. Morishima et al. (Eds.): APWeb 2016 Workshops, LNCS 9865, pp. 191–203, 2016.
DOI: 10.1007/978-3-319-45835-9_17

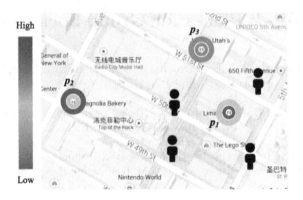

Fig. 1. Motivating example of GkP query (Color figure online)

Specifically, assume that a group of users/friends are seeking a place to meet-up. Ideally, the place should be relatively close to everyone (spatial proximity), and also frequently visited by groups of size similar to theirs (social fitness). Motivated by this real application scenario, we propose to study *group-based geo-social top-k places* query, namely, GkP query, where the ranking of a POI is a combination of factors from spatial proximity and social fitness.

Figure 1 depicts a vivid example of GkP query, where four friends are looking for a restaurant to get-together. The figure shows users' current locations, as well as three restaurants, i.e., p_1, p_2, and p_3. To show the popularity and suitability of the restaurants, we associate each place with a colored circle - from green to red, the visiting frequency grows from low to high. The outer circle denotes the total visiting frequency, while the inner circle denotes the frequency for groups of four users. If we are equally interested in spatial proximity and social fitness, p_3 is the best answer, as it is not far from users and it is the mostly visited by groups of four users. If we care more about spatial proximity, p_1 is the best, since it minimizes the total travel distance. Additionally, p_2 is not preferable, because it is far away and unsuitable for groups of four.

While spatial proximity is easy to express, modeling social fitness is a non-trivial task. First and foremost, data availability is a major concern, since we need to extract the visiting frequency of group users to POIs. This is an obscure task, since users may check-in at the same POI at different time of the same day, and friends may attend the same social event without prior arrangements. We overtake the issue by using the following approach: (1) retrieve data using the public APIs of existing mobile social network applications, where people can co-check-in at a place, e.g., group check-in of Facebook; and (2) utilize data mining techniques to infer events happened by groups of friends [11]. Besides, it is more challenging to decide which group sizes are relevant to the specified user groups. For instance, given a group size m, the social fitness of a place is determined not only by the visiting frequency of size-m groups, but also groups of sizes $m + 1$ and $m - 1$, or $m + 2$ and $m - 2$, etc. This is intuitive, as a popular restaurant for groups of four, can also be suitable for a group of three or five. We address this challenge by adapting ideas from document retrieval and constructing relevance vectors for POIs. To effectively deal with GkP queries, we present two *index-free* rudimentary solutions- one is distance-driven, and the other is relevance-driven, which greedily consider spatial proximity and social fitness, respectively. Preliminary experiment results confirm the usability of GkP query and solutions.

Contributions. In summary, we make the following contributions:

- We motivate and formulate the GkP query that considers both spatial proximity of users and social fitness of POIs.
- We propose two baseline algorithms, distance-driven and relevance-driven, respectively, for processing GkP queries.
- We conduct preliminary experimental study on real-life datasets, and report insight into the performance of the solutions.

Related Work. Check-in based recommendations arise with the emergence of Geo-social networks. [2,13] recommend POIs based on information such as past check-ins and preferences, etc. Utilizing geo-tagged images and check-ins, [6] recommends *areas of interest*. These methods overlook the real-time nature of the problems, where users' current locations are changing regularly.

Aggregate nearest neighbor query [8] was introduced to retrieve POIs with the smallest aggregate distance. TripRouter [5] investigated routes (order lists of POIs) recommendation based on users' spatial proximity and POIs' popularity, and later planned visiting time was incorporated [4]. Moreover, [10] defines the *off-trending score* of a POI to estimate how busy it is. These approaches do not consider the suitability of POIs to a specified group of users.

Efforts were dedicated on a reverse problem that finds groups of users to attend an event at a POI; for example, *circle of friend* query [7], *socio-spatial group* query [12], *geo-social skyline* query [3], etc. Recently, [1] presented a framework that segregates the social, geographical and query processing modules.

Organization. Section 2 formulates the GkP query, and the modeling of spatial proximity and social fitness are discussed in Sect. 3. Then, Sect. 4 presents the rudimentary solutions. Section 5 reports the preliminary experiment results, followed by conclusion and discussion on future work in Sect. 6.

2 Problem Statement

Let $P = \{p_1, p_2, \ldots, p_n\}$ be a set of POIs. Each $p \in P$ is a pair (l_p, r_p), where l_p denotes the location of p, and r_p represents the fitness (to be defined shortly) associated with p. Given a set of m query points $Q = \{q_1, q_2, \ldots, q_m\}$ that represents the m users' locations, and an integer k, a GkP query retrieves a ranked list of k POIs from P that have the highest scores according to

$$\mathsf{rank}(p, Q) = \alpha \cdot D(p, Q) + (1 - \alpha) \cdot R(p, Q), \qquad (1)$$

Equation (1) is a linear combination of a proximity score, computed by function $D : P \times Q \rightarrow [0, 1]$, and a fitness score, measured by function $R : P \times Q \rightarrow [0, 1]$. The scores are normalized across the dataset, and parameter $\alpha \in (0, 1)$ is specified by users implying their preferences. It is intuitive that the lower the score of a POI, the higher it is ranked (Fig. 2).

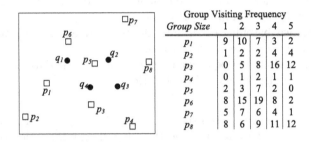

Fig. 2. Running example of GkP query

Example 1. *Figure 1 depicts the locations of 8 POIs $P = \{p_1, \ldots, p_8\}$, and 4 users. For each POI, the table besides shows the visiting frequencies of groups of various sizes (1–5 users). For example, the visiting frequency of p_1 by size-3 groups is 7. Assume in Table 1 are the values of $D(p, Q)$ and $R(p, Q)$, $\alpha = 0.5$, and $k = 3$. The GkP query returns p_5, p_3, and p_6 as the answers.*

Table 1. Ranks of POIs

p	$D(p,Q)$	$R(p,Q)$	rank	p	$D(p,Q)$	$R(p,Q)$	rank
p_1	0.346	0.358	0.352	p_5	0.306	0.180	0.243
p_2	0.251	0.559	0.405	p_6	0.307	0.325	0.316
p_3	0.227	0.261	0.244	p_7	0.307	0.449	0.378
p_4	0.276	0.458	0.367	p_8	0.272	0.410	0.341

3 Modeling Proximity and Fitness

While spatial proximity is straightforward, the modeling of social fitness becomes intriguing. We first discuss social fitness, followed by spatial proximity.

3.1 Social Fitness

We measure the fitness of a POI to Q, or size-m groups, utilizing *relevance*. Intuitively, the relevance of p to size-m groups, denoted as $r_p(m)$, can be computed by comparing (1) the visiting frequency of size-m groups at p with groups of other sizes; and (2) the visiting frequencies of all POIs for size-m groups. By collecting the relevance of p to all sizes of groups, we have a set of relevance $\{r_p(1), \ldots, r_p(m), \ldots, r_p(m_{\max})\}$, where $1 \leq m \leq m_{\max}$, and $m_{\max}$ is the largest group size in question.

This formulation recalls the document retrieval problem, where we try to score documents based on the similarity of the query term to the keywords of the documents. Analogously in our setting, we can regard the given group size m as the query term, and each relevance vector as a document with $r_p(m)$ as its keywords. Based on this observation, we utilize the *term weight evaluation* method [9] used in language model to define relevance. Formally, we present the following definition.

Definition 1 (Relevance Vector). *The relevance vector associated with p is $r_p = \{r_p(1), \ldots, r_p(m), \ldots, r_p(m_{\max})\}$, where $1 \leq m \leq m_{\max}$, $m_{\max}$ is the largest group size, and*

$$r_p(m) = (1 - \lambda) \cdot \frac{f_p(m)}{\sum_{i=1}^{m_{\max}} f_p(i)} + \lambda \cdot \frac{f(m)}{\sum_{i=1}^{m_{\max}} f(i)}, \qquad (2)$$

where $f_p(m)$ (resp. $f(m)$) is the visiting frequency of size-m groups to p (resp. all POIs), the meanings of the summations are similarly understood thereby, and $\lambda \in (0,1)$ is a smoothing parameter.

The two terms in Eq. (2) imply the *maximum likelihood estimate* of size-m groups for p and all POIs, respectively. Immediate is that $r_p(m)$ can also be obtained by using TF/IDF method in document retrieval. Due to the interest of space, we omit this method in this paper.

Example 2. *Further to Example 1, the group visiting frequency of 8 POIs are listed. Take the size-1 group at p_1 as an example. We have $f_{p_1}(1) = 9$, $\sum_{i=1}^{5} f_{p_1}(i) = 31$, and $f(1) = 33$, $\sum_{i=1}^{5} f(i) = 225$. As $\lambda = 0.5$, we can calculate $r_{p_1}(1) = (1 - 0.5) \times \frac{9}{31} + 0.5 \times \frac{33}{225} = 0.218$.*

Relevance measure only the correspondence between p and individual group sizes. As mentioned before, the social fitness to Q is also influenced by the relevance of other groups with size close to m. To reflect this observation in the formulation of social fitness, we present a formula below, which is based on the intuition that the relevance of groups with sizes close to m plays a greater role in the overall social fitness. In other words, the contribution of relevance of other groups gradually decreases with the absolute size difference.

Definition 2 (Synthetic Relevance). *The synthetic relevance of a POI p regarding group size m, denoted as $sr_p(m)$, is defined as*

$$sr_p(m) = \frac{1}{3} \cdot \sum_{i=1}^{m_{\max}} \frac{r_p[i]}{(|m - i| + 1)^2}. \tag{3}$$

Example 3. *Further to Example 2, we can now compute the synthetic relevance of every POI, as shown in Table 2. Then, take p_1 as an example, and assume $R_{\min}$ is 0.1. Given a query Q of size 4, the synthetic relevance of p_1 equals $R(p_1, 4) = \frac{1}{3} \cdot (\frac{0.218}{(|4-1|+1)^2} + \frac{0.270}{(|4-2|+1)^2} + \frac{0.246}{(|4-3|+1)^2} + \frac{0.157}{(|4-4|+1)^2} + \frac{0.108}{(|4-5|+1)^2}) = 0.096.$*

Table 2. Synthetic relevance of POIs

Size	p_1	p_2	p_3	p_4	p_5	p_6	p_7	p_8
1	0.328	0.207	0.169	0.183	0.256	0.264	0.293	0.252
2	0.411	0.310	0.294	0.345	0.372	0.396	0.400	0.310
3	0.389	0.360	0.382	0.465	0.507	0.453	0.409	0.372
4	0.289	0.400	0.441	0.364	0.328	0.326	0.326	0.367
5	0.200	0.335	0.337	0.281	0.183	0.198	0.199	0.306

Denote $\frac{r_p[i]}{(|m-i|+1)^2}$ as $\sigma(m)$. It can be inferred that from 1 to m, $\sigma(m)$ monotonically increases with m, and then decreases from $m+1$ to $m_{\max}$. This is a interesting characteristic that fits our assumption nicely. Moreover, the values of Eq. (3) is limited within [0,1). Next, we proceed to define social fitness.

Definition 3 (Social Fitness). *The social fitness p to Q, denoted as $R(p, Q)$, is defined as*

$$R(p, Q) = \frac{R_{\min}}{\Gamma(sr_p(m))}, \tag{4}$$

where the value is normalized by a constant $R_{\min}$ such that

$$\Gamma(sr_p(m)) = \begin{cases} sr_p(m), & sr_p(m) > R_{\min}; \\ R_{\min}, & otherwise. \end{cases}$$

In implementation, we choose a minimum positive synthetic relevance as $R_{\min}$. Subsequently, the lower the social fitness, the better p towards Q. Note that since relevance can be derived without queries, we pre-compute them for POIs in our implementation.

3.2   Spatial Proximity

To measure the spatial proximity of a POI to a set of query locations, we adopt the aggregate distance [8]. Given a monotonically increasing function f, the aggregate distance between p and Q is denoted as $ad(p, Q) = f(d(p, q_1), \ldots, d(p, q_m))$, where $d(p, q_i)$ denotes the Euclidean distance between p and q.

Under different application scenarios, function f can be *sum*, *max*, or *min*. Without loss of generality, we choose *sum* for exposition, i.e., $f = \sum_{i=0}^{m} d(p, q_i)$, since *sum* is more widely used in real-life applications. Nonetheless, the proposed solutions can be easily extended to support *min* and *max* functions.

Definition 4 (Spatial Proximity). *The spatial proximity of a POI p to Q, denoted by $D(p, Q)$, is defined as $D(p, Q) = \frac{ad(p,Q)}{|Q| \cdot d_{\max}}$, where $d_{\max}$ is a constant factor used for normalization, e.g., the maximum Euclidean distance between any two points.*

For spatial proximity, the smaller the aggregate distance between p and Q, the lower the score of p, and hence, the higher p is ranked.

4   Rudimentary Solutions

This section presents two baseline solutions from the perspectives of distance and relevance, respectively.

4.1   Distance-Driven Solution

The distance-driven solution (DDS) considers spatial proximity first to derive the answers. In general, it maintains a size-k priority queue $\mathcal{P}$, and uses the ranking score in Eq. (1) as the priority[1]. Then, it retrieves POIs of minimum spatial proximity $D(p, Q)$ by iterations, while keeping the lower bound of social fitness $\underline{R}(p, Q)$ for unseen POIs for early-stopping.

The pseudocode of DDS is encapsulated in Algorithm 1. It takes as input a set of query locations Q, a set of POIs and an integer k, and outputs a ranked list $\mathcal{P}$ of size k. In initialization, it sets up a priority queues $\mathcal{P}$ of capacity k for keeping the top-k results and a list L for all POIs in P sorted according to $R(p, Q)$ (Lines 1 and 2). Recall that $ad(p, Q)$ in $D(p, Q)$ is a monotonically increasing function. We employ an existing technique to select a POI being the aggregate nearest neighbor [8], in order to find the POI with the minimum $D(p, Q)$ each time. For each p returned, we first remove it from L (Line 4). Then, if $\mathcal{P}$ is not filled up, we direct enqueue p; otherwise, we need to determine if it is necessary to compute further (Lines 5–9). In particular, it uses the ranking score of the k-th POI in $\mathcal{P}$ as threshold θ, and only POIs with ranking score lower than θ are enqueued. If higher than θ, the algorithm terminates, as all remanning POIs have higher ranking scores than those in $\mathcal{P}$.

---

[1] We implemented priority queues with min heaps such that the smaller the priority of an element, the higher it is ranked.

Algorithm 1: DistanceDrivenSolution(Q, P, k)

Input   : Q is a set of locations; P is a set of POIs; k is an integer.
Output : $\mathcal{P}$ are k descendently ranked POIs.
1 initialize a priority queue $\mathcal{P}$ of capacity k;
2 construct a sorted list L according to $R(p, Q)$;
3 **foreach** POI p returned by ANN query **do**
4   remove p from L;
5   **if** $\mathcal{P}.length() < k$ **then** enqueue p into $\mathcal{P}$;
6   **else**
7          $\theta \leftarrow$ retrieve the k-th element in $\mathcal{P}$, $s \leftarrow \alpha \cdot D(p, Q) + (1 - \alpha) \cdot R(p, Q)$;
8   **if** $s > \theta$ **then** **return** $\mathcal{P}$;
9   **else** enqueue p into $\mathcal{P}$;

The cost for constructing L is $O(|P| \log |P|)$. Assume the cost of each ANN query ρ. In the worst case the overall complexity is $O(\rho |P| \log |P|)$.

Example 4. *Further to Example 3, the searching process of DDS for top-3 results is shown in Table 3. In particular in step-5, the ranking score of current p equals 0.331, which is higher than $\theta = 0.316$, and thus, the search terminates.*

Table 3. Searching states of DDS

Step	p	$D(p, Q)$	$R(p, Q)$	θ	$\mathcal{P}$
1	p_5	0.180	0.227	$+\infty$	p_5
2	p_3	0.261	0.227	$+\infty$	p_5, p_3
3	p_6	0.325	0.251	$+\infty$	p_5, p_3, p_6
4	p_1	0.358	0.251	0.316	p_5, p_3, p_6
5	p_8	0.410	0.251	0.316	p_5, p_3, p_6

4.2   Relevance-Driven Solution

In contrast to DDS, relevance-driven solution (RDS) maintains k POIs with the current lowest ranking score in a priority queue $\mathcal{P}$. A sorted list of POIs is prepared in ascending order of their social fitness. By doing this, RDS incrementally visits POIs with minimum $R(p, Q)$ in the order of the list.

The major steps of RDS is described in Algorithm 2, whose input and output are identical to DDS. Specifically, it first initializes a priority queue $\mathcal{P}$ of capacity k for keeping the top-k results; similarly, we sort all POIs according to its social fitness in L (Lines 1–2). For each new POI p in L, RDS first removes it from L to avoid duplicate examination. Then, if the $\mathcal{P}$ is not filled up yet, p is directed

---

Algorithm 2: RelevanceDrivenSolution(Q, P, k)

Input   : Q is a set of locations; P is a set of POIs; k is an integer.
Output : $\mathcal{P}$ are k descendently ranked POIs.
1 initialize a priority queue $\mathcal{P}$ of capacity k;
2 construct a sorted list L according to $R(p, Q)$;
3 **while** $L \neq \emptyset$ **do**
4 | $p \leftarrow$ get the first POI and remove it from L;
5 | **if** $\mathcal{P}.length() < k$ **then** enqueue p into $\mathcal{P}$;
6 | **else**
7 | | $p' \leftarrow$ retrieve the k-th element in $\mathcal{P}$;
8 | | **if** $R(p, Q) > R(p', Q)$ **then return** $\mathcal{P}$;
9 | |_ **else** enqueue p into $\mathcal{P}$;

---

enqueued (Line 5). In other case, we already have k POIs, and hence, the last one is used for early-stopping. That is, the algorithm compares $R(p, Q)$ with the social fitness of the k-th POI in $\mathcal{P}$. If the former is larger, it implies that all the POIs remained in L have a higher ranking score than those in $\mathcal{P}$, and thus, the algorithm terminates (Line 8). Otherwise, p is enqueued in the $\mathcal{P}$ (Line 9).

The cost for constructing L is $O(|P| \log |P|)$, and in the worst case we need to enqueue all POIs into $\mathcal{P}$ once. Therefore, the overall complexity is $O(|P| \log |P|)$.

Example 5. *Further to Example 3, the searching process of RDS for top-3 results is listed in Table 4. Although $\mathcal{P}$ no longer changes after step-6, it has to continue checking the remaining POIs till $R(p, Q)$ is larger than that of the head of L.*

Table 4. Searching states of RDS

Step	p	$R(p, Q)$	$R_{\min}$	$\mathcal{P}$	Step	p	$R(p, Q)$	$R_{\min}$	$\mathcal{P}$
1	p_3	0.227	$+\infty$	p_3	5	p_5	0.306	0.367	p_5, p_3, p_8
2	p_2	0.251	$+\infty$	p_3, p_2	6	p_6	0.307	0.341	p_5, p_3, p_6
3	p_8	0.272	$+\infty$	p_3, p_8, p_2	7	p_7	0.307	0.316	p_5, p_3, p_6
4	p_4	0.276	0.405	p_3, p_8, p_4	8	p_1	0.346	0.316	p_5, p_3, p_6

5   Empirical Studies

We implemented the two algorithms DDS and RDS using C++ with STL support, and all algorithms were ran in main memory where data also resided. Algorithms were run on a PC with Intel i5 2.93 GHz CPU, 3 GB memory, and

Windows XP. Queries with same parameters were run for 100 times, the average values are reported. We compare *response time* and *node hitting times*. Note that DDS uses the output of ANN queries [8] as candidates, in which case node hitting times means the number of visited candidates. For RDS, it is the number of POIs visited by the algorithm.

Datasets. Two typical geo-social network datasets were involved: (1) BrightKite[2](B) contains 4,747,287 check-in records from March, 2008 to October, 2010, each comprising user ID, check-in time, and location ID, as well as social ties among users; and (2) Gowalla[3](G) contains similar types of information.

In order to obtain group visit information, we use an existing algorithm [11] to find *group events* of each POI using check-in information. Group visit events extracted from two datasets are depicted in Table 5. The two datasets showcase different characteristics after extracting the group events. We chose the region covering most of United States, from $-130°$ to $-74°$ in the longitude and from $23°$ to $54°$ in the latitude.

Table 5. Statistics of group events

Group size	BrightKite	Gowalla	Group size	BrightKite	Gowalla
1	2289100	2635821	11	8	90
2	84982	167198	12	2	65
3	11529	11059	13	4	40
4	2771	2950	14	2	42
5	834	1144	15	5	32
6	297	608	16	2	37
7	105	347	17	1	18
8	58	221	18	2	27
9	27	143	19	1	18
10	13	95	20	0	14

Given a query Q, the aggregate distance of all query points in Q influences the spatial proximity to POIs. Therefore, we randomly generated queries in region sizes of 500^2, $1,000^2$, $1,500^2$, $2,000^2$, and $2,500^2$, respectively. Concerning real-life applications, we set $|Q|$ from 4 to 20. Table 6 shows the parameter settings, and the default parameters are in bold.

Effect of k. Figures 3(a) and (b) show the performance results of changing k from 10 to 50. Since Gowalla contains more POIs than BrightKite, the algorithms

[2] http://snap.stanford.edu/data/loc-brightkite.html.
[3] http://snap.stanford.edu/data/loc-gowalla.html.

Table 6. Parameter settings

Parameter	Range
k	**10**, 20, 30, 40, 50
α	**0.1**, 0.3, 0.5, 0.7, 0.9
$|Q|$	**4**, 8, 12, 16, 20
$|P|$	**400K**, 800K, 1200K, 1600K, 2000K
Region size	**500^2**, 1000^2, 1500^2, 2000^2, 2500^2

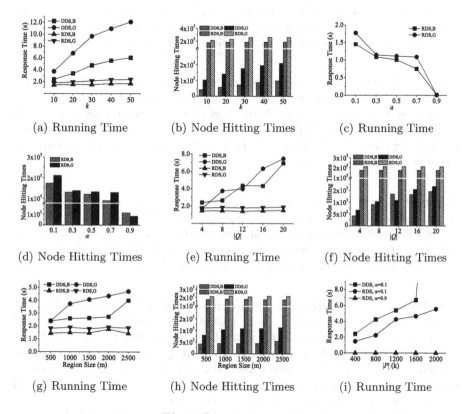

(a) Running Time   (b) Node Hitting Times   (c) Running Time

(d) Node Hitting Times   (e) Running Time   (f) Node Hitting Times

(g) Running Time   (h) Node Hitting Times   (i) Running Time

Fig. 3. Experiment results

run faster on BrightKite than Gowalla, and the number of node hit is also less on Gowalla. Specifically, RDS retrieves POIs by comparing POIs with the current k-th result, where the POIs are ordered by social fitness. If the proportion of spatial proximity is much smaller than suitability score, the algorithm is easier to be terminated according to Algorithm 2. The running time of DDS is higher than RDS, because DDS needs more time to retrieve aggregate nearest neighbors iteratively. It is also noted that, while the running time of DDS is higher than RDS, DDS hits less nodes than RDS, since ANN queries cost a lot of time.

Effect of α. As mentioned above, RDS is sensitive to the proportion of social fitness as per Eq. (1), this set of experiments further demonstrate our argument. As shown in Fig. 3(c), when α is small, spatial proximity plays an important role in ranking value, RDS is inefficient in query processing. In particular, the algorithm needs to visit all POIs in the dataset (cf. Fig. 3(d)), and thus, takes more time. Reversely, with α increases, social fitness is more important than spatial proximity, and thus, becomes a leading factor to ranking score. Since DDS is driven by distance, it is also sensitive to α. The smaller α, the faster DDS. In our experiment, we only got the results for DDS when $\alpha=0.1$, where the response time is 2402.9 ms on BrightKite, 3735.0 ms on Gowalla; and node hitting times is 412.6 on BrightKite, 1020 on Gowalla, respectively. The results for higher α are more than 2 h, and are unacceptable in real-life applications.

Effect of Group Size. The group size denotes the number of query points, which influences the aggregate distances and the dimensions that take effects in relevance vectors. However, it has little effect on RDS. The running time of RDS is stably with $|Q|$ in Figs. 3(e) and (f). On the other hand, different group sizes affect the efficiency of ANN queries. That is, the more users in the group, the longer time it takes to finish.

Effect of Group Region. Group region determines the dispersity of query points. Figures 3(g) and (h) read that response time of DDS increases with region size, while for RDS it remains stable. Similar to group size $|Q|$, group region influences the aggregate distance from query Q to POIs. As a consequence, group region affects DDS but having not impact on RDS.

Scalability. For this experiment, we extended BrightKite as follows. For each POI, we randomly generated 2, 3, 4 and 5 locations around it, and hence, we had five datasets of increasing sizes, i.e. with about 400k, 800k, 1,200k, 1,600k and 2,000k POIs, respectively. For each new POI, we generated the group visiting frequency in each group size under normal distribution. As shown in Table 5, both datasets have few group visit events when group size is larger than 20, and thus, we chose 20 as the length of relevance vectors.

Figure 3(i) depicts the results of response time on different datasets. Let $\alpha = 0.1$ and 0.9, and we fix $|Q| = 4$. As discussed above, DDS is sensitive to α, and we could not get the exact results in reasonable time. Thus, we omit the case when $\alpha = 0.9$. Moreover, when $|P| = 2,000k$, the running time of DDS reaches 37.7 s, which is not depicted in Fig. 3(i) either to avoid under-representation of other results. While both algorithms scales linearly with $|Q|$, they heavily rely on proper settings of α. This fact needs to be exploited when designing advanced algorithms for handling GkP queries on massive datasets.

6 Conclusion

In this paper, we have formulated the GkP query problem, and appropriately modeled the two aspects - social fitness and spatial proximity. Additionally, we introduced two baseline solutions to handle GkP queries, and conducted preliminary experimental studies. The empirical evaluation demonstrates that the proposed algorithms are effective and sufficient on real-life data. Currently, the rudimentary algorithms are index-free, and hence, we are conceiving a tailored index to boost the performance of GkP query processing.

Acknowledgement. This work was in part supported by NSFC Nos. 61402494 and 61402498, NSF of Hunan No. 2015JJ4009.

References

1. Armenatzoglou, N., Papadopoulos, S., Papadias, D.: A general framework for geo-social query processing. PVLDB **6**(10), 913–924 (2013)
2. Berjani, B., Strufe, T.: A recommendation system for spots in location-based online social networks. In: SNS, p. 4 (2011)
3. Emrich, T., Franzke, M., Mamoulis, N., Renz, M., Züfle, A.: Geo-social skyline queries. In: Bhowmick, S.S., Dyreson, C.E., Jensen, C.S., Lee, M.L., Muliantara, A., Thalheim, B. (eds.) DASFAA 2014, Part II. LNCS, vol. 8422, pp. 77–91. Springer, Heidelberg (2014)
4. Hsieh, H., Li, C.: Mining and planning time-aware routes from check-in data. In: CIKM, pp. 481–490 (2014)
5. Hsieh, H.-P., Li, C.-T., Lin, S.-D.: Exploiting large-scale check-in data to recommend time-sensitive routes. In: UrbComp, pp. 55–62 (2012)
6. Liu, J., Huang, Z., Chen, L., Shen, H.T., Yan, Z.: Discovering areas of interest with geo-tagged images and check-ins. In: MM, pp. 589–598 (2012)
7. Liu, W., Sun, W., Chen, C., Huang, Y., Jing, Y., Chen, K.: Circle of friend query in geo-social networks. In: Lee, S., Peng, Z., Zhou, X., Moon, Y.-S., Unland, R., Yoo, J. (eds.) DASFAA 2012, Part II. LNCS, vol. 7239, pp. 126–137. Springer, Heidelberg (2012)
8. Papadias, D., Tao, Y., Mouratidis, K., Hui, C.K.: Aggregate nearest neighbor queries in spatial databases. ACM Trans. Database Syst. **30**(2), 529–576 (2005)
9. Ponte, J.M., Croft, W.B.: A language modeling approach to information retrieval. In: SIGIR, pp. 275–281 (1998)
10. Sklar, M., Shaw, B., Hogue, A.: Recommending interesting events in real-time with foursquare check-ins. In: RecSys, pp. 311–312 (2012)
11. Wei, L.-Y, Yeh, M.-Y., Lin, G., Chan, Y.H., Lai, W.J.: Discovering point-of-interest signatures based on group features from geo-social networking data. In: TAAI, pp. 182–187 (2013)
12. Yang, D., Shen, C., Lee, W., Chen, M.: On socio-spatial group query for location-based social networks. In: KDD, pp. 949–957 (2012)
13. Ying, J.J., Kuo, W., Tseng, V.S., Lu, E.H.: Mining user check-in behavior with a random walk for urban point-of-interest recommendations. ACM TIST **5**(3), 40:1–40:26 (2014)

Temporal Spatial-Keyword Search
on Databases Using SQL

Jingru Wang, Jiajia Hou, Feiran Huang, Wei Lu[✉], and Xiaoyong Du

DEKE, MOE and School of Information,
Renmin University of China, Beijing 100872, China
{wangjru,houjiajia,huangfeiran,lu-wei,
duyong}@ruc.edu.cn

Abstract. Massive amount of textual content is associated with location and time tags, generated on webs related to restaurant, group-buying or social networking services. Often, users tend to retrieve up-to-date information with location and text proximity to some specified descriptions. To accelerate the search process, the state-of-the-art methods resort to design new index structures and probing algorithms. Nevertheless, efficient solutions fully supported by existing RDBMS still remain an open problem. To address this problem practically, in this paper, we propose TSKSQL, a solution that processes temporal spatial-keyword similarity search using SQL statements only. The novelty and advantages of TSKSQL are listed below. (1) We design a novel signature generation scheme that is able to properly capture texture, locational and temporal information properly. We index objects based on their generated signatures using a single B^+-Tree with the ability to process similarity queries by simply probing the B^+-Tree. (2) We propose various optimization techniques based on RDBMS so that both CPU and I/O costs can be reduced significantly. (3) We deploy TSKSQL over a real RDBMS, PostgreSQL. We conduct extensive experiments and the results show that TSKSQL demonstrates a good efficiency and stability.

1 Introduction

With the growing advances of positioning technologies like GPS, tracking the location of mobile objects to push Location-based Services (LBS) has been applicable [1]. Combined with such technologies, textual objects are conveniently associated with spatial and temporal tags, which are generated on webs such as tweets, news and group-buying every day. Particularly, these location tags consist of geographical and keyword terms, directly supported by the attributes or highly structured map-based geometric data. Recently, lots of commercial interests and the user preferences emerge in location based (LB) information related to, for example, businesses and entertainment centers, accommodation and public services. Investigated in a lot of the Excite search engine, it is discovered about one fifth of all queries were geographical [2]. These query requests contribute to a primitive operation in similarity search, based on a large variety of complex databases related to keywords and spatial locations. For example, Flickr or other companies offer API, providing the LB sharing series, which

© Springer International Publishing Switzerland 2016
A. Morishima et al. (Eds.): APWeb 2016 Workshops, LNCS 9865, pp. 204–216, 2016.
DOI: 10.1007/978-3-319-45835-9_18

helps users to search for photos or other objects by typical keywords and a specified spatial and time range. The mass of objects related to multi-source description information aggravate the complex for queries and analysis.

Textual, geographic and temporal query techniques are well researched independently. For the spatial index the existing indices can be categorized in R-tree based indices, grid based indices and space filling curve based indices. For text index, these indices include inverted file based and signature file based indices. In addition, hybrid index structures [3] are generated by tightly combination of a spatial and a text index. The papers that present the existing geo-textual indices often report on experimental studies that suggest that the proposed indices are competitive with baseline indices. While the state of affairs makes it fail to index complex objects with more information such as time tags. The main challenge lies in the combination of textual and spatial-temporal constraints, i.e., finding restaurant that contains query terms *coffee*, *pizza*, and are close to the intended location in some time intervals. For example, Fig. 1 (a) shows us the objects belonging to R with time and text labels. One pivot is selected with the distances calculated respect to the other objects. Via the confined threshold, the nearest objects will generate a collection as a candidate set as shown in Fig. 1(b).

(a)

objects	labels	time
$o_1(1, 2)$	city, color, tourism, skyline	8:00
$o_2(2, 1)$	travel, wallpaper	18:00
...	...	...
$o_n(3, 3)$	holiday, New York	...
...	...	...
$p(2.5, 2.5)$	color, wallpaper, America	3:00

(b)

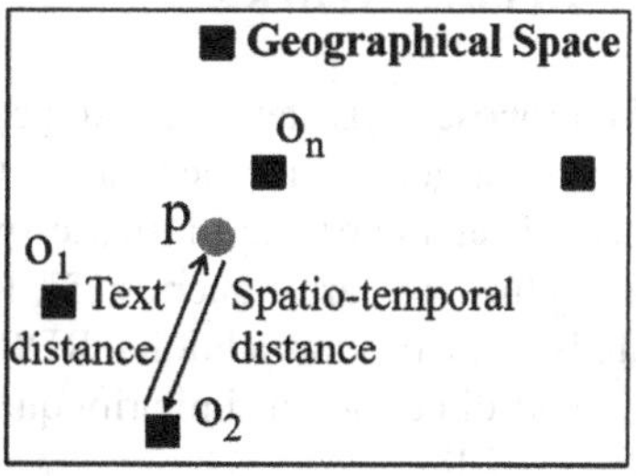

Fig. 1. (a) The objects belonging to the database with text, location and time tags. (b) The objects map in the geographical space with multi-dimensional distances.

In this paper, we propose Temporal Spatial-Keyword SQL (TSK-SQL), a new solution for similarity search in metric spaces utilizing SQL in advantage of fully support by existing RDBMS. Here we use the similarity function as UDFs, via which users can make easy SELECT-FROM-WHERE (SFW) enquiries. We develop a B + -tree based index structure to proceed the similarity queries supported widely and efficiently by RDBMS. As we can see, TSK-SQL can proceed similarity queries using the conventional database techniques only, which makes it overcome the limitations of existing indexing methods and can support multiple types of similarity queries. To process the TSK-SQL queries efficiently, we provide a signature generation scheme, considering the combination of the location, text and time similarity. Comparing the index probing method for location, temporal and text similarity separately, the performances such as IO cost and query efficiency will be enhanced. Our contributions can be summarized as the follows points:

(1) TSK-SQL is a universal framework which enables the objects with multiple tags
     such as, geographical, textual even time, can be indexed in the metric spaces
     based on B^+-tree and process similarity queries based on index scan.
(2) The TSK-SQL is deployed on top of PostgreSQL and processed based on
     extensive experiments on various real datasets, which verify the higher efficiency
     compared with the sequential scan over all datasets.
(3) Blending the temporal, location and text similarity will benefit the IO cost and
     efficiency for processing querying.

The organization of the paper is shown as follows. Section 2 shows the related
works for reviewing the approaches to querying temporal spatial-keywords. Section 3
gives the definitions for TSK-SQL including database setting, problem definition and
similarity search definition. Section 4 presents the index building method including the
signature generation and the B^+-tree building process. Section 5 provides querying
process with detailed SQL statements shown. Section 6 we conduct the experiments
and compare the experimental data based on the different databases. Section 7 comes to
a summary for the TSKT-SQL method and the potential improvements.

2 Related Work

We propose SQL statements to process the fusion of location, time and text similarity
queries in general metric spaces. Our work is related to the works on metric access
methods and querying in metric-space based on the existing RDBMS [4], such as the
perceptual similarity queries [5], RDBMS similarity-awareness building [6] and possibilistic queries in traditional RDBMS [7]. Besides, the index building and the mixture
of multi-dimensional similarity queries get relation to the works such as ST-SJOIN and
RSTkNN [8].

Over decades, solutions focus on building new indexing techniques as native
engines to get better efficiency. Some optimizing applications based on their cost
models are achieved, such as VP-tree and its variants [9]. Considering restricted
Euclidean spaces, solutions based on *Tries* and *inverted indexes* [10] have been proposed using the edit distance in *text* spaces. Unlike these solutions, the SQL-based
Solutions [11] are alternative ones with some appealing advantages. Recently, iDis-
tance [12] provides an efficient method for similarity queries in multiple Euclidean
spaces based on B^+-tree. In spatial databases based on existing RDMBS, the generalized search tree (GiST) building on the R-tree [13] and its variants will provide a
height-balanced search tree for users. Based on SQL statements, GiST index can
provide the similarity queries in the spatial (Euclidean) spaces. For text spaces, the
SQL statements can be employed to answer the similarity queries. However, failing to
conduct a query in metric spaces, the application of these works is restricted in text
spaces which cannot be mapped into an arbitrary metric space. Our work contributes to
answering the similarity queries in metric spaces for both spatial and textual queries.

To further accelerate the query processing, the fusion of multi-dimensional queries
[14] is utilized which provides the fusion parameters adjusting the importance of
spatio-temporal proximity factor and the textual similarity factor. And this parameter is
also a user-defined parameter which can adjust the query time.

3 TSK-SQL

3.1 Problem Definition

In this section, we give the problem definition. It is assumed that each geo-temporal-textual object associated with a text description, time tag and location information expressed by the attribute (latitude, longitude).

Dataset Setting: Let D be the geo-temporal-textual dataset. Each object $o \in D$ is defined as <o.key, o.loc, o.time>, where o.key represents the keyword descriptions; o. loc is the geographical location information consisting of longitude and latitude; o.time is the time information.

    The TSK-SQL is conducted as follows. Given dataset named p and a query object q, the similarity metric for p and q is represented by the multi-dimensional distances. TSK-SQL searches for similar objects judging by spatial, textual and time distance no larger than the user-defined thresholds.

Problem Definition: Given two objects o_1 and o_2 belonging to spatial-temporal textual dataset D, $Sim(o_1, o_2)$ represents the comprehensive distance for objects o_1 and o_2 in metric spaces. Although D includes multiple dimensional terms, the spatial, textual and time similarity can be mapped and combined in a metric space.

$$Sim(o_1, o_2) = \alpha_1 SimSpatial(o_1, o_2) + \alpha_2 SimTextual(o_1, o_2) \ldots + \alpha_N SimN(o_1, o_2)$$
$$+ (1 - \alpha_1 - \alpha_2 - \ldots - \alpha_N) SimTemporal(o_1, o_2) \tag{1}$$

$$SimSpatial(o_1, o_2) = \frac{\sqrt{(o_1.x - o_2.x)^2 + (o_1.y - o_2.y)^2}}{Smax} \tag{2}$$

$$SimTextual(o_1, o_2) = \frac{Levenshtein(o_1.i, \quad o_2.i)}{Kmax} \tag{3}$$

$$SimTemporal(o_1, o_2) = \frac{|o_1.t - o_2.t|}{Tmax} \tag{4}$$

    In Eq. (1), the similarity metric, spatial-textual-time similarity, is obtained. The parameters $\alpha_1, \alpha_2, \ldots, \alpha_N \in [0,1]$ and $\alpha_1 + \alpha_2 + \ldots + \alpha_N < 1$, which are used to adjust the importance of spatial, textual and time similarity. In addition, the parameter α_1, α_2 and α_N can be adjusted by users. SimN in Eq. 1 represents the extensively dimensional similarity metric. In metric space, the rules for Sim are shown as follows:(a) $Sim(o_1, o_2) > 0$ (non-negative); (b) when $o_1 = o_2$, $Sim(o_1, o_2) = 0$ (c) $Sim(o_1, o_2) = Sim(o_2, o_1)$ (symmetry); (d) $Sim(o_1, o_2) \leq Sim(o_1, o_3) + Sim(o_2, o_3)$ (triangle inequality).

    As shown in Eq. (2), we choose the Euclidean distance to measure the similarity of location of two objects, $\sqrt{(o_1.x - o_2.x)^2 + (o_1.y - o_2.y)^2}$. S_{max} is the maximal distance of pairs of arbitrary distinct objects in D. Using S_{max}, the spatial can be normalized into a range [0, 1]. Textual similarly shown in Eq. (3), the textual description

SimTextual(o_1, o_2) can be normalized. Levenshtein$(o_{1.i}, o_{2.i})$ is the edit distance of two textual descriptions, which is widely used in textual similarity computing. *Kmax* is the maximal textual distance of pairs of distinct objects in D for normalization. Similarly, time similarity is computed by the time difference normalized by T_{max} shown in Eq. (4).

Similarity Search Definition: Given a query object q, a data set D, and threshold θ. The spatial keyword similarity search is identified by the distance of objects in D relative to q in a range $(0, \theta]$.

For Sim(o_1, o_2), rules (a), (b) and (c) are clearly met. In addition, the spatial, temporal and textual distance in metric space can satisfy the triangle inequality respectively. For the liner superposition of them, it still satisfies the triangle inequality in the metric space. As shown in Fig. 2, combining the pruning rule and building index, distinct candidate sets will be generated with size diminished significantly.

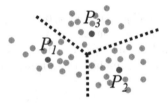

Fig. 2. Pivots based partitioning in the whole dataset.

4   Index Building

In our work, query process based on SQL includes index building process and index probing process. The index building consists of pivot selection, mapping the database, signature generation and B$^+$-tree building. For users SQL requests, the terminals will probe the index based on the UDFs including α_1, α_2 and threshold etc. The whole process is conducted by mere SQL statements in STW style, which really improves the efficiency and user experience.

4.1   Index Building

One universal approach for temporal spatial keyword query is sequential scan. However, the sequential scan is adapted to the small database, with time cost increased with the size of database. Here we use it as an evolution method instead of querying method. In existing RDBMS, the generalized search tree (known as GiST) can be build on the R-tree and its variants. However, R-tree based index is limited to low dimensional query not applicable in our case. To take advantage in dynamic insertion and deletion in SQL, the B$^+$-tree are employed in our experiments.

How to index the multi-dimensional objects is still a problem, in which each dimension's data type differ from others. To answer the TSK query efficiently, we propose an effective signature generation scheme combined with textual, spatial and temporal terms in different data spaces. UDFs include the importance factors adjusted by users.

Mapping Column Generation: Based on pivot selected, we utilize the mapping scheme to map the multi-dimensional space to a metric space. In this means, we generate a new column I in a storage type <Pid, Sim(o, p)>. Pid identifies the pivots we select randomly in the database. Sim(o, p) includes the any object o and a pivot p, which can be calculated by Eqs. (1)–(4). Then we can map the multiple dimensional information into one dimensional metric space for D.

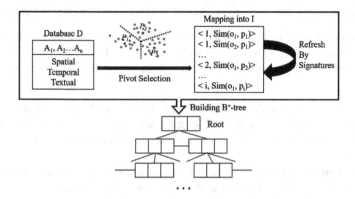

Fig. 3. The B^+-tree building process.

Signature Generation Scheme: To accelerate querying process, the signatures should be generated. Signatures should be pair-wise comparable in separated intervals labeled by the pivot based partition. These signatures are easily used for pruning and partitioning the database. Generally, an analytical expression for signatures is shown as,

$$V(r) = i * a + |r, p_i| \qquad (5)$$

where a is a large value to make V(r) distinct by i. However, Eq. (5) put a big obstacle in finding a proper a. For a universal way, we define a new piecewise function for Eq. (5). Utilizing the mapping scheme, the multi-dimensional spaces mapped to a single dimensional space. Based on the mapping principle, the pivot ID and the distance to pivot for any object are selected as the signatures. Given the signatures <i, Sim_i> and <j, Sim_j>, where i is labeled by the pivot and Sim is obtained by Eq. (1). The comparable difference for <i, Sim_i> and <j, Sim_j> is defined as diff <i, j>.

$$\text{diff} <i,j> \begin{cases} >0 & i = j \, or \, Sim_i > Sim_j \, when \, i = j \\ =0 & i = and \, Sim_i = Sim_j \\ <0 & other \, conditions \end{cases} \qquad (6)$$

We maintain the pivot ID and distance in a new column I. These signatures are comparable by Eq. 6.

Theorem 1: Given a partition P_i, $\forall r \in P_i$, the necessary condition for $|q, r| \leq \theta$:

$$|p_i, q| - \theta \leq |p_i, r| \leq |p_i, q| + \theta$$

One object should just assign to one partition, for no intersection between any two partitions. Considering this rule, the boundary of the intervals should not overlap each other. Based on Theorem 1 and similarity search definition, r is qualified as a candidate if $Min_i = |p_i, q| - \theta \leq |p_i, r| \leq |p_i, q| + \theta = Max_i$. Given a partition P_i, we judge the object as a candidate with signatures located in $[Min_i, Max_i]$ belonging to $[0, 1]$.

Index Building Steps: To build index based on the complex objects, the first step is to map them to one-dimensional values in the metric space. To build a comparable index, we can conduct the partitions on R. There are some detailed steps to build the index as shown in Fig. 3:

1. **Choose Pivots:** We randomly choose some objects as the pivots from the whole dataset, which label the partitions. Using the selected pivots, we generate the pivot table as the Ptable. This table stores the pivot ID in integer data type and original attributes.
2. **Do Partition:** For any object in the dataset, we compute the distances to each pivot. Based on the distances, we choose the ones nearest the pivots.
3. **Associate I to the R:** We generate the < Pid, Sim(Pid, o) > stored in a new column I, applied to the dataset table R.
4. **Building B$^+$-Tree Index:** UDFs are integrated as the comparison rules. Then the B$^+$-tree can be built on R. The following SQL statements illustrate the building details.

```
update table R set (refid,dist)=(
    select(s.rid,sim(S.[A],P.[A])
    from ptable S
    order by sim(S.[A],P.[A])
    limit 1);
CREATE INDEX I-INDEX ON R
USING BTREE (I ASC NULL LAST);
ALTER TABLE R CLUSTER ON I;
```

5   Query Process

In DBMS, to facilitate the operation, we implement the UDFs where we design the distance function of two distinct complex objects. Users merely submit the SQL statement (SELECT-FROM-WHERE) to database to search the objects whose signatures located in the threshold based boundaries.

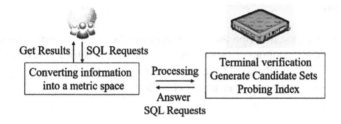

Fig. 4. The query process based on SQL.

As shown in Fig. 4, the query rewriting component will firstly translate UDF SIMQ into a sequence of range search conditions over the index. In that means, the requests are converted into a metric space. Before starting to answer any similarity queries, we achieve the range of each partition based on Theorem 1 and create a temporary table to store the min and max boundary values.

Observed in experiments, the optimization of the number of pivots depends on the database size. Sometimes it is necessary to select thousands of pivots, leading to a large number of search range conditions. Increasing search range conditions result in the reduction of number of candidates, however, potentially high computation cost. To avoid duplicated scan, one-directional index probing over index of R can improve the performance. To this consideration, we build a composite index over attributes (PID, Max, Min, QID) shown as in Table 1.

Table 1. A temporary table with the search ranges.

PID	Max	Min	QID
1	Max_1	Min_1	1
...	...	...	...
p	Max_p	Min_p	1

Due to the temporary table containing the range (Min, Max) for each pivot, we can check the objects whether in the range or not. When the objects are judged out of ranges, they are discarded directly. Otherwise, we will utilize the Sim functions and definitions above to verify the candidateship. The following SQL statements illustrate the query process details.

```
SELECT      R.loc, R.keywords
FROM        R, SearchRangeTable SRT, QueryTable QT
WHERE       SRT.QID=QT.QID AND I
BETWEEN     SRT.min and SRT.max AND Sim(q[A], R.[A])< θ;
```

6 Experiments

In this section, we first describe the configurations of our experiments, including two data sets, similarity functions, methods, and performance metrics. Then we study the parameters that potentially affect the performance of TSK-SQL. Subsequently, we compare TSK-SQL with the other approaches in database.

6.1 Data Sets and Similarity Functions

Restaurant: Restaurant information is collected in a geo-textual dataset, captured from the DaZhongDianPing of Beijing, a Chinese Consumer guide web. The location is attributed by (longitude, latitude) and the keywords are Chinese words. The data volume is 65535. We use the Eq. 1 as the similarity function, and give location and text the same weight with $\alpha_1 = \alpha_2 = 0.5$.

Flickr: Flickr is a geo-textual-temporal dataset, which is the online photo management and sharing application in the world. The dataset consists of the photo ids, locations, keywords and the time tags. The data volume is 140000. We use the Eq. 1 as the similarity function, and give location, text and time with different weight as $\alpha_1 = \alpha_2 = 0.3$, $\alpha_3 = 0.4$.

The distributions of these 2 real datasets are shown in Table 2. We randomly select 100 objects from each data set as queries, with the average elapsed time obtained for each query object.

We list the thresholds that are commonly set in existing work across various data sets in Table 2 and the threshold highlighted in bold is default in the experiments. All experiments are conducted on a PC with Intel E5620 2.4 GHz of CPU, 8 GB of memory, and CentOS 5.5 operating system. In addition, all experiments of SKSQL are executed in PostgreSQL 9.4.5.

Table 2. The two datasets for restaurant information in Beijing and Flickr.

Dataset	Similarity function	Data volume	Size (M)	Dimension	Language	Data format	Threshold θ
restaurant	Equations 1–3	65535	7.51	3	Chinese	UTF-8	0.0025, 0.001, 0.0005
Flickr	Equations 1–4	140000	7.03	4	English	ANSI	0.005, 0.001, 0.005

6.2 Evaluation of TSKSQL

In this study, we evaluate the effectiveness of the index method as follows. In Fig. 5, we alter the number of pivots and threshold values with the time consumptions for the query process tested. For every single figure, the increase of number of pivots contributes to the increase of index building time consumption, however, the general

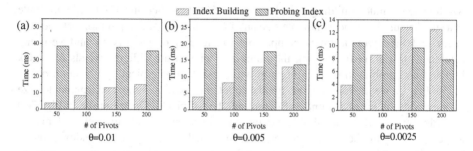

Fig. 5. The time consumption for index building and index probing at (a) θ = 0.01, (b) θ = 0.005 and (c) θ = 0.0025.

reduction of probing index time consumption. Smaller thresholds will accelerate both the index building and probing process. However, when it comes to a certain threshold, the two consumptions will be comparable shown in Fig. 5(c). In other words, the threshold contributes more to the index building.

We leave the number of pivots as the tuning parameter, which varies in range (50,100, 150, 200) for restaurants and (50, 100, 200, 300, 400, 500, 1000) for flicker. We evaluate the performance of all approaches in terms of average elapsed time, average candidate set size and average I/O consumptions. The experimental results are shown in Fig. 6. In Fig. 6(a) and (b), the running time are compared with varying threshold and pivots. Generally, for English and Chinese tag distance computations, the index building time is different. And additional temporal information in Flickr database

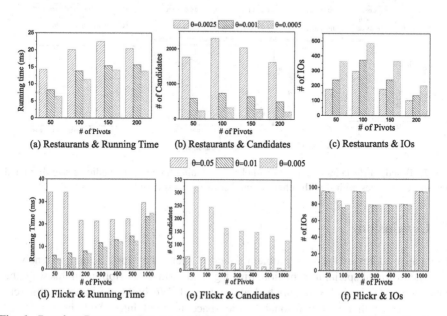

Fig. 6. Based on Restaurant Dataset or Flickr, the running time (a, d), candidate size (b, e) and IO size (c, f) varies with the number of pivots.

will donate the index building complex. In Fig. 6, the smaller threshold will contribute to a smaller running time, candidate size and I/Os. The cost of computation between the query and the pivot becomes comparable to the cost of identifying and verifying candidates in Fig. 6(d). Varying the number of pivots, the different trends for index building and probing time consumption will present some typical optimization point.

In Fig. 7, we investigate the trends about the running time and candidate size varying with the threshold under different number of pivots. Ones can see in Fig. 7(a) and (d), for a certain threshold, the running time varies with the selected pivots. Moreover, due to the UDFs, larger thresholds will donate heavier index probing consumption and weaken the filter power. Under fixed number of pivots, the running time, as well as the candidate size shown in Fig. 7(b) and (e), increases over the threshold. Arising from the weak filter power, the IO consumptions tend to stable for large thresholds in Fig. 7(c) and (f). The pruning mechanisms will lead to the drastic changes of IO consumptions for the low thresholds. Combining the cost of running time and IOs, optimizations for the threshold will be achieved for different datasets as around 0.002 (Restaurant dataset) and below 0.01 (Flickr dataset).

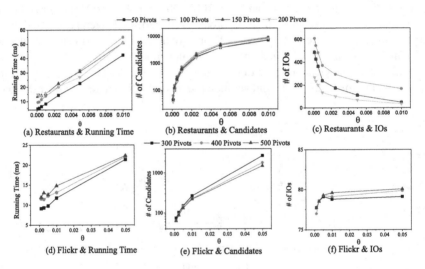

Fig. 7. Based on Restaurant Dataset or Flickr, the running time (a, d), candidate size (b, e) and IO size (c, f) varies with θ with different number of pivots selected.

7 Conclusion

This paper addresses the new problem temporal spatial-keyword Search, extensively with the fusion of spatial information, time tags and textual description. In this way, the construction of the index is enriched and extended. We build the index in different data spaces, with one-dimensional metric space mapped into. And the signatures are generated for improving the query process and IO consumption performances.

The TSKSQL method presented in this paper resolved the query problem based on SQL. Users can merely submit SELECT-FROM-WHERE statements, with the efficiency and user experience improved. Several users defined functions are used. Based on the B^+-tree and the pruning rules we proposed, the TSK search gets a high performance and can be used in existing RDBMS. This method is universal and easily extended by other information tags.

In the future work, higher dimensional query will be conducted and optimized based on our method. It requires more databases and platforms tested and usage in more other fields such as biomedical DNA queries. The pivot selection is conducted randomly, which demands more efficient algorithms. The alternative method for pruning should be investigated further.

Acknowledgment. The corresponding author of this paper is Wei Lu and this work is supported in part by the funding under the National Nature Science Foundation of China No. 61502504, and the Research Funds of Renmin University of China No. 15XNLF09.

References

1. Gruteser, M., Grunwald, D.: Anonymous usage of location-based services through spatial and temporal cloaking. In: Proceedings of 1st International Conference on Mobile Systems, Applications and Services, pp. 31–42. ACM (2003)
2. Sanderson, M., Kohler. J.: Analyzing geographic queries. In: SIGIR Workshop on Geographic Information Retrieval, pp. 8–10 (2004)
3. Zhou, Y., Xie, X., Wang, C., Gong, Y., Ma, W.-Y.: Hybrid index structures for location-based web search. In: Proceedings of 14th ACM International Conference on Information and Knowledge Management, pp. 155–162. ACM (2005)
4. Naughton, J.F.: Technical perspective: natural language to SQL translation by iteratively exploring a middle ground. ACM SIGMOD Rec. **45**(1), 5 (2016)
5. Bedo, M.V.N., dos Santos, D.P., Ponciano-Silva, M., de Azevedo-Marques, P.M., Traina Jr., C.: Endowing a content-based medical image retrieval system with perceptual similarity using ensemble strategy. J. Digit. Imaging **29**(1), 22–37 (2016)
6. Al Marri, W.J., Malluhi, Q., Ouzzani, M., Tang, M., Aref, W.G.: The similarity-aware relational database set operators. Inf. Syst. **59**, 79–93 (2016)
7. Medina, J.M., Barranco, C.D., Pons, O.: Evaluation of indexing strategies for possibilistic queries based on indexing techniques available in traditional RDBMS. Int. J. Intell. Syst. (2016)
8. Choudhury, F.M., Culpepper, J.S., Sellis, T., Cao, X.: Maximizing bichromatic reverse spatial and textual k nearest neighbor queries. Proc. VLDB Endow. **9**(6), 456–467 (2016)
9. Fu, A.W.-C., Chan, P.M.-S., Cheung, Y.-L., Moon, Y.S.: Dynamic vp-tree indexing for n-nearest neighbor search given pair-wise distances. VLDB J.—Int. J. Very Larg. Data Bases **9**(2), 154–173 (2000)
10. Jayalakshmi, T., Chethana, C.: A semantic search engine for indexing and retrieval of relevant text documents. Int. J. **4**(5), 1–5 (2016)
11. Egenhofer, M.J.: Spatial SQL: a query and presentation language. IEEE Trans. Knowl. Data Eng. **6**(1), 86–95 (1994)

12. Dobrota, M., Bulajic, M., Bornmann, L., Jeremic, V.: A new approach to the QS university ranking using the composite I-distance indicator: uncertainty and sensitivity analyses. J. Assoc. Inf. Sci. Technol. **67**(1), 200–211 (2016)
13. De Felipe, I., Hristidis, V., Rishe, N.: Keyword search on spatial databases. In: 2008 IEEE 24th International Conference on Data Engineering, pp. 656–665. IEEE (2008)
14. Lu, J., Lu, Y., Cong, G.: Reverse spatial and textual k nearest neighbor search. In: Proceedings of 2011 ACM SIGMOD International Conference on Management of Data, pp. 349–360. ACM (2011)

Features of Rumor Spreading on WeChat Moments

Wangchun Jiang[1], Bin Chen[1(✉)], Lingnan He[2], Yichong Bai[3],
and Xiaogang Qiu[1]

[1] College of Information System and Management,
National University of Defense Technology, Changsha 410073, China
nudtcb9372@gmail.com
[2] The School of Communication and Design, Sun yat-sen University,
Guangzhou 510275, China
[3] Fibonacci Consulting Co. Ltd., Towcester, UK

Abstract. WeChat is a mobile social media software launched by Tencent in 2011 that has 600 million monthly active users in August 2015. It is used in over 200 countries and regions with more than 20 different language versions. WeChat Moments (WM), viewed as a kind of realization of its social networking, provides users a way to post, view and share links of web pages in HTML5. The rumor spreading on WM, apart from the traditional traits of rumor spreading, gets its new spatiotemporal features. For better management and control of rumor spreading on WM, study for more knowledge about its properties is required. In this paper, 10 WM pages are used to analyze the properties, which contains approximately 6.5 million page views records. With the analysis of overall diffusion temporal characteristics, we propose a rumor spreading lifecycle with three different phases, i.e., the development phase, the explosion phase and the decline phase. By analyzing the diffusion region in different time, it is found that the rumor spreading regions in different time experience little change from the very beginning, and the cities in most frequently observed provinces like Guangdong are extracted for further analysis. It is concluded that the rumor spreading region has a positive correlation with its population and GDP. Moreover, the spatial and temporal characteristics of different spreading levels are studied, which leads to the conclusion that for most users only two steps are required to get access to the rumor that interests them on WM.

Keywords: WM · Rumor spreading · Lifecycle · Spreading region · Spreading level

1 Introduction

Served as a social media tool, WeChat, which was first released in 2011 and viewed its monthly active users reaching 600 million in August 2015 for the first time, has become a necessity for people's daily life. More than 20 language versions have been introduced to over 200 countries and regions since it was created, which helped it

© Springer International Publishing Switzerland 2016
A. Morishima et al. (Eds.): APWeb 2016 Workshops, LNCS 9865, pp. 217–227, 2016.
DOI: 10.1007/978-3-319-45835-9_19

become the most popular mobile messaging application in China [1]. Apart from the original chat function, WeChat Moment (WM) is an implementation of private online social network, which allows users to post, view and share links of Web pages in HTML5 (H5, WM pages) [2]. This kind of function facilitates users' online social communication, and makes the information diffusion more convenient and efficient. In the meantime, utilizing the wide propagation of WM, the rumor tends to spread in the form of web pages in H5 on WM, which may undermine the health and comfortable social network environment. Therefore, the study of rumor spreading features on WM is valued.

In the study, 10 WM rumor pages with more than 6.5 million page view records from November 2015 to April 2016 are used to investigate the features. Three aspects and findings of our research are as follows.

(1) **Rumor spreading lifecycle:** The analysis of rumor diffusion trend on WM via diffusion graph by time is conducted, and then the rumor diffusion lifecycle is proposed and analyzed.
(2) **Rumor spreading regions by time:** The diffusion regions of rumor on WM by time with geographical statistics data are examined and the conclusion about which provinces are included in the most wide-spreading regions is made.
(3) **Rumor spreading level characteristics of time and region:** Spatial and temporal features of different diffusion levels of rumor pages spreading on WM are studied in this part.

2 Background

2.1 Rumor on WeChat Moments

Rumor on WM is a kind of false, aggressive and purposeful information diffused via WeChat Moments. It is likely to distort the truth, impact users on their value of life and even damage their characteristics [3]. With the rising level of rumormongers' knowledge, rumors on WM become increasingly informative and anonymous. Some rumors are so tempting and they seem to be so real that people view them on the internet can hardly tell whether they are true or not. Consequently, people would rather choose to believe them under this circumstance, which results in the wide spreading of rumors. What's worse, this endangers both the online social network among users and the real society.

Compared with traditional rumor traits, rumors on WM spread at a faster speed with more influential effects on people. Considering the features of WM pages diffusion, the rumors on WM are more likely to affect the community of users with strong relationship, which means effect in this way is more significant than traditional ones.

2.2 Related Works

With the increasing open social networks and anonymous online community, research on online information diffusion has attracted more and more researchers. For example,

Nicole B. Ellison explored the definition, history and scholarship of social network sites [4], Faust provided a way to analyze social networks [5]. Social media like Twitter [6], Facebook [7] and Sina Weibo [8] provide users with a platform where they can exchange messages easily. However, this kind of communication mechanism can hardly get user's private information under protection. Different from the open social media, anonymous online community takes privacy protection of users into consideration. QQ and WeChat [9] are good examples of anonymous online community. Moreover, WeChat is mostly based on the real relationship of daily life, which can be mapped to the strong online relationship. Some works have been done about the information diffusion and application of WeChat [10].

Advance of information communication technologies promotes the analysis of big data. For example, spatial analysis of urban emergency events are investigated from a novel perspective with the mobile social media data [11]. Social media big data mining is also valued in the study of crowdsourcing recently [12]. Online data of web events are well studied for the keyword system [13].

However, there are few researches concentrating on the rumor spreading on WeChat Moments. Thus, we are attracted by the problem: what features of rumor spreading in such a strong relationship network will be?

3 Methods and Experiments

3.1 WeChat Moments Dataset

The WM page is the web page that spreads on the WeChat Moments, which is usually launched by Tencent or other third-party web developer for the purpose of marketing, politics and culture propagation. Because no Application Program Interface (API) is provided to record the page information in WeChat, we crawled the data with the help of Fibonacci Consulting Co. Ltd. Datasets including 10 rumor pages are chosen to study rumor spreading in WeChat. The whole diffusion process in WM is recorded in the dataset from November 2015 to April 2016.

All the page IDs and their titles are listed in Table 1.

The format of page view record in the dataset from Fibonacci Consulting Co. Ltd. is described as follow:

$$< P_{id}, \ S_{id}, \ IP, \ Add, \ V_{id}, \ E, \ T >$$

Where P_{id} is the ID of the WM page, which is an identification of the page created by the development platform; S_{id} is the ID of user who posts the page; IP is the IP address of the user who views the page; Add is the geographical address of the viewer; V_{id} is the ID of the user who views the page; E is the event type of the user, which includes "view", "share", "exist"; T is the local time when the page is viewed.

Table 1. Page ID and titles

Page code	Page ID	Title
Page 1	11804d95-5118-4286-9d2d-1ca1f69c72d4	Beijing Secret, View Now! (Delete Soon!)
Page 2	126c0e23-d2d1-4b2e-986c-cf9634cc731a	Significant Notification, You MUST know!
Page 3	604a2960-2fd9-4dc8-bb6e-cd389cbc911b	Top 4 women zodiac bring good luck to husband!
Page 4	687afb6d-6c3c-43fb-b3b1-d36740da3053	Emergency: Death Coming! View Now...
Page 5	77283692-bd29-4221-a7f1-0c732589c25b	Letter designed for you. Worth reading! Finish it
Page 6	7ac4565f-07ab-418a-9ae0-5c7a6f17785c	Suggestion: save it for a rainy day, little time wasted
Page 7	b036998e-ecf2-42cf-b4ad-2e76cef5c5e2	These four pictures can save life, share it!
Page 8	b848ea0c-0c7f-4aaa-a5 cd-254b0cc4d5b1	Diabetes can be cured, tell others! You are so kind
Page 9	c3feec83-d60e-465d-add9-722722d8cf74	News 9.00 last night caused a sensation in China!
Page 10	fa1bfd82-e9dc-4e51-a867-cb9037949bd8	(SECRET) It's Awesome! View now, delete soon

Page 1 is chosen as an example to demonstrate the rumor page spreading in our work.

3.2 Rumor Spreading Lifecycle

With the statistic work of all 10 pages, we find that the number of page views by day can be divided into three steps. Take page 1 as an example, whose variation curve of daily number of page views is given in Fig. 1.

In Fig. 1, the horizontal axis denotes the time and the vertical axis denotes the number of page views. It can be seen from Fig. 1 that there are three obvious different phases for the number of page views variation. Thus the spreading of the rumor is divided into three phases according to the lifecycle theory [14]. From point A to point B is the **development phase**, in which the number of page views increases at a slow speed. The **explosion phase** is the period from point B to point C, in which the number of page views witnesses a sharp increment and the number of page views is larger than that of the development phase. After that period, the number of page views stays in a low level and varies slowly, and it comes to the last period of the lifecycle - **decline phase**.

As is shown in Fig. 1, it takes almost one month before page 1 spreads widely in a fast speed. That is to say, after the page is launched, it is not likely to be popular on the

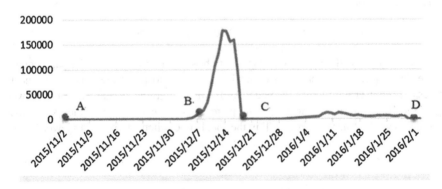

Fig. 1. The number of page views of page 1 by day

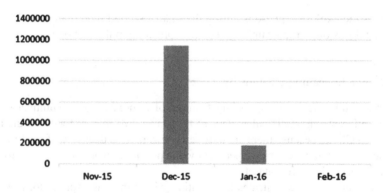

Fig. 2. The number of page views of page 1 by month

WM quickly. Moreover, Fig. 1 also indicates that the number of page views in explosion phase accounts for the majority of the total number of view. To get a better view about this phenomenon, we check the number of page views variation by month.

In Fig. 2, the horizontal axis denotes the time of month and the vertical axis denotes the number of page views. The monthly number of page views reaches the top with over 1.1 million view records in December 2015, which is the second month after its launch. It accounts for 86.3 % of the total number of page views. We get the monthly number of page views of all 10 pages and the percentage of number of page views in their explosion phases in Table 2. It can be seen that the number of page views in explosion phase accounts for over 50 % of total views for most pages. Note that for

Table 2. Monthly number of page views and percentage of explosion phase number of page views

Number of page views	Page 1	Page 2	Page 3	Page 4	Page 5
Nov-15	1	7	52512	646997	1475545
Dec-15	1145838	0	11145	87065	128612
Jan-16	181538	7700	40477	36796	143181
Feb-16	136	4425	20319	23150	53794
Mar-16	0	771	4138	3184	7808
Apr-16	0	658	2585	2272	5190
Total	1327513	13561	131176	799464	1814130
Percentage	86.32 %	56.78 %	40.03 %	80.93 %	81.34 %
Number of page views	Page 6	Page 7	Page 8	Page 9	Page 10
Nov-15	2002212	1644513	515176	1	185
Dec-15	1468864	611042	191860	0	15968
Jan-16	5	587865	766570	3651	52353
Feb-16	2	248276	989	20	39413
Mar-16	1	72685	2	0	6567
Apr-16	0	17674	0	0	5137
Total	3471084	3182055	1474597	3672	119623
Percentage	57.68 %	51.68 %	51.99 %	99.43 %	43.77 %

most pages the explosion phase is during the first or second month after the launch. It means that diffusion of rumor finishes its main spreading in the first one or two months.

3.3   Rumor Spreading Regions by Time

In order to study the rumor spreading features of region, the daily number of page views in different regions is calculated. In this paper, we mainly focus on the rumor spreading in China, because there are only few viewers (less than 1 % of total for every page) locate in foreign countries. Specifically, the provinces where viewers are from are traced with the help of IP dataset.

The viewer's address indicates the location where the page spread to. Hence, by examining the region of viewers, we can study the facts like where the page is first created, which province has the most rumor viewers, and what the connection is between rumor viewer location and the local economic features.

To further illustrate the statistical results, the number of page views of Page 1 in different phases is plotted in the digital map of Fig. 3 ((a) Development Phase, (b) Explosion Phase, (c) Decline Phase). According to the statistics, Page 1 is launched in Guangdong Province, and propagated to the adjoining province Hunan, and then to other provinces like Jiangsu, Liaoning, Beijing and Shanxi. As time goes by, the diffusion of page enters the Explosion Phase, during which more viewers are witnessed

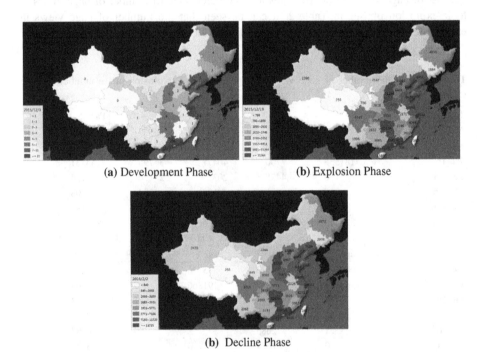

(a) Development Phase   (b) Explosion Phase

(b) Decline Phase

Fig. 3. Page 1 number of page views geographical distribution in different phase: (a) development phase; (b) explosion phase; (c) decline phase

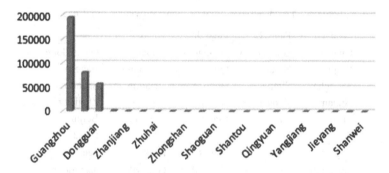

Fig. 4. Viewer distribution of page 1 in Guangdong

in the provinces mentioned above. The rumor was also viewed by WeChat users in the central and western regions. When it reaches the last phase of the diffusion, the rumor viewed region distribution maintains only with the increment of number of page views.

After being launched, the rumor page may be shared and viewed by viewers in the local region, and then spreads to other places. The majority of viewers is located in the east part of China. The economy in the east is much better than west, so people there can access network easier, which is necessary for the availability of rumor on the WM. Moreover, people in developed regions are more eager to propagate information. Additionally, the population in the east part of China is much bigger than that of the west. So we can deduce that there exists a correlation between the propagation of rumor and economy, as well as the population. To get a better view about this, we study the geographical features of rumor spreading in Guangdong Province.

Guangdong Province has the most viewers in Page 1 spreading, so we take a specific look at the viewer distribution in cities in this province. The number of page views of each city in Guangdong Province is presented Fig. 4. It depicts that viewer in Guangzhou accounts for more than half of the total viewers in Guangdong, followed by which are Shenzhen, Dongguan and Foshan. Taking the economy and population of these cities into considerations, we can find that the ranking has a positive correlation with the GDP and population, which supports our deduction proposed before.

Moreover, in order to figure out whether the regional features of rumor spreading have relationship with the type and content of rumor, top 5 viewer amount provinces of 10 pages are counted and listed in Table 3. Except for Page 3, other pages top five provinces account for over 60 % of total number of page views, which implies that viewers of certain rumor pages show a geographic aggregation. Among all the 10 pages, Guangdong Province ranks the first all the time. This is a sign that people in Guangdong are more likely to view the rumor pages than people in other provinces. The number of page views in Beijing and Jiangsu is big considering the showing frequency in the table, followed by Shanghai, Henan and Shandong with four times. It is assumed that rumors are viewed more frequently in these regions due to two facts namely the economy and the population, which are based on the fact that Guangdong, Shanghai and Beijing are developed region. These regions are not only rich but also have large population.

Table 3. Top 5 number of page views provinces of all pages

Page 1	Page 2	Page 3	Page 4	Page 5
Guangdong	Guangdong	Guangdong	Guangdong	Guangdong
Beijing	Henan	Qinghai	Liaoning	Jiangsu
Shanghai	Sichuan	Heilongjiang	Tianjin	Shandong
Hunan	Jiangsu	Henan	Jilin	Zhejiang
Shanxi	Guizhou	Liaoning	Beijing	Beijing
78.25 %	73.15 %	47.50 %	73.89 %	60.22 %
Page 6	Page 7	Page 8	Page 9	Page 10
Guangdong	Guangdong	Guangdong	Guangdong	Guangdong
Sichuan	Shandong	Jiangsu	Henan	Zhejiang
Shanghai	Beijing	Beijing	Jiangsu	Henan
Zhejiang	Jiangsu	Shandong	Hubei	Jiangsu
Beijing	Hebei	Liaoning	Shanghai	Shandong
76.98 %	65.03 %	75.73 %	82.41 %	69.75 %

3.4   Spatial and Temporal Features of Different Rumor Spreading Levels

The spreading level of rumor is an information diffusion concept which consists of the information shared by users. It concerns users who share the page rather than those who only view it. As can be seen in Fig. 5, the circle in different color represents different users. Take Page 1 for example, it is posted by U_0, and then viewed by U_{11}, U_{12} and U_{13}. Though all of them view the page, but only U_{11} and U_{13} share it, so U_{11} and U_{13} are in the spreading level one, but U_{12} is not included.

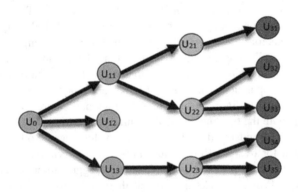

Fig. 5. Spreading levels

In order to get a better understanding about how the spatial features of different spreading levels will be like, we study the viewer information in every spreading level and then analyze the geographical distribution.

Page 1 is chosen to study the regional diffusion features in different spreading levels. Six spreading levels are obtained based on the statistical data of Page 1. The 1st

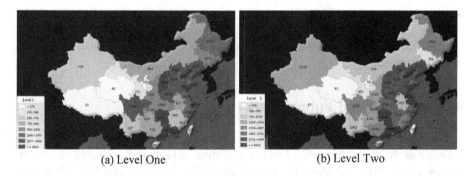

(a) Level One   (b) Level Two

Fig. 6. Viewer distribution of page 1 in different spreading level: (a) level one; (b) level two

and 2nd level regional distribution results are showed in Fig. 6 ((a) Level One; (b) Level Two). As is shown in the figures, the viewers of level one and level two mainly locate in the developed regions like Guangdong, Shanghai and Beijing. Except for the number of page views, no obvious regional distribution differences can be found between these two spreading levels. It indicates that the rumor spreads in almost the same mode in every level. This means if we get access to the one of the spreading level of the rumor, we can predicate that the viewers are almost in the same region in the next spreading levels.

Furthermore, the temporal features of rumor in different spreading levels are studied. Table 4 shows the intervals of Page 1 in different spreading levels. In Table 4, minInterval represents the minimum time it takes for the page to be shared in different levels, and the midInterval, maxInterval and aveInterval is the median, maximum and average of time respectively. The totalUser and userRatio denotes the number of users and their percentage of total in every level. As can be seen, in the spreading level one, it takes over 8 h for the first user to share the page, and the last record of the one who shares the page in level one is 1377.699 h after the page launch. The average time taken to share the page in spreading level one is 266.5 h, and that of other levels are 173.6 h, 88.6 h, 59.5 h, 6.2 h and 779.9 h respectively. Considering that there is only one user in level 6, we can exclude it. Thus, there is an obvious trend that the higher the spreading level is, the less time it takes for the page to be shared by users.

Additionally, among those who share the page, there are 392 users in level one and 512 in level two, which account for 78.8 % of the total number together. Thus, we can

Table 4. Interval of Page 1 in different spreading levels

Level	minInterval/h	midInterval/h	maxInterval/h	aveInteval/h	totalUser	UserRatio
Level one	8.631	244.916	1377.699	266.503	392	0.342
Level two	0.371	163.659	1248.424	173.596	512	0.446
Level three	0.202	74.833	671.562	88.558	198	0.173
Level four	2.4888	32.6769	639.215	59.535	42	0.036
Level five	0.757	11.564	11.564	6.161	2	0.002
Level six	779.906	779.906	779.906	779.906	1	0.001

assume that there for most of the rumors, it only takes twice sharing to reach the majority of the users who are interested in the topic and willing to share. It also suggests that the users who are interested in the rumor are close to each other in the WeChat Moments.

4 Conclusion and Future Work

In this paper, we study the features of rumor spreading on WeChat Moments. With the statistics analysis, the lifecycle of rumor spreading is proposed, including the development phase, explosion phase and decline phase. The fact is observed that during the explosion phase the number of page views is much bigger than other phases and has a sharp increase in the beginning. This could help with the control and management of the diffusion of rumor. Moreover, the regional features of rumor diffusion is examined with the data counting. After being launched, the rumor page is propagated to different regions, and then the main spreading areas experience little changes. It is found that the developed provinces that with lager population are more likely to be the most wide-spreading regions for rumor. At last, we study the diffusion features of time and region in different spreading levels. It is found that the rumor spreading region in different spreading level tends to be similar, and that for most rumors, only two sharing actions are required to reach the majority of the users who would share them. Thus WeChat Moments plays the role of a filter which could choose the users who have the same interests in the rumor and finally share it.

In order to achieve the final goal of control and management of rumor on WM, further study is required. Therefore, to make the work more convincing, more samples, i.e., rumor pages, are needed in further study. Apart from the networking knowledge related to the spreading filed, rumor spreading models based on the integration of the network and user agents should be built, which is supposed to simulate the operation of rumor from a thorough view and make the study results more authentic.

Acknowledgement. The authors would like to thank the National Natural Science Foundation of China under Grant Nos. 71303252, 61503402, 61403402, 91024032. We also thank Fibonacci Consulting Co. Ltd. for the big dataset.

References

1. List of virtual communities with more than 100 million active users. Wikipedia (2016). https://en.wikipedia.org/wiki/List_of_virtual_communities_with_more_than_100_million_active_users
2. Li, Z., Chen, L., Bai, Y., et al.: On diffusion-restricted social network: a measurement study of WeChatMoments (2016)
3. Li, L., School of Humanities, Southeast University: Hermeneutics structural analysis of online rumor. J. Northeast. Univ. **17**, 221–225 (2015)
4. Ellison, N.B., et al.: Social network sites: definition, history, and scholarship. J. Comput.-Mediat. Commun. **13**(1), 210–230 (2007)

5. Wasserman, S., Faust, K.: Social network analysis. Encycl. Soc. Netw. Anal. Min. **22**(Suppl 1), 109–127 (2011)
6. Cha, M., Haddadi, H., Benevenuto, F., Gummadi, P.K.: Measuring user influence in Twitter: the million follower fallacy. In: ICWSM, vol. 10, no. 10–17, p. 30 (2010)
7. Acquisti, A., Gross, R.: Imagined communities: awareness, information sharing, and privacy on the Facebook. In: Danezis, G., Golle, P. (eds.) PET 2006. LNCS, vol. 4258, pp. 36–58. Springer, Heidelberg (2006)
8. Rauchfleisch, A., Schäfer, A.R.M.S.: Multiple public spheres of Weibo: a typology of forms and potentials of online public spheres in China. Inf. Commun. Soc. **18**(2), 139–155 (2015)
9. Liao, D.H., Luo, X.L.: Application of WeChat in the working process of college group study. J. Jiangxi Univ. Tradit. Chin. Med. (2015)
10. Tong, H.: Research on WeChat according to communication study and its influence. Chongqing Soc. Sci. (2013)
11. Xu, Z., Zhang, H., Sugumaran, V., et al.: Participatory sensing-based semantic and spatial analysis of urban emergency events using mobile social media. Eurasip J. Wirel. Commun. Netw. **2016**(1), 1–9 (2016)
12. Xu, Z., Liu, Y., Yen, N., et al.: Crowdsourcing based description of urban emergency events using social media big data. IEEE Trans. Cloud Comput. 1 (2016)
13. Xuan, J., Luo, X., Zhang, G., et al.: Uncertainty analysis for the keyword system of web events. IEEE Trans. Syst. Man Cybern. Syst. **46**, 1 (2015)
14. Phases, Lifecycle. "Lifecycle phases." Websphere Digital Media Enable Solutions

Distance-Based Continuous Skylines on Geo-Textual Data

Jialiang Chen[1], Jiping Zheng[1,2($\boxtimes$)], Shunqing Jiang[1], and Xianhong Qiu[1]

[1] College of Computer Science and Technology,
Nanjing University of Aeronautics and Astronautics,
Nanjing, People's Republic of China
{chenjialiang,jzh,jiangshunqing,qiuxh}@nuaa.edu.cn
[2] School of Computer Science and Engineering,
University of New South Wales, Sydney, Australia

Abstract. Various kinds of data from real applications are usually associated with geographic information as well as textual descriptions. Existing methods mostly consider static query points not supporting moving context. In this paper, we study distance-based continuous skyline queries on geo-textual data. That is, given a set of geo-textual data and a distance constraint, the skyline queries continuously return the objects that are not dominated by others when the query point is moving within the distance constraint. We only consider distance and text relevance dimensions and two algorithms are introduced to calculate initial skyline results and continuous skylines efficiently. Also, grid file indexes are exploited to accelerate continuous skyline query processing. Experimental results on real datasets demonstrate the efficiency and effectiveness of our proposed methods.

Keywords: Continuous skyline queries · Geo-textual data · Uncertain motion model

1 Introduction

Recently, massive data that associated with geographic information are generated by current popular applications, such as *Airbnb*, *Google Maps* and *Instagram*. Besides the location information, these data (or points of interests) are usually enhanced with textual descriptions. For example, in *Airbnb* and *Agoda*, people add tags or tips to the hotels that they have stayed while others can search hotels by some keywords. In *Instagram*, people share photos associated with their locations and textual descriptions. In addition, points of interests that are closer tend to be more important. Consider the following example: A tourist visiting HongKong is looking for a restaurant for dinner. He prefers to choose a closer one in the range of 10 km. In addition, restaurants associated with the following keywords: { "pizza", "steak", "ice-cream" } are particularly interested in because of his tastes. Since he is traveling by car or keeps moving, the distances between him and restaurants vary over time. In this example, existing skyline processing researches [1,11] can only invoke a snapshot skyline query processing technique periodically and require the high costs of computation to answer

© Springer International Publishing Switzerland 2016
A. Morishima et al. (Eds.): APWeb 2016 Workshops, LNCS 9865, pp. 228–240, 2016.
DOI: 10.1007/978-3-319-45835-9_20

continuous queries. Also, no text relevant skyline queries [4,10,12] consider the movement of a query while users in the real world are likely to be with a moving context. Indeed, all of above guarantee no distance constraint scenarios.

In this paper, we propose distance based continuous skyline queries over a moving query on geo-textual data, which enables users to retrieve interested objects continuously considering both textual descriptions and geographic information. We solve the problem by exploiting the motion features of query points. Since the maximum moving speed of each query is limited and the location does not change abruptly over continuous temporal scenes, we first propose an uncertain motion model to predict the potential region for the query point in the coming future. Next we investigate the connection between the spatial locations of objects and their dominance relationship, which provides an indication of where to find changes in the skyline and update them. Besides, we add a distance constraint to filter out points of interests too far in the distance which are usually meaningless. Finally, we provide an innovative algorithm to support the processing of distance-based continuous skyline queries on geo-textual data. Throughout, we promote our solutions to allow fuzzy queries by combining the keyword-matching technique with the text relevance functions depending on the edit distance technique.

The rest of this paper is organized as follows. The most related researches in skyline queries as well as in spatial keyword searching are listed in Sect. 2. Next a detailed description of distance-based continuous skyline on geo-textual data including problem definition, description of the uncertain motion model and the steps of d_r-$CGTS$ algorithms are presented in Sect. 3. The performance of our proposals on real data sets is evaluated in Sect. 4, followed by the conclusion of this paper in Sect. 5.

2   Related Work

The skyline query was first introduced to the database community by Borzsonyi et al. [1] in 2001. Consequent researches focus on efficient skyline query processing [11]. Then continuous skyline query processing was first carried out by Huang et al. [8]. They considered the distance to a query point as the unique dynamic attribute and maintained continuous skyline results by event driven mechanisms. Lee et al. [9] studied the skyline problem when all the attributes of a data point are dynamic, and presented several rules to retrieve skyline candidates. Cheema et al. [2] proposed a safe zone for a query to cut down the cost of continuous skyline query processing. As long as the query point stays in the safe zone, the results are guaranteed to remain correct. Instead, we assume skyline query processing in a constrained area only querying data objects within it.

Spatial keyword search extends classic keyword search to retrieve objects considering relevance to a set of keywords as well as proximity to the location of the query points. Felipe et al. [6] first carried out keyword search on spatial databases. Cong et al. [5] presented the popular IR-tree index, which supports the ranking of objects based on a weighted sum of spatial distance and textual relevance. Based on the above in spatial keyword search, Choi et al. [4] et al. firstly gave the definition of keyword-matched skyline and retrieved the result by strict keyword-matching technique. Shi et al. [12] studied the textually related spatial skyline queries and evaluated several classic models for keyword-matching elaborately. Li et al. [10] looked into the skyline problem for geo-textual data and improved the query efficiency by utilizing an inverted K-D tree. In our work, since only considering distance and text relevance dimensions, we adopt grid file index for simplicity.

3   Continuous Distance-Based Skyline Queries on Geo-Textual Data

3.1   Problem Definition

Definition 1 (Geo-Textual Object). A geo-textual object is defined as $p(\lambda, \mathcal{W})$, where $p.\lambda$ is p's spatial location and $p.\mathcal{W}$ is a string vector consisting of n keywords($w_i \in \mathcal{W}|w_1, w_2....w_n$).

Definition 2 (Geo-Textual Query). A geo-textual query is defined as $q(\lambda, d_r, \mathcal{W})$, where $q.\lambda$ is the center of a circle, $q.d_r$ stands for the corresponding radius of constrained disk area and $q.\mathcal{W}$ contains a set of query keywords.

Based on the above definition, given a geo-textual query $q(\lambda, d_r, \mathcal{W})$ and a geo-textual object $p(\lambda, \mathcal{W})$, we use Euclidean distance to study the spatial relationship. That is, the distance between p and q can be denoted as follows:

$$d(p.\lambda, q.\lambda) = \sqrt{(p.x - q.x)^2 + (p.y - q.y)^2} \tag{1}$$

where $q.x$ and $q.y$ are coordinates of q's location.

We select keywords of an object which has the minimum edit distance with the query keywords to calculate the textual relevance. Furthermore, as a query contains more than one keyword, we average the textual relevance of different keywords. Consider a geo-textual query q with a single keyword $q.\mathcal{W} = w$ and a geo-textual object p with $p.\mathcal{W} = \{w_1, w_2, \ldots, w_m\}$, the textual relevance $s(p.\mathcal{W}, q.\mathcal{W}))$ can be estimated by:

$$s(p.\mathcal{W}, q.\mathcal{W}) = \omega(p.w^*) \times \left(1 - \frac{ed(q.w, p.w^*)}{len(q.w)}\right) \tag{2}$$

where w^* is the keyword in $p.\mathcal{W}$ which has the minimum edit distance with $q.w$. $\omega(p.w^*)$ stands for the weight of w^*, $ed(q.w, p.w^*)$ represents the edit distance between $q.w$ and $p.w^*$ and $len(q.w)$ represents the length of the query keyword $q.w$.

Similarly, if a query q contains multiple keywords, $q.\mathcal{W} = \{w_1, w_2, \ldots, w_n\}$, we have

$$s(p.\mathcal{W}, q.\mathcal{W}) = \sum_{k=1}^{n} \left(\omega(p.w^*) \times \left(1 - \frac{ed(q.w_k, p.w^*)}{len(q.w_k)}\right)\right) / n \tag{3}$$

Definition 3 (Geo-Textual Dominance). For two geo-textual objects p_i and p_j, $p_i \prec p_j \Leftrightarrow d(p_i.\lambda, q.\lambda) \leq d(p_j.\lambda, q.\lambda)$ and $s(p_i.\mathcal{W}, q.\mathcal{W}) \leq s(p_j.\mathcal{W}, q.\mathcal{W})$ and at least one $<$ holds.

Generally, the results that far away from the query are usually not interested by users. In the example described in Sect. 1, retrieving the candidate restaurants that are far away from the user is simply a waste of time and incurs an additional processing cost. For this reason, we give our definition of distance based geo-textual skyline as follows:

Definition 4 (Distance Based Geo-Textual Skyline). Given a query point q, a set of objects D and a distance constraint d_r, an object p in D is a distance-based geo-textual skyline object if and only if $d(p, q) < d_r$ and $\forall p' \in D, \nexists\, p' \prec p$.

Definition 5 (Continuous Distance Based Geo-Textual Skyline). Given a query point q, a set of objects D and a distance constraint d_r. The spatial location of the query $q.\lambda$ changes continuously whereas the keywords $q.\mathcal{W}$ remain constant. Continuous distance-based geo-textual skyline always returns all the objects belong to distance-based geo-textual skyline in each moment.

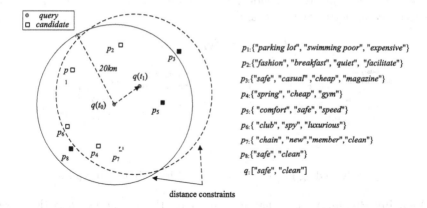

Fig. 1. Example of distance based continuous skyline queries on geo-textual data

Figure 1 provides an example of continuous distance-based skyline queries on geo-textual data. A moving user wants to find hotels containing the following keywords: {"safe", "clean"} within 20 km from his location. For simplicity, we consider the weights of all keywords are equal. At time t_0, the user is at position $q(t_0)$, $\{p_5, p_7, p_8\}$ are returned since they have higher textual relevance or closer to the query q among all the objects within the restricted range. At time t_1, the user moves to a new position $q(t_1)$ which is closer to p_3 than p_7. Thus, p_3 is better than p_7 and p_7 is geo-textual dominated by p_3. Besides, p_8 is out of the constraint range. Then the new skyline is $\{p_3, p_5\}$.

3.2 Uncertain Motion Model

In this paper, we use an uncertain motion model for the position of a query object q. Let q be a query point in Euclidean space and q's position at time t is denoted as $q(t).\lambda$. The motion M of query point q is a finite sequence of positions sampled at discrete time instances: $M = \langle q(t_0).\lambda, q(t_1).\lambda, \ldots, q(t_N).\lambda \rangle$, where $t_{i-1} < t_i$. The interval between two consecutive instances is represented as $s = [t_i, t_j]$, where $i < j$. We place no lower or upper bounds on the sizes of time intervals. Assume that the maximum moving speed of an object q equals to v_{max} and the motion direction is unconstrained. Then in a time interval $s = t_i - t_{i-1}$, any two predictions of $q's$ actual position, denoted by $q_1(t_i).\lambda$ and $q_2(t_i).\lambda$. The maximum displacements between the two predictions can be expressed as follows:

$$drift_{max}(q_1(t_i).\lambda, q_2(t_i).\lambda) = 2v_{max}s \qquad (4)$$

Our motion model includes two phases: Expanding and Relocating.

Expanding Phase. An equivalent way to describe the drift bound mentioned above is in terms of a bound on the possible locations of $q(t_i)$ in an expanding phase. As shown in Fig. 2, given a query q with a maximum moving speed v_{max}, any time t_i and a time interval s, in an expanding phase, the estimated location of q of any direction after an elapsed time of s is defined as $\hat{q}(t_i + s).\lambda = q(t_i).\lambda \pm v_{max}s$. Let $B(q, r)$ denote a Euclidean ball of radius r centered at point $q.\lambda$. From the above definitions, we can obtain

$$\hat{q}(t_i + s).\lambda \in B(\hat{q}(t_i), v_{max}s) \qquad (5)$$

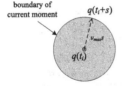

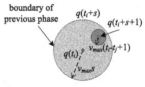

Fig. 2. Expanding phase   **Fig. 3.** Relocating phase

Relocating Phase. Assume that at time $t_i + s$ in the expanding phase described above, the accurate position of q at time $t_j (t_i < t_j$ and $t_j \le t_i + s)$ can be obtained. Thus the new obtained accurate position will be utilized to reconfigure the center of the uncertain motion model (relocating) while the radius of Euclidean ball will be accordingly updated to $v_{max}(t_i - t_j + 1)$ (as shown in Fig. 3), this process is called a relocating phase.

Therefore, the Euclidean ball keeps expanding and relocating alternatively in the whole query processing guaranteeing the correctness of query position predictions.

3.3 Change of Skyline

Considering the characteristics of the uncertain motion model, the skyline results must be influenced by the uncertainty of query position in continuous query processing. Let q be a geo-textual query in an expanding located at $q.\lambda$ with its distance constraint $q.r$. Initially, $q.r = q.d_r$. We have following lemmas to describe these possibilities in detail. Note that the lemmas are only proved to be correct under the MinMax decision criterion [7].

Lemma 1. *Let $S(t)$ be the skyline at time t in an expanding phase. $|S(t)|$ is the cardinality of $S(t)$. Then, if $t_2 > t_1$, $|S(t_2)| > |S(t_1)|$.*

It is obvious as $q.r$ increases existing dominance between two objects p_i and p_j will not stand while no dominance will be added under MinMax decision criteria. Thus skyline results increase in a monotonic way. Lemma 1 offers convenience for skyline maintenance. That is, when a new geo-textual object is accessed, we only need to verify whether it is able to enter the skyline rather than considering all of the possibilities.

Lemma 2. *Let S be the current skyline in an expanding phase. Then, if the radius $q.r$ increase to $d_r + d_v$, for an object p, a prerequisite of entering the skyline is: $\exists sk \in S, d(p.\lambda, q.\lambda) - d(sk.\lambda, q.\lambda) < 2 * (d_r + d_v)$.*

We prove Lemma 2 by contradiction. Assume that an object p is currently dominated by a skyline object sk and $d(p.\lambda, q.\lambda) - d(sk.\lambda, q.\lambda) > 2 * (d_r + d_v)$. If the dominance relationship between sk and p is changed, $d(p.\lambda, q.\lambda) - d(sk.\lambda, q.\lambda) \leq 2 * (d_r + d_v)$ holds, which obviously conflicts with the given prerequisite. So we know that Lemma 2 is right. That is to say, during the process of $q.r$ increases to $d_r + d_v$, only the objects $\{\forall p \in D | \exists sk \in S, d(p.\lambda, sk.\lambda) < 2 * (d_r + d_v)\}$, have potential to affect the skyline results.

Lemma 3. *Let S_r and S_e be the skyline of a relocating phase and of the latest moment in the previous expanding phase respectively. Then, we have $S_r \subseteq S_e$.*

Let $q.\lambda$ and $q.R$ be the center and the radius of the query q in an expanding phase respectively. Then we enter the relocating phase, the query center changes to $q'.\lambda$ and the new radius is $q'.r = q'.d_r$. There are three situations:

1. Assume that there is a skyline object sk and a nonskyline object p, $sk \prec p$. Then we have $d_s + R < d_p - R$, where $d_s = d(sk.\lambda, q.\lambda)$ and $d_p = d(p.\lambda, q.\lambda)$. If the query q still satisfies the motion model, $d(q.\lambda, q'.\lambda) + r < R$ holds. We can obtain $d_s + R < d_p - R \Rightarrow d_p - d_s > 2 * (d(q.\lambda, q'.\lambda) + r) \Rightarrow d_s + r < d_p - r$, and the original dominance relationship between sk and p remains unchanged;
2. Assume that there are two skyline objects sk_1 and sk_2, which cannot dominate each other (sk_1 can not dominate sk_2 in distance but has an advantage at textual relevance). Similarly, we use $d_1(d'_1)$ and $d_2(d'_2)$ to denote their distances to $q.\lambda(q'.\lambda)$. In the previous expanding phase, $d_1 + 2R > d_2$ since sk_1 can not dominate sk_2 in distance. When q enters the relocating phase, as mentioned in Situation 1, $q'.\lambda$ must appear in the estimated region, we have $d_1 + d(q.\lambda, q'.\lambda) + 2r < d_2$ and $r < R$. Consider the following situation: $d_1 + 2R > d_2$ but $d_1 + 2r < d_2$, despite the movement of the query, if $d'_1 + 2r > d'_2$ holds, sk_2 will be dominated by sk_1 and leave the skyline.

3. If there are two nonskyline objects p_1 and p_2, it is obvious that the change of the relationship between the two objects cannot affect the skyline.

When the query point is relocated, some skyline objects in the skyline may leave while no objects can be skyline points. We know that Lemma 3 is right.

3.4   Continuous Distance-Based Skyline Computation

We now address the issues of continuous distance-based skyline query processing on geo-textual data. Based on the observations in Sect. 3.3, we compute the skyline on-the-fly only considering those objects with possibilities to change the skyline in each moment. Specifically, before maintaining skyline continuously, the initial distance-based skyline results need to be retrieved. Then we enter an expanding phase and start to maintain the skyline results. As the estimated radius of the query increases continuously, the objects that may cause influence to skyline (determined by Lemma 2) are visited. When new location information of the query q is determined, we enter the relocating phase and refresh the query position $q.\lambda$ as well as the query radius $q.r$. The new initial skyline for the coming expanding phase can be fetched from the skyline results at the last moment of the previous expanding phase (proved in Lemma 3). The skyline results are kept updated efficiently by executing expanding and relocating alternately. Since the query point is moving in a planar area, we adopt the uniform $2D$ grid file which is dividing the data space into $h \times v$ cells to speed up the query processing as shown in Fig. 4.

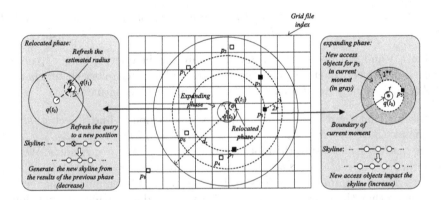

Fig. 4. Distance-based continuous skyline computation

Initial Skyline Computation. The initial skyline computation framework is presented in Algorithm 1. Given a query $q = (\lambda, d_r, \mathcal{W})$ with a maximum moving speed v_{max}, our solution first invokes textual relevant function to compute the initial skyline ISK according to query keywords $q.\mathcal{W}$ and the distance constraint d_r. An empty list L is obligated for holding the coming skyline. Then all cells of

---

Algorithm 1. Initial Skyline Computation

Input: $q = (\lambda, d_r, \mathcal{W})$, v_{max}.
Output: Initial Skyline ISK.

1 List $L = \emptyset$, Heap $H = \emptyset$;
2 **for** *each cell$_i$* **do**
3 | **if** $mindist(cell_i, q.\lambda) < d_r$ **then**
4 | | insert $cell_i$ as an entry to H;

5 **while** H *is not empty* **do**
6 | remove top entry e;
7 | **if** e *is a cell* **then**
8 | | $\forall p \in e$, insert into H;
9 | **else**
10 | | check e with L, insert or delete if necessary;

11 **return** L;

---

the grid file index which minimum distance to $q.\lambda$ not beyond d_r will be inserted into an empty heap H. After that, while the heap H is not empty, geo-textual objects in a cell are sequentially compared to the current skyline objects in L, which is adjusted with deletion or insertion if necessary. After all cells are visited, the objects in the list L are the skyline results ISK.

Continuously Update. The continuous skyline query processing starts with an expanding phase. To guarantee the completeness and correctness of skyline results, the search radius of the skyline d_s is dynamically adjusted as the radius of motion model increases. For example, the initial radius of the uncertain motion model is zero while d_s is equal to d_r. Then if the radius of uncertain area is increasing to R, d_s will be updated to $d_r + R$.

Inspired by Lemma 3, our method avoids repeating traversal of the whole dataset by space division and only focuses on the objects that are possible to affect the skyline. We store the skyline objects with their distances to the query for helping to judge whether objects can enter skyline or not as well as to predict the accurate time that candidate objects enter the skyline by computing the variation in distance between the initial moment and the current moment. We classify the new accessed objects as follows.

- p_{in}. An object p accessed at present is not dominated by the corresponding skyline object, and after further checking, it is not dominated by any other skyline objects.
- p_{cache}. An object p accessed at present is still dominated by some skyline objects, but after further checking, it is not dominated by any other skyline objects, before the query radius increased to d_r, the unique dominance relationship between p and the corresponding skyline object will be broken.
- p_{prune}. An object p accessed at present dominated by a skyline object or may not break the dominance relationship with the corresponding skyline before the query radius increase to d_r.

In each moment, objects belong to p_{cache} with their specific times impacting the skyline will be added to the cache queue. By checking the cache queue,

---

Algorithm 2. d_r-$CGTS$

Input: $q = (\lambda, d_r, \mathcal{W})$, v_{max}, ISK, R.
Output: Current Skyline CSK.

```
 1  cache queue Q = ∅;
 2  CSK = ISK;
 3  if R < d_r and no new location of q arrives then
 4  │   if R == d_r then
 5  │   │   return CSK;
 6  │   else
 7  │   │   check Q;
 8  │   │   for each cell e: ∃sk, mindist(e, q.λ) − d(sk, q) < 2 * v_max and
    │   │       mindist(cell_i, q.λ) < d_r + R do
 9  │   │   │   for each object p in cell e do
10  │   │   │   │   if p is a p_in then
11  │   │   │   │   │   add p to CSK;
12  │   │   │   │   else if p is a p_cache then
13  │   │   │   │   │   insert p into Q;
14  │   │   │   │   else
15  │   │   │   │   │   p is a p_prune, ignore;
16  │   │   return CSK;
17  else
18  │   refresh q.λ, R;
19  │   empty Q;
20  │   compute new ISK by CSK;
21  │   return CSK;
```

---

we still need to deal with new accessed objects in each moment. The steps of the distance-based continuous geo-textual skyline query processing is shown in Algorithm 2. From line 3 to line 16, the algorithm is in an expanding phase. The cache queue is checked first and then the new accessed objects are distinguished for being disposed in corresponding way. After that, the current skyline CSK is return. From line 17 to line 20, if new location information of the query q is determined, the algorithm enters the relocating phase. The returned skyline objects are refined from the previous ones, which will be treated as the new ISK of the coming expanding phase. Meanwhile, the cache queue will be emptied.

4   Experimental Evaluation

This Section experimentally evaluates the performance of the proposed algorithms. As this is the first attempt for continuous skyline query processing on geo-textual data, we could not directly compare with any previous technique. Thus, we provide two baseline methods BNL^+ and $D\&C^+$, which are promoted from BNL and D&C [1] respectively but adopting grid file indexes to compare with our method. To be fair, the above algorithms adopt the same textual relevance functions. It is worth noting that the two baseline methods cannot correctly tell when the skyline changes as our method does. In all experiments, we focus on both CPU time and I/O counts. We conduct our experiments on real datasets: FSQ and TWE [3] where FSQ is a real-life dataset collected from

Table 1. Parameter and ranges

Parameter	Range (Default*)
Cardinality of datasets	100 K, 200 K, 300 K, 500 K*, 1 M
Radius of query range (km)	10, 20*, 30, 50, 100
Ratio of relocating	10 %, 20 %*, 30 %, 40 %, 50 %

Foursquare containing 1.1 million worldwide POIs and TWE is a larger real-life dataset that comprises 40 million tweets with GPS coordinates. Default values for parameters are shown in Table 1. All the algorithms are implemented in C++ with STL library. Experiments are performed on a PC with Intel Core i3-3240 3.40 GHz dual CPU and 4G memory running a Windows 7 operating system. The disk page size is fixed to 4096 bytes.

The Effect of Cardinality. In this experiment, we evaluate the scalability of our method by varying the size of datasets between 100 K and 1 M. We select objects from FSQ and TWE randomly. By default, the query range is 20 km while the relocating ratio is set to 20 %. The results of this experiment are shown in Fig. 5. We can see that as the size of datasets increases, the growth rate of our proposed algorithm has a clear advantage. Figure 5(a) and (b) shows that the I/O counts of our method is nearly only a half of the other two methods. In Fig. 5(c) and (d), the runtime of our method is dramatically smaller. This phenomenon shows that our proposed algorithm has a good scalability.

The Effect of Query Range. In this round of experiment, we investigate the effect of the query range. Figure 6(a) and (b) shows that the I/O cost of the

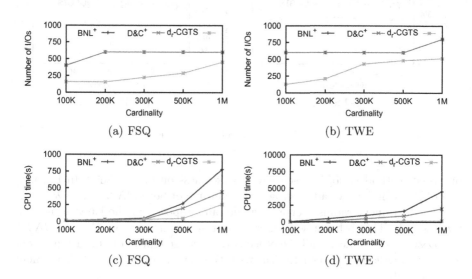

Fig. 5. Effect of Cardinality

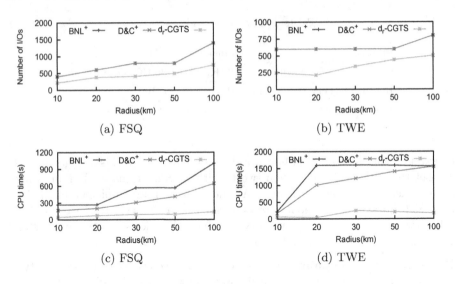

Fig. 6. Effect of query range

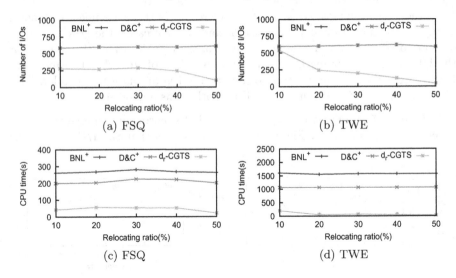

Fig. 7. Effect of relocating ratio

proposed method is not too sensitive to skewness on query range. In Fig. 6(c) and 6(d), as the query radius grows, the runtime of both BNL^+ and $D\&C^+$ is longer when query radius increases while our proposed method performs relatively steady. That is because a wider query range contains more objects, BNL^+ and $D\&C^+$ need to access all the objects in the range repeatedly in each moment while our method only need to deal with the new access ones in each moment incrementally.

The Effect of Relocating Ratio. This experiment is organized to study the effect of the relocating ratio. we fix the query range to 20 km while the number of objects is 500 K. Since the relocating is performed randomly in our simulation, we take twenty times of tests and get the average cost as our final results. The query range is 20 km while the the the size of datasets is 500 K. Figure 7 presents the runtime and I/O cost of 100 query times when we vary the relocating ratio of the query from 10 % to 50 %. As the relocating ratio increases, the cost of BNL^+ and $D\&C^+$ are steadily high while that of our method decreases. The reason is that, skyline results of a relocating phase can be obtained from the former results in our method, which costs almost negligible overhead.

5 Conclusions

This paper studies the distance constrained continuous skylines on geo-textual data. We utilize *disk* uncertain motion model to represent a query object, which integrates the uncertainty of location into the skyline. Thus the retrieved objects are still spatially close and textually relevant to the potential query point in the whole processing. Our solution does not need to do overmuch keyword-matching or compute the skyline from scratch at every time instance. Instead, the possible change from one time to another is predicted and processed on specified part of the dataset accordingly making the distance-based geo-textual skyline results efficiently updated. Empirical studies on real datasets demonstrate that our solution has both lower elapsed time and I/O cost.

Acknowledgment. This work is partially supported by Natural Science Foundation of Jiangsu Province of China under grant No. BK20140826, Funding of Graduate Innovation Center in NUAA under grant No. KFJJ20151604.

References

1. Börzsöny, S., Kossmann, D., Stocker, K.: The skyline operator. In: ICDE, pp. 421–430 (2001)
2. Cheema, M.A., Lin, X., Zhang, W., Zhang, Y.: A safe zone based approach for monitoring moving skyline queries. In: EDBT, pp. 275–286 (2013)
3. Chen, L., Cong, G., Cao, X., Tan, K.-L.: Temporal spatial-keyword top-k publish/subscribe. In: ICDE, pp. 255–266 (2015)
4. Choi, H., Jung, H., Lee, K.Y., Chung, Y.D.: Skyline queries on keyword-matched data. Inf. Sci. **232**, 449–463 (2013)
5. Cong, G., Christian, S., Wu, D.: Efficient retrieval of the top-k most relevant spatial web objects. In: VLDB, pp. 337–348 (2009)
6. Felipe, I., Hristidis, V., Naphtali, R.: Keyword search on spatial database. In: ICDE, pp. 656–665 (2008)
7. Hjaltason, G.R., Samet, H.: Distance browsing in spatial databases. In: TODS, pp. 256–318 (1999)
8. Huang, Z., Lu, H., Ooi, B.C., Tung, A.K.H.: Continuous skyline queries for moving objects. TKDE **18**(12), 1645–1658 (2006)

9. Lee, M.-W., Hwang, S.-W.: Continuous skylining on volatile moving data. In: ICDE, pp. 1568–1575 (2009)
10. Li, J., Wang, H., Li, J., Gao, H.: Skyline for geo-textual data. GeoInformatica **20**(3), 1–17 (2016)
11. Papadias, D., Tao, Y., Fu, G.: Progressive skyline computation in database systems. TODS **30**(1), 41–82 (2005)
12. Shi, J., Wu, D., Mamoulis, N.: Textually relevant spatial skylines. IEEE Trans. Knowl. Data Eng. **28**(1), 224–237 (2016)

Improving Urban Traffic Evacuation Capability in Emergency Response by Using Smart Phones

Ping Zhang[1], Yi Liu[1], Rui Yang[1], Hui Zhang[1(✉)], and Zengli Gong[2]

[1] Institute of Public Safety Research, Department of Engineering Physics,
Tsinghua University, Beijing, China
zhangp14@mails.tsinghua.edu.cn,
{liuyi,ryang,zhhui}@tsinghua.edu.cn
[2] Beijing Legalsoft Ltd., Beijing, China
gongzengli@gmail.com

Abstract. This article presents a social network based methodology for improving urban traffic evacuation capability in emergency response by using smart phones. Considering destructive and unexpected characteristics of natural hazards or man-made disasters, the effected people cannot evacuate efficiently when they face the unknown impacts of these events. Therefore, a smart phone application, called *EMAPP*, is developed to tackle this difficulty. An overall description including design architecture and system modules is provided. Optimal shelter choice strategy is given by using the modified Dijkstra's algorithm. The Nagel-Schreckenberg model loaded by vehicle arrival rate is implemented to produce the spatio-temporal diagrams of the vehicles. Both traffic congestion and cascading failure during real-time emergency evacuation are analyzed. The main issues are devoted to link the affected people, geographic information and traffic conditions through the smartphone application. Therefore, in emergency evacuation, the affected people can receive mutual help and urban resilience can be enhanced.

Keywords: Social network · Spatio-temporal analysis · Emergency evacuation · Traffic control · GIS · Mobile phone application

1 Introduction

Natural hazards and man-made disasters may lead to the disruption of urban system with numerous casualties and property losses. Characteristics of these catastrophes and accidents are distinct, which may bring different types of destruction like communication interruption, building collapse and traffic breakdown. Victims may be trapped in the affected areas without help and notification. They need to be evacuated to shelters under authoritative evacuation instructions. However, real-time traffic condition varies rapidly and evacuees encounter in road congestion frequently in emergency evacuation. Furthermore, the damage of telecom base station may cause network paralysis during natural disasters such as earthquake and Typhoon. Victims have difficulties to locate their positions and navigate their directions. Due to the shortage of appropriate

A. Morishima et al. (Eds.): APWeb 2016 Workshops, LNCS 9865, pp. 241–252, 2016.
DOI: 10.1007/978-3-319-45835-9_21

evacuation information, victims have difficulties to carry out self-help or mutual-aid. A few scenarios are provided to illustrate the situations that decision makers and victims may be encountered.

- During earthquake, landslide or building fires, not only disaster-induced collapse but also falling debris of the buildings may cause significant safety problem [1]. Flying debris can destroy cars and roads, which bring traffic congestion and hinder emergency evacuation. Efficient evacuation instruction should notify the drivers take a detour to keep away from the vulnerable buildings.
- During flood, hurricane or tsunami, natural hazards can be predicted. Then, a large area of residents need to be transported to the safety areas before disaster strikes. Therefore, efficient countermeasures, including evacuation shelter choice and timely route selection, are greatly needed.
- During toxic chemical leakage, nuclear proliferation or terrorist bombing, such emergency will bring panic to the city dwellers without pre-warning. Residents need to avoid the hazardous areas during evacuation. Also, they need to know the status of their family members and relatives.

In order to improve city community resilience, which can be prepared for and resisted to rapid changing environment, it is needed to perform evacuation research to minimize the loss from disasters. Meanwhile, the primary goal of emergency services is to reduce the loss of life and property, especially in the crowded neighborhoods, where response time is vital important [2]. To illustrate the complex evacuation process, Stepanov [3] depicted seven evacuation phases including incident detection, issuing evacuation order, delivering order/message to public via transmitters, preparation for evacuation, movement through evacuation network, arrival at the safety zone and verification phase. Evacuation is one of the indispensable parts of large-scale disaster response, which is determined by spatio-temporal analysis based on individual agents under different disaster circumstances [4]. After evacuation order is issued, evacuees and vehicles will follow the evacuation instructions to the designated locations. A large amount of researches concentrate on the aspects of the shortest path design, maximum road network flow, minimum cost flow, reversible lane design and traffic signal problems. Inevitably, congestion takes place as soon as evacuation begins. Even a car breakdown may result in the cascading problem to real-time evacuation.

2 Related Work

2.1 Traditional Method

Traffic evacuation research can be divided into two categories. On the one hand, the structure of urban traffic turns into a classical graph theory problem. Let $G = \{V, E\}$ depicts the physical topological structure of traffic network, where V is the vertex that denotes the location of each intersection with latitude and longitude. E is the edge that represents the pairwise relationship between two adjacent vertices. Based on the graph theory, many studies turn into mathematical programming or optimizing problems. Objective functions are mainly total network clearance time and the proportion of evacuees be rescued in evacuation. To improve the efficiency and accuracy of decision making, optimization models are used, such as, the genetic algorithm, particle swarm optimization algorithm, neural network algorithm and tabu search method. On the other hand, vehicles are treated as the particles with distinct locations and velocities. Traffic flow is formed when mutual interaction between vehicles is taken place. Then, the relationship among velocity, density and flow is analyzed by the hydrodynamic functions. These functions eventually attribute to differential equations and are solved numerically.

However, actual evacuation is a full of uncertainty since personal reaction and psychology are very much different. Therefore, many researchers investigate the social relationship and decision making that probably influence the evacuation process [5]. Also, efficient crisis management requires a high level of response, and precise knowledge on how many people exposed in the incident area [6]. Nowadays, more and more people are accustomed to the Internet. It seems reasonable and appropriate to draw support from increasingly ubiquitous portable, wireless devices such as smart phones [7]. These devices, which contain versatile sensors like GPS, are very important sources of spatial information [8]. Several projects like real-time urban monitoring in Rome and PLAN (Personal Localized Altering Network) in New York have already come true [9, 10].

2.2 Smart Phones Used in Evacuation

With the rapid development of telecommunication technologies and GIS tools, alternative approaches are carried out in analyzing the structure of cities [11]. Smart phones used in disaster management provide different types of data and information, which improve the effectiveness of traditional evacuation. The data and information can be divided into three categories.

- Trajectories of the crowd and positions of rescue vehicles;
- Real-time status of the affected area added with geographic tag;
- Social media used in emergency evacuation.

Social media can provide comprehensive information in emergency evacuation [12]. Evacuation instructions, including evacuation shelter site choice and optimal route selection, are vital for evacuees. However, instruction is hard to disseminate without developing strong social network to promote resident-to-resident collaboration [7].

3 Framework and Modules

3.1 System Architecture

The proposed architecture integrates communication, GIS, risk management and social network. A smart phone application, named *EMAPP*, is produced to analyze the spatio-temporal data in emergency. It contains five modules, namely Geo-database, Prediction, Information Release, Social Network and Scenario modules. System architecture is depicted in Fig. 1.

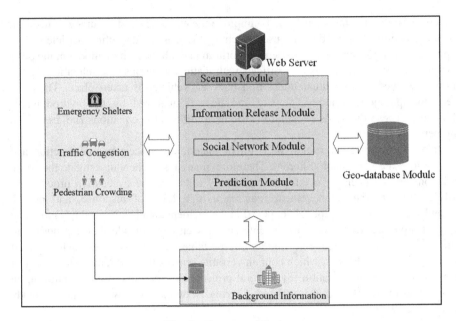

Fig. 1. System architecture

3.2   Geo-Database Module

With the growing usage of GPS-enabled smart phones, a great volume of traffic and geographic data are generated. A central challenging is how to represent the actual emergency management scenario through spatio-temporal data [13]. Storing all kinds of data, however, unrelated to disaster scenario, produce a burden to the local technical department. To tackle the dilemma, we integrate three kinds of spatio-temporal data: users' trajectories, vehicle locations and traffic conditions. The matching of such data can facilitate real-time evacuation, and provide a new perspective of how evacuees may interact with each other in the affected area.

3.3   Prediction Module

EMAPP can perceive emergency before it evolves into disaster and make useful prediction with the feasibility of Geo-database module.

- Trajectory Prediction and Abnormal Clustering Identification

Users' movements and mobility patterns can be analyzed based on the daily use of *EMAPP*. Therefore, evacuation route and the nearest shelter are recommended. Meanwhile, heat map displayed in *EMAPP* depicts the population distribution based on the online users' number and their geographic positions. During a large-scale activity, when the travelers' number and density exceed a predefined threshold, it becomes necessary to warn the users to leave the high-risk area.

- Traffic Congestion Prediction

When the moving speed of a user in accordance with a car and the user's location is located on the road, we can then claim the smart phone is located in the vehicle. The pedestrian crowded problem is changed into a traffic congestion problem. The real-time traffic condition data can therefore be updated. The pedestrian crowded and traffic congestion mechanisms are very similar.

- Emergency Information Collection

Emergency information flow is coming from many resources. *EMAPP* is designed with an incident reporting interface. When unexpected threats happen, such as fire or terrorist attack, users can be timely reporting by uploading scenario picture tagged with spatio-temporal information with brief description text. All information will be filtered and analyzed to establish situation awareness by emergency agencies.

3.4   Information Release Module

Gathering spatial related disaster response data like the locations of the shelters and emergency medical services are beneficial to the city dwellers. Such information will help the evacuees make correct decision during emergency. It will result in decreasing the evacuation time under the exposure of risk. *EMAPP* extended by coupling the static information with online communication means, such as, social media and SMS text message can disseminate a seasonable notification to warn the evacuees. The way to select an evacuation shelter and traffic jam encountered during evacuation will be explained in Sect. 4.

3.5   Social Network and Scenario Module

Information dissemination via website and social media is quicker than official notification. Communities can share information simultaneously to respond to a crisis, regardless of its type and magnitude [7]. Community neighbors are capable of contacting with each other and providing mutual support by establishing social network through *EMAPP*. They can broadcast rescue messages to their friends in case of trapped in a disaster zone. If the disaster type changes, the scenario module can be changed in accordance with the disaster type.

4   Modeling and Simulation

4.1   Extraction of Significant Locations

A pilot study is carried out and the participants are mainly students from the Department of Engineering Physics in Tsinghua University. Forty students have installed *EMAPP* on their smart phones for about one month. Figure 2 partially depicts their daily usages on the GaoDe Map. The campus, which located in the northwest of Beijing, is selected as a study area. In this study, we only focus on their daily usages in the campus, the trajectories outside are not considered.

With the help of users' daily spatio-temporal data sets, four significant locations are extracted by the k-means clustering. Crowded areas are identified and marked in Fig. 3. It is undoubted that the higher regional density is, the risker the area is. Meanwhile, it is necessary to protect the crowded places from terrorist attack and prevent the crowd from stamping. Alternative route recommendation can be made by *EMAPP* to help the users avoid these areas as much as possible.

Fig. 2. Pilot study area in Beijing, China

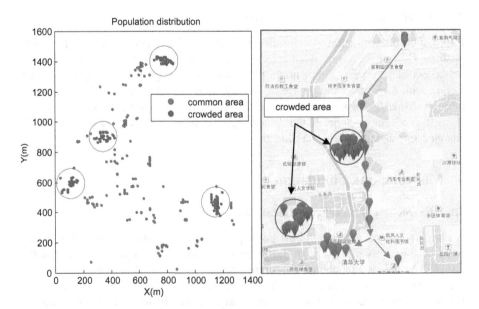

Fig. 3. Extraction of significant locations and a student's daily routine

A student's daily routine is demonstrated by analyzing the spatio-temporal data. The student lives in the dormitory and has a class in the morning and afternoon respectfully. By using the real-time crowd information, two congestion sites will be encountered on his/her way to the class. Therefore, the student is warned or selects another route.

4.2 Evacuation Shelter Selection

An optimal distribution of the shelters in the urban region can greatly reduce the network clearance time, i.e., the time needed to escape from the residential area to temporary shelters. In this paper, five shelters are designated fairly uniform by considering full usage of community emergency resources [14]. To be simplified, the city dwellers will arrive at the nearest shelter by taking the shortest route. The Dijkstra's algorithm is modified by pre-calculating geographic distance between two crossroads according to their latitude and longitude. The following pseudo-code depicts the logical calculation step.

Algorithm: Pseudo-code for Modified Dijkstra's Algorithm

Input: $G = (V, E, Shelters)$: A geography graph

Output: dist[V\Shelters, Shelters]: distance between each vertex to the nearest shelter

```
1   Precompute geography distance of each edge
2   for all v∈V \{Shelters ∪ suc[Shelters]} do
3       for all s∈Shelters do
4           dist[v,s] ← ∞            // initialize the distance matrix
5           pre[v] ← null            // initialize the precursor nodes
6       end for
7   end for
8   while V\Shelters is not null do
9       for all s∈Shelters do
10          u ← vertex in V with smallest dist[]
11          if dist[u,s] = +∞ then
12              break
13          end if
14          V ← V\{u}                // remove the existing nodes
15          for all neighbor v of u
16              alt ← len[u,s] + distance_between(u,v)
17              if alt < len[v,s] then
18                  len[v,s] ← alt       // update the shortest length
19                  pre[v] ← u           // update the precursor nodes
20              end if
21          end for
22      end for
23      dist[v,s] ← Minᵥ(len[v,s])
24  end while
```

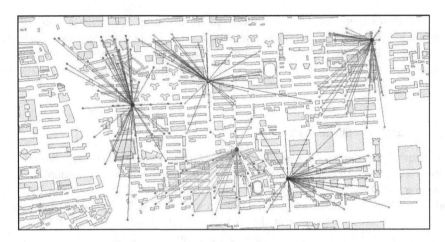

Fig. 4. Emergency evacuation shelter selection

The distance between each vertex to the nearest shelter is calculated and demonstrated in Fig. 4.

4.3   Traffic Evacuation in the Affected Area

Large-scale emergency evacuation consists of two steps. Step 1: the core area evacuation, evacuees are notified and move to the assigned shelters. Step 2: All the evacuees take public transportation from the shelters to safer places. Meanwhile, the status of network periphery affected by congestion changes over time, the spatio-temporal trend will also be considered in the routing selection [15, 16]. Duanmu [17] provides an arrival rate function (1) and accumulative rate function (2) in 24 h.

$$A(t) = \frac{a_i}{b_i} t^{a_i-1} e^{-(t^{a_i}/b_i)} \tag{1}$$

$$F_i(t) = 1 - e^{-(t^{a_i}/b_i)} \tag{2}$$

They assume that approximately 10 % of the evacuees will arrive prior to 8:00, 80 % of the evacuees will arrive from 8:00 to 16:00, and another 10 % of the evacuees will arrive at the last eight hours of the day. Therefore, using the values in function (2) ($F(8) = 0.1$ and $F(16) = 0.9$), two constants can be calculated: a is 4.45 and b is 99310. In this paper, 20,000 vehicles are presumed to arrive at the affected area and their arrival rates obeying the two functions (see Fig. 5). The Nagel-Schreckenberg model loaded by vehicle arrival rate is implemented to produce the spatio-temporal diagrams. The model contains indispensable four rules [18, 19].

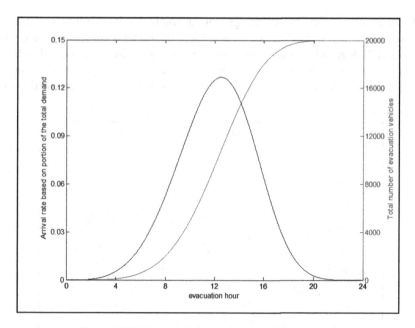

Fig. 5. Vehicles arrival rate and accumulative number

Rule 1: Acceleration:

$$v_j(t) \rightarrow v_j(t + \frac{1}{3}) = \min\{v_j(t) + 1, v_{\max}\}$$

Rule 2: Breaking:

$$if \ v_j(t + \frac{1}{3}) > d_j(t) \quad then \quad v_j(t + \frac{2}{3}) = d_j(t) \quad else \ v_j(t + \frac{2}{3}) = v_j(t + \frac{1}{3})$$

Rule 3: Randomization:

$$v_j(t + \frac{2}{3}) \xrightarrow{p} v_j(t + 1) = \max\left\{0, v_j(t + \frac{2}{3}) - 1\right\}$$

with probability p

Rule 4: Driving:

$$\text{car } j \text{ moves } v_j(t + 1) \text{ cells}$$

where $d_j(t)$ denotes the distance between car j and car $j+1$. The time step corresponds to 1 s in real time. Vehicles are treated as agents, and the study road length equals to 750 m, which contains 100 cells. The maximum velocity Vmax equals to *three* (3 * 7.5 * 3.6 = 81 km/h). The simulation time is 24 h. The experiment results are extracted for every 60 s. Two-randomization probabilities are chosen as 0.2 and 0.5 and different simulation results are compared.

From numerical simulation, the greater randomization probability is the higher congestion is, which means that slow cars induce the traffic bottleneck extremely (see Figs. 6 and 7). Meanwhile, the congestion wave propagates in the opposite direction of travelling. With the GPS sensors, smart phones can detect the early stage of congestion and capture the dynamic traffic data in the city [9]. The users can be detoured to other

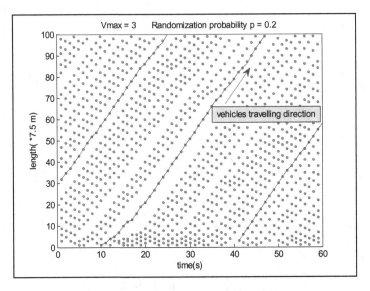

Fig. 6. Spatio-temporal diagram (Vmax = 3, p = 0.2)

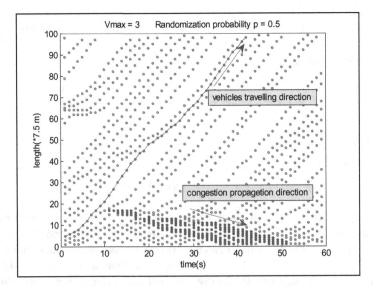

Fig. 7. Spatio-temporal diagram (Vmax = 3, p = 0.5)

itineraries to mitigate the congestion by smart phone notification. Meanwhile, the users can send their massages through *EMAPP* to other evacuees to prevent the overcrowded and avoid cascading failure.

5   Conclusion

In this paper, we present social network based emergency evacuation terminal application, named *EMAPP*, to improve urban traffic evacuation capacity. Its modules and functions are described. By collecting users' daily trajectory data, the application can push the congestion information and provide suitable emergency shelter location. The development of disaster can also be analyzed by spatio-temporary geographic data. Specially designed modules are devoted to the users, which can be used for aiding community by sharing information with each other and by providing channels to the city dwellers for uploading information. The evacuees can make a strategic decision depending on disaster scenarios.

The focus of this paper lies on proper evacuation shelter and route selection based on the users' trajectories. Modified Dijkstra's algorithm is provided to identify the nearest shelter by calculating the shortest path based on the geospatial data. After that, traffic congestion is analyzed immediately. The methodology presented in this paper produces a realistic result, which will yield better suggestion since arterial roads are of great importance in evacuation. Vehicles with low velocity or high randomization probability can be distinguished, which may cause traffic bottleneck and terrible cascading consequence. Integration of *EMAPP* and hazard scenario data can recommend the drivers to take a detour when the traffic jams happen.

In summary, this article presents social network based terminal for providing spatio-temporal analytic support to improve city evacuation capability for different disaster scenarios. Future research will focus on analyzing the users' behaviors and selection strategies. Whenever a major disaster happens, we expect that the usage of this emerging technology can provide valuable information to the victims and emergency agencies.

Acknowledgements. The research is partially funded by the National Natural Science Foundation of China (Grant No. 91024032, No. 91224008).

References

1. Xu, Z., et al.: Simulation of earthquake-induced hazards of falling exterior non-structural components and its application to emergency shelter design. Nat. Hazards **80**(2), 935–950 (2016)
2. Oxendine, C., Sonwalkar, M., Waters, N.: A multi-objective, multi-criteria approach to improve situational awareness in emergency evacuation routing using mobile phone data. Trans. GIS **16**(3), 375–396 (2012)
3. Stepanov, A., Smith, J.M.: Multi-objective evacuation routing in transportation networks. Eur. J. Oper. Res. **198**(2), 435–446 (2009)

4. Winter, S., et al.: Get me out of here: collaborative evacuation based on local knowledge. In: Proceedings of the 3rd ACM SIGSPATIAL International Workshop on Indoor Spatial Awareness, pp. 35–42. ACM (2011)

5. Murray-Tuite, P., Wolshon, B.: Evacuation transportation modeling: an overview of research, development, and practice. Transp. Res. Part C: Emerg. Technol. **27**, 25–45 (2013)

6. Steenbruggen, J., Tranos, E., Nijkamp, P.: Data from mobile phone operators: a tool for smarter cities? Telecommun. Policy **39**, 335–346 (2015)

7. Jaeger, P.T., et al.: Community response grids: e-government, social networks, and effective emergency management. Telecommun. Policy **31**, 592–604 (2007)

8. Alamdar, F., Kalantari, M., Rajabifard, A.: Towards multi-agency sensor information integration for disaster management. Comput. Environ. Urban Syst. **56**, 68–85 (2016)

9. Calabrese, F., et al.: Real-time urban monitoring using cell phones: a case study in Rome. IEEE Trans. Intell. Transp. Syst. **12**(1), 141–151 (2011)

10. Fry, J., Binner, J.M.: Elementary modelling and behavioural analysis for emergency evacuations using social media. Eur. J. Oper. Res. **249**(3), 1014–1023 (2016)

11. Iovanovici, A., et al.: A hierarchical approach in deploying traffic lights using complex network analysis. In: Proceeding of the 18th International Conference on System Theory, Control and Computing, pp. 791–796 (2014)

12. Xu, Z., et al.: Crowdsourcing based description of urban emergency events using social media big data. IEEE Trans. Cloud Comput. **PP**(99) (2016)

13. Xu, Z., et al.: Participatory sensing-based semantic and spatial analysis of urban emergency events using mobile social media. EURASIP J. Wirel. Commun. Netw. **2016**(44), 1–9 (2016)

14. Zhang, P., Zhang, H., Guo, D.: Evacuation shelter and route selection based on multi-objective optimization approach. In: 1st International ACM SIGSPATIAL Workshop on the use of GIS in Emergency Management (EM-GIS), Seattle, Washington, USA (2015)

15. Wang, Z., Zlatanova, S.: Multi-agent based path planning for first responders among moving obstacles. Comput. Environ. Urban Syst. **56**, 48–58 (2016)

16. Asif, M.T., et al.: Spatial and temporal patterns in large-scale traffic speed prediction. IEEE Trans. Intell. Transp. Syst. **15**(2), 794–804 (2014)

17. Duanmu, J., et al.: Buffering in evacuation management for optimal traffic demand distribution. Transp. Res. Part E: Logistics Transp. Rev. **48**(3), 684–700 (2012)

18. Nagel, K.: A cellular automaton model for freeway traffic. J. Phys. I Fr. **2**(12), 2221–2229 (1992)

19. Barlovic, R., et al.: Metastable states in cellular automata for traffic flow. Eur. Phys. J. B – Condens. Matter Complex Syst. **5**(3), 793–800 (1998)

Context Enhanced Keyword Extraction for Sparse Geo-Entity Relation from Web Texts

Li Yu[1], Feng Lu[1,2(✉)], Xueying Zhang[3], and Xiliang Liu[1,4]

[1] State Key Laboratory of Resources and Environmental Information System,
Institute of Geographic Sciences and Natural Resources Research,
Chinese Academy of Sciences, Beijing 100101, China
{yul,luf,liuxl}@lreis.ac.cn

[2] Jiangsu Center for Collaborative Innovation in Geographical Information
Resource Development and Application, Nanjing 210023, China

[3] Key Laboratory of Virtual Geography Environment,
Nanjing Normal University, Nanjing 210046, China
zhangsnowy@163.com

[4] Fujian Collaborative Innovation Center for Big Data Applications
in Governments, Fuzhou 350003, China

Abstract. Geo-entity relation recognition from rich texts requires robust and effective solutions on keyword extraction. Compared with supervised learning methods, unsupervised learning methods attract more attention for their capability to capture the dynamic feature variation in text and to discover additional relation types. The frequency-based methods of keyword extraction have been widely studied. However, it is difficult to be applied into geo-entity keyword extraction directly because of the sparse distribution of geo-entity relations in texts. Besides, there are few studies on Chinese keyword extraction. This paper proposes a context enhanced keyword extraction method. Firstly the contexts for geo-entities are enhanced to reduce the sparseness of terms. Secondly two well-known frequency-based statistical methods (i.e., DF and Entropy) are used to build a large-scale corpus automatically from the enhanced contexts. Thirdly the lexical features and their weights are statistically determined based on the corpus to enhance the distinction of the terms. Finally, all terms in the enhanced contexts are measured with the lexical features, and the most important terms are selected as the keywords of geo-entity pairs. Experiments are conducted with mass real Chinese web texts. Compared with DF and Entropy, the presented method improves the precision by 41 % and 36 % respectively in discovering the keywords with sparse distribution and generates additional 60 % correct keywords for geo-entity relation recognition.

Keywords: Geographical information retrieval · Geo-entity relation · Keyword extraction · Text mining · Context enhancement

© Springer International Publishing Switzerland 2016
A. Morishima et al. (Eds.): APWeb 2016 Workshops, LNCS 9865, pp. 253–264, 2016.
DOI: 10.1007/978-3-319-45835-9_22

1 Introduction

The web provides important and even exclusive resources for geographic information retrieval and knowledge discovery [1]. At the same time, geo-entity relations are commonly used in describing the locations of entities and geographical phenomena which are crucial for building geographic knowledge systems [2]. To better understand the geographic semantics embedded in rich web texts, it's a pressing need for robust and effective solutions in geo-entity relation extraction.

The frequently used supervised learning methods which perform well with specified static texts behave poorly in extracting geo-entity relations from web texts [3]. Firstly, building massive patterns or corpora are expensive and training models is time-consuming, the massive web texts cannot be processed in real-time with supervised methods [4]. Secondly, web texts may cover various domains with strong hetero-geneities, leading to a poor portability for model training [5]. Thirdly, the dynamic nature of web texts constantly generates additional relation types which cannot be captured by predefined patterns and pre-trained models [6]. The unsupervised learning methods have attracted more attentions in the field of web texts mining because they don't need large scale patterns and corpora. Additionally, they can be utilized for additional relation exploring, which are more suitable for dynamic text mining [7].

Keywords play an important role in relation recognition with unsupervised learning methods, which provide rich clues to describe the relations between entities [8]. Unsupervised methods regard keyword extraction as a ranking task and extract the top-ranked as keywords [9]. The existing keyword extraction methods for relation recognition are mainly based on frequency statistics. These methods are based on the hypothesis that there exist a large number of redundant terms which imply the relations for a specific entity pair. However, this hypothesis is not appropriate to extract key-words for geo-entity based on the following reasons: Firstly, the specific geo-entity pair rarely co-occurs in one sentence based on our experiments [10]. Besides, the number of terms in the context of the specific geo-entity pair is very limited, which makes the terms rather sparse. Secondly, the synonymy exacerbates the problem of sparseness [11]. Thirdly, there is a strong correlation between the types of geo-entity and the terms [12]. For example, "flow into" can only describe the relation between water bodies, not buildings. However, it is not applicable for semantic relations which are not restricted by the type of geo-entity pair. Therefore, only frequency statistic is hard to distinguish the keywords from others and will not work well in recognizing geo-entity relations with sparse distribution. Besides, different languages vary in word segmentation, part-of-speech (POS) tagging and syntactic analyzing, which have a great influence on keyword extraction. Compared with English, a character-based language like Chinese needs a different strategy of keyword extraction for geo-entity relation.

This paper focuses on how to extract keywords from mass Chinese web texts for recognizing geo-entity relations with extremely sparse distribution. Our contributions are as follows:

(1) We propose the context enhanced method to reduce the term sparseness of key-word extraction. To the best of our knowledge, the sparse distribution of geo-entity relation is firstly presented in the field of geo-entity relation

recognition. We also prove sparseness reduction is essential for generating high-quality keywords and achieving an unsupervised recognizing method of sparse geo-entity relation.

(2) In order to reveal the specific characteristics of the given web texts and deal with heterogeneous web texts, we use feature selection and weight statistics to increase the distinctions between the terms in context. Different with the frequency-based methods, we additionally explore multiple lexical features in real-time and dynamically adjust their weights.

(3) Our method significantly outperforms other comparing algorithms (DF and Entropy), and has the ability of discovering additional keywords that is appropriate to dynamic text mining.

The remainder of this paper is organized as follows. A context enhanced methodology of keyword extraction for sparse geo-entity relation is presented in Sect. 2. The experiments and discussion are presented in Sect. 3. Conclusion is drawn in Sect. 4.

2 Methodology

2.1 Definitions

Input: Chinese texts crawled from assigned websites. One piece of texts is shown below.

> 中关村位于**海淀区**，邻近**北京大学**和**清华大学**。此外，
> 中关村是**中国**的科技中心，被誉为"**中国的硅谷**"。
>
> *Zhongguancun is located in **Haidian District**, along with the proximity to **Peking University** and **Tsinghua University**. Besides, **Zhongguancun** is a technology hub in **China**, and is referred to as "**China's Silicon Valley**".*

Output: a set of keywords for geo-entity pairs.

Geo-entity pair (e_1, e_2): two geo-related entities co-occurring in one sentence. The first geo-entity appearing in one sentence is paired with other geo-entities in the same sentence. For example, (中关村Zhongguancun, 海淀区Haidian District), (中关村Zhongguancun, 北京大学Peking University) and (中关村Zhongguancun, 清华大学Tsinghua University) are geo-entity pairs in the first sentence.

Geo-entity relation r: a state of connectedness between geo-entities, divided into two types, spatial relations and semantic relations. Spatial relations consist of topological, directional and distance relations, such as *"within"*, *"south"* and *"10 kilometres"*. Semantic relations are *"hypernym"*, *"hyponym"*, *"equal"*, to name a few. Both of them can be represented as a set of facts with the form (e_1, r, e_2). The examples of fact are

(中关村, 相邻, 北京大学) and (中关村, 别名, 中国的硅谷), which are (Zhong-guancun, adjacent, Peking University) and (Zhongguancun, alias, China's Silicon Valley) in English.

Term t: a phrase or a word with semantic information in a sentence, such as "位于", "科技中心"("be located in", "technology hub" in English) and so on.

Context c: all terms existing before, between and after the specified geo-entity pair in a sentence except for other geo-entities in the same sentence, with the stop words filtered. The stop words are function words, such as "被", "并", "都" ("by", "and", "both" in English) and so on. For example, the context of (中关村, 海淀区), (中关村, 北京大学) and (中关村, 清华大学) contains 2 terms, (位于, 邻近) which are (be located in, proximity) in English.

Keyword k: the terms picked out from context as indicators in relation expressions. For example, the term "proximity" picked out from the context (be located in, proximity) is a keyword revealing the topological relation *"adjacent"* for the geo-entity pair (Zhongguancun, Peking University) (Table 1).

Table 1. Examples of geo-entity pairs and corresponding keywords.

Geo-entity pairs	Keywords
(中关村, 海淀区) (Zhongguancun, Haidian District)	(位于) (*be located in*)
(中关村, 北京大学) (Zhongguancun, Peking University)	(邻近) (proximity)
(中关村, 清华大学) (Zhongguancun, Tsinghua University)	(邻近) (proximity)
(中关村, 中国) (Zhongguancun, China)	(科技中心) (technology hub)
(中关村, 中国的硅谷) (Zhongguancun, China's Silicon Valley)	(誉为) (as)

2.2   Sparseness Reduction

The terms in the context of a specific geo-entity pair are usually sparse. Merging the contexts of geo-entity pairs with the same type will reduce the sparseness of terms in one context. This requires a fine-grained mapping table connecting types to geo-entities. In this paper, an online Chinese encyclopaedia (Baidu Baike[1]) is used for obtaining the type labels of each geo-entity. Similar to Wikipedia, Baidu Baike attaches each piece of web texts with multiple type labels according to the ranked importance for each entry. For example, the entry "Beijing" has 4 type labels, "municipality", "ancient capital", "China" and "first-tier city".

The process of sparseness reduction for terms is shown in Fig. 1. Firstly, we search the geo-entities in Baidu Baike one by one, and obtain the corresponding label types.

---

[1] http://baike.baidu.com.

Secondly, all type labels of the specified geo-entity are assessed by using their orders and frequencies, and the most important label is picked out as the geo-entity type. After all geo-entity is assigned its type, the type of geo-entity pair (e_x, e_y) can be decided with the name $T_{xy} = $ <type$_{ex}$, type$_{ey}$>. Thirdly, we merge the contexts of geo-entity pairs with the same type, and the number of terms in context will be increased. This process enhanced the information used to extract keywords for geo-entity pairs. Moreover, the term's semantics are also fused with the help of the synonym dictionary $CiLin^2$ to reduce the sparseness of terms.

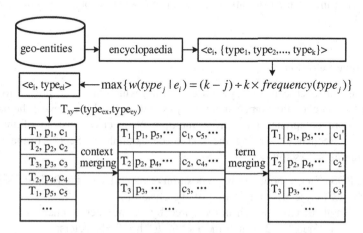

Fig. 1. Sparseness reduction for terms in contexts.

2.3   Corpus Generation

A large-scale corpus is needed to select the effective features for keyword extraction. It is generated automatically based on two well-known frequency-based statistical methods, namely the DF (Domain Frequency) and Entropy. DF and Entropy methods are used for extracting keywords from the entire web texts. The intersection of these two resulted keyword sets forms the corpus for feature selection. DF is shown in formula (1). Entropy is shown in formula (2)–(3).

$$DF_t = \frac{f_{t,T_i}}{\sum_{j=1}^{N} f_{t,T_j}} \tag{1}$$

$$S_{i,j} = \exp(\frac{\ln 0.5}{\overline{D}} \times D_{i,j}) \tag{2}$$

$$Entropy_t = \begin{cases} -\sum_{i=1}^{N}\sum_{j=1}^{N}(S_{i,j}\log S_{i,j} + (1-S_{i,j})\log(1-S_{i,j})), & 0 < S_{i,j} < 1 \\ 0, & others \end{cases} \quad (3)$$

In formula (1), $f_{t,Ti}$ denotes the frequency of term t appearing in the contexts of geo-entity pairs with the type $T_i \in TS$. TS is the type set of geo-entity pairs with the size of N. In formula (2), $S_{i,j}$ denotes the similarity between the context p_i and p_j, which is measured by the average distance of all contexts and the distance $D_{i,j}$ between p_i and p_j after removing the term t from all contexts. Formula (3) denotes the entropy of term t measured by $S_{i,j}$.

2.4 Feature Selection

Feature selection is crucial for keyword extraction, which has been proved to have a positive effect on classification accuracy [13] as well as be able to reveal the nature of keywords more comprehensively from multiple perspectives instead of the single aspect "term frequency". Taking the text piece example in Sect. 3.1, the selected features are defined as follows.

(1) The POS of term (noun, verb, preposition or others). e.g., the POS of "邻近" is a verb in Chinese with a meaning of 'be close to'.
(2) The length of term, which is measured by the number of characters. e.g., the length of "邻近" is 2, which means "邻近" has 2 characters.
(3) The location of term (left of e_1, between e_1 and e_2, or right of e_2). e.g., the location of "邻近" is between the geo-entity pair (e_1 = 中关村, e_2 = 北京大学).
(4) The previous term just before e_1. e.g., the previous term just before e_1 = 中关村 is null.
(5) The next term just after e_1. e.g., the next term just after e_1 = 中关村 is "位于".
(6) The previous term just before e_2. e.g., the previous term just before e_2 = 北京大学 is "邻近".
(7) The next term just after e_2. e.g., the next term after e_2 = 北京大学 is "和".
(8) The distance between the term and e_1. e.g., the distance between "邻近" and e_1 = 中关村 is 3. Note that the distances in features (8)–(11) are measured by the number of elements after word segmentation.
(9) The distance between the term and e_2. e.g., the distance between the term "邻近" and e_2 = 北京大学 is 0.
(10) The distance between the term and the head of sentence. e.g., the distance between the term "邻近" and the head of sentence is 4.
(11) The distance between the term and the tail of sentence. e.g., the distance between the term "邻近" and the tail of sentence is 4.

2.5   Term Assessing

After selecting features, the process of term assessing is conducted, this considers the influence of the length, POS, location and distance of the terms, shown in formula (4)–(8). These lexical features are statistically determined according to the credible results of two frequency-based statistical methods and changed with the input texts in real time.

$$wgt^{(t)} = \theta_{LEN} \times (\theta_{POS} + \theta_{LOC} + \theta_{DIS}) \tag{4}$$

$$\theta_{LEN} = \begin{cases} 1, & \min < length(t_{pos}) < \max \\ 0, & others \end{cases} \tag{5}$$

$$\theta_{POS} = p(t_{POS}) \tag{6}$$

$$\theta_{LOC} = \begin{cases} p(t_{loc}|tp(e_1)) \\ p(t_{loc}|tn(e_1)) \\ p(t_{loc}|tp(e_2)) \\ p(t_{loc}|tn(e_2)) \end{cases} \tag{7}$$

$$\theta_{DIS} = \begin{cases} p(dis(e_1)|t_{loc}) \\ p(dis(e_2)|t_{loc}) \\ p(dis(head)|t_{loc}) \\ p(dis(tail)|t_{loc}) \end{cases} \tag{8}$$

In formula (4), $wgt^{(t)}$ denotes the weight of term t for the specified geo-entity pair, considering the importance of length θ_{LEN}, part-of-speech θ_{POS}, location θ_{LOC} and distance θ_{DIS}. Formula (5) denotes the weight of the length of term t affected by the POS of t (t_{pos}). The length of each type of POS has its own valid range. The $wgt^{(t)}$ will be equal zero if the length of t with t_{pos} is out of the range. Formula (6) denotes the weight of POS, which is the probability of the event that the POS of t, namely (t_{pos}), is equal to the specific part-of-speech. Formula (7) denotes the weight of relative location affected by the previous and next terms of geo-entity. t_{loc} denotes relative location of term t, which can be left, between or right. $tp(e_1)$ denotes the previous term of e_1, $tn(e_1)$ denotes the next term of e_1. For example, $p(t_{loc} = between|tp(e_1))$ denotes the probability that the term t located between e_1 and e_2 is the keyword when the previous term of e_1 is a specific term. Formula (8) denotes the weight of distance affected by the location of term. $dis(e_1)$ denotes the distance between t and e_1. $dis(e_2)$ denotes the distance between t and e_2. $dis(head)$ denotes the distance between t and the head of the sentence. $dis(tail)$ denotes the distance between t and the tail of the sentence. For example, $p(dis(e_1)|t_{loc} = between)$ denotes the probability that the term t with a definite distance to e_1 is the keyword when t is located between e_1 and e_2.

All terms in contexts are assessed by formula (4) and ranked in descending order. After ranking, a local ordered list of terms is generated for each geo-entity pair, which indicates the decreasing importance of the terms for geo-entity relation expression. The most important term is picked out as the keyword of the specified geo-entity pair.

3   Experiments

3.1   Dataset

All the articles on Chinese national geography are crawled from Encyclopaedia of China[3], with 2.3 million words in total. These articles describe the geographic, cultural and historical knowledge of toponyms, which provide rich information for geo-entity relation extraction. These articles are pre-processed using GATE[4] and 31,065 geo-entity pairs are generated. They are randomly divided into 3 groups to check the robustness of the proposed method.

3.2   Baselines

The proposed method is compared with DF and Entropy. Specifically, DF method extends the classic TFIDF using the frequency of the terms in the context of the type-specific entity pairs, which would favor specific relational terms as opposed to generic ones. Entropy method converts the context to a vector of terms and assesses the discrimination of each term based on the informatics theory, which would provide useful heuristic information for keyword extraction.

3.3   Metrics

Because the number of the keywords in the experiment is unknown, we can only define the precision as shown in formula (9). *Cnt(right set)* denotes how many the extracted keywords are correct. *Cnt(result set)* denotes the total number of keywords in the results.

$$Precision = \frac{Cnt(right\ set)}{Cnt(result\ set)} \tag{9}$$

We randomly sample part of data from the results, and manually evaluate them by two people, and evaluate the coherence of their annotation by *kappa* coefficient (κ) as formula (10). P_0 denotes the relative annotation agreement between the two people, P_e denotes the hypothetical probability of chance agreement. If $\kappa > 0.8$, the annotations

---

[3] http://www.360doc.com/content/11/0110/01/694750_85358960.shtml.

[4] https://gate.ac.uk/.

are accepted and the mean precision of the two evaluations is calculated. Otherwise, evaluation is conducted again.

$$\kappa = \frac{P_0 - P_e}{1 - P_e} \tag{10}$$

3.4   Results

3.4.1   Keyword Extraction

We utilize the proposed method with the first group as an example. The results are shown in Fig. 2. The terms in context are ordered by their descending importance ranks, the one with the maximal weight is picked out as the keyword for each pair of geo-entities. Note that some geo-entity pairs own multiple keywords because multiple terms in one context have the equal weight. For example, the geo-entity pair (*Zhejiang Province, Qiandao Lake*) has keywords "artificial-lake" and "reservoir".

	e_1	e_2	terms in context	keyword
1				
2	Pukou	Yangtze River	north, locate	north
3	Pulan	Menshi	west, coal-mining, have	west
4	China	Mount Putuo	buddhism, four, mount	buddhism
5	Longsha Park	Wangjiang Tower	scenic, have	scenic
6	Tsitsihar	Songnen plain	locate	locate
7	Qimen County	Mount Qishan	near, have	near
8	JiangSu Province	Qidong City	govern, granary, cotton-area	govern
9	Zhejiang Province	Qiandao Lake	artificial-lake, reservoir	artificial-lake, reservoir
10	Qiantang River	Xin'an River	upstream, origin	upstream
11	Mount Qingcheng	Mount Tiancang	contain	contain
12	Qingtian County	Shimen Cave	relic, have	relic
13	Wuding River	Luhe River	tributary	tributary
14	Mount Tianshan	Turpan	basin, locate	basin
15	Mount Data	Qianfo Cave	main-pick, north, south, east	main-pick
16	Qin	Cangjiangou		name

Fig. 2.   Examples of extracted keywords in the first group of data.

3.4.2   Additional Keywords

Compared with the corpus, some new geo-entity pairs and keywords in each group are extracted, as shown in Fig. 3. In the horizontal axis, pair denotes geo-entity pair, type (kw) denotes the number of keyword's types, and the index numbers correspond to each group. The vertical axis denotes how many new objects are extracted. For example, in the first group, 35.4 % additional geo-entities pairs and 31.3 % additional keyword's types are generated with our method.

The extraction percentage of additional geo-entity pairs is almost the same in the three methods. Additionally, the DF explores the largest number of new types of

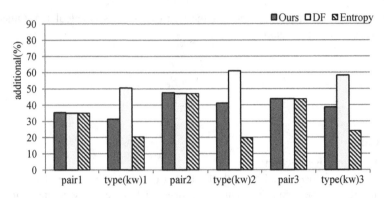

Fig. 3. Additional geo-entity pairs and keywords

keywords (average 56.6 % in three groups), while the Entropy misses the most of the keywords.

3.4.3 Precision

The extracted keywords are evaluated manually and the *kappa* coefficient κ is calculated. The additional objects are evaluated to assess the ability of a keyword extraction method adapting to the unknown data in the corpus. 100 additional geo-entity pairs with additional types of keywords are sampled randomly from the results, and added into the evaluation set. Then two people simultaneously check if the extracted keyword in the evaluation set is the relational term of one specific geo-entity pair. The *kappa* coefficient κ with a value 0.83 declares a high coherence and proves the validity of the evaluation.

Table 2. The precision of three methods for all additional extracted keywords (%)

Precision(%)	Ours	DF	Entropy
new(kw)	60.3	31.7	26.7
AVG	85.5	44.1	49.4

Table 2 shows that how many geo-entity pairs with the additional types of keyword are extracted correctly (new(kw), in short), and the mean of all results which contains the existed keywords and the new discovered ones extracted correctly (AVG, in short). The proposed method gets an average precision of 85.5 %, which is about 41 % and 36 % higher than DF and Entropy. More importantly, the precision of new types of keywords extracted with the presented method is 60.3 %, surpassing by 28 % and 33 % with DF and Entropy respectively. Although DF method obtains the largest number of new types of keywords (shown in Fig. 3), it has the low precision of new types of keywords (31.7 %). Moreover, Entropy method misses the most keywords and has the lowest precision.

3.4.4 Discussion

As mentioned in Sect. 1, the frequency-based methods for keyword extraction are derived from TF-IDF and Entropy. TF-IDF is under the premise that entity relations would appear frequently in massive texts. And Entropy is dependent on the hypothesis that the relational terms used to describe the specific relation appear more often than others. Both TFIDF and Entropy assess the importance of terms by frequency statistic. Unfortunately, there is usually no significant frequency difference between keywords and other terms because the keywords are sparsely distributed. Thus, it is difficult to distinguish the keywords from contexts using the frequency-based methods. Therefore, TFIDF (including DF) and Entropy do not perform well in keyword extraction for sparse geo-entities, especially on the additional types of keywords.

On the contrary, we extract keywords not only with the term frequency, but also the lexical features to reveal the specific characters of the given texts. Besides, the reliability is kept with combining the types of geo-entities with the lexical features, which produces massive keywords with a higher quality dealing with the sparse geo-entity relations. Moreover, our method can discover additional keywords from the original web texts, which is a step forward comparing with supervised learning methods.

However, there are still two kinds of keywords we can't effectively deal with: (1) Keywords with semantic constraints. Sometimes relations depend on time, spatial or semantic constraints, which no longer meet the format of the triplet. For example, the sentence "艾比湖蒙古语称为艾比淖尔(Aibi Lake is called Ebi Bur in Mongol)." expresses the facts (Aibi Lake, alias in Mongol, Ebi Bur). Our method can extract the keywords "be called" which is the meaning of "alias", but miss the semantic constraint. More features should be considered when dealing with keywords with semantic constraints, such as grammatical structure, semantic coherence and so on. Besides, dependency parsing is also an effective solution for completing relation expression. (2) Implicit keywords. One sentence implies a kind of relation between two geo-entities, whereas the keywords describing this relation do not appear in the sentence. For example, the sentence "The water resources of Min River are 13.32 million kilowatt, accounting for 18.85 % of water resources of Sichuan Province" describes a topological relation (Min River; Sichuan Province; within), but there are no terms meaning "within" in the sentence. Geometric information from geographical knowledge bases (such as Geonames and OpenStreetMap) would be beneficial to extract implicit spatial keywords.

Note that the main contribution of this study is to alleviate the influence of context sparseness. The proposed method solves this problem with the help of a fine-grained mapping table and an open synonym dictionary. Because the languages only influence the feature selection and the weights of features, specific features should be selected in the context enhanced method for different languages.

4 Conclusion

This paper proposed a context enhanced method to extract the keywords from mass web texts to recognize geo-entity relations with sparse distributions. We adopt two strategies to reduce the sparseness of terms in contexts. The first is a fine-grained type table used to merge the contexts for increasing the number of terms, and the second is semantic fusion conducted to reduce the sparseness of terms in all contexts. Moreover, we consider the global and local features by introducing the characteristics of length, part-of-speech, position and distance of terms to improve the performance. It is demonstrated that the proposed method can efficiently enhance the ability of discovering geo-entity relation keywords with sparse distributions. This method also generates massive additional keywords which is helpful to realize the unsupervised learning methods of geo-entity relation recognition.

Acknowledgments. This work was partially supported by the National High-Tech Research and Development Program of China (2013AA120305) and the National Natural Science Foundation of China (41271408).

References

1. Jones, C.B., Purves, R.S.: Geographical information retrieval. Int. J. Geogr. Inf. Sci. **22**(3), 219–228 (2008)
2. Kordjamshidi, P., Otterlo, M.V., Moens, M.F.: Spatial role labeling: towards extraction of spatial relations from natural language. ACM Trans. Speech Lang. Process. **8**(3), 1–39 (2011)
3. Purves, R.S., Clough, P., Jones, C.B.: The design and implementation of SPIRIT: a spatially aware search engine for information retrieval on the Internet. Int. J. Geogr. Inf. Sci. **21**(7), 717–745 (2007)
4. Zhu, S.N., Zhang, X.Y., Zhang, C.J.: Syntactic pattern recognition of geospatial relations described in natural language. In: Proceedings of 2010 International Conference on Broadcast Technology and Multimedia Communication, 13 December, pp. 354–357. CNKI, Chongqing (2010)
5. Li, W.W., Goodchild, M.F., Raskin, R.: Towards geospatial semantic search: exploiting latent semantic relations in geospatial data. Int. J. Digit. Earth **7**(1), 17–37 (2014)
6. Loglisci, C., Ienco, D., Roche, M., et al.: Towards geographic information harvesting: extraction of spatial relational facts from web documents. In: 2012 IEEE 12th International Conference on Data Mining Workshops, 10 December, pp. 789–796. IEEE, Brussels (2012)
7. Turney, P.D., Pantel, P.: From frequency to meaning: vector space models of semantics. J. Artif. Intell. Res. **37**, 141–188 (2014)
8. Zhang, W.R., Sun, L., Han, X.P.: A entity relation extraction method based on Wikipedia and pattern clustering. J. Chin. Inf. Process. **26**(2), 75–127 (2012)
9. Liu, Z.Y., Sun, M.S.: Can prior knowledge help graph-based methods for keyword extraction? Front. Electr. Electron. Eng. **7**(2), 242–253 (2012)
10. Vasardani, M., Winter, S., Richter, K.F.: Locating place names from place descriptions. Int. J. Geogr. Inf. Sci. **27**(12), 2509–2532 (2013)
11. Shen, M.M., Liu, D.R., Huang, Y.S.: Extracting semantic relations to enrich domain ontologies. J. Intell. Inf. Syst. **39**(3), 749–761 (2012)
12. Zhang, X.Y., et al.: SVM based extraction of spatial relations in text. In: 2011 IEEE International Conference on Spatial Data Mining and Geographical Knowledge Services, 29 June–01 July, pp. 529–533. IEEE, Fuzhou (2011)
13. Naughton, M., Stokes, N., Carthy, J.: Sentence-level event classification in unstructured texts. Inf. Retrieval **13**(2), 132–156 (2010)

A Stacked Generalization Framework for City Traffic Related Geospatial Data Analysis

Xiliang Liu[1,2], Li Yu[1], Peng Peng[1], and Feng Lu[1,3(✉)]

[1] State Key Laboratory of Resources and Environmental Information System, IGSNRR, Chinese Academy of Sciences, Beijing, China
{liuxl,yul,pengp,luf}@lreis.ac.cn
[2] Fujian Collaborative Innovation Center for Big Data Applications in Governments, Fuzhou, China
[3] Jiangsu Center for Collaborative Innovation in Geographical Information Resource Development and Application, Nanjing, China

Abstract. Analyzing traffic related geospatial data often lacks in priori knowledge and encounters parameter setting problems due to the dynamic characteristics of city traffic. In this paper, we propose a pervasive, scalable framework for city traffic related geospatial data analysis based on a stacked generalization. Firstly we analyze the optimal linear combination based on stepwise iteration, and also prove its theoretical validity via error-ambiguity decomposition. Secondly we integrate six classical approaches into this framework, including linear least squares regression, autoregressive moving average, historical mean, artificial neural network, radical basis function neural network, support vector machine, and conduct experiments with a real city traffic detecting dataset. We further compare the proposed framework with other four linear combination models. It suggests that the proposed framework behaves more robust than other models both in variance and bias, showing a promising direction for city traffic related geospatial data analysis.

Keywords: City traffic · Geospatial data · Ensemble learning · Stacked generalization · Robustness

1 Introduction

With the development of information and communication technologies, more and more sensors (e.g., loop detectors, floating cars and smart phones) have been applied to detect city traffic, providing more abundant data resources for intelligent transport system and other related fields [1]. These data can be transformed into time-labelled geospatial data so as to characterize the operating parameter including traffic flow, link travel time, intersection delays, and so on. However, during the process of city traffic analysis, the time-labelled geospatial data still cannot be utilized directly owing to the following three obstacles:

- First, limited by the transmission bandwidth, energy consumption and storage pressures, the sampling rate of these sensors cannot be high [1], leading to the data sparseness and data missing problems in a given spatial-temporal slice. The

A. Morishima et al. (Eds.): APWeb 2016 Workshops, LNCS 9865, pp. 265–276, 2016.
DOI: 10.1007/978-3-319-45835-9_23

communication failure and random disturbance of the device itself can also deteriorate this situation, causing errors in original data.

- Second, the spatial-temporal distribution of these geospatial data among a city or a given region is heterogeneous owing to the dynamic characteristics of city traffic. This phenomenon as well makes the data sparseness and data missing problems even worse.
- Third, the deficiency of priori knowledge for the specific traffic phenomenon leads to various models, and each model is designed only for a particular situation. The model selection and parameter setting problems become an unavoidable step in the modeling of geospatial data.

The classical approaches for city traffic analysis are based on a specific single model. For example, Rohini estimates the average link travel time using a linear least squares regression model [2]. The machine learning strategies such as artificial neural network and support vector machine, are also employed in city traffic analysis. A single model is only one-sided reflection for the city traffic conditions, and cannot express the dynamic characteristics of city traffic. At the same time, the parameter setting and over-fitting problems (e.g. both ANN and SVM have) of the single model cannot be neglected.

Some researchers seek to model the city traffic via a hybrid way based on mathematical statistics. Hibon *et al.* analyze the principle in hybrid model selection, and consider the hybrid model behaves more accurate than the single model because the result of the hybrid model occupies a better confidence interval [3]. However, this hybrid method simply averages the original multiple methods, or add up all the methods using a weighted linear regression. Two defects using this hybrid method cannot be ignored:

- The combination of the original methods needs the computation of all the geospatial data. Once the computation is done, the weights for the original methods are fixed. This kind of hybrid method cannot meet the need of online applications and complex urban transportation analysis.
- The traffic data are often internally correlated in spatial and temporal dimensions. Hence the independent and identically distributed (i.i.d) precondition and random process hypothesis cannot be applied in the hybrid modeling of city traffic related geospatial data. This condition restricts the generalization of the hybrid method based on mathematical statistics.

In this paper, in order to reduce the influences from the dynamic nature of city traffic, we propose a pervasive, scalable framework for city traffic related geospatial data analysis based on Stacked Generalization (also known as Stacking) [4]. Theoretically, we analyze the optimal linear combination strategy based on a stepwise iterative way. We also mathematically prove the effectiveness of Stacking based on error-ambiguity decomposition. Furthermore, we evaluate the performance of the proposed Stacking framework and conduct experiments with a real city traffic related geospatial dataset comparing with other single models and hybrid models. Final results reveal that the proposed framework behaves more robust than other models both in variance and bias, showing a promising direction for city traffic related geospatial data analysis.

The reminder of the paper is organized as follows. Section 2 introduces Stacked Generalization framework in details, including the optimal linear combination strategy and the mathematical justification of the effectiveness of the Stacking framework. Section 3 carries out the experiments based on a real city traffic dataset in Beijing comparing with other single models and hybrid models. Section 4 discusses and concludes modeling of Stacking framework.

2 The Stacked Generalization Framework

2.1 Modeling of Stacked Generalization

Stacked Generalization is a branch of ensemble learning which places emphasis on the combination of heterogeneous models. Compared with homogeneous ensemble learning methods (e.g., Boosting, Bagging, etc.), Stacked Generalization can tolerate more different models, and has a wider coverage for the original problem space, hence the effect of Stacked Generalization is generally better than homogeneous ensemble learning methods [5]. Another advantage of Stacked Generalization lies in that this method cannot easily get over-fitted [6]. Based on "weak learner" theory [7], there hardly exists an "*ideal*" model to cope with all the conditions for citywide traffic analysis. However, a batch of models which can achieve a general level can be easily obtained from the literatures. This situation is just the case for the application of Stacked Generalization.

Generally speaking, the structure of Stacked Generalization framework consists of two layers. The first layer is Level-0 learner. The output of Level-0 learner and its corresponding feature vectors are transmitted to the second layer (the Level-1 learner) as the input data. A new learning strategy is then formed to combine different models. Finally, the training result of the Level-1 learner is generated as the final output of Stacked Generalization framework. A more detailed description is as follows.

The original dataset $D = \{(x_i, y_i), i = 1, 2, \ldots, m\}$ on R^n is given as the input of the Level-0 learner. Here x_i stands for the ith input vector and y_i the corresponding feature label. Firstly resample D for K times, and in each resampling D is separated into two parts: the training dataset D_k and the test dataset $D_{-k}(D_{-k} = D - D_k, k = 1, 2, \ldots, K)$. N different models L $(L = L_1, \ldots, L_N)$ are constructed based on D_k and D_{-k} in Level-0 learner. The test result T_k corresponding to the test dataset D_{-k} in each resampling is then generated $(T_k = \{(x_j^k, y_j^k), j = 1, 2, \ldots, |D_{-k}|\}, k = 1, 2, \ldots, K)$. T_k and D_{-k} compose a new training sample M_k $(M_k = D_{-k} + T_k)$. All the training samples M constitute the training dataset for the Level-1 learner $(M = \cup M_k, k = 1, 2, \ldots, K)$. Based on M, the Level-1 learner is again trained based on N different models L (other learning strategies are also welcomed.). The training result of the Level-1 learner is generated as the final output of Stacked Generalization framework. The logic structure of Stacked Generalization is shown in Fig. 1.

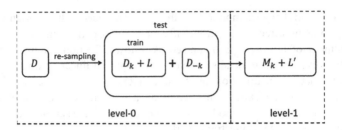

Fig. 1. The logic structure of stacked generalization

2.2   Optimal Linear Combination Based on Stepwise Iteration

The aim of the Level-1 learner is to find the optimal hybrid solution among all the basic models. Traditional solutions seek to solve this problem by simple averaging all the models employed in Level-1 learner. In this paper, in order to obtain a better effect, we design a new learning strategy for the Level-1 learner based on stepwise iteration.

Let L ($L = L_1, \ldots, L_N$) be the basic models in Level-0 learner and M the training dataset for the Level-1 learner ($M = \cup M_k$, $k = 1, 2, \ldots, K$). In Level-1 learner, the model which obtains the minimum mean absolute error (MAE) is selected as the first model in the combination:

$$L_1^c = arg \min E(L) \tag{1}$$

Then the model which can reduce the training error the most is selected as the next model for the Level-1 learner:

$$L_2^c = p_2 L_1^c + (1 - p_2) arg \min E(p_1 L_1^c + (1 - p_1)l) \tag{2}$$

Following this way, until all the N different models L is analyzed:

$$L_N^c = p_N L_{N-1}^c + (1 - p_N) arg \min E(p_{N-1} L_{N-1}^c + (1 - p_{N-1})l) \tag{3}$$

Here $l \in L$, p is the weight coefficient, $p_i \in [0, 1]$, $i = 1, \ldots, N$. Each p is calculated as follows [5]:

$$p_i = \frac{E_{i+1} - E_i}{2\Delta} + 0.5 \tag{4}$$

E_{i+1} and E_i are the normalized errors for L_{i+1}^c and L_i^c. Δ represents the variance between two consecutive basic models:

$$\Delta = E((L_{i+1}^c - L_i^c)^2) \tag{5}$$

2.3   Theoretical Validity via Error-Ambiguity Decomposition

Error-ambiguity decomposition technique is a frequently used tool to analyze the effectiveness in machine learning field. In this paper we analyze the theoretical validity of the proposed Stacked Generalization framework as follows.

Let α be a basic model of Stacked Generalization framework. The output of α is $V^{\alpha}(x)$. Let $\bar{V}(x)$ be the total output:

$$\bar{V}(x) = \sum_{\alpha} w_{\alpha} V^{\alpha}(x) \tag{6}$$

Here w is the weight for each basic model, $\sum_{\alpha} w_{\alpha} = 1$. The ambiguity of α is defined as:

$$A^{\alpha}(x) = (V^{\alpha}(x) - \bar{V}(x))^2 \tag{7}$$

The ambiguity of Stacked Generalization framework is then expressed as:

$$\begin{aligned}
\bar{A}(x) &= \sum_{\alpha} w_{\alpha} A^{\alpha}(x) \\
&= \sum_{\alpha} w_{\alpha} (V^{\alpha}(x) - \bar{V}(x))^2
\end{aligned} \tag{8}$$

For a given input vector x, the square error of α is defined as:

$$E^{\alpha}(x) = (f(x) - V^{\alpha}(x))^2 \tag{9}$$

The square error of Stacked Generalization framework is also defined as:

$$E(x) = (f(x) - \bar{V}(x))^2 \tag{10}$$

The ambiguity of Stacked Generalization framework $\bar{A}(x)$ can be decomposed as:

$$\begin{aligned}
\bar{A}(x) &= \sum_{\alpha} w_{\alpha} A^{\alpha}(x) = \sum_{\alpha} w_{\alpha} (V^{\alpha}(x) - \bar{V}(x))^2 \\
&= \sum_{\alpha} w_{\alpha} V^{\alpha}(x)^2 - 2\bar{V}(x) \sum_{\alpha} w_{\alpha} V^{\alpha}(x) + \sum_{\alpha} w_{\alpha} \bar{V}(x)^2 \\
&= \sum_{\alpha} w_{\alpha} V^{\alpha}(x)^2 - \bar{V}(x)^2
\end{aligned} \tag{11}$$

In the same way, $\sum_{\alpha} w_{\alpha} E^{\alpha}(x) - E(x)$ can also be decomposed as:

$$\begin{aligned}
&\sum_{\alpha} w_{\alpha} E^{\alpha}(x) - E(x) \\
&= \sum_{\alpha} w_{\alpha} (f(x) - V^{\alpha}(x))^2 - (f(x) - \bar{V}(x))^2 \\
&= \sum_{\alpha} w_{\alpha} V^{\alpha}(x)^2 - \bar{V}(x)^2
\end{aligned} \tag{12}$$

From Eqs. (11) and (12), we can conclude that:

$$\bar{A}(x) = \sum_{\alpha} w_{\alpha} E^{\alpha}(x) - E(x) \tag{13}$$

Note that $\bar{E}(x) = \sum_\alpha w_\alpha E^\alpha(x)$, Eq. (13) can then be rewritten as;

$$E(x) = \bar{E}(x) - \bar{A}(x) \tag{14}$$

Apply Eq. (14) to the original dataset $S_i = \{(x_i, y_i)\}|_{i=1,2,\ldots,N}$:

$$\begin{cases} E^\alpha = \int P(x)E^\alpha(x)dx = \sum_{i=1}^{N} P(x_i)E^\alpha(x_i) \\ A^\alpha = \int P(x)A^\alpha(x)dx = \sum_{i=1}^{N} P(x_i)A^\alpha(x_i) \\ E = \int P(x)E(x)dx = \sum_{i=1}^{N} P(x_i)E(x_i) \end{cases} \tag{15}$$

In Eq. (15), E^α is just the generalized error which stands for the difference of the original model α. According to (15), the relation between E^α, A^α and E can be summarized as:

$$E = E^\alpha - A^\alpha \tag{16}$$

Equation (16) demonstrates that the generalized error of Stacked Generalization framework **E** is smaller that each of the basic models. When the differences A^α between basic models enlarge, **E** will be reduced. This is also the advantage of Stacked Generalization in heterogeneous ensemble learning.

3 Experiments

3.1 Stacked Generalization Framework

In the implementation of Stacked Generalization framework, the resampling strategy in Level-0 is LOO-CV (Leave-One-Out Cross Validation). The LOO-CV strategy can guarantee that there are no random factors influencing the data during the experiment. The flow of the Stacked Generalization framework is presented in Fig. 2.

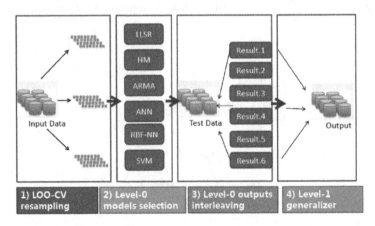

Fig. 2. Stacked generalization framework flowchart

3.2   Hybrid Models Based on Mathematical Statistics

In order to further test the effect of Stacked Generalization framework, we compare with other four traditional hybrid models based on mathematical statistics, namely the equal weights method (EW), the optimal weights method (OW), the minimum variance method (MV) and the minimum error method (ME). The EW method is widely accepted. Let $Y = \{Y_i\}|_{i=1,2,...M}$ be the outputs of M different models, and $w = \{w_i\}$ the weights for the hybrid model. The w for OW is expressed as $w = M_v^{-1}I_m(I_m'M_v^{-1}I_m)^{-1}$, where I stands for the Identity Matrix. The w for MV is calculated as follows:

$$
\begin{cases}
Min f = w_i M_v w_i^T \\
\sum_{i=1}^{M} w_i = 1, 0 \le w_i
\end{cases}
\tag{17}
$$

The w for ME is expressed as:

$$
\begin{cases}
Min \ f = \sum_{i=1}^{M} w_i|\hat{y}_i - y_i| \\
\sum_{i=1}^{M} w_i(\hat{y}_i - y_i) = \sum_{i=1}^{M} (\hat{y}_i - y_i) \\
\sum_{i=1}^{M} w_i = 1, 0 \le w_i
\end{cases}
\tag{18}
$$

3.3   Dataset Description

We employ a real city traffic dataset, namely the intersection delay data which cover 400 main intersections on the main roads (the expressways, the arterial streets and collector streets) in Beijing. These intersections can be regarded as on the same level according to Beijing's road network. The intersection delay data are derived from FCD from March to June in 2011. Each record in the intersection delay data contains a sequence of delays in each direction (left, right and straight) for a given intersection during 96 time periods (time window bandwidth is 15 min starting from 0:00 every day). All the data are subdivided according to different weekdays (Monday to Sunday) and weekends. For more details of the intersection delay data, please refer to [1]. Figure 3 illustrates the study area and 400 main intersections.

The purple points are the selected intersections. Some significant landmarks are also labeled with their names.

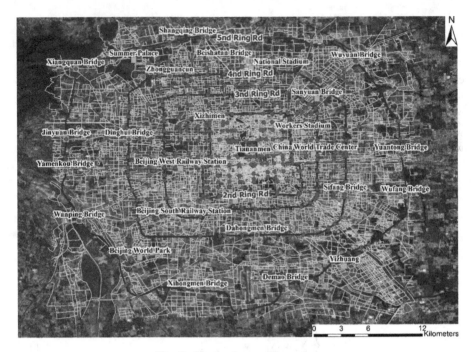

Fig. 3. The study area illustration

3.4   Individual Model Selection and Parameter Tuning

According to literature review, we select six classical different models for intersection delay analysis, namely linear least squares regression (LLSR), autoregressive moving average (ARMA), historical mean (HM), artificial neural network (ANN), radical basis function neural network (RBF-NN), support vector machine (SVM).

We takes the first three time periods' intersection delay values as the input, while the fourth time period's intersection delay value as the output. In HM, K represents the number of the historical time periods (Here K is 3). The LLSR leads to the prediction scheme by means of linear regression with time-varying coefficients.

The left four models need to adjust their own parameters respectively. For a specific model we set the selection criterion: if this combination can satisfy 90 % of all the turning conditions (i.e., different turn types among 400 main intersections during 96 time periods in a week) within an error range of 20 s, this combination is added to the candidate list; If there exist multiple choices, the most simple one is chosen from the list. In order to find the best combination of p and q in ARMA(p,q), we test all the feasible combinations among the range of [1, 10]. The BIC value (Bayes Information Criterion) of each combination is compared. Finally the combination of $(1, 1)$ is selected according to the selection criterion. For the ANN model, we adopt the simple MLP (Multilayer Perceptron) structure. In order to determine the hidden neuron number, we use a simple grid search approach with the number ranging from 1 to 20. According to the selection criterion, the topological structure is finally set as 3-5-1. Specifically, we produce the RBF-NN with almost zero error on training vectors

(1.51e-6). It contains as many radial basis transfer function neurons as input vectors. During the test among 400 main intersections, the spread rate of RBF-NN model is determined as 0.90 to ensure that the network function is smoother with better generalization. For SVM model, we choose radius basis function as SVM's kernel function. With the grid search method, the best penalty parameter and the RBF kernel parameter is selected according to the selection criterion. In the end the penalty parameter is set as 3.50, while the RBF kernel parameter is set as 0.15, respectively.

3.5   Evaluation Metrics

We evaluate the effects of the 11 models (including six different single models, four statistical hybrid models and the stacked generalization framework) using two metrics: the RMSE (Root Mean Square Error) and the MAE (Mean Absolute Error, MAE). The RMSE shows the degree of dispersion of samples and reflects the model's generalization ability. The MAE measures how close the eventual outcomes are to the real value, and shows the offset between the real values and the estimations.

Additionally, in order to get a stable result, for a specific single model or a statistical hybrid model, we randomly separate the original intersection data as the training data and test data with a ratio of 7:3 for ten times. The averaged RMSE and MAE in ten tests are regarded as the final result for each specific model.

3.6   Experiment Results

3.6.1   Comparison Between Single Models and Stacked Generalization Framework

The RMSE comparison between six different single models and the proposed Stacked Generalization framework is shown in Fig. 4.

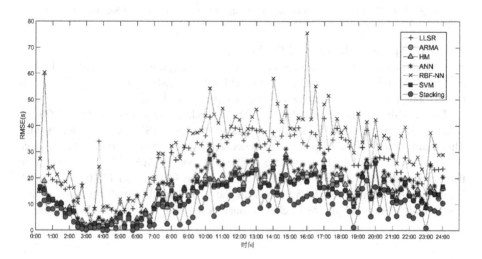

Fig. 4. The effect comparison between single models and Stacking (RMSE)

In Fig. 4, RBF-NN behaves the worst due to the over-fitting problem. The proposed framework behaves the best in most cases, showing a better generalization ability in intersection delay analysis.

3.6.2 Comparison Between Hybrid Models and Stacked Generalization Framework

We also compare the RMSE values between four different statistical hybrid models and the proposed Stacked Generalization framework. The result is shown in Fig. 5.

In Fig. 5, the ME hybrid method behaves the worst, while the proposed Stacked Generalization framework again shows better RMSE results in most cases. This demonstrates the advantage of the proposed Stacked Generalization framework over traditional statistical hybrid models.

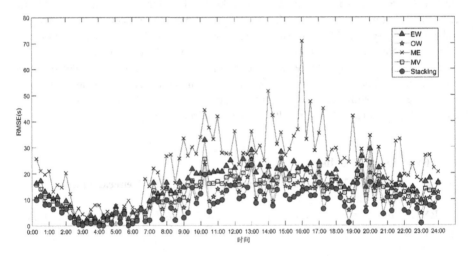

Fig. 5. The effect comparison between statistical hybrid models and Stacking (RMSE)

3.6.3 Comparison Between all the Models

In order to clearly demonstrate the comparisons, we aggregate the RMSE and MAE results of 11 models (including six different single models, four statistical hybrid models and the stacked generalization framework) into Fig. 6.

Figure 6 shows that among the 11 different models, the proposed Stacked Generalization framework behaves the best according to the RMSE and the MAE results. This means that with the help of the framework, we can generally control the variance within about 10 s and the bias within 5 s. The OW model's MAE (4.97 s) is similar to the framework (4.95 s). However, the RMSE of the OW model (12.61 s) is much larger than the framework (9.98 s). Not all the hybrid models perform better than a single model. For example, ME behaves much worse than the simple HM method.

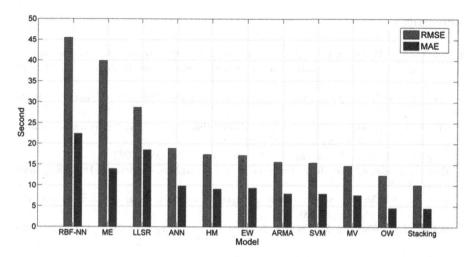

Fig. 6. The effect comparison between all models

4 Discussion and Conclusion

In this paper, we propose a Stacked Generalization framework for city traffic related geospatial data analysis. We analyze the optimal linear combination based on stepwise iteration and redesign the learning strategy. We also prove its theoretical validity via error-ambiguity decomposition. Six simple models, including LLSR, ARMA, HM, ANN, RBF-NN and SVM, are constructed as the basic models. Four statistical hybrid models, namely EW, OW, ME, and MV are selected to compare the effects based on the criteria of RMSE and MAE. We conduct experiments with a real city traffic dataset. Final results show the proposed framework outperforms other models both in variance and bias, showing a promising direction for city traffic related geospatial data analysis.

Based on mathematical proof, the Stacked Generalization framework simplifies the modeling of city traffic related geospatial data with no need to test all possible combinations. It also save the parameter tuning step. Furthermore, the Stacked Generalization framework provides a pervasive, scalable framework for city traffic related geospatial data analysis, which means any new promising models can be easily incorporated.

In the future, we plan to apply the Stacked Generalization framework to other related research fields, and test its ability with more models and datasets.

Acknowledgement. This research is supported by the National Natural Science Foundation of China (41271408, 41401460), and the Chinese Postdoctoral Science Foundation (2015M581158).

References

1. Liu, X.L., Lu, F., Zhang, H.C., Qiu, P.Y.: Intersection delay estimation from floating car data via principal curves: a case study on Beijing's road network. Front. Earth Sci. **7**(2), 206–216 (2013)
2. Rohini B.: Predicting speeds on urban streets using real-time GPS data. In: Masters Abstracts International, pp. 41–04 (2000)
3. Hibon, M., Evgeniou, T.: To combine or not to combine: selecting among forecasts and their combinations. Int. J. Forecast. **21**(1), 15–24 (2005)
4. Wolpert, D.H.: Stacked generalization. Neural Netw. **5**, 241–259 (1992)
5. Zhou, Z.H.: Ensemble Methods: Foundations and Algorithms. Chapman & Hall/CRC, Boca Raton (2012)
6. Jose, V., Winkler, R.: Simple robust averages of forecasts: some empirical results. Int. J. Forecast. **24**, 163–169 (2008)
7. Helmbold, D., Warmuth, M.: On weak learning. J. Comput. Syst. Sci. **50**(3), 551–573 (1995)

Detection of Statistically Significant Bus Delay Aggregation by Spatial-Temporal Scanning

Xia Wu[1], Lei Duan[1,2(✉)], Tinghai Pang[1], and Jyrki Nummenmaa[3,4]

[1] School of Computer Science, Sichuan University, Chengdu, China
2013wuxia@gmail.com, pthaike@gmail.com
[2] West China School of Public Health, Sichuan University, Chengdu, China
leiduan@scu.edu.cn
[3] School of Information Sciences, University of Tampere, Tampere, Finland
jyrki.nummenmaa@uta.fi
[4] Sino-Finnish Centre, Tongji University, Shanghai, China

Abstract. Public bus service plays an indispensable role in modern urban traffic system. With the bus running data, the detection of the statistically significant aggregations of bus delay is useful for optimizing the bus timetable, so that the service quality can be improved. However, previous studies have not considered how to detect bus delay aggregation using statistical hypothesis testing. To fill that gap, this paper considers the detection of bus delay aggregation from bus running data. We present RSTV-Miner, a mining method using statistical hypothesis testing, for detecting statistically significant bus delay aggregation. Our empirical study on real data demonstrates that RSTV-Miner is effective and efficient.

Keywords: Bus delay aggregation · Spatial-temporal analysis · Traffic data mining

1 Introduction

Public bus, which is one of the most widely used transportation tools for most people, plays an important role in the modern urban traffic system. The on-time performance is a critical factor affecting people's willingness to take buses. Naturally, people prefer to take the buses that have high on-time rate, i.e., the buses run in accordance with the timetable, since people can avoid unnecessary waiting time and estimate the exact time to the destination. Intuitively, the bus drivers can avoid the situation of ahead of schedule by slowing down. However, there are many causes of bus delay [1], for the case of behind schedule, the bus drivers cannot simply catch up time by speeding up due to some limitations such as maximum speed limit and road condition. Thus, the detection of bus delay

This work was supported in part by NSFC 61572332, the Fundamental Research Funds for the Central Universities 2016SCU04A22, and China Postdoctoral Science Foundation 2014M552371, 2016T90850.

A. Morishima et al. (Eds.): APWeb 2016 Workshops, LNCS 9865, pp. 277–288, 2016.
DOI: 10.1007/978-3-319-45835-9_24

Table 1. Samples of Tampere bus data

Stop code	Latitude	Longitude	Delay	Arrival	Line	Date	Stop name
1500	61.49855	23.73550	60	00:31:31	4Y	2015-9-27	Ammattikoulu
3084	61.47992	23.80464	15	19:21:52	102	2015-10-23	Kuoppamaentie
0098	61.50003	23.73738	−34	00:09:48	3Y	2015-8-27	Savilinna

aggregations, which is the basis for optimizing the bus timetable, can improve the bus service quality.

Recently, the city of Tampere, Finland, released as open data [2] the locations of its buses at every second. In particular, the bus data includes information on, for each bus and each bus stop, whether a bus was on schedule and how much was the delay if it was not on time. Table 1 lists several samples of Tampere bus data. Each record contains the information of a bus arriving at a bus stop. For example, by the first record in Table 1, we can see that a bus of Line 4Y arrives at Stop Ammattikoulu (code: 1500, location: 61.49855"N, 23.73550"E) at 00:31:31 AM on September 27, 2015 with 60 s behind schedule. As shown in the last record in Table 1, the value of "Delay" is minus if the bus arrives ahead of schedule, there are also other details not mentioned.

Motivated by the real-world requirement shown above, we try to detect the aggregation of bus delay from the bus running data in this work. Intuitively, it is hard to avoid all bus delays, since the real-world is complex and uncertain. Instead of finding all frequent bus delay cases, we focus on detecting the statistically significant aggregations of delay. Specifically, we apply the spatial-temporal scanning method, which has been verified effective in the early warning of infection diseases outbreak, to the bus running monitoring data, and test the significance level of each aggregation of bus delay in both temporal dimension and spatial dimension. To the best of our knowledge, there is no previous work on detecting the bus delay aggregation using statistical hypothesis testing. We will review the related work systematically in Sect. 3.

To tackle the detection of bus delay aggregation, we need to address two technical challenges. First, how to perform spatial-temporal scanning on the bus running data efficiently. Second, how to perform statistical hypothesis testing for a pair of a given zone and a time interval.

The main contributions of this paper include: (1) introducing a novel data mining problem of bus delay aggregation detection; (2) designing an efficient and effective algorithm for detecting statistically significant bus delay aggregations; (3) conducting extensive experiments using real data to evaluate our proposed algorithm, and demonstrating visually that some interesting results can be found by our algorithm.

The rest of the paper is organized as follows. We formulate the problem of bus delay aggregation mining in Sect. 2, and review related work in Sect. 3. In Sect. 4, we present the critical techniques of our method. We report experiment and case study in Sect. 5, and conclude the paper in Sect. 6.

2   Problem Definition

In this section, we give a formal definition for statistically significant bus delay event aggregation. To that end, we will also need to define several concepts concerning spatial-temporal scanning with respect to "time interval" and "zone".

We start with some preliminaries. We use a series of continuous non-negative integers starting from 0 to denote the time points; we use t_{max} to denote the maximum time point. Without loss of generality, we assume that the smaller the value, the earlier the time point, and that the interval between any two consecutive time points is a constant.

For brevity, we denote $[0, t_{max}]$ by $\widetilde{T}$. A *time interval* T is a sub-interval of $\widetilde{T}$ (denoted by $T \sqsubset \widetilde{T}$) of the form $T = [T.t_s, T.t_e]$ satisfying $0 \leq T.t_s < T.t_e \leq t_{max}$. The *time span* of T, denoted by $||T||$, is the number of time points in T, that is, $||T|| = T.t_e - T.t_s + 1$.

For a given bus, we use $AT(u)$ and $ET(u)$ to denote the real arrival time point and the expected arrival time point at Stop u, respectively. The delay time at Stop u, denoted by $\Delta(u)$, is $AT(u) - ET(u)$. Let θ be the time threshold. If $\Delta(u) \geq \theta$, we say that a *bus delay event* happens at Stop u.

We denote the *position of bus stop* u by its geographic coordinates of the form of $P(u) = (u.lng, u.lat)$. For two bus stops u_1 and u_2, the geographical distance between them, denoted by $Dis(u_1, u_2)$, is

$$Dis(u_1, u_2) =$$
$$2 \times R \times sin^{-1}\sqrt{(sin\frac{x}{2}) + cos(u_1.lat \times \frac{\pi}{180}) \times cos(u_2.lat \times \frac{u_2.lat}{180}) \times (sin\frac{y}{2})^2} \tag{1}$$

where

$$x = (u_1.lat \times \frac{\pi}{180}) - (u_2.lat \times \frac{\pi}{180})$$
$$y = (u_1.lng \times \frac{\pi}{180}) - (u_2.lng \times \frac{\pi}{180})$$
$$R = 6.37130$$

Please note that Eq. 1 is an approximate function to calculate the distance between two objects on the earth.

Let $\widetilde{S}$ be the *study area* that we take into consideration. A *zone* S is a subarea of $\widetilde{S}$ (denoted by $S \sqsubset \widetilde{S}$), such that at least one bus stop locates within S. As all observations happen at bus stops, interchangeably, S will be used to denote a set of bus stops within the zone.

Given zone S and time interval T, we define $\mathcal{N}(S, T)$ to be the number of bus arrival events happened, and $\mathcal{D}(S, T)$ to be the number of bus delay events observed. Intuitively, $\mathcal{D}(S, T) \ll \mathcal{N}(S, T)$.

Without loss of generality, we apply log-likelihood ratio statistic to measure the significance of the spatial-temporal aggregation of bus delay events. Specifically, given zone S and time interval T, the likelihood of the happening of bus delay aggregation within S during T, denoted by $\mathcal{L}(S, T)$, is

$$\mathcal{L}(S,T) =$$

$$
\begin{cases}
\begin{aligned}
&\mathcal{D}(S,T) \times log(r_1) + (\mathcal{D}(\widetilde{S},\widetilde{T}) - \mathcal{D}(S,T)) \times log(r_2) \\
&-\mathcal{D}(\widetilde{S},\widetilde{T}) \times log\frac{\mathcal{D}(\widetilde{S},\widetilde{T})}{\mathcal{N}(\widetilde{S},\widetilde{T})}
\end{aligned} & ,r_1 > r_2 \\
0 & ,r_1 \leq r_2
\end{cases} \tag{2}
$$

where,

$$r_1 = \frac{\mathcal{D}(S,T)}{\mathcal{N}(S,T)}$$

$$r_2 = \frac{\mathcal{D}(\widetilde{S},\widetilde{T}) - \mathcal{D}(S,T)}{\mathcal{N}(\widetilde{S},\widetilde{T}) - \mathcal{N}(S,T)}$$

Given a set of bus running records within area $\widetilde{S}$ during time interval $\widetilde{T}$, the problem of detecting statistically significant bus delay aggregation is to find the pair of (S,T), such that $\mathcal{L}(S,T) = \max\{\mathcal{L}(S',T') \mid S' \sqsubset \widetilde{S}, T' \sqsubset \widetilde{T}\}$, and $\mathcal{L}(S,T)$ is statistically significant.

Table 2 lists the frequently used notations of this paper.

Table 2. Summary of notations

Notation	Description
θ	Time threshold
$\widetilde{T}$	The maximum time interval
$\widetilde{S}$	The study area
(S,T)	A pair of a zone and a time interval
$\mathcal{D}(S,T)$	The number of bus delay events happened within S during T
$\mathcal{N}(S,T)$	The number of bus arrival events happened within S during T
$\mathcal{L}(S,T)$	The likelihood of bus delay aggregation happened within S during T

3   Related Work

Urban traffic analysis is an important and valuable problem in daily life. Some applications have been applied to help government or company to improve the public transportation service and provide a more convenient traffic experience. For example, bus travel time prediction [3–6] can assist people to get a better schedule when they go out; bus delays prediction [7] can improve the traffic operation. According to our review, there do not exist any works about bus delay aggregation detection.

Aggregation detection is widely studied in disease outbreak monitoring and has attracted extensive attentions from both research and industry. There are large number of studies about the spatial aggregation [8] and temporal-spatial aggregation [9] on the disease detection such as cancer [10], diabetes [11], and sclerosis [12], which is an important method for us to control and prevent the

---

Algorithm 1. Framework of RSTV-Miner

Input: bus data D, study spatial-temporal area $(\widetilde{T}, \widetilde{S})$, delay threshold θ, maximum
    size of zone α, Monte Carlo times M.
Output: a spatial-temporal area (S', T') with maximum log-likelihood $\mathcal{L}(S', T')_{max}$.
1: $index\_Rtree(\alpha, \theta, D)$; //refer to Section 4.1
2: $\{(S, T)\}_{real} \leftarrow ST\_Scan(\widetilde{S}, \widetilde{T})$; //refer to Algorithm 2
3: **for** each pair (S, T) in $\{(S, T)\}_{real}$ **do**
4:    $\{(S, T)\}_{monte} \leftarrow MonteCarol((S, T), M)$; //refer to Section 4.3
5: **end for**
6: $(S', T') \leftarrow \{(S, T)\}_{monte}$; //get a zone has maximum log-likelihood
7: **return** (S', T');

---

disease outbreaks. Especially, more and more applications are adapting cluster detection to deal with some problems, such as terrorism outbreaks [13], air pollution [14], and crime location [15].

Some typical methods are used to deal with aggregation detection problems. Scan statistics are effective tools in these methods [16,17]. Some works focus on detecting the change in the spatial pattern of a disease [18]. Wallenstein [19] proposed the method to cluster in time by scan statistic. Kulldorff *et al.* [20,21] proposed a temporal-spatial scanning statistic method to find a time periodic geographical disease.

4 Design of RSTV-Miner

In this section, we present our method, RSVT-Miner, for mining bus delay aggregation from bus dataset. In general, the framework of RSTV-Miner includes: R-tree index structure, spatial-temporal scan, and statistical test. Technically, the key issues of RSTV-Miner are generation and effective scan of index. Algorithm 1 presents the procedure of our method.

4.1 R-Tree Index Structure and Representation

In this study, we partition a spatial study area into $m \times n$ 2-dimensional grids. Each grid covering a set of bus stops within a zone and we get a set of zones $\widetilde{S} = \{S_1, S_2, \ldots, S_i\}$. We generate R-tree index using these zones. Then we use these zones as a minimal unit of space in the following study. In this paper, we need to measure the size of a zone when detecting bus delay aggregation. To address this issue, in our method, each zone is a rectangle and the side length of it is equal to the distance between two nearest bus stops.

To detect the aggregation of bus delay, we need to structure an index for zones. At this moment, using each zone to structure the index and searching for its neighbors is a time-consuming process. In addition, the computation cost is very high. This does not allow us to search all sub-areas of $\widetilde{S}$. To address this issue, we use R-tree to structure index that will help us to group nearby

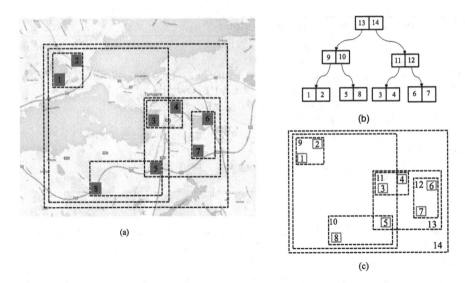

Fig. 1. R-tree index structure demonstrate

zones and retrieve data quickly according to their spatial locations. And to be more statistical significance, when generating an R-tree, we just use zones which overcast at least one bus stop. As demonstrated in Fig. 1, we give an example of R-tree structure in which red rectangles represent the zones overcasting bus stops. We start to build R-tree by using the zones which have partitioned. As illustrate Fig. 1(c), we use R-tree structure, so that a spatial search requires to visit only a small number of nodes.

4.2 Spatial-Temporal Scan

Spatial-temporal clustering is a process of grouping objects based on their spatial and temporal similarity. We need a statistical data to express clustering degree for detecting bus delay aggregation. To address this issue, we use log-likelihood ratio to test the spatial and temporal similarity in Tampere. We propose a approach to analyze spatial-temporal data at a higher level of abstraction by grouping the data according to its similarity into meaningful clusters. Given a spatial-temporal study area (S, T), we can calculate log-likelihood ratio for a zone $\mathcal{L}(S, T)$.

Example 1. Given a spatial-temporal study area $(\widetilde{S}, \widetilde{T})$. Figure 2 presents an example to illustrate the problem definition. As shown, we build the spatial-temporal area as the 3D space C. Given two spatial-temporal area (S_1, T_1), (S_2, T_2) in C. To calculate $\mathcal{L}(S_1, T_1)$ and $\mathcal{L}(S_2, T_2)$ for spatial-temporal area $(S_1, T_1), (S_2, T_2)$ by Eq. 2, and if the result is $\mathcal{L}(S_1, T_1) > \mathcal{L}(S_2, T_2)$, (S_1, T_1) can be considered it has a higher clustering degree than (S_2, T_2). If we check all the subspace in C, we can find the largest outlier space cluster which has a biggest log-likelihood ratio. We can consider it has the bus delay aggregation on this spatial-temporal area.

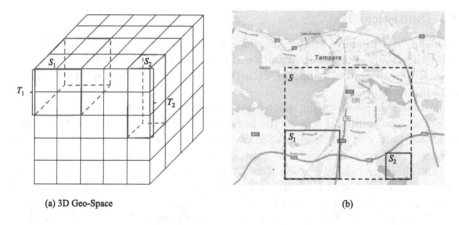

(a) 3D Geo-Space   (b)

Fig. 2. Illustration of bus delay aggregation

We apply spatial-temporal scan to Tampere bus data by R-tree index, as illustrated in Fig. 1 (b). In this method, we use R-tree to retrieve the spatial dimension. To attach temporal dimension with spatial dimension, we divide temporal area into time slots. There are many combinations of spatial-temporal entries (S, T). It is time consuming to retrieve all the combinations, so we just retrieve the spatial data attached consecutive time slots in rush hour at Tampere. We only scan the region indexed by R-tree that side length is no more than maximum pre-set value, so that we never retrieve more than 50 % of total testing area at risk. Algorithm 2 gives an implementation of spatial-temporal scanning. We propose this method as following: (1) retrieve R-tree to find every space dimension zone; (2) attach all time slots with each zone, and use log-likelihood to test this spatial-temporal area clustering degree; (3) repeat the two steps for each zone and generate a collection set of spatial-temporal clusters.

Algorithm 2. Spatial-temporal scanning

Input: R-tree index for $\widetilde{S}$, temporal area $\widetilde{T}$
Output: spatial-temporal set $\{S, T\}$ has maximum log-likelihood
1: **for** each S_i in $\widetilde{S}$ **do**
2:    **for** each T in $\widetilde{T}$ **do**
3:       calculate $\mathcal{L}(S_i, T)$;
4:    **end for**
5:    $(S_i, T) \leftarrow max(\{\mathcal{L}(S_i, T)\})$;
6:    $\{(S, T)\}_{max} \leftarrow addToList((S_i, T))$;
7: **end for**
8: **return** $\{(S, T)\}_{max}$;

4.3 Statistical Test

To ensure our model is statistic significance, we use Monte Carol model to simulate the result. Poisson distribution [22] is widely used to model underlying distribution of spatial-temporal data. We use it to simulate spatial-temporal data of bus delay.

We can get the clustering spatial-temporal area (S, T) with maximum $\mathcal{L}(S, T)$ by our spacial-temporal scan method, written as $\mathcal{L}(S, T)_{real}$. In order to validate that the result can not be simulated, we must test the significance of the result. For every zone, we calculate the expectation of bus delay. And then we generate the simulated delay of each zone by poisson distribution with delay expectation. Then we use our spacial-temporal scan method to get all the $\mathcal{L}(S, T)$ values in this simulate data, denoted as $\mathcal{L}(S, T)_{simu}$. We conduct this test and get the result $\{\mathcal{L}(S, T)\}_{simu}$. If the test is significant at 5 percent level, which means $\mathcal{L}(S, T)_{real}$ ranks top 5 percent of $\{\mathcal{L}(S, T)\}_{simu}$, we can conclude that $\mathcal{L}(S, T)_{real}$ satisfies the statistic significant.

5 Experiments

In this section, we report a systematic empirical study using Tampere bus data set to verify the bus delay aggregation result by RSTV-Miner. All experiments were conducted on a PC computer with an Intel Core i7-3770 3.40 GHz CPU, and 16 GB main memory, running Windows 7 operating system. All algorithms were implemented in C++.

To mine bus delay aggregation of Tampere, we scan every working day of data set. When travel the R-tree, we abandon the grid whose area is more than half of testing space. Using R-tree index to reduce the time of traverse can make an efficient way to spatial-temporal scanning. We use Monte Carol method to validate the output of model with simulation times $M = 100$. By comparison, if the real result area larger than the top-5 simulated result, the result is statistic significance.

At the beginning of our experiment, we need to confirm the threshold θ which estimates whether a bus delay event happened. In our experiment, we find when we change θ, spatial-temporal clustering degree change. To set θ, Fig. 3 presents some results on the Tampere map. When $\theta = 270$, we can get maximum log-likelihood at the same spatial-temporal testing area.

When traveling R-tree index for each zone, we set a maximum value of side length as α to avoid travel the zone which is more than half of Tampere at risk. As listed in Table 3, Spatial area changes with α when we fixed other parameters, study on 14th August, 9:00~13:00. When $\alpha > 120$, the result zone area is nearly half of the Tampere area and the finding zone area does not change.

As listed on Table 4, we list results on consecutive days, from 26th August to 28th August, these results have been checked by Monte Carol simulation. The bus delay aggregation of specify spatial-temporal area has a larger degree. To mine the bus delay aggregation, the most clustering spatial-temporal area, listed in Table 4, has the higher log-likelihood compared to other spatial-temporal area

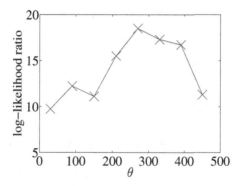

Fig. 3. Threshold θ variation with log-likelihood ratio test

Table 3. Result zone area variation with α

α	Side length of zone	Result zone area	$\mathcal{L}$
30	3 km	3.75 km^2	14.8657
60	6 km	14.28 km^2	29.0666
90	9 km	62.15 km^2	11.9916
120	12 km	62.15 km^2	14.1069
150	15 km	167.50 km^2	18.3807
180	180 km	167.50 km^2	17.6174
210	210 km	167.50 km^2	45.2287
240	240 km	167.50 km^2	35.8306

on the same day. We can find that these zones attached to spatial-temporal area are nearby the center square, a bridge, some traffic hubs and narrow places of Tampere, as illustrated in Fig. 4 which presents the results from 26th August to 28th August. These results are in accordance with the previous studies [1] and our general knowledge of Tampere traffic.

Table 4. Spatial-temporal scanning result

Fig	Date	Time interval	$(lat_1, lng_1, lat_2, lng_2)$	$\mathcal{L}$
(a)	26th Oct, 2015	10:30~11:00	(61.5192, 23.6172, 61.5747, 23.6797)	13.8912
(b)	26th Oct, 2015	16:30~17:30	(61.4987, 23.6092, 61.5327, 23.6997)	29.0666
(c)	27th Oct, 2015	10:30~12:00	(61.4977, 23.7022, 61.5197, 23.8457)	11.9916
(d)	27th Oct, 2015	18:00~18:30	(61.4987, 23.6092, 61.5327, 23.6997)	14.1069
(e)	28th Oct, 2015	10:30~11:00	(61.5137, 23.6127, 61.5747, 23.7037)	18.3807
(f)	28th Oct, 2015	16:00~19:00	(61.4957, 23.5957, 61.5227, 23.6457)	17.6174

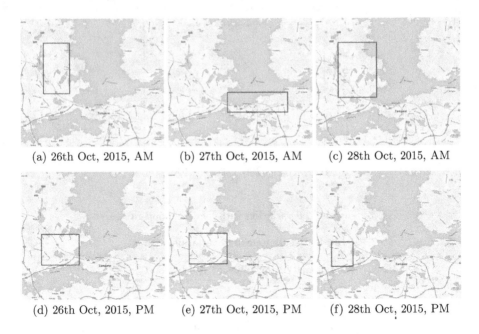

(a) 26th Oct, 2015, AM   (b) 27th Oct, 2015, AM   (c) 28th Oct, 2015, AM

(d) 26th Oct, 2015, PM   (e) 27th Oct, 2015, PM   (f) 28th Oct, 2015, PM

Fig. 4. Spatial-temporal area detection

6   Conclusions

In this paper, we study a problem of mining bus delay aggregation which is useful for optimizing the bus delay timetable. To mine these clusters of bus delay and present the result sets concisely, we propose an algorithm called RSTV-Miner. RSTV-Miner has three components:R-tree index structure, spatial-temporal scan and statistical test. We evaluate our method using the open data set released by city of Tampere, Finland recently. Our experiment verifies the bus delay aggregation in spatial-temporal area by RSTV-Miner. And it is useful for traffic schedule structure to find the traffic congestion place in Tampere.

In our work, we apply spatial-temporal scanning in our algorithm that help us to learn the aggregation of bus delay which is useful for traffic schedule construction. We use statistical hypothesis test to detect the clustering degree of bus delay. Mining this interest problem in our work, we find the aggregation of bus delay in both temporal dimension and spatial dimension. After finding the aggregation, we obtain many clusters of bus delay on spatial-temporal area using RSTV-Miner. When scanning area, we partition study area into zones, which omits some details about bus stops and affects the efficiency of algorithm. This lead us to do more future work on mining bus delay. In the future, we could also do more data mining on experiment results to predict bus delay and traffic congestion.

References

1. Syrjärinne, P., Nummenmaa, J., Thanisch, P., Kerminen, R., Hakulinen, E.: Analysing traffic fluency from bus data. IET Intell. Transport Syst. **9**(6), 566–572 (2015)
2. Syrjärinne, P., Nummenmaa, J.: Improving usability of open public transportation data. In: 22nd ITS World Congress, pp. 5–9 (2015)
3. Mazloumi, E., Rose, G., Currie, G., Sarvi, M.: An integrated framework to predict bus travel time and its variability using traffic flow data. J. Intell. Transp. Syst. **15**(2), 75–90 (2011)
4. Padmanaban, R., Divakar, K., Vanajakshi, L., Subramanian, S.: Development of a real-time bus arrival prediction system for indian traffic conditions. IET Intell. Transport Syst. **4**(3), 189–200 (2010)
5. Yu, B., Lam, W.H., Tam, M.L.: Bus arrival time prediction at bus stop with multiple routes. Transp. Res. Part C: Emerg. Technol. **19**(6), 1157–1170 (2011)
6. Chien, S.I.J., Kuchipudi, C.M.: Dynamic travel time prediction with real-time and historic data. J. Transp. Eng. **129**(6), 608–616 (2003)
7. Abdelfattah, A., Khan, A.: Models for predicting bus delays. Transp. Res. Rec. **1**(1623), 8–15 (1998)
8. Kulldorff, M.: A spatial scan statistic. Commun. Stat.-Theory Methods **26**(6), 1481–1496 (1997)
9. Takahashi, K., Kulldorff, M., Tango, T., Yih, K.: A flexibly shaped space-time scan statistic for disease outbreak detection and monitoring. Int. J. Health Geographics **7**(1), 1 (2008)
10. Michelozzi, P., Capon, A., Kirchmayer, U., Forastiere, F., Biggeri, A., Barca, A., Perucci, C.A.: Adult and childhood leukemia near a high-power radio station in Rome, Italy. Am. J. Epidemiol. **155**(12), 1096–1103 (2002)
11. Green, C., Hoppa, R.D., Young, T.K., Blanchard, J.: Geographic analysis of diabetes prevalence in an urban area. Soc. Sci. Med. **57**(3), 551–560 (2003)
12. Sabel, C., Boyle, P., Löytönen, M., Gatrell, A.C., Jokelainen, M., Flowerdew, R., Maasilta, P.: Spatial clustering of amyotrophic lateral sclerosis in finland at place of birth and place of death. Am. J. Epidemiol. **157**(10), 898–905 (2003)
13. Gao, P., Guo, D., Liao, K., Webb, J.J., Cutter, S.L.: Early detection of terrorism outbreaks using prospective space-time scan statistics. Prof. Geogr. **65**(4), 676–691 (2013)
14. Zou, B., Peng, F., Wan, N., Mamady, K., Wilson, G.J.: Spatial cluster detection of air pollution exposure inequities across the united states. PLoS ONE **9**(3), e91917 (2014)
15. Helbich, M., Leitner, M.: Evaluation of spatial cluster detection algorithms for crime locations. In: Gaul, A., Geyer-Schulz, A., Schmidt-Thieme, L., Kunze, J. (eds.) Challenges at the Interface of Data Analysis, Computer Science, and Optimization, pp. 193–201. Springer, Heidelberg (2010)
16. Naus, J., Wallenstein, S.: Temporal surveillance using scan statistics. Stat. Med. **25**(2), 311–324 (2006)
17. Naus, J.I.: The distribution of the size of the maximum cluster of points on a line. J. Am. Stat. Assoc. **60**(310), 532–538 (1965)
18. Rogerson, P.A., Yamada, I.: Monitoring change in spatial patterns of disease: comparing univariate and multivariate cumulative sum approaches. Stat. Med. **23**(14), 2195–2214 (2004)

19. Wallenstein, S.: A test for detection of clustering over time. Am. J. Epidemiol. **111**(3), 367–372 (1980)
20. Kulldorff, M., Heffernan, R., Hartman, J., Assunçao, R., Mostashari, F.: A space-time permutation scan statistic for disease outbreak detection. PLoS Med. **2**(3), e59 (2005)
21. Kulldorff, M.: Prospective time periodic geographical disease surveillance using a scan statistic. J. R. Stat. Soc.: Ser. A (Stat. Soc.) **164**(1), 61–72 (2001)
22. Ahrens, J.H., Dieter, U.: Computer methods for sampling from gamma, beta, poisson and bionomial distributions. Computing **12**(3), 223–246 (1974)

Acquisition and Representation of Knowledge for Academic Field

Jie Yu$^{(\boxtimes)}$, Haiqiao Wu, Chao Tao, and Lingyu Xu

School of Computer Engineering and Science, Shanghai University, Shanghai,
People's Republic of China
jieyu@shu.edu.cn

Abstract. With the rapid development of Internet, a large number of academic resources are available for researchers. How to organize these resources and represent them well is a big challenge. This paper proposes a novel method of acquiring and representing academic knowledge with cognitive characteristic and provides base for personalized academic services. In this paper, hierarchical knowledge for a specific research field is built according to the features of academic papers. Phrase is regarded as the center and clustering technique is applied with the neighboring condition of a phrase. In addition, semantic relationship between words and phrases is obtained. The experimental results illustrate the effectiveness of the method.

Keywords: Cognitive · Academic field · Semantic relationship · Hierarchical knowledge representation

1 Introduction

With the rapid development of information technology and the popularity of the Internet, data is growing at an unprecedented rate. The era of big data has come and data has changed its role from a simple processing object began to a basic resource [1].

Under the background of the information explosion, information trek and information overload on the Internet has become an increasingly serious problem [2]. Information trek is that users in the complex information Internet space lost its course and do not know they are now in what position in the information space, then cannot return to a node and forget their goals. Information overload, it is due to the complexity and breadth of information provided by Internet, not takes into account the viewer's level of knowledge and cognitive ability, so causing the viewer cannot correctly understand and use the information. In this case, the information obtained from the traditional information technology can also bring a lot of useless, wrong and confusing information garbage.

Take the academic fields an example, almost all year SCI number of papers has increased over the previous year on the last 20 years. Especially in the last 10 years, a large number of Chinese scholars joined the ranks of academic papers published in international, leading to the number of obvious growth trend. The rapid increase of information, on one hand, brings convenience to the user; on the other hand, lets users

A. Morishima et al. (Eds.): APWeb 2016 Workshops, LNCS 9865, pp. 289–297, 2016.
DOI: 10.1007/978-3-319-45835-9_25

face the problem of information trek and information overload. How to effectively utilize the mass information becomes an urgent problem to be solved.

At present, academic knowledge mostly illustrates in the form of knowledge map. While knowledge can be represented, but not show the hierarchical and cognitive characteristics, so it cannot give the user personalization recommendation and guide the user adaptive learning, thereby resulting in the problem of information trek.

For the above-mentioned situation, this paper proposes a hierarchical knowledge representation for a specific research field according to the features of academic papers. Phrase is regarded as the center and clustering technique is applied with the neighboring condition of a phrase. In addition, semantic relationship between words and phrases is obtained. The method has two characteristics:

- Semantics. As the phrase has better semantic than the word, it has stronger field characteristic and phrases with word relative to them can adequately express the semantics of a research field.
- Cognition. It can express the domain information in a hierarchical way, which is currently not available in the knowledge representation.

The rest of this paper is organized as follows. Related work is introduced in Sect. 2. Section 3 describes our approach on how to build the academic knowledge map. Experimental analysis is given in Sect. 4. Finally, we conclude our work in Sect. 5.

2 Related Work

The representation of knowledge in the academic domain is mostly demonstrated in the form of knowledge map. [3] draw search engine academic knowledge map, combined with structural pattern in this area, research focus and the status quo analysis. The academic study of search engines generally can be divided into four sub-areas: search engine key technologies, personalized, professional, intelligent search engine research, search engine application, and commercial profit model research, basic knowledge and theoretical research. [4] put forward the recommendation engine academic research analysis, by drawing knowledge map of the field in the recommendation engine analyzed, and discussed the current situation and characteristics of the domestic research in the field of recommendation engine. [5] presented the knowledge map analysis of the present situation of library management in our country. In the way of knowledge map, the paper discussed the research efforts of library management in the field of distribution, academic representatives, periodicals distribution and related important academic literature, and analyzed the hot area of research and frontier issues on library management in the recent years. [6] came from the perspective of knowledge map drawing and analysis, using the comparison of the strategic map to draw the prediction theory on the research hotspot and the application prospect, and the research status of the domestic life cycle theory is grasped by the analysis method of the concept network. It can improve the understanding of the domestic life cycle theory. [7] proposed a practical methodology to capture and represent organizational knowledge. The methodology uses a knowledge map as a tool to represent knowledge. While these knowledge maps can be demonstrated knowledge in the field, but their biggest problem is that there is no cognitive and users cannot get personalized recommendation services due to their cognitive level. For example, in an academic field, it is obvious that a novice and a veteran with a certain level are not on the same level, so they are supposed to direct to different positioning and recommended with different knowledge. Therefore, stratified knowledge is need for personalized academic services to recommend the appropriate level of information to the corresponding level of the people.

In view of this situation, we have adopted the title, abstract, to obtain the knowledge of academic field, and then cluster different phrases to get different levels of the academic division. Using the value of the semantic relationship between the phrases, it can get different levels of content. Based on the hierarchical knowledge, for different levels of users, different levels of content are recommended to different users according to their own cognitive level.

3 Method Introduction

3.1 Method Summary

In academic papers, the field characteristic of the phrase is stronger than that of the word. It covers areas of high quality information in a condensed content. Therefore, we put forward that the phrase is regarded as the center, through the phrase clustering analysis, different cognitive levels are obtained. By using the values of relationship between the semantic units, the hierarchical knowledge map is acquired.

Our method takes the phrase as key unit, because the phrase in the academic field has more field information than the word. Table 1 gives some experimental results. The corpus is extracted from papers of the American computer association special interest group information retrieval session (SIGIR). One thousand six hundred and ninety articles are collected from the published literature in the range of 2007 to 2013. The abstracts and titles of these documents constitute the corpus. The weights of words and phrases in the corpus are calculated. Weights of the top ten words and phrases are given in Table 1.

Table 1. Top 10 words and phrases

Ranking	Word	Ranking	Phrase
2	Rank	1	Information retrieval
3	Query	5	Web search
4	Search	11	Search engine
6	Document	12	Search result
7	Learning	23	Language model
8	Retrieval	40	Query expansion
9	Web	48	Test collection
10	Model	56	Question answering
13	Relevance	57	Topic model
14	Based	60	Collaborative filtering

It can be seen from the table that the word ranking is generally higher than the phrase, but the word cannot well reflect the semantic nature of knowledge. For example, although the word *rank* is ranking higher than the phrase *collaborative filtering* in the field of information retrieval, *collaborative filtering* involves much more semantics than *rank*.

In our method, weight values of phrases and words are calculated first and the semantic relations between semantic units are obtained. Then K-means clustering method is applied to obtain hierarchical domain knowledge based on the phrases, which are described in the form of feature vectors. Finally, according to the values of semantic relationships between phrases, we obtain hierarchical knowledge map. Therefore, there are three key issues that obtaining of weight values of semantic unit, discovering and measuring relation between unit and clustering to get hierarchy, respectively, which will be presented in the next subsection.

3.2   Implementation of Key Issues

3.2.1   Acquisition of Semantic Units and Weight Calculation

In this paper, we regard the semantic unit as a word or phrase. Phrase is defined as follows: There is set S, which consists of all the word except for stop words. The phrase is from the subset of $S \times S = \{(x, y) | x, y \in S \cap x \neq y\}$. Here, x and y are neighboring words, the ones whose co-occurrence frequency is bigger than threshold are chosen.

Because it is the access to the academic field of knowledge and representation, so the first is to determine the source corpus [8]. In the process of acquisition and representation of knowledge in the academic field, the quality and reliability of data sources directly affect the result. Theoretically, corpus acquisition has many choices, including academic content, title, a reference to the relationship between authors, publishers, abstracts and so on. Academic articles have their own unique characteristics, abstract, key words and title are natural language vocabulary, which express the concept of literature subject. A set of key words appearing more frequently in the field of academic research can reveal the characteristics and relation between the results of these studies then get the law of development and the development direction of academic research and the like. In this paper, we extract the semantic units from the abstract of academic articles. However, there are a certain number of units, which are irrelevant to the specific field. Therefore, we use article title to filter this kind of unit.

As the processing of the data is derived from the text information, so, the method of processing is selected as the TF-IDF algorithm [9]. TF-IDF algorithm is a kind of weighted technology of text mining. The main idea is if a high-frequency words or phrases occur in the article, and rarely in other articles, then that word or phrase has a good ability to distinguish between articles and suitable for classification. Frequency *TF* represents the frequency of the term t appearing in the corpus statistics. Inverse Text Frequency is $IDF = \log(N/N_t)$ [10], where N represents the total number of the training set, N_t represents the number of document t. Its main point is that the more specific terms appearing in a few documents, its weight is higher than the weight of the words that appear in many documents. If it occurs only in a small number of documents, the amount of information it involves is higher, such words would have a strong ability to distinguish between categories and suitable for feature selection. The formula TF-IDF algorithm is as follows.

$$w = \frac{n_i}{\sum_1^m n_j} * \log\frac{D}{d} \tag{1}$$

Where n_i represents the word i occurs n times in the text, $\sum_1^m n_j$ represents the number of all words in the text that appears in total. d represents the number of the words appearing in the background text, D represents the total number of background text.

3.2.2   Calculation of Semantic Relations

In the calculation of semantic relations, the paper uses a semantic unit co-occurrence method. In the field of information retrieval, the general research of semantic unit co-occurrence is based on statistical methods. It is based on such a basic assumption: two words often appear together (co-occurrence) in the same window unit of text (such as a sentence, a paragraph, etc.); it is considered that the two words in meaning are interrelated [11]. The greater the co-occurrence number is, the closer the relation is. Based on this assumption, we obtain the semantic relations between them by using the statistical calculation of the large-scale real data. The formula used is given as follows.

$$P(T_i, T_j) = \frac{C(T_i, T_j)}{\sum_{T'_i, T'_j} C\left(T'_i, T'_j\right)} \tag{2}$$

In formula (2), $C(T_i, T_j)$ is the frequency in the training corpus, semantic unit T_i and T_j appearing simultaneously in the same window. $\sum_{T'_i, T'_j} C\left(T'_i, T'_j\right)$ represents the sum of co-occurrence frequency of the entire semantic unit.

Here, the semantic relations include two cases: the relationship between phrases and phrases, the relationship between phrases and words. These two different relationships were obtained and then analyzed. When the value is greater than or equal to the threshold value, it is considered that the semantic relationship exists. Otherwise, there is no relation between the semantic units.

3.2.3   Clustering Semantic Units

In this paper, the sample features of semantic units are represented as vector U *(weight, neighbornum, relationvalue)*, where

- *weight* represents the weight value of the semantic unit;
- *neighbornum* represents the number of its neighbors;
- *relationvalue* represents the total link number of the semantic unit.

The selection of these three elements is based on the thought relation density of a unit can reflects the level of a unit. A unit that has great number of neighbors usually is a general concept. In addition, the unit which has high total link number but few neighbor is often a specific term in the field, such as a technique name.

After getting the vector of each unit, we use the clustering method for K-means clustering [12]. First k semantic units are randomly selected from the corpus as the initial cluster centers. For the rest of the other semantic unit, which is calculated the distance to the cluster center, and the distance formula is $\sqrt{(x-x')^2+(y-y')^2+(z-z')^2}$. The coordinates (x, y, z) represents the center of the cluster, (x', y', z') denotes the coordinates of the semantic unit. Secondly, according to the smallest distance, adjust the cluster. Then calculate the new cluster center of each cluster. Constantly repeat this process until the new cluster center no longer occurs [13].

After clustering, the different levels of the field are obtained. Combined with the value of the semantic unit relationship given by Sect. 3.2.2, the content of different levels can be obtained, and finally become a hierarchical knowledge map.

4 Experimental Analysis

4.1 Calculating Weight of Unit and Relation Between Units

This paper aims at the academic field of knowledge acquisition and display. The experimental materials are the academic papers from the Association for Computing Machinery of special interest group on information retrieval conference. There are totally 1690 articles from 2007 to 2013. The corpus is through the web crawler, extraction of the abstracts and titles of these documents, preprocessing, filtering and in the form of text to save. Using Cartesian product processing, the analysis and calculation are carried out in the text. Then filter out the parts that do not meet the requirements and save the rest of phrases.

TF-IDF algorithm is used to deal with the saved phrases and words, and the weights of the phrases and words are obtained. According to the arrangement of the weights of the size descending, the result is shown in Table 2 (part of the word and phrase).

Table 2. Weight values of the top 20 words and phrases

Unit	Weight	Unit	Weight
Information retrieval	0.041	Search engine	0.021
Rank	0.036	Search result	0.021
Query	0.035	Relevance	0.017
Search	0.030	Based	0.017
Web search	0.028	Approach	0.015
Document	0.025	Text	0.015
Learning	0.024	Recommendation	0.014
Retrieval	0.022	User	0.014
Web	0.022	Information	0.014
Model	0.021	Classification	0.012

According to the formula (2), we can get the semantic relationships between phrases and phrases, phrases and words. Table 3 and Table 4 give the results of the top 10. It can be seen that the greater the value of the relationship, the more tightly binding between semantic units.

Table 3. Top 10 relationship between phrases and phrases

Phrase	Phrase	Weight
Information retrieval	Language model	0.269
Search result	Result diversification	0.269
Named entity	Entity recognition	0.192
Information retrieval	Interactive information	0.154
Query performance	Performance prediction	0.154
Information retrieval	Retrieval evaluation	0.115
Information retrieval	Cross-language information	0.115
Information retrieval	Distributed information	0.115
Document retrieval	Spoken document	0.115
Latent semantic	Semantic analysis	0.115

Table 4. Top 10 relationship between phrases and words

Phrase	Word	Weight
Information retrieval	Model	0.308
Information retrieval	Learning	0.269
Information retrieval	Query	0.231
Information retrieval	Rank	0.231
Information retrieval	Term	0.192
Web search	Query	0.192
Information retrieval	Framework	0.154
Information retrieval	Exploiting	0.154
Information retrieval	Probabilistic	0.154
Information retrieval	Statistical	0.154

4.2   Clustering of Semantic Units

According to the clustering method in Sect. 3.2.3, the clustering results can be displayed as follows (Fig. 1).

It can be seen that, by clustering algorithm, the semantic units have clustered into three layers. The semantic unit center of the first layer is *information retrieval*, which belongs represents the green region. This is easy to understand, since the concept *information retrieval* in the field of information retrieval is very common and does not mean any specific methods and names. The semantic unit center of the second layer is *search engine* and *search result*, which belongs to the blue area. Those two words are not a specific method but less general in the field of information retrieval. The third layer of the semantic unit center is *collaborative filtering*, which belongs to the green area. The phrase is a specific method in the field of information retrieval. Here, each layer represents a different level, which corresponds to different cognitive level.

By clustering, we can find the level of research area, and the result of the hierarchical knowledge map obtained by the combination of the formula (2). As shown in the Fig. 2. In the knowledge map, we can see the relationship between the semantic units.

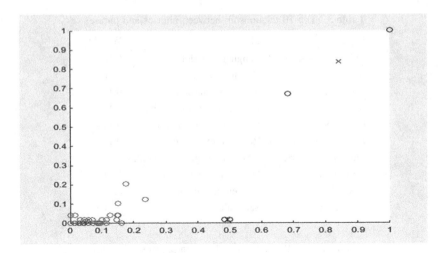

Fig. 1. Results of clustering

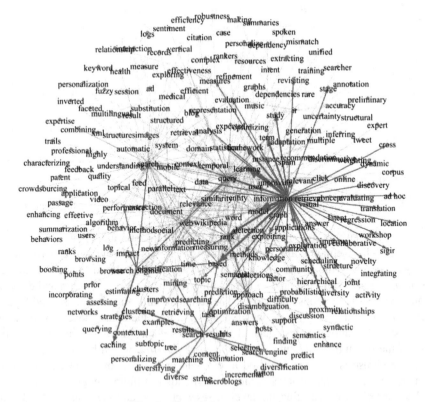

Fig. 2. Knowledge representation

5 Conclusions

With the rapid development of Internet, how to organize the large amount of academic resources and represent them well has caught much attention. In this paper, we represent academic knowledge in a hierarchical form, which provides great cognitive characteristic. In this method, phrase is regarded as the center and clustering technique is applied with the neighboring condition of a phrase. In addition, semantic relationship between words and phrases is obtained. The experimental results illustrate the effectiveness of the method.

References

1. Meng, X.F., Ci, X.: Big data management: concepts, techniques and challenges. Comput. Res. Dev. **50**(1), 146–169 (2013)
2. White, M.E.: What information explosion. Can. Vet. J. La Rev. Vet. Can. **30**(8), 626–628 (1989)
3. Yang, L., Yuqing, S.: Search engine on academic knowledge map research. Inf. Knowl. (6), 105–110 (2010)
4. Guohe, F., Xiaoting, L.: Analysis of knowledge map of domestic recommendation engine in academic research. Inf. Sci. (1) (2012)
5. Xiaomei, H.: Knowledge map analysis of the present situation of library management in our country. Library (6), 114–117 (2011)
6. Feicheng, M., Juncheng, W., Yutao, Z.: Drawing of knowledge map of domestic life cycle theory – Based on the strategic map and conceptual network analysis. Inf. Sci. (4), 481–487 (2010)
7. Kim, S., Suh, E., Hwang, H.: Building the knowledge map: an industrial case study. J. Knowl. Manag. **7**(2), 34–45 (2003)
8. Zhang, H., Ling, T.: Application of bibliometric in the research of subject hot spots. In: The Thirteenth National Conference on Medical Informatics of the Chinese Medical Association (2007)
9. Nguyen, L.A.: Proposal of discovering user interest by support vector machine and decision tree on document classification. In: International Conference on Computational Science and Engineering, pp. 809–812 (2009)
10. Jones, K.S.: A statistical interpretation of term specificity and its application in retrieval. J. Doc. **60**(5), 493–502 (1972)
11. Lund, K., Burgess, C.: Producing high-dimensional semantic spaces from lexical co-occurrence. Behav. Res. Methods **28**(2), 203–208 (1996)
12. Hartigan, J.A., Wong, M.A.: Algorithm AS 136: a K-means clustering algorithm. Appl. Stat. **28**(1), 100–108 (1979)
13. Hartigan, J.A., Wong, M.A.: A K-means clustering algorithm. Appl. Stat. **28**(1), 100–108 (2013)

Using Learning Features to Find Similar Trajectories

Peiguo Fu[1(✉)], Haozhou Wang[2], Kuien Liu[2], Xiaohui Hu[1], and Hui Zhang[1]

[1] Science and Technology on Integrated Information System Laboratory,
Institute of Software Chinese Academy of Sciences, Beijing, China
{peiguo12,hxh,zhanghui}@iscas.ac.cn
[2] Pivotal.inc, San Francisco, USA
{hawang,kliu}@pivotal.io

Abstract. In the last decade, the trajectories data have been collected by many applications and such trajectories contain rich information that can be used to detect events especially for anomaly event detections. However, there are still many challenges on this problem, the major one is how to identify the similar trajectories on semantic level. In this work, we extract the nature features from raw trajectories and use them to do the semantic trajectory similarity search. To achieve this, we propose a PLS algorithm to detect such semantic similar trajectories efficiently and effectively. We also leverage the DBSCAN to help extract the information from large trajectory data. The results of our algorithm are demonstrated by the real world dataset.

Keywords: Feature extraction · Trajectory compression · Trajectory partition · Similarity calculation

1 Introduction

The Global Positioning System (GPS) is now widely used in many industry areas such as deliveries, vehicles tracking and freight transport. The newly technologies include chip development, wireless communication and so on that allow the GPS devices to report their location in real time. Trajectories, which are collected by such devices, contain important spatio-temporal information and play a significant role in these areas. Since the trajectory data can be used to management the vehicles and predict the behaviour of certain vehicles. Moreover, these data can also be used as event detection to detect unusual event or accident. Currently, not only industries have many interest to analysis trajectory data, but many academic researches are also focusing on this area such as designing effective trajectory indexing structures [1,2], trajectory query processing [3,4], trajectory uncertainty management [5,6], and mining knowledge/patterns from trajectory data [7,8]. Meanwhile, there are still many open issues in trajectory analysing, especially for trajectory similarity search in semantic level without extra knowledge (e.g. road network or check-in data).

© Springer International Publishing Switzerland 2016
A. Morishima et al. (Eds.): APWeb 2016 Workshops, LNCS 9865, pp. 298–309, 2016.
DOI: 10.1007/978-3-319-45835-9_26

The similar trajectories in semantic level means these trajectories have the similar object or have the same behaviors. For example, a person drives his car from his/her home to the shopping center to buy something everyday, there trajectories can be considered as semantic similar. If there is a stronger drives a car that follows this person's trajectory, it should be detected as a dis-similar semantic trajectory even this trajectory is "shape" similar with previous trajectories. It is easy to see that such semantic trajectory can be used to event detection to help improve the performance of event detection. However, to calculate semantic similarity trajectories, we are facing some challenges. The first one is that, normally, to calculate the similarity among trajectories, a distance measure for example Euclidean distance, DTW [21], LCSS [22] or EDR [23] will be used. However, such distance measures are only designed to detect the "shape" similarity between given trajectories, and will not be able to find the similar semantic trajectories. The second one is to extract the semantic information from raw trajectory data as we cannot rely on any extra knowledge. This is because the extra knowledge may not always available and updated in any of cases. The last one is the searching performance due to the volumes of trajectory dataset is very large in nature. To address these challenges, in this preliminary study, we propose a new algorithm, which leverages the inner features of raw trajectory data and extracts the useful features information to speed up the similar semantic trajectory search. Moreover, we also combine the DBSCAN [24] to help the algorithm to extracts the required features from raw trajectory dataset. The experiments with real world dataset shows our method can use the found features to do the semantic trajectory similarity search with the good results. To summarize, our major contributions of this work are: (1) we defined the semantic trajectory similarity search and identify the challenges of this problem. (2) we propose an efficient algorithm to solve this problem. (3) we conduct an extensive experiments with real world large dataset to demonstrate our proposed algorithm.

The rest of this paper is organized as follows. We first give some definitions in Sect. 2. We propose our algorithm in Sect. 3 and finalise the experiments in Sect. 4. The literature review are listed in Sect. 5. Finally, we conclude our work in Sect. 6.

2   Problem Statement

In this section, the terms and notations that used in this paper are first introduced and listed in Table 1.

2.1   Preliminary Concepts

Definition 1. *(Phase Change) A phase change is the special features of a moving object, which is denoted as PC. A PC indicates the status of a moving object that changes at a certain period of time and in a certain area. A PC contains three values, id, t and a, where id is the id of moving object and t is time of the status changed and a is the area.*

Table 1. Summarize of notations

Notation	Definition
T	A raw trajectory
ap	An anchor point
PC	The special features of a moving object
E	An entry area
AT	A anchor trajectory

The speed changing or the direction changing will be a status changing for a moving object. For example, The status of a ship includes sailing, entering, docking, departing etc.

Definition 2. *(Entry Area) An entry area is a fixed spatial area in the space, where the moving objects have a series of state transition in this area when they are entering or leaving. Specially, it also contains the status of speed = 0 of the moving object.*

The symbol of the set of entry areas are denotes as E. The status of a moving object between two different entry areas e_i and e_{i+1} may have more than one status transition. That means that there could be a series of status transition $\overline{ST} = \{st_1, st_2, \ldots, st_m\}$ when the moving object travels from e_i to e_{i+1}.

So we rewrite the raw trajectory T into a phase changed based trajectory $\overline{AT}$. Such trajectories are so called anchored trajectories. The size $|\overline{AT}|$ denotes the number of phase changed locations of $\overline{AT}$.

3   Learning Features to Find Similar Trajectories

In this section, we will describe the detail of our algorithm. We will be more information to the algorithm in detail by the content of three parts include feature extraction, data processing and similarity calculation etc.

3.1   Feature Extraction

In this subsection, we present the main features that will be used to describe the trajectories. The features can be mainly divided into two types: routing features (which describe where the moving object travels),and moving features (which describe how the moving object travels).

Routing Features. Routing features describe the characteristics related to where the moving object travels. Thus, as we focus on trajectories collected from vessels, the natural routing features are the information about the routes they travel on. Route information can directory affect the moving patterns of the trajectories. So in our paper, we identify and use 2 kinds of route information (type and direction) s the routing features, shown in the Table 2. These features can be extracted from the AIS data, and well distinguish different kinds of routes.

Type: The type of the vessel is a important feature which can affect how the route changes. Different kinds of vessels have different routes when they travel in the ocean.

Direction: The direction feature indicates the traffic direction of the route. There are two values of direction, i.e. 1 (start-destination route) and -1 (destination-start route) as we defined in this paper.

Moving Feature. Moving objects have different moving features to describe how the objects travel. Many articles do research on extracting various moving information from trajectories. In our paper, we propose four types of moving features such as speed, course, stop points and number of phase changes to describe the motion behavior of a moving object (Table 3).

Table 2. Summarize of notations

Feature type	Example	Numeric
Type	Cargo	No
Direction	1(−1)	No

Table 3. Summarize of notations

Feature type	Example	Numeric
Speed	100	Yes
Course	100	Yes
Stop points	5	Yes
Number of phase changes	10	Yes

Speed: The speed of a moving object is one of the most important moving features. For instance, if the speed of a vessel is higher or lower than the average speed of trajectories on the same trajectory, the speed feature can significantly distinguish from others.

Course: The course of the moving object is another important moving feature of a trajectory. Similar to speed feature, if the course of a vessel is higher or lower than the average course of trajectories on the same trajectory, the course feature can significantly distinguish from others.

Stop points: Stop points are places where the moving object stays for a certain period of time as speed $= 0$. In our paper, stop points is different with the start and destination points, it only represents the stay points of the trajectory between start and destination. Stop point is a sharp phase change of the moving object, which is usually abnormal. There are many reasons for the occurrence of stay points.

Number of phase changes: A phase change is a important indicator of the moving status. So if a trajectory have more frequently phase changes, it maybe abnormal compared with other trajectories.

3.2 Data Processing

Data Filling. We divided the trajectories of same type of ship which have the same origin and destination as a set, and then to analysis the trajectories in the set. However, due to susceptible to weather, water, and other factors, the signal transmission can easily be affected, the ship's track records are not as good as comprehensive data on land, there may be exists trace missing problem. In order to increase the accuracy of calculating the similarity value, we need to fill a vacancy for lost data.

When there exist a huge time interval or spatial separation between two continuous points of a trajectory. There may be exist the records missing problem. So in order to enhance the accuracy of the similarity calculation results, we must fill the missing records. In this paper, we use the time-aware and space-correlation collaborative algorithm to solve the trace missing problem, we also use the historical records and other type ship records to calibrating trajectory data.

Suppose that a raw trajectory $T = \{p_1, p_2, \ldots, p_n\}$ start at p_{start} and end at p_{end}, and the time interval or spatial distance is much greater than a given value between two continuous points as p_i and p_{i+1}. if there exist some historical points location between p_i and p_{i+1}, we will use the historical points to predict the missing points in this trajectory. Firstly, we use the anchor points which located at the location of missing points as the baseline value, and use a exponential function as the adaptive function to calibrating the results. But in some times, there maybe no records and no historical points of this type route in the location where missing records. So we need to use other types of records to predict the results. We also use a exponential function to adjust the results. And the calculation formula as follows:

$$p_{predict} = \lambda_1 * ap + \lambda_2 * p_h * f_1 * f_2 + (1 - \lambda_1 - \lambda_2) * p_o * f_3 \qquad (1)$$

where $p_{predict}$ is the missing point which need to be predicted. λ_1 and λ_2 are the adjustment factors to changing the proportion of value ap, p_h and p_o. ap is the anchor point located at the location. p_h is the historical record. p_o is other type vessel record. Function f_1 and f_2 are the adjustment functions to calibrating the time and distance Influence between $p_{predict}$ and p_h. Function f_3 is the adjustment function to calibrating the difference between different types of vessels. Function f_1, f_2 and f_3 are defined as follows:

$$f_1 = e^{-\alpha|t_{p_{predict}} - t_{p_h}|} \qquad (2)$$

$$f_2 = e^{-\beta \sqrt[2]{(la_{p_{predict}} - la_{p_h})^2 + (lon_{p_{predict}} - lon_{p_h})^2}} \qquad (3)$$

$$f_3 = e^{-\gamma} \qquad (4)$$

Trajectory Compression. Because of the high rate at which AIS data is collected, the amount of AIS data is large. Because of the large amount of data and the regularity of vessels, we can compress the data to a much smaller volume without losing important information. In fact, the ultimate criterion for the quality of compression is in the extent to which the data can be compressed without damaging the use of the trajectory data for further processing. So in this paper, we use the features extracted from the raw trajectories as the metrics to compress the trajectories.

Using AIS messages a moving object trajectory of a vessel can be constructed. Usually we use the latitude, longitude and time to represents a trajectory. As we described above, a moving object is represented by a sequence of points: $T = \{p_1, p_2, \ldots, p_n\}$ where each point consists of a geospatial coordinate set and a timestamp, i.e. $p_i = (o, l, t, s, c)$. $i \in \{1, 2, \ldots, n\}$.

In the field of moving object databases different techniques have been studied to compress trajectory data, and the most common method is Piecewise Linear Segmentation(PLS). The PLS-algorithm compresses a trajectory T into linear segments by recursively keeping the points that have maximum error higher than a fixed threshold. Thus, the goal of the algorithm is to reduce the number of points in a trajectory while keeping the maximum deviation, or error, from the original trajectory within the threshold. So we use PLS algorithm to compress the trajectories.

Compression with PLS using any of these error measures can lead to problems with regards to retaining stops in trajectories. It is possible for a trajectory to be reduced in such a way that in the compressed trajectory it appears as if the vessel moves slowly, whereas in the original uncompressed trajectory the vessel stopped moving for a period of time. Knowing whether a vessel stops or not is important in the behavior analysis of vessels, thus we would like to retain this information during compression. The pseudo code for this algorithm is given below.

Algorithm 1. pls (T, ϵ)

Require: T, ϵ
Ensure: T_C
  $d_{max} \leftarrow 0, i_{max} \leftarrow 0$
  for $i \leftarrow 2$**to**$(end - 1)$ **do**
    $d = E(T(i), T(1), T(end))$
    if $d > d_{max}$ **then**
      $i_{max} \leftarrow i$
      $d_{max} \leftarrow d$
    end if
  end for
  if $d_{max} \geq \epsilon$ **then**
    A = **pls**(T(1,i_{max}),ϵ)
    B = **pls**(T(i_{max},end),ϵ)
    T_C = A,B(2,end)
  else
    T_C = T(1),T(end)
    $N \leftarrow n$
  end if
  return T_C

From trajectories compress method, we can get a much smaller volume data without losing important information because the features which measure the travel behaviors all have been retained. And in next part we will use the features to describe the travel behaviors of the trajectories.

After we filling and compress the raw trajectory, we have a new trajectory which have fewer points but don't lose the routing features and behavior features of the raw trajectory. So in next part, we will calculate similarity between different trajectories with anchor trajectories which act as the reference system to distinguish the abnormal trajectories. When calculating the similarity between different tracks, the processed new trajectories would be used.

3.3   Similarity Calculation

There are multiple approaches for performing the outlier detection tasks on vessel trajectory data. We decided to take a similarity measure based approach. We use similarities defined on alignments between the points of two trajectories. Alignment measures are flexible in dealing with trajectories of different length in terms of the number of points, time, and distance traveled. The compression detailed in the previous section reduces the number of points substantially, which makes alignment computation faster. However, compression can have a potentially negative influence on the quality of the alignments. We investigate this influence, and the performance of alignment measures in general, in this section.

First, we cluster the raw trajectories data into clusters using DBSCAN algorithm, and use the geometric centers of the clusters as the anchor points. And use the anchor points to construct the new trajectories as the Anchor Trajectories. When calculating the similarity between two different trajectories we use the anchor trajectories as the reference trajectories. At the calculation of the similar value of a trajectory, we use the time-aware and space-correlation collaborative algorithm to calculate the similarity, and also use the historical records and other type ship records to calibrating the value of similarity.

In order to calculate the similarity, we use the Anchor Trajectories (denotes as AT) as the reference system. Then we calculate the similarity between anchor trajectory and the new trajectory. Considering the actual situation, the new trajectory also been impacted by the near time trajectories, especially in the relatively short time interval. So the impaction of the near time trajectories must be take into account. The specific formula is as follows:

$$Sim_T = \lambda * Sim_{AT} + (1 - \lambda) * Sim_{T'} * f_1 \tag{5}$$

where λ is the adjustment factor to changing the proportion of value Sim_{AT} and $Sim_{T'}$. Function f_1 is the adjustment function to calibrating the time impaction between trajectories T' and T as we defined in former section. In order to maintain consistency, the parameter used in this section is the same as we used in former section. And we use the DTW(dynamic time warping) algorithm to calculate the values of Sim_{AT} and $Sim_{T'}$. The Sim_{AT} and $Sim_{T'}$ are calculated as follows:

$$Sim_{AT} = \frac{DTW(T, AT)}{|T| + |AT|} \qquad (6)$$

$$Sim_{T'} = \frac{DTW(T, T'))}{|T| + |T'|} \qquad (7)$$

where $|T|$, $|AT|$ and $|T'|$ are the number of points of trajectories T, AT and T' respectively.

After we get the similarity values of every trajectory, the lower the score of the similarity is, the higher the degree of outliers.

4   Experiment

In this section, we conduct extensive experiments to validate the effectiveness of our algorithm. All experiments have been performed through the real data on a workstation with 12 Intel Xeon 3.50 GHz CPUs and 32 GB main memory and 64 bit Windows10 as operating system. And the algorithm has been implemented in JDK8.

4.1   Experiment Setup

We cluster the raw data into clusters using DBSCAN, and use the geometric centers of the clusters as the anchor points. We use a real-world trajectory data set generated by vessels in East China region over one month. This data set has more than 40,000 trajectories. Since the amount of data is too large, in order to facilitate the calculation, we use the 'passenger ship' type trajectories which include about 600,000 records as the experimental data. In our algorithm, we set the weight of $\lambda_1 = 0.8$, $\lambda_2 = 0.1$, $\lambda = 0.9$, $\alpha = \beta = \gamma = 0.085$ and $\epsilon = 200$.

4.2   Performance Evaluation

Figure 1(a) represents the effectiveness of using our feature learning algorithm and Fig. 1(b) shows the result that direct comparison without our algorithm. The black dots represent the normal trajectories, and the red line represents the abnormal trajectories. From the two pictures we can see that, applying our method significantly outperforms the basic approach. That's because we use the time-aware and space-correlation collaborative algorithm which solve the trace missing problem, and we also use the historical records and other type ship records to calibrating trajectory data. After we calculate a more precisely value to fill a vacancy for lost data, it can obviously increase the accuracy of calculating the similarity value. Simultaneously, as we use the time-aware and space-correlation collaborative algorithm to calculate the similarity, and use the historical records and other type ship records to calibrating the value of similarity, we can have a more precisely similarity of the trajectory. That's why our algorithm can have a much better result.

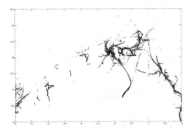
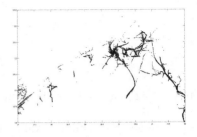

(a) Result with our algorithm   (b) Result without our algorithm

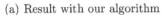

Fig. 1. The comparing results with our algorithm and without our algorithm

In addition, after we compress the large amount of data into a much smaller volume data without damaging the use of the trajectory data for further processing, our algorithm can obviously reduce the operation time. In fact, by increasing the number of raw trajectories, the computation time of our approach increases very slowly compared to the basic one. This is an expected behavior since by considering much smaller points, the number of involved in the calculation points decreases.

5   Related Works

In the past few years, a lot of research works focused on the trajectory analyzing. Representative work includes designing effective trajectory indexing structures [1,2], trajectory query processing [3,4], uncertainty management [5,6], and mining knowledge/patterns from trajectories [7,8].

Effective index structures [1–4,9–14] are built to manage trajectories and support high performance trajectory queries. Data mining methods are applied on trajectories to detect important PoIs and find the popular route from a source to a destination [7,15–18]. Attentions are also drawn to semantic representation or interpretation of trajectory data by associating or annotating GPS locations with semantic entities [19,20].

The existing trajectory abnormal detection algorithms focused on how to find the most representative trajectory out of a set of trajectories. Given a set of trajectory data, [25] apply a piecewise linear segmentation method to compress the trajectory and then use a similarity based approach to perform the clustering, classification and outlier detection tasks using kernel methods. In [26], the author propose an online method that is able to detect anomalous trajectory "on-the-fly" and to identify which parts of the trajectory are responsible for its anomalousness.

Given a set of trajectories, [27] proposed a solution to cluster the trajectories into several groups, and represent each group by its most central trajectory. The assigning trajectory sample points to some semantical anchor points, i.e., PoIs, share the similar motivation of some research works of construction semantic trajectories, [28] summarized a set of trajectories by providing a symbolic route to represent the cardinal trajectory directions.

And also a few works have been conducted on trajectory segmentation. In literature [29], the authors proposed a method to segment heterogeneous trajectories into several parts according to different means of transportation, e.g., by bike and by car. This trajectory segmentation method can hardly be applied on a trajectory generated by the same transportation. In literature [24], they propose a partition-and-summarization approach to use the semantic to segment and summarize individual trajectory.

Dedicated algorithms are independently designed for trajectory annotations with geographic regions or lines. Regarding trajectory annotation with geographic regions, studies [20,30] focused on computing topological correlations (called spatial predicates) between trajectories and regions. Regarding trajectory annotation with geographic lines, many works [31–34] have been focusing on identifying the correct road segment on which a vehicle is traveling. [31] used only geometric information of the underlying road network and apply distance measurements to generate line annotation. [32] accounted for the connectivity and contiguity of the road networks, rather than only the geometric distances. [33,34] studied generating annotations for low-sampling-rate trajectories.

6   Conclusion

In this paper, we propose a trajectory abnormal detection system. This system can detect the abnormal trajectories of vessels use the AIS record of the vessels through our feature learning algorithm. Firstly we use the DBSCAN algorithm to cluster the large number of historical data into clusters and use the geometric centers of the clusters as the anchor points to have anchor trajectories. We use the time-aware and space-correlation collaborative algorithm, and also use the historical records and other type ship records to calibrating trajectory data and to solve the trace missing problem. Simultaneously, we use the PLS algorithm to process the raw trajectory data which can be compressed without damaging the use of the trajectory data for further processing. Through this step we can compress the data to a much smaller volume without losing important information, it is a important step to speed the algorithm's operation time. And last, we use the DTW algorithm to calculate the similarity of between trajectories and anchor trajectories as we use anchor trajectories as the reference system. We made use of the real-life data for our algorithm, experimental results show that our algorithm has good detection effect, higher efficiency and stronger scalability.

Acknowledgments. The authors would like to acknowledge the support of the project which is provided by the National Natural Science Foundation of China under Grant (No. U1435220)(No. 61503365).

References

1. Cai, Y., Ng, R.: Indexing spatio-temporal trajectories with Chebyshev polynomials. In: Proceedings of the 2004 ACM SIGMOD International Conference on Management of Data, pp. 599–610. ACM (2004)
2. Wu, D., Yiu, M.L., Jensen, C.S., et al.: Efficient continuously moving top-k spatial keyword query processing. In: 2011 IEEE 27th International Conference on Data Engineering (ICDE), pp. 541–552. IEEE (2011)
3. Chen, L., Ozsu, M.T., Oria, V.: Robust and fast similarity search for moving object trajectories. In: Proceedings of the 2005 ACM SIGMOD International Conference on Management of Data, pp. 491–502. ACM (2005)
4. Vlachos, M., Kollios, G., Gunopulos, D.: Discovering similar multidimensional trajectories. In: Proceedings of the 18th International Conference on Data Engineering, pp. 673–684. IEEE (2002)
5. Zheng, K., Trajcevski, G., Zhou, X., et al.: Probabilistic range queries for uncertain trajectories on road networks. In: Proceedings of the 14th International Conference on Extending Database Technology, pp. 283–294. ACM (2011)
6. Zheng, K., Zheng, Y., Xie, X., et al.: Reducing uncertainty of low-sampling-rate trajectories. In: 2012 IEEE 28th International Conference on Data Engineering (ICDE), pp. 1144–1155. IEEE (2012)
7. Jeung, H., Yiu, M.L., Zhou, X., et al.: Discovery of convoys in trajectory databases. Proc. VLDB Endowment 1(1), 1068–1080 (2008)
8. Zheng, K., Zheng, Y., Yuan, N.J., et al.: On discovery of gathering patterns from trajectories. In: 2013 IEEE 29th International Conference on Data Engineering (ICDE), pp. 242–253. IEEE (2013)
9. Wang, H., Zheng, K., Xu, J., et al.: SharkDB: an in-memory column-oriented trajectory storage. In: Proceedings of the 23rd ACM International Conference on Conference on Information and Knowledge Management, pp. 1409–1418. ACM (2014)
10. Ni, J., Ravishankar, C.V.: Indexing spatio-temporal trajectories with efficient polynomial approximations. IEEE Trans. Knowl. Data Eng. 19(5), 663–678 (2007)
11. Chakka, V.P., Everspaugh, A.C., Patel, J.M.: Indexing large trajectory data sets with SETI. Ann Arbor 1001, 48109-2122, 12 (2003)
12. Cudre-Mauroux, P., Wu, E., Madden, S.: Trajstore: an adaptive storage system for very large trajectory data sets. In: 2010 IEEE 26th International Conference on Data Engineering (ICDE), pp. 109–120. IEEE (2010)
13. Frentzos, E., Gratsias, K., Pelekis, N., Theodoridis, Y.: Nearest neighbor search on moving object trajectories. In: Medeiros, C.B., Egenhofer, M., Bertino, E. (eds.) SSTD 2005. LNCS, vol. 3633, pp. 328–345. Springer, Heidelberg (2005)
14. Saltenis, B.S., Jensen, C.S., Leutenegger, S.T., et al.: Indexing the positions of continuously moving objects, pp. 331–342. ACM (2000)
15. Lee, J.G., Han, J., Whang, K.Y.: Trajectory clustering: a partition-and-group framework. In: Proceedings of the 2007 ACM SIGMOD International Conference on Management of Data, pp. 593–604. ACM (2007)
16. Jeung, H., Shen, H.T., Zhou, X.: Convoy queries in spatio-temporal databases. In: IEEE 24th International Conference on Data Engineering, ICDE 2008, pp. 1457–1459. IEEE (2008)
17. Li, Z., Ding, B., Han, J., et al.: Swarm: mining relaxed temporal moving object clusters. Proc. VLDB Endowment 3(1-2), 723–734 (2010)

18. Zheng, B., Zheng, K., Sharaf, M.A., et al.: Efficient retrieval of top-k most similar users from travel smart card data. In: 2014 IEEE 15th International Conference on Mobile Data Management (MDM), vol. 1, pp. 259–268. IEEE (2014)

19. Yan, Z., Spaccapietra, S.: Towards semantic trajectory data analysis: a conceptual and computational approach. In: VLDB Ph.D. Workshop (2009)

20. Spaccapietra, S., Parent, C., Damiani, M.L., et al.: A conceptual view on trajectories. Data Knowl. Eng. **65**(1), 126–146 (2008)

21. Kruskal, J.B.: An overview of sequence comparison: time warps, string edits, and macromolecules. SIAM Rev. **25**(2), 201–237 (1983)

22. Kearney, J.K., Hansen, S.: Stream editing for animation. University of Iowa, Dept. of Computer Science, No. TR-90-08 (1990)

23. Chen, L., Ng, R.: On the marriage of Lp-norms and edit distance. In: Proceedings of the Thirtieth International Conference on Very Large Data Bases, vol. 30, pp. 792–803. VLDB Endowment (2004)

24. Su, H., Zheng, K., Zeng, K., et al.: Making sense of trajectory data: a partition-and-summarization approach. In: 2015 IEEE 31st International Conference on Data Engineering (ICDE), pp. 963–974. IEEE (2015)

25. De Vries, G.K.D., Van Someren, M.: Machine learning for vessel trajectories using compression, alignments and domain knowledge. Expert Syst. Appl. **39**(18), 13426–13439 (2012)

26. Chen, C., Zhang, D., Castro, P.S., et al.: iBOAT: isolation-based online anomalous trajectory detection. IEEE Trans. Intell. Trans. Syst. **14**(2), 806–818 (2013)

27. Evans, M.R., Oliver, D., Shekhar, S., et al.: Summarizing trajectories into k-primary corridors: a summary of results. In: Proceedings of the 20th International Conference on Advances in Geographic Information Systems, pp. 454–457. ACM (2012)

28. Andrae, S., Winter, S.: Summarizing GPS trajectories by salient patterns. na (2005)

29. Yan, Z., Chakraborty, D., Parent, C., et al.: SeMiTri: a framework for semantic annotation of heterogeneous trajectories. In: Proceedings of the 14th International Conference on Extending Database Technology, pp. 259–270. ACM (2011)

30. Nergiz, M.E., Atzori, M., Saygin, Y.: Towards trajectory anonymization: a generalization-based approach. In: Proceedings of the SIGSPATIAL ACM GIS 2008 International Workshop on Security and Privacy in GIS and LBS, pp. 52–61. ACM (2008)

31. Bernstein, D., Kornhauser, A.: An introduction to map matching for personal navigation assistants (1998)

32. White, C.E., Bernstein, D., Kornhauser, A.L.: Some map matching algorithms for personal navigation assistants. Transp. Res. Part C: Emerg. Technol. **8**(1), 91–108 (2000)

33. Newson, P., Krumm, J.: Hidden Markov map matching through noise and sparseness. In: Proceedings of the 17th ACM SIGSPATIAL International Conference on Advances in Geographic Information Systems, pp. 336–343. ACM (2009)

34. Lou, Y., Zhang, C., Zheng, Y., et al.: Map-matching for low-sampling-rate GPS trajectories. In: Proceedings of the 17th ACM SIGSPATIAL International Conference on Advances in Geographic Information Systems, pp. 352–361. ACM (2009)

An Algorithm for Mining Moving Flock Patterns from Pedestrian Trajectories

Yang Cao[✉], Jia Zhu, and Fang Gao

School of Computer Science, South China Normal University,
Guangzhou, China
{caoyang, jzhu}@m.scnu.edu.cn, xpycy@21cn.com

Abstract. Statistics from the research show that the majority of pedestrians actually do not walk alone, but in groups. Detecting pedestrians moving together through public spaces can provide valuable information to many location-aware applications. In this paper, we use the term "degree of freedom" to reflect the characteristics of pedestrian freedom of movement, and propose a definition of freedom moving flock pattern and a corresponding extraction algorithm. Furthermore, we evaluate the proposed algorithm by applying it to two real pedestrian trajectory datasets. The results show that the algorithm is capable of extracting the freedom moving flock patterns that are common in real-world scenarios.

Keywords: Flock pattern · Moving flock · Pedestrian trajectory · Trajectory mining

1 Introduction

With the increasing deployment and use of location detection devices (GPS, GSM, RFID, etc.), trajectory data of moving objects are currently collected in growing amounts. These data describe changes of spatial positions and hold valuable information about the movement behavior of moving objects. There have been emerging interests in efficient mining methods for mining interesting patterns from such unstructured data streams [1]. Many spatio-temporal patterns have been proposed [1–6]. Recently, diverse studies have focused in identifying group behavior patterns of moving objects whose share a strong relationship and interaction within a defined spatial region during a given time duration. Examples include the convoy [3, 7], swarm [8, 9] and flock patterns [1, 2, 6, 10, 11]. The difference between all those patterns is the way they define the relationship between the moving objects [10].

In this paper, we are interested in mining flock pattern from pedestrian trajectories which has demonstrated to be useful in security and surveillance applications [12, 13], e.g. potentially identify suspicious behavior within large number of people. Moreover, further pedestrian behavior analysis with other spatial data is helpful to understand the interaction of pedestrian motion and traffic networks, which provide valuable reference for the design of urban infrastructures, traffic management or crowd safety during emergency events or evacuation processes.

© Springer International Publishing Switzerland 2016
A. Morishima et al. (Eds.): APWeb 2016 Workshops, LNCS 9865, pp. 310–321, 2016.
DOI: 10.1007/978-3-319-45835-9_27

The flock pattern is defined by a set of objects that travel together for a specified time duration [11]. Recent papers on flock detection have focused either on algorithms using the mappings of data domain [5] or finding maximal duration flocks [14]. However, most of these algorithms do not consider the characteristics of different mobile objects (e.g. animals, pedestrians and vehicles). And very few research efforts have been devoted in studying the flock patterns among pedestrians. Because flock pattern detection is particularly relevant due to the characteristics of the moving objects, how they interact each other and how they move together [15, 16]. It is important to make a distinction between pedestrians and other moving objects. Considering the freedom of pedestrian movement, we propose a definition of freedom moving flock pattern and its corresponding extraction algorithm in this paper.

This paper is organized as follows. Sect. 2 highlights related works. Sect. 3 introduces the definitions of pedestrian flock pattern mining including degree of freedom and freedom moving flock pattern. Sect. 4 presents the flock pattern extraction algorithm. Sect. 5 shows the experimental results. Finally, Sect. 6 concludes this paper.

2 Related Works

Since the first proposal of the flock pattern by Laube and Imfeld [17], several papers have been published addressing the problem of finding flock patterns, in which a disk with a predefined diameter is used to identify groups of trajectories moving together in the same direction [1, 2, 10, 11]. Vieira et al. [10] were the first to present an exact solution for reporting flock patterns in polynomial time and also for those that can work effectively in real time. Another class of flock patterns is the Maximal Length (or Duration) Flocks [14, 18–20]. These patterns are very similar to the original flock, but there is no defined time window. Therefore, the patterns are only defined by a diameter ε and a minimum number of objects μ.

Previous researches show that the majority of pedestrians walk in groups through urban spaces rather than alone [21, 22]. Moussaid et al. [22] show that up to 70 percent of the observed pedestrians in a commercial street are walking in groups. Further, especially if felt in a dangerous situation, people display affiliative behaviors, as argued for by Mawson [23].

To monitor and infer collective behavior patterns from pedestrians, a variety of different sensor modalities have been considered and investigated, such as video surveillance systems [24, 25], Call-data records (CDRs) [26, 27], mobile social media data [28, 29] and location detection devices [30–32]. Kjærgaard et al. [30] detects pedestrian flocks by fusion of multi-modal sensors in mobile phones. Wirz et al. [31] presents an online method to detect pedestrian flocks in urban canyons by smoothed spatio-temporal clustering of GPS Trajectories. Wachowicz et al. [32] introduced a moving flock definition, along with a method for finding moving flock patterns from pedestrian datasets.

Our proposed algorithm for the purpose of finding pedestrian flock patterns has been mainly inspired by the works of Vieira et al. [10] and wachowicz et al. [32], and it is further described in the next sections.

3 Preliminaries

In this section, we prepare some technical definitions that are needed for describing the following algorithms.

The basic idea behind a flock pattern is that a highly correlated group of objects travel together within a small neighbor during a certain length of time. We have adopted the concept of flock pattern [10, 11] as described below.

Definition 1. Given a set of trajectories T, a minimum number of trajectories $\mu > 1(\mu \in N)$, a maximize distance $\varepsilon > 0$ defined over the distance function d and a minimum duration $\delta > 1 (\delta \in N)$. **A *Flock($\mu$, ε, δ)* pattern** reports all sets F of trajectories where: for each set $f_k \in F$, the number of trajectories in f_k is greater or equal to $\mu(|f_k| \geq \mu)$ and there exist δ consecutive time stamps $t_j, \ldots,t_{j+\delta-1}$ in which there is a disk of center $c_k^{t_i}$ and diameter ε that covers all trajectories of $f_k^{t_i}$ which is the flock f_k in time $t_i, j \leqslant i \leqslant j + \delta$.

The minimum number of trajectories μ refers to the minimum number of the members in a flock. The maximize distance ε defines the closeness of members at some time instances. The minimum duration δ is the minimum time interval in which the flock members are close together.

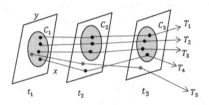

Fig. 1. Flock pattern example

Figure 1 shows an example of flock pattern in the two-dimensional space. The flock is formed by trajectories with identifiers $\{T_1, T_2, T_3\}$ covered by the disks $\{C_1, C_2, C_3\}$ at the time interval $I = [t_1, t_3]$. The trajectory T_4 leaves the pattern at time t_2, which does not stay in the pattern during the consecutive time interval I. The trajectory T_5 only join in the pattern at time t_1 and leave at t_2 and t_3. Refer to Definition 1, trajectory T_4 and T_5 are not included in the flock pattern. However, in comparison with other moving objects (e.g. vehicles), pedestrians have more freedom in movement. The trajectories similar to T_4 always appear in group movement of pedestrians especially in an open space, or in a loose group, which should be accepted into the pedestrian flock.

Considering the freedom of pedestrian movement, we extend Definition 1 to obtain Definition 4. In order to formally define the freedom moving flock, we define the notion of degree of freedom and flock's spatial extent.

Definition 2. Given a *Flock(μ, ε, δ)* pattern in a time interval I, the **degree of freedom** of the trajectory T_i in the *Flock(μ, ε, δ)*, denoted by DOF_i, is defined by the proportion of I_{join}^i to I, that is,

$$DOF_i = I_{join}^i / I \tag{1}$$

where I_{join}^i is the total amount of time during which the trajectory T_i is contained inside the disks of the flock.

The notion of a flock's spatial extent is used to define moving flocks [32], of which flock members should not solely remain close together (i.e. within a specified radius), but should also move together (i.e. not remain stationary in one location) for the time interval.

Definition 3. Given $Flock(\mu, \varepsilon, \delta)$ pattern in a time interval I, its **spatial extent** $ext(I)$, is defined as $ext(I) = \max\{l, w\}$ where l and w are the length and the width of the minimum bounding rectangle (MBR) of the sub-trajectories belonging to the flock.

Definition 4. Given a set of trajectories T, a minimum number of trajectories $\mu > 1(\mu \in N)$, a maximize distance $\varepsilon > 0$ defined over the distance function d, a minimum duration $\delta > 1\,(\delta \in N)$ and a minimum degree of freedom DOF_{min}, a **freedom moving flock pattern** in a time interval I, denoted by $Flock_{free}$ $(\mu, \varepsilon, \delta, DOF_{min})$, reports all sets F of trajectories where: (1) for each set f_k in F, the number of trajectories in f_k is greater or equal to $\mu(|f_k| \geq \mu)$, (2) there exist δ consecutive time stamps $(t_j, ...,t_{j+\delta-1}) \subset I$ which there is a disk of diameter ε that covers most trajectories of $f_k^{t_i}$ which is the flock f_k in time t_i, (3) for each trajectory T_i in f_k, $DOF_i \leq DOF_{min}$, (4) the spatial extent $ext(I) \geq \varepsilon$.

The minimum degree of freedom DOF_{min} reflects the lower limit of the time that the moving member should stay in the flock. The flock extent $ext(I)$ is the minimum distance of the pedestrian moving in the flock.

In comparison to Definition 1, Definition 4 emphasizes that flock members have more freedom. They should move together for a long time but need not stay in the flock all the time. The members can leave the flock for a while, but the leaving time should be restricted by the DOF_{min}. This situation is common in pedestrian group movement.

4 The Flock Pattern Extraction Algorithm

In the following section we present the four-step pattern extraction algorithm for freedom moving flock, which includes spatial neighbor computation, membership persistence analysis, DOF filtering and pruning.

4.1 Spatial Neighbor Computation

Two moving pedestrians are referred to as spatial neighbors for a specific time instance if their locations for this time instance are close. In this step, the location proximity between the trajectory points co-occurring in time is calculated. Given any two pedestrian trajectories T_i and T_j, $d(T_i, T_j)$ is the Euclidean distance between T_i and T_j at time t. If $d(T_i, T_j) \leq \varepsilon/2$, where ε is the distance threshold of the flock, the trajectories T_i and T_j are referred to as spatial neighbors at time t.

The pseudo-code description of the spatial neighbor computation algorithm is given in Algorithm 1. The output of algorithm is the total spatial neighbor set $N(T) = \{N(T_1),$ $\ldots, N(T_n)\}$, where $N(T_i)$ is the spatial neighbor set of trajectory T_i in the time interval I.

Algorithm 1. The spatial neighbor computation algorithm

Input: the trajectory set $T=\{T_1, \ldots, T_n\}$ in the time interval $I= [t_1, t_m]$, the maximize distance ε of the flock, the minimum trajectory number μ in the flock
Output: the total spatial neighbor set $N(T)$
1   $N(T)=\varnothing$
2   for ($i=0$; $i<T$.length; $i++$)
3       $N(T_i) =\varnothing$ // $N(T_i)$ is the spatial neighbor set of trajectory T_i in the time interval I
4   for each time stamps $t_j \in I$
5           $N_{t_j}(T_i)=\varnothing$ // $N_{t_j}(T_i)$ is the spatial neighbor set of trajectory T_i at the time t_j
6   for ($k=0$;$k<T$.length; $k++$)
7   if ($k!=i$)
8   find the points $p_f \in T_i$, $p_g \in T_k$ in time t_j
9   if $d(p_f, p_g) \leq \varepsilon/2$ // $d(p_f, p_g)$ is the distance between the trajectory points p_f and p_g
10                      $N_{t_j}(T_i) = N_{t_j}(T_i) \cup \{T_k\}$
11   end if
12   end if
13   end for
14   if $|N_{t_j}(T_i)| \geq \mu$
15              $N(T_i)= N(T_i) \cup \{N_{t_j}(T_i)\}$
16   end if
17   end for
18      $N(T)= N(T) \cup \{N(T_i)\}$

4.2   Membership Persistence Analysis

This step, membership persistence analysis, is to check whether the trajectory neighbors at a specific time instance continue to be close to each other for other adjacent time instances. As said above, pedestrians have more freedom in movement. It is permitted that the members leave the flock for a short time. Considering this characteristic of pedestrians, we use the Jaccard measure [33] to calculate the similarity between the spatial neighbor sets at adjacent time instances.

Given the spatial neighbor set of the trajectory T_i at adjacent time t_j and t_{j+1}, the Jaccard measure is calculated by

$$jaccard\left(N_{t_j}(T_i), N_{t_{j+1}}(T_i)\right) = \frac{\left|N_{t_j}(T_i) \cap N_{t_{j+1}}(T_i)\right|}{\left|N_{t_j}(T_i) \cup N_{t_{j+1}}(T_i)\right|} \tag{2}$$

If $jaccard\left(N_{t_j}(T_i), N_{t_{j+1}}(T_i)\right) \geq \sigma$ (σ is a threshold value that is normally set as 50 %), $N_{t_j}(T_i)$ and $N_{t_{j+1}}(T_i)$ will be merged, that is $N_{I_{t_j}}(T_i) = N_{t_j}(T_i) \cup N_{t_{j+1}}(T_i)$

and $I_{t_j} = \{t_j, t_{j+1}\}$. This merging process is performed in a recursive manner until the longest duration flocks are found. If the time duration is lesser than the user-defined threshold δ, the flock will be disregarded. Then the subsequent time stamp $t_{j+|I_{t_j}|-1}$ are chosen to continue the merging process until the last time stamp of the trajectory. All spatial neighbor sets in $N(T)$ generated in the preceding step will be checked and merged to extract the candidate flocks.

The pseudo-code description of the membership persistence analysis algorithm is given in Algorithm 2. The outcome of this step is the candidate flock set $CF(T, I)$.

Algorithm 2. The membership persistence analysis algorithm

Input: the total spatial neighbor set $N(T)$, the time interval of the trajectory I, the minimum duration δ, the parameter σ
Output: the candidate flock set $CF(T, I)$
1 $CF(T, I)=\varnothing$
2 for each $N(T_i) \in N(T)$
3    $CF(T_i, I)=\varnothing, j=1$ // $CF(T_i, I)$ is the candidate flock set related to the trajectory T_i
4   while $(j<|I|)$ // the loop to find the candidate flocks from $N(T_i)$
5      $N_{I_{t_j}}(T_i)=N_{t_j}(T_i),\ I_{t_j} = \{t_j\},\ k=j$
6   while $(k<|I|)$ // the loop to find the longest duration flock from t_j
7   if $jaccard\left(N_{t_k}(T_i), N_{t_{k+1}}(T_i)\right) \geq \sigma$
8          $N_{I_{t_j}}(T_i)=N_{I_{t_j}}(T_i) \cup N_{t_{k+1}}(T_i),\ I_{t_j} = I_{t_j} \cup \{t_k\},\ k++$ // merging process
9   else
10   break // disregard the candidate
11   end if
12   end while
13   if $\left(\left|I_{t_j}\right| \geq \delta\right)$ and $(<N_{I_{t_j}}(T_i),\ I_{t_j}> \notin CF(T_i, I))$
14        $CF(T_i, I)= CF(T_i, I) \cup \{<N_{I_{t_j}}(T_i),\ I_{t_j}>\}$
15   end if
16      $j=k+1$
17   end while
18    $CF(T, I)= CF(T, I) \cup \{CF(T_i, I)\}$
19 end for

4.3 DOF Filtering

In the preceding step, we use Jaccard measure as merging criterion. It will cause a new problem that some moving objects only stay in the candidate flock for a short time. In the real-world situation, these objects join in the flock occasionally and should not be a part of the group. Therefore, in this step, we use a *DOF* threshold (i.e. DOF_{min}) to filter the candidate flocks extracted from the preceding step.

The pseudo-code description of the *DOF* filtering algorithm is given in Algorithm 3. The outcome of this step is the filtered candidate flock set $FCF(T, I)$.

Algorithm 3. The *DOF* filtering algorithm

Input: the candidate flock set $CF(T, I)$, the *DOF* threshold DOF_{min}, the minimum number of trajectories in the flock μ
Output: the filtered candidate flock set $FCF(T, I)$
1 $FCF(T, I) = CF(T, I)$
2 for each $CF(T_i, I) \in FCF(T, I)$ // traversing all flocks found in the above step
3   for each $<N_{I_{t_j}}(T_i), I_{t_j}> \in CF(T_i, I)$
4   for each T_k in the candidate flock $N_{I_{t_j}}(T_i)$
5   compute the total time that T_k stay in the flock, i.e. I^k_{join}
6        $DOF_k(I_{t_j}) = |I^k_{join}| / |I_{t_j}|$ //compute the DOF_k of T_k in the flock $N_{I_{t_j}}(T_i)$
7   if $DOF_k(I_{t_j}) < DOF_{min}$
8   delete T_k from the flock $N_{I_{t_j}}(T_i)$
9   end if
10   end for
11   if the number of trajectories in the flock $N_{I_{t_j}}(T_i)$ is less than μ
12   delete $<N_{I_{t_j}}(T_i), I_{t_j}>$ from $CF(T_i, I)$
13   end if
14   end for
15   if $CF(T_i, I) = \varnothing$
16   delete $CF(T_i, I)$ from $FCF(T, I)$
17   end if
18   end for

4.4   Pruning

Algorithm 4. The pruning algorithm

Input: the filtered candidate flock set $FCF(T, I)$, the maximize distance ε
Output: the final flock set $F(T, I)$
1 $F(T, I) = FCF(T, I)$
2 for each $CF(T_i, I) \in F(T, I)$ // traversing all flocks filtered in the above step
3   for each $<N_{I_{t_j}}(T_i), I_{t_j}> \in CF(T_i, I)$
4   compute the extent of the flock $<N_{I_{t_j}}(T_i), I_{t_j}>$, i.e. $ext(I_{t_j})$
5   if $ext(I_{t_j}) < \varepsilon$
6   delete $<N_{I_{t_j}}(T_i), I_{t_j}>$ from $CF(T_i, I)$ // delete the stationary flock
7   end if
8   end for
9   if $CF(OT_i, I) = \varnothing$
10   delete $CF(T_i, I)$ from $FCF(T, I)$
11   end if

The above steps still produce stationary patterns as well. Hence, the final step is to pruning stationary patterns. The extent of each filtered flock (i.e. the notion in Definition 3) has been computed. Patterns with a short extent (i.e. having an extent smaller than ε) are considered as stationary flock patterns and will be disregarded.

The pseudo-code description of the Pruning algorithm is given in Algorithm 4. The outcome of this step is the final flock set $F(T, I)$.

5   Experiments

In order to verify the efficiency of the proposed algorithms, we run several experiments with two pedestrian trajectory datasets under different parameters. The first dataset (denoted by NO. 1) has 2010 locations generated by 12 people in the campus of South China Normal University, which record the walking trajectories of some friend. The second dataset (denoted by NO. 2) has 1376 locations generated by 7 people between the university and the supermarket, which record a round trip for shopping.

The trajectory data is displayed in Fig. 2, which the black and red arrows indicate the moving direction and the red bubbles show the POIs near the origin and the destination of the trajectories.

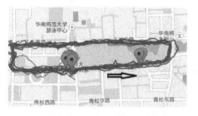

    (a) Trajectory dataset No.1   (b) Trajectory dataset No.2

Fig. 2. The experimental trajectory data (blue lines). Color figure online

In order to improve the analysis accuracy, several trajectory data preprocessing steps [34] are performed on the trajectory data, which are outlier cleaning and Gaussian smoothing. Since most trajectory points are recorded at different time intervals or are removed as error in preprocessing, missing data imputation is also performed to ensure that the movement of pedestrians co-occurring in time will also have trajectory points co-occurring in time. Here we use interpolation [35] to approximate the missing data.

We tested several values for the DOF_{min}, μ, δ, ε parameters. The ranges of values for two dataset are shown in Table 1, where bold values represent default values. For instance, for the Dataset NO. 1 when the DOF_{min} varies from 0.1 to 1, with increments of 0.1, the default values for μ, δ and ε are 3, 30 and 20, respectively.

Figures 3 and 4 show the total number of patterns discovered from the datasets when DOF_{min}, μ, δ and ε are varied.

Shown in Figs. 3(a) and 4(a), as the minimum degree of freedom DOF_{min} increases, which means that more restrictions on pedestrians' freedom in the flock, a smaller

Table 1. Parameters values for two datasets

	DOF_{min} [default]	μ [default]	δ [default]	ε [default]
Dataset NO. 1	0.1, 0.2, ..., 1 [0.5]	2, 3, ...,12 [3]	10, 20,..., 720 [30]	5, 10, ..., 150 [20]
Dataset NO. 2	0.1, 0.2, ..., 1 [0.5]	2, 3, ..., 7 [2]	3, 10, ..., 100 [3]	10,20,..., 400 [80]

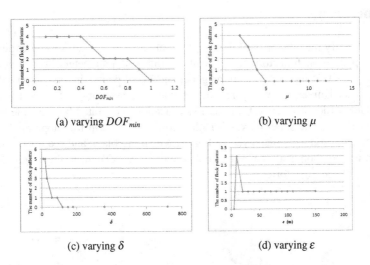

(a) varying DOF_{min} (b) varying μ

(c) varying δ (d) varying ε

Fig. 3. The number of flocks when varying (a) DOF_{min} (b) μ, (c) δ, (d) ε for the dataset NO. 1

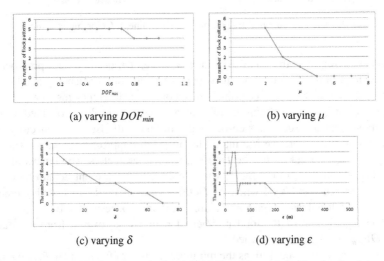

(a) varying DOF_{min} (b) varying μ

(c) varying δ (d) varying ε

Fig. 4. The number of flocks when varying (a) DOF_{min} (b) μ, (c) δ, (d) ε for the dataset NO. 2

number of flocks are found. When DOF_{min} is set to 1, the criterions of the freedom moving flock pattern are the same with those of the normal moving flock pattern [32], which pedestrians cannot leave the flock during the time of the flock.

As the experimental results of Figs. 3(b), (c) and 4(b), (c) shown, when the minimum number of objects (μ) increases or the minimum duration (δ) increases, a smaller number of flocks are found. When μ becomes greater than 5, no flock is found from the datasets. It is specific to the context and nature of moving objects. Early observations have shown that pedestrian groups composed of two to four members are the most frequent, while groups of size five and larger are rare [22].

Moreover, in order to extract reasonable flock patterns, the value of δ of Fig. 3(c) is larger than that of Fig. 4(c), while the value of ε of Fig. 3(d) is less than that of Fig. 4 (d). Considering the meaning of these parameters, we can infer that the pedestrian group in dataset NO. 2 is looser than the group in dataset NO. 1. It is consistent with the moving purpose and the environment of two datasets.

By the support of these experiment data, we choose $DOF_{min} = 0.5$, $\mu = 3$, $\delta = 30$, $\varepsilon = 40$ for the dataset NO. 1, while $DOF_{min} = 0.5$, $\mu = 2$, $\delta = 30$, $\varepsilon = 80$ for the dataset NO. 2. The flock patterns (shown with red lines) extracted from two datasets are visualized in Fig. 5. As we can see, the pedestrian flocks extracted from the two datasets is reflecting the real situation. Experiments on the real trajectory datasets show that our methods can effectively extract flock patterns for different variations of the flock parameters.

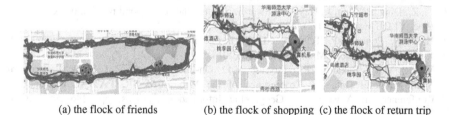

(a) the flock of friends   (b) the flock of shopping (c) the flock of return trip

Fig. 5. The freedom moving flock patterns extracted from dataset NO. 1 and NO. 2

6 Conclusion

Discovering pedestrian flock patterns is useful for several applications ranging from tracking suspicious activities to crowd safety. However previous few research efforts have been devoted in studying flocking associated to pedestrian movement. Considering the freedom characteristic of pedestrian movement, we propose a definition of freedom moving flock pattern and its corresponding extraction algorithm in this paper.

Experiments on real trajectory datasets show that our methods can effectively mining pedestrian trajectory data and discovery freedom moving flock patterns. As future work we will examine cost models to enable the user pick the most efficient algorithm based on the context and nature of pedestrians.

Acknowledgements. This research was supported by the Major Project of High Resolution Earth Observation System (No. 11-Y20A40-9002-15/17)

References

1. Geng, X., Takagi, T., Arimura, H., Uno, T.: Enumeration of complete set of flock patterns in trajectories. In: Zhang, C., Basalamah, A., Hendawi, A. (Eds.) Proceedings of the 5th ACM SIGSPATIAL International Workshop on GeoStreaming, pp. 53–61. ACM, New York (2014)
2. Gudmundsson, J., van Kreveld, M.: Computing longest duration flocks in trajectory data. In: GIS 2006, pp. 35–42, New York, USA (2006)
3. Jeung, H., Yiu, M.L., Zhou, X., Jensen, C.S., Shen, H.T.: Discovery of convoys in trajectory databases. PVLDB **1**(1), 1068–1080 (2008)
4. Li, Z., Ding, B., Han, J., Kays, R.: Swarm: mining relaxed temporal moving object clusters. In: VLDB 2010, Singapore, pp. 723–734 (2010)
5. Romero, A.: Mining moving flock patterns in large spatio-temporal datasets using a frequent pattern mining approach. Master thesis, University of Twente (2011)
6. Geng, X., Uno, T., Arimura, H.: Trajectory pattern mining in practice - algorithms for mining flock patterns from trajectories. In: Proceedings of the International Conference on Knowledge Discovery and Information Retrieval and the International Conference on Knowledge Management and Information Sharing, pp. 143–151 (2013)
7. Jeung, H., Yiu, M.L., Zhou, X.F., Jensen, S.C., Shen, H.T.: Discovery of convoys in trajectory databases. Proc. VLDB Endow. **1**, 1068–1080 (2008)
8. Li, Z., Ding, B., Han, J., Kays, R.: Swarm: mining relaxed temporal moving object clusters. Proc. VLDB Endow. **3**(1-2), 723–734 (2010)
9. Hai, P.N., Poncelet, P., Teisseire, M.: All in one: mining multiple movement patterns. Int. J. Inf. Technol. Decis. Mak. **13**(8), 1–40 (2014)
10. Vieira, M.R., Bakalov, P., Tsotras, V.J.: On-line Discovery of Flock Patterns in Spatio-temporal Data. In: Proceedings of the 17th ACM SIGSPATIAL International Conference on Advances in Geographic Information Systems, pp. 286–295. ACM, New York, USA (2009)
11. Tanaka, P.S., Vieira, M.R., Kaster, S.D.: Efficient algorithms to discover flock patterns in trajectories. In: GeoInfo, pp. 56–67 (2015)
12. Makris, D., Ellis, T.: Path detection in video surveillance. Image Vis. Comput. **20**(12), 895–903 (2002)
13. Piciarelli, C., Foresti, G.L., Snidaro, L.: Trajectory clustering and its applications for video surveillance. In: IEEE International Conference on Advanced Video and Signal based Surveillance (AVSS), Como, Italy, pp. 40–45 (2005)
14. Arimura, H.,Takagi, T.: Finding all maximal duration flock patterns in high-dimensional trajectories. Manuscript, DCS, IST, Hokkaido University, April 2014
15. Laube P., Kreveld M., Imfeld, S.: Finding REMO - detecting relative motion patterns in geospatial lifelines. In: Developments in Spatial Data Handling, pp. 201–215 (2005)
16. Gudmundsson J., Kreveld M. van, Speckmann B.: Efficient detection of motion patterns in spatio-temporal data sets. In: Proceedings of the 12th Annual ACM International Workshop on Geographic Information Systems, pp. 250–257. ACM (2004)
17. Laube, P., Imfeld, S.: Analyzing relative motion within groups of trackable moving point objects. In: Geographic Information Science, pp. 132–144 (2002)

18. Turdukulov, U., Calderon Romero, U., Turdukulov, U., Huisman, O., Retsios, V.: Visual mining of moving flock patterns in large spatio-temporal data sets using a frequent pattern approach. Int. J. Geogr. Inf. Sci. **28**(10), 2013–2029 (2014)
19. Rosero, O.E.C., Romero, A.O.C.: Performance analysis of flock pattern algorithms in spatio-temporal databases. In: Latin American Computing Conference, pp. 1–6 (2014)
20. Gudmundsson, J., Kreveld, M.: Computing longest duration flocks in trajectory data. In: Proceedings ACM GIS 2006, pp. 35–42. ACM (2006)
21. Aveni, A.F.: The Not-so-lonely crowd: friendship groups in collective behavior. Sociometry **40**(1), 96–99 (1977)
22. Moussaid, M., Perozo, N., Garnier, S., Helbing, D., Theraulaz, G.: The walking behaviour of pedestrian social groups and its impact on crowd dynamics. PLoS ONE **5**(4), e10047 (2010)
23. Mawson, A.: Understanding mass panic and other collective responses to threat and disaster. Psychiatry **68**(2), 95–113 (2005)
24. Ge, W., Collins, R.T., Ruback, B.: Automatically detecting the small group structure of a crowd. In: Applications of Computer Vision (WACV), pp. 1–8 (2009)
25. Pellegrini, S., Ess, A., Van Gool, L.: Improving data association by joint modeling of pedestrian trajectories and groupings. In: Daniilidis, K., Maragos, P., Paragios, N. (eds.) ECCV 2010, Part I. LNCS, vol. 6311, pp. 452–465. Springer, Heidelberg (2010)
26. Girardin, F., Vaccari, A., Gerber, A., Ratti, C.: Quantifying urban attractiveness from the distribution and density of digital footprints. J. Spat. Data Infrastruct. Res. **4**, 175–200 (2009)
27. Vaccari, A., Liu, L., Biderman, A., Ratti, C., Pereira, F., Oliveirinha, J., Gerber, A.: A holistic framework for the study of urban traces and the profiling of urban processes and dynamics. In: IEEE International Conference on Intelligent Transportation Systems (2009)
28. Xu, Z., Liu, Y., Yen, N., Mei, L., Luo, X., Wei, X., Hu, C.: Crowdsourcing based description of urban emergency events using social media big data. IEEE Trans. Cloud Comput. **8**(99), 1 (2016)
29. Xu, Z., Zhang, H., Sugumaran, V., Choo, K.K.R., Mei, L., Zhu, Y.: Participatory sensing-based semantic and spatial analysis of urban emergency events using mobile social media. EURASIP J. Wirel. Comm. Netw. **2016**, 44 (2016)
30. Kjærgaard, M.B., Wirz, M., Roggen, D., Tröster, G.: Mobile sensing of pedestrian flocks in indoor environments using WiFi signals. In: 2012 IEEE International Conference on Pervasive Computing and Communications, Lugano, pp. 95–102 (2012)
31. Wirz, M., Schläpfer, P., Kjærgaard, M.B., Roggen, D., Feese, S., Tröster, G.: Towards an online detection of pedestrian flocks in urban canyons by smoothed spatio-temporal clustering of GPS trajectories. In: Proceedings of the 3rd ACM SIGSPATIAL International Workshop on Location-Based Social Networks, pp. 17–24. ACM, New York (2011)
32. Wachowicz, M., Ong, R., Renso, C., Nanni, M.: Finding moving flock patterns among pedestrians through collective coherence. Int. J. Geogr. Inf. Sci. **25**(11), 1849–1864 (2011)
33. Jaccard, P.: The distribution of the flora in the alpine zone. New Phytol. **11**(2), 37–50 (1912)
34. Cao, Y., Huang, H., Gartner, G.: A signal-loss-based clustering method for segmenting and analyzing mixed indoor/outdoor pedestrian GPS trajectories. In: Liu, C. (ed.) Principle and Application Progress in Location-Based Services, pp. 3–19. Springer International Publishing, Heidelberg (2014)
35. Idrissov, A., Nascimento, M.A.: A trajectory cleaning framework for trajectory clustering. In: Proceedings Mobile Data Challenge by Nokia Workshop, in Conjunction with International Conference on Pervasive Computing, Newcastle, UK (2012)

Author Index

Printed in the United States
By Bookmasters